The Book Buyer's Advisor

The Definitive Guide to Discovering the Year's Best Books

Edited by Bill Ott
American Library Association's BOOKLIST *Magazine*

Triumph Books, Inc.
CHICAGO

Library of Congress Catalog Card Number: 90-062533

International Standard Book Number: 0-9624436-1-1 (paper)
                                      0-9624436-2-X (cloth)

Triumph Books, Inc.
644 South Clark Street Suite 2000
Chicago, IL 60605

Printed in the United States of America

CONTENTS

INTRODUCTION

Popular opinion has it that books just aren't much good anymore. Whether one talks to curmudgeonly English professors who think that *Ulysses* was our last good novel, or to alternative press advocates convinced that today's conglomerate-owned trade publishers can't tell books from dollar signs, or to independent bookstore owners fighting extinction against Goliath-like chain stores, the message is the same: books as we know and love them are in danger. And yet, that frail, constantly beleaguered but somehow resilient species—the good book—always finds a way to survive, whether the would-be assassin is a conglomerate or a computer.

There is no denying that the doomsayers, with the exception, perhaps, of the curmudgeonly professor, have a point. There are in the neighborhood of 50,000 new books published every year, and the amount of ephemera— from celebrity exercise books to yet another prepackaged techno-thriller— has reached epidemic proportions. Yes, there is definitely more trash out there today, but does that necessarily mean that there are fewer good books, or that the bad will always engulf the good, like an evil version of Pac-Man? It may offend our sensibilities, but perhaps Amy Tan's *Joy Luck Club* can coexist peacefully on the same bookstore shelves with Vanna White's autobiography. It was Yeats, after all, who observed that "Love has pitched his mansion in / The place of excrement." If love, why not books?

Only time will tell if Pac-Man or Yeats' Crazy Jane provides the more appropriate metaphor for the health of the trade publishing industry, but the average reader can't be expected to spend much time worrying about such larger issues as the future of literature in a bottom-line world. No, what the average reader wants is something to read, and the biggest problem standing in the way of finding it is not that good books don't exist anymore, but that they're surrounded by so many bad ones.

If a good book can be likened to a treasure, then clearly what we need is a reliable treasure map. But *reliable* is the key; there's so much hype out there, books start to look like nothing but fool's gold. Walking the aisles at a recent American Booksellers Convention in Las Vegas—where fool's gold is a way of life—a naive book editor might easily have concluded that Donald Trump and country singer Ronnie Milsap were major American authors. It's even harder for the general reader. Bombarded by subway billboards and television commercials proclaiming the arrival of one more weighty tome on thin thighs, it's no wonder more of us don't conclude that the written word has been trivialized beyond redemption.

But it really isn't so. The first thing a quick perusal of *The Book Buyer's Advisor* should suggest is that, in the opinions of the reviewers and editors at BOOKLIST magazine, there are more good books published in one year than anyone has time to read. That fact alone should give the determined reader renewed confidence. Each year the BOOKLIST staff wades through those 50,000 new books in search of what's good across the gamut of fiction and nonfiction. Librarians, who have been reading BOOKLIST since it first appeared as an American Library Association publication in 1905, use our reviews to help them decide which books will line the shelves of the nation's public and school libraries. If it works for them—and 85 years of nonstop publication indicates it does—there's no reason why it can't also work for the book-buying public, whose access to information about the range of new books is surprisingly limited.

General readers usually find out about books from newspapers and mass-market magazines, where very little space is available for reviews. To supplement those sources, we offer this one-volume survey of the previous year's publishing output. The reviews you'll find on the following pages are shorter than the ones you'll encounter in most newspaper book sections, but brevity has its advantages. By limiting our comments to a succinct statement as to why we think a particular book merits attention, we allow you the freedom to browse at will, sampling our reviews as one would an hors d'oeuvres platter. All book reviewers would be wise to remember, after all, that the main entrée is always the book itself, not the review.

In the course of one year, BOOKLIST usually reviews about 7,000 books, a total that includes children's books, reference books, and many special-ized titles designed to fill particular subject needs in libraries. That 7,000 has been whittled down to 1,000 for inclusion in this premiere edition of *The Book Buyer's Advisor*. The titles were selected with the tastes of the book-loving general reader in mind, the kind of person who reads not just to find out how to do something but to be entertained and enlightened—and to feel the sublime rhythm of well-crafted words rolling off the page. Naturally, the attempt has been made to pick the *best* 1,000 books reviewed over a year's time, but in making such a subjective judgment, the radically different tastes of the reading public have been taken into account. Thus, John Updike appears here, but so, too, does Jackie Collins, a trendsetter in her chosen field, the "fashion-and-passion" novel. Occasionally a title has also been included not because of its quality but because it's such a disappointment. Robert Ludlum fans, for example, can be expected to queue up in great numbers for any new espionage novel by the author of *The Bourne Identity*. In his latest book, however, in the opinion of our reviewer, Ludlum is way off stride. We include such reviews as a kind of Buyer Beware service: this book isn't what you think it is. But our more important function is alerting readers to books they might not hear about anywhere else. Every year a very few unheralded but richly deserving books somehow manage to emerge from the pack—*The Joy Luck Club* is a classic example—but there are many, many more that go virtually undiscovered. Finding these inadequately promoted, under-reviewed gems is what we do best at BOOKLIST—and what *The Book Buyer's Advisor* can do for you. Whether it's 74-year-old Eleanore Devine's collection of taut, sensuous short stories, *You're Standing in My Light*, or obscure Yugoslavian Danilo Kis's *Hourglass*, the anguished story of a Hungarian's last months before being sent to a Nazi concentration camp, the following pages are filled with just the kind of books serious readers long for—vivid, fully realized expressions of the mess and muddle of being human, captured in all its irony, comedy, tragedy, and pathos.

Such books are a treasure worth looking for and a delight to find. Happy hunting.

Bill Ott

How to Use *The Book Buyer's Advisor*

The reviews included here are organized first under nonfiction and fiction and then by broad subject categories, which appear alphabetically. Ideally, of course, the volume is designed to encourage browsing: find a subject area that interests you, and start flipping pages. For those searching for a specific book, however, the author and title indexes should ensure easy access. A note about biographies: the most difficult organizational decision an editor faces is deciding when to consider a book "Biography" and when to group it with the subject most related to the life being studied. For the purposes of this book, all lives of sports figures have been classified under "Sports & Recreation," all lives of musicians appear under "Music," and, in general, other biographical and autobiographical works are considered "Biography."

All reviews are prefaced by the following bibliographical information: author or editor, which appears in boldface; title, which appears in italics; and publisher, price, and number of pages. When no author or editor is listed on the book's title page, the title appears in boldface. Publisher, price, and pagination all refer to a book's original publication, usually in hardcover. Many of the titles included here are now available as paperback reprints, but current information on paperback availability is constantly changing. Consult your local bookseller for up-to-date data.

The editor's choices for the best books within each subject category are indicated by a large check mark (✔) appearing to the left of the author's or editor's name.

Acknowledgments

There would be no *Book Buyer's Advisor* without the ongoing excellence of the BOOKLIST magazine adult books staff—Martin Brady, editor; Brad Hooper and Ray Olson, associate editors; John Brosnahan, Denise Perry Donavin, and Donna Seaman, assistant editors; and Chris Anderson and Angus Trimnell, publishing assistants. This group has written more than half of the reviews that appear in these pages. The remaining reviews were written by free-lancers, whose names appear following their work and who also deserve thanks for doing well the hardest thing that can be asked of any writer: have an opinion and make someone care about it.

Special thanks are also due Stuart Whitwell, BOOKLIST managing editor, who designed this book and produced camera-ready pages using the desktop publishing program Ventura Publisher; Phil Herbst, a copy editor and proofreader with the kind of eye for detail that no computer will ever replace; and Ben Segedin, BOOKLIST layout and copy editor, who took time away from other duties to nurse a gargantuan manuscript through more revisions than any of us cares to remember.

NONFICTION

Art

Adams, Henry.
Thomas Hart Benton: Drawing from Life.
Abbeville, $49.95. 208p.

Adams, the author of a recent illustrated biography—*Thomas Hart Benton: An American Original*—now looks further into the artist's life and work with this study of Benton's drawings, studies, and illustrations. This book, a companion to a traveling exhibition, examines just how Benton worked, drawing from life and later incorporating many of these quick studies into his larger paintings and murals. Adams also pays attention to the development of Benton's style as the painter moved from modernism to regionalism. A notable series of illustrations, both of drawings and studies and of the finished works they preceded, illuminates both Adams' points and Benton's art. —*John Brosnahan*

Aslet, Clive.
The American Country House.
Yale, $45. 320p.

The importation of the concept of the country house from Great Britain and Europe to nineteenth-century America is charted in this social and architectural history. Aslet covers the great American country houses built from the mid-nineteenth through the early twentieth centuries. Britisher Aslet, who is the author of *The Last Country Houses*, easily transfers his expertise on style from England to the New World and describes many of the monumental homes that the Vanderbilts, Hearsts, and Rockefellers commissioned and then used as symbols of their wealth and privilege. While the inspiration for these homes may have come from overseas, Aslet points out the specifically American spirit and purpose they represent. The text is well illustrated with numerous color and black-and-white photographs. Readers interested in the American country house should also consult Mark Allan Hewitt's *The Architect and the American Country House*, also published by Yale and intended as a companion volume to Aslet's study. Whereas Aslet focuses on the social milieu of the country house, Hewitt emphasizes the architects who designed these elaborate retreats, from Julia Morgan to Frank Lloyd Wright. —*John Brosnahan*

Art

Ballinger, James K.
Frederic Remington.
Abrams, $39.95. 160p.

The main theme of this exemplary review of the career of the best-known artist of the Old West is Remington's struggle for acceptance by the fine-art establishment. Remington achieved popularity early with his magazine illustrations of cowboys, cavalrymen, and Indians—subjects he retained after the frontier they represented was finally closed. He modified his painting style from romantic realism to an atmospheric impressionism and expanded his media to include sculpture. He tried out new settings—more contained and tranquil eastern landscapes to counterpoint his kinetic western scenes. Lamenting that the bulk of previous books on Remington have concentrated on his life rather than his art, Ballinger documents and scrutinizes Remington's changes, clearly demonstrating the artist's growth. But development and, needless to say, popularity did not ensure highbrow acceptance either then or since. This entry in the Library of American Art series splendidly abets *Frederic Remington: The Masterworks* in finally winning the long fight for Remington's recognition as a great American master. —*Ray Olson*

✓ **Cikovsky, Nicolai.**
Winslow Homer.
Abrams, $39.95. 160p.

The latest of the Library of American Art monographs on the transcendent masters of American art is the best thus far. It's really a matter of rising to the occasion. In own time, Homer (1836–1910) was considered the finest American painter, and subsequent decades have seen no reason to demote him. Cikovsky gracefully and absorbingly discusses Homer's life and art, which are inextricable if for no other reason than that he was reticent to the point of hermeticism about his nonprofessional life. Indeed, he was famously reclusive during the latter half of his life. But his oils, prints, and watercolors are full of self-expression. Early on, Cikovsky holds, they attest in both method and form Homer's adherence to the same aesthetic principles of modernity, democracy, and nationality that animated his analogue in American letters, Walt Whitman. The work from the middle of his career reflects a classical balance and formalism that the autodidactic artist only then imbibed from Japanese prints and those paragons of nineteenth-century inspiration, the Elgin marbles. Finally, in his last years, Homer devoted his oils to "his most deliberated expressions of emotion and ideas," his watercolors to "the purity of unmediated sensation, of the power and pleasure of seeing for its own sake." A marvelous critical biography of interest to anyone concerned with American art. —*Ray Olson*

Gilot, Francoise.
Matisse and Picasso: A Friendship in Art.
Doubleday, $30. 304p.

Gilot, painter, poet, and Picasso's companion from 1946 to 1954, wrote about their relationship in *Life with Picasso*. Here, in a meandering, generously designed and illustrated memoir, she describes the "difficult and rare friendship" shared by the two giants of twentieth-century art: Picasso and Matisse. Gilot, decades younger than both men, functioned as "arbiter, hostage, ambassador of good will, and agent provocateur" for the two geniuses whose rivalry evolved into respect. She analyzes their contrasting personalities and approaches to painting and discusses their inspirations and intent. While Matisse is serene and benevolent, expressing a "unity of spirit," Picasso is volatile and demanding, instilling his work with "existential anxiety." Gilot describes the elderly Matisse at work on his famous cutouts, shares his letters to her, and reconstructs conversations the three of them had about art. A unique and intimate portrait of the two artists that includes a self-portrait—the author is an interesting subject in her own right. —*Donna Seaman*

Green, Oliver.
Art for the London Underground: London Transport Posters 1908 to the Present.
Rizzoli, $29.95. 144p.

Although it's not in the elephantine format of the usual poster book, this all-color mounting of 80 years of the art placed before London's subway commuters by the city's transport system must be reckoned one of the finest poster albums of recent years. Green precedes the generous helping of posters with a thumbnail history of the underground's long project to advertise its services to its users, and he accompanies each two-page spread of illustrations with at least one terse, informative note. The posters are presented chronologically and, what's better, laid out and reproduced with such care and flare that each page, whether it displays one, two, or more images, is a work of framing quality in itself. Relatively few of the artists represented are big names, but among the latter, many readers who know zip about art will recognize Len Deighton, who fashioned a collagelike vision called "London's Country Village Life" for the underground in 1957, five years before launching his spy-thriller career with *The Ipcress File.* —*Ray Olson*

✓ Hambourg, Maria Morris and Phillips, Christopher.
The New Vision: Photography between the World Wars.
Abrams, $60. 318p.

Cataloging an exhibition of the same name, this splendid volume brings together some 400 photographs—American and European, fine art and commercial—from the interwar period. The exhibition's particular genius lies in identifying themes of the era—the machine, the city, surrealism, abstractions, and portraits—and illustrating them with both fine art and more

Art

practical, often advertising, images. Hambourg, associate curator of photography at New York's Metropolitan Museum, brilliantly carries forward the interest of her former superior at the Museum of Modern Art, John Szarkowsi, in the illusionary aspects of all kinds of photography, bringing it to bear on some of the photos at hand in a superb essay, "From 291 to the Museum of Modern Art: Photography in New York, 1910–1937." Phillips contributes another strong essay on European photography of the period. A must for all lovers of fine-art photography. —*Gretchen Garner*

Hobbs, Anne Stevenson, ed.
Beatrix Potter's Art.
Viking/Warne, $24.95. 192p.

Those who think of Beatrix Potter only in terms of Peter Rabbit will be pleasantly surprised when perusing this well-conceived and beautifully designed book. Hobbs, curator of the National Art Library's Beatrix Potter Collection at the Victoria and Albert Museum in London, has selected a variety of items from Potter's drawings and paintings—from still-life studies to sketches of animals, Lake Country landscapes, pictures of her famous book characters, and detailed botanical pieces. Each of the entries is captioned, telling where and when the work was done, the size, the medium, and, at times, incidental remarks. A lengthy introduction discusses the artist's background and influences. A satisfying browsing item but also a resource for appreciators of fine art. —*Barbara Elleman*

Hughes, Robert.
Nothing If Not Critical: Selected Essays on Art and Artists.
Knopf, $24.95. 415p.

Art critic and cultural observer Hughes collects his essays on art and artists, mainly from his ongoing contributions to *Time*, the *New Republic*, and the *New York Review of Books*. Acerbic and appreciative in equal measure, Hughes' views of art history and the current art scene are notable for both their style and content, his critical judgments presented in the most persuasive manner and often with seething disdain and dismissal. Although the author seems more comfortable in the aesthetic clime before the turn of the current century, Hughes dutifully reports on the latest hot young artist to strike the fancy of the New York tastemakers. If Hughes often seems to style himself as a modern-day Berenson for a middlebrow audience, he certainly provokes ample attention both to his subjects and to himself. —*John Brosnahan*

Kelly, Franklin.
Frederic Edwin Church.
Smithsonian Institution Press, $50. 210p.

The author of *Frederic Edwin Church and the National Landscape* recruits the manager of Olana, Church's fabulous New York estate, and paleontologist Stephen Jay Gould to write additional essays for this catalog of an exhibition of 49 paintings by the most successful nineteenth-century American landscapist. Church's pictures of the mountainous South American tropics sold at record prices in their time and were widely reproduced. Gigantic canvases, they maintain the power to stun. They also advance, as do Church's northeastern U.S. and arctic scenes, the conception of a harmonious, unitary nature that the artist imbibed from the great philosopher of science, Alexander von Humboldt. Darwin, who also admired the German, blasted Humboldt's ideas with his own of a competitive, fragmented evolutionary process. He also undercut the spiritual optimism of Church's visionary landscapes, and as the star of Darwinism rose, Church's declined along with that of sanguine, liberal scientific thought. Quite aside from this (Gould's) fascinating argument in intellectual history, the book brilliantly displays the exhibition's riches and documents Church's efflorescence as a landscapist and his later obsession with his estate. —*Ray Olson*

✓ **Kruger, Barbara and Linker, Kate.**
Love for Sale: The Words and Pictures of Barbara Kruger.
Abrams, $29.95. 96p.

Without a doubt, Barbara Kruger is one of the most exciting visual artists of the 1980s. Her large pictures, combining found photographs and bold, simple texts, engage almost every viewer. Her works are always puzzles, asking for solutions, but are never so difficult as to be ignored. Dealing with gender ("What big muscles you have!" "Your comfort is my silence," "I am your reservoir of poses") or money and consumerism ("Buy me, I'll change your life," "We get exploded because they've got money and god in their pockets," "You make history when you do business"), Kruger combines imagery that is somehow familiar with challenging assertions that synergistically create new, discomforting meanings. Experienced in publishing, Kruger knows about the picture-log of our culture, and with a mind educated by feminism and semiotics, she knows about communication and especially about pronouns. This retrospective survey—designed very much in her own style, with bold graphics in red and everything else in black and white, and accompanied by Kate Linker's informative essay—is a valuable, important book. —*Gretchen Garner*

Mapplethorpe, Robert.
Some Women.
Little, Brown/Bulfinch Press, $50. 120p.

Controversy dogs photographer Robert Mapplethorpe even in death as censorship problems continue to raise havoc with public showings of his work. The present volume, however, includes none of the more notorious images of homoeroticism and sadomasochism that helped to make his problematic reputation. Instead, Mapplethorpe concentrates here on the female form—from the naked blissful innocence of young girls to the ultimate grande dame/crone in the person of sculptor Louise Nevelson. Celebrity portraits and nude figure studies—in a few cases these two categories overlap—are the prime exhibits. The artist's familiar style, with its careful arrangements and controlled poses, allied to these traditional subjects makes a strong art-for-art's-sake case for Mapplethorpe's late work. A series of portraits of singer Patti Smith—the photographer's friend and more—taken in 1987 and 1988 closes the volume and, more symbolically, Mapplethorpe's career as an artist. Joan Didion's introduction suggests a subtext for these pictures, but like the connection between Mapplethorpe and his sitters, it's not necessarily a cordial agreement, but perhaps a case of wills in conflict. —*John Brosnahan*

Marchesseau, Daniel.
The Intimate World of Alexander Calder.
Abrams, $85. 398p.

The private side of Alexander Calder's art is shown in items from the American sculptor's own home as well as in items from the private collections of his family and friends. Many of these pieces exhibit Calder's fondness for a joke—usually an embellishment of the most ordinary object with an imaginative send-up. Although some of the objects are more "serious" pieces of jewelry or small-scale mobiles, the sense of joy and fun infuses every page: Calder's witty and playful creations are illustrated in color plates and documentary photographs. While this is not a scholarly volume, it intimately reveals a further side of Calder's role as an artist; it is also a book that covers an area relatively uncharted, since only minor attention has been given to the objects featured here (apart from some of the jewelry and *Calder's Circus*, which is on display at the Whitney Museum). The text, which seems not to have been thoroughly proofread for this English translation, could have been arranged better to follow the illustrations more closely, but Calder's spontaneous magic overcomes this minor distraction. —*John Brosnahan*

Moore, Gene and Hyams, Jay.
My Time at Tiffany's.
St. Martin's, $60. 232p.

Moore's displays for Tiffany's Fifth Avenue store have already been celebrated in Goldman's *Windows at Tiffany's: The Art of Gene Moore* (1980), but another retrospective look—through the windows and at the wonders Moore has created—is always welcome. Moore himself, with the help of Jay Hyams, supplies the text this time; in Goldman's book, he only gave brief commentaries on particular displays. And while Tiffany remains the focus of Moore's story, his whole career as artist-turned-window-designer is retold here, with discussions of work done for other department stores and clients. Although the narrative sometimes becomes repetitive ("and then I used stuffed birds on real tree trunks"), there are enough fascinating anecdotes to maintain interest, especially when Moore tells about the many now-famous artists he has worked with. The illustrations are an additional invitation into Moore's tiny world, although many are photographed merely in black and white. —*John Brosnahan*

Newhall, Nancy.
From Adams to Stieglitz: Pioneers of Modern Photography.
Aperture, $39.95. 170p.

Nancy Newhall knew and wrote about the titans of photography in the mid-twentieth century as she and her husband, photo historian Beaumont Newhall, helped to chart and expand the growth of the medium from World War II until her untimely death in a freak rafting accident in 1974. This fourth entry in Aperture's series, Writers and Artists on Photography, includes book and portfolio notes, magazine articles, and biographical material on Peter Henry Emerson, Paul Strand, Alvin Langdon Coburn, Ansel Adams, Edward and Brett Weston, Minor White, and others. Of particular interest are illuminating biographical notes on Alfred Stieglitz, whose stature as a pivotal figure in American art is substantial. Newhall brings warmth, wit, and intelligence to her exploration of Stieglitz and his turbulent personality and to many issues of the medium to which she was so firmly devoted. —*John Alderson*

Pfeiffer, Bruce Brooks.
Frank Lloyd Wright Drawings: Masterworks from the Frank Lloyd Wright Archives.
Abrams, $65. 304p.

From the archives of the Frank Lloyd Wright Foundation comes this stupendous collection of architectural drawings and renderings covering the American architect's long, illustrious, and often controversial career. Wright's impressive drafting skill, heretofore too little recognized, is dramatically illustrated throughout the volume, as is the equally distinguished work now attributed to his associates. The examples include drawings for projects and completed buildings, with samplings of preliminary sketches, engineering studies, and presentation renderings for residential, public, commercial, and high-rise buildings. In his introduction, Wright scholar Pfeiffer supplies insight into how the architect used these drawings in his work and also adds commentary to each individual piece. —*John Brosnahan*

✓ **Porter, Eliot and Gleick, James.**
Nature's Chaos.
Viking, $29.95. 128p.

Here is another stunner from the most popular and polished of contemporary nature photographers. This collection consists of 110 images harvested from four decades' work. The common subject is natural pattern—the apparently chaotic arrangements of, say, a river system, cracks in a bed of dried mud, a cloud, or lichen on rocks that such disciplines as fractal geometry and fluid dynamics are helping us see as more complex—though often protean and unique—expressions of order. Accompanying Porter's pix is Gleick's piquant little essay on the science of chaos and how its discoveries and conundrums are reinforcing the premodern wisdom of Heraclitus, who declared that one

Art

could not step into the same river twice. Good reading, good viewing. —*Ray Olson*

Rogers, Malcolm, ed.
Camera Portraits: Photographs from the National Portrait Gallery 1839–1989.
Oxford, $60. 320p.

From queen of the B-movies Joan Collins to just plain Queen Elizabeth, British photographers capture Brit celebs in this collection of portraits exhibited to mark the 150th anniversary of photography. Drawn from the archives of the National Portrait Gallery, these examples find equal distinction on both sides of the lens, with the work of some of the best-known camera artists matched with some of the country's most striking personalities. The range of subjects—from Thomas Carlyle to Sting—is enormous, from the historical as well as other viewpoints. Although for American viewers a few subjects will be unknown, photogenic qualities are unmistakable. (For example, Cecil Beaton's style as photographer and androgynous beauty place him in the unique position of being both artist and model.) The range of technique from daguerreotype to Cibachrome print also documents the development of photography in a significant manner, as do the commentaries on the photographers and their work. —*John Brosnahan*

Sabbagh, Karl.
Skyscraper.
Viking, $22.95. 365p.

The companion volume to a PBS television series, *Skyscraper* tells the story of how a New York City high rise is planned, designed, and built. The real estate deal that produced Worldwide Plaza on Manhattan's West Side is but the start of the story, however, for Sabbagh investigates many related issues that have an impact on the final structure: architectural considerations, community input and opposition on neighborhood "improvements," engineering technology, financing, and the sheer physical feat of constructing a 45-story building. Sabbagh is especially good at explaining some of the finer points of construction and design technology and at describing the many things that could and did go wrong to delay the building's completion. Profiles of the people who worked on the project, from real estate mogul William Zeckendorf to construction workers, fill out this dramatic story. —*John Brosnahan*

Sandler, Martin W.
American Image: Photographing One Hundred Fifty Years in the Life of a Nation.
Contemporary, $40. 272p.

Not the first book to seize upon photography's sesquicentennial as pretext for an American history picture book, Sandler's is, however, the most attractive one yet. His main text traces the nation's development and how photographers and photography fit into it. His captions generally emphasize the kinds of subjects and events depicted rather than the specific pictures. He downplays technical and aesthetic matters—verbally, that is, for the quality of his selections and their reproduction (not to mention, in the cases of relatively less distinguished images, their placement on the pages) is stunningly high. The only regrets to have are that there aren't more pictures in the book and that it isn't even bigger than its present 9-by-12-inch dimensions. Many of the photos are oft-published warhorses (with good reason: they're excellent), but a lot aren't, too. Shove those *American Heritage* coffee-tablers aside to make room for this first-rate history picture book. —*Ray Olson*

Schaub, George.
Using Your Camera.
Amphoto, $27.50. 144p.

Words like *software* and *program,* once technojargon to photographers, are common terms in the microchip world of today's 35mm cameras. This generously illustrated, breezy volume acquaints us with the modern single-lens-reflex (SLR) camera, how to understand and control various metering systems and focus techniques for sharpness over a particular area, the selection of accessories, films, lenses, contrast control—indeed, all the building blocks necessary for taking good pictures, all presented with clarity, authority, and sensitivity. An excellent reference and introduction for the amateur photographer. —*John Alderson*

✔ **Szarkowski, John.**
Photography until Now.
Museum of Modern Art, $60. 344p.

Marking the one hundred fiftieth anniversary of the invention of photography and the fiftieth of MOMA's photo department, curator Szarkowski traces the interlocking of technology and vision as, together, they have driven the photographic enterprise to date and does it with perception, depth, clarity, and wry good humor. He extensively covers photomechanical reproduction and its impact on photography's dominance as *the* twentieth-century illustrative medium, but more importantly, he offers an overview that, like no other, thoughtfully balances technology, concept, and intuition in its purview. Using many excellent but not widely published pictures, he also helps us to view the medium afresh. A major work, not to be missed. —*John Alderson*

Tucker, Paul Hayes.
Monet in the '90s.
Yale, $45. 340p.

Tucker concentrates on Monet's series painting from the 1890s—those notable sequences of studies of grainstacks, poplar trees, and the facade of Rouen Cathedral depicted at various times of the day and year. The publication of Tucker's book coincided with the recent Monet exhibition that drew large crowds in Boston, Chicago, and London; the value of the book, however, will extend well beyond the show's closing. Tucker relates the paintings to the

Art

social context of the period as well as to changes in critical and public response occasioned by Monet's growing reputation as an impressionist master. The individual paintings within the series are also examined and analyzed as to technique and style, again both within the context of Monet's art and the history of modern painting. —*John Brosnahan*

Wissinger, Joanna.
Victorian Details: Enhancing Antique and Contemporary Homes with Period Accents.
Dutton, $22.50. 160p.

A source book of ideas and addresses for ways to re-create the popular Victorian look in either authentically restored or modern settings. Wissinger covers exterior architectural details, interior design, and garden landscaping while identifying the major components of the Victorian style and suggesting how the same effect can be achieved through antique or reproduction materials. Although the author doesn't assume a purist attitude, she expertly catalogs a whole range of Victorian styles and industriously searches for their contemporary equivalent. The large number of color illustrations helps to portray this sympathetic approach and to visualize the Victorian age's varied palette and enthusiasm for mass detail. —*John Brosnahan*

Biography

Albert, Carl.
Little Giant: The Life and Times of Speaker Carl Albert.
Univ. of Oklahoma, $24.95. 379p.

Carl Albert offers an intimate account of his long and distinguished tenure as one of America's foremost lawmakers. Born and raised in rural Oklahoma, Albert had an exemplary congressional career that spanned three decades and five administrations. First elected to the House of Representatives in 1947, he immediately became one of the legendary Sam Rayburn's most dedicated protégés. As Democratic House whip (1955–62), majority leader (1962–71), and, finally, Speaker of the House (1971–77), Albert displayed a rare combination of political savvy and integrity, establishing him as a dynamic and respected party leader. In addition to detailing his own life and work, the author provides a fascinating overview of key governmental players and the often arcane legislative process. A forthright self-portrait of a major twentieth-century politico. —*Margaret Flanagan*

Alexander, Shana.
When She Was Bad: The Story of Bess, Hortense, Sukhreet & Nancy.
Random, $19.95. 304p.

Bess Myerson, Judge Hortense Gable, her strange daughter, Sukhreet, and Nancy Capasso—the principal players in the odd affair known as the Bess

Mess—have all found a place in that special corner of the American consciousness reserved for scandals of the rich and famous. For those few who don't read the tabloids while waiting in line at supermarkets, here are the unsavory facts: former Miss America Bess Myerson became romantically involved with a married sewer contractor, Andy Capasso. Judge Gable, who was presiding over the Capasso divorce, had her own problems—mainly a brilliant yet emotionally unstable daughter who needed a job. Eventually Sukhreet found one with Myerson, who was then New York City's cultural affairs commissioner. Coincidence? Maybe; at least the jury could find no provable wrongdoing. Alexander is interested not so much in the legal wranglings as in what brought this unlikely quartet into such uncomfortable juxtaposition. Focusing on the juicy theme of women "brought low by love," she spins a good story, but we instantly become leery when the inevitable psychological probing begins. Alexander clearly has her favorites: Sukhreet and Nancy. Whether this reflects reality or the author's attempt to shape the tale to fit her interpretation is difficult to say, but anyone who has seen Sukhreet babbling away on television will be surprised at how much leeway she gets here. Whatever the book's shortcomings as psychobiography, though, it has all the ingredients of a winner: love, hate, sex, greed, mother-daughter relations—the full gamut of best-selling emotions. —*Ilene Cooper*

Ambrose, Stephen E.
Nixon: The Triumph of a Politician 1962–1972.
Simon & Schuster, $24.95. 736p.

The first volume of this planned three-part project, *Nixon: The Education of a Politician 1913–1962*, succeeded as a masterly introduction to the life and career of the thirty-seventh president of the U.S. This second volume, as proficiently and objectively rendered as the first, develops themes set down in its predecessor: namely, the personal and political effect of Nixon's major personality traits (his awkwardness in dealing with people on an individual basis coupled with an ability to manage himself before a crowd; impressive intelligence and leadership qualities but an inability to cultivate close relationships). The time covered in this second installment spans the years from Nixon's defeat in the 1962 California gubernatorial race to his reelection to the presidency in 1972. What Ambrose perceives in the man during this decade is an outstanding diplomat with moral emptiness; but given Ambrose's great attention to prose style as well as historiographical substance, admiration on the part of the reader is not a prerequisite to admiring the book. —*Brad Hooper*

✓ **Bair, Deirdre.**
Simone de Beauvoir.
Summit, $24.95. 750p.

Bair's biography of the French author, philosopher, and feminist aims to restore the balance between interest in de Beauvoir's personal life—as the lifelong companion of Jean-Paul Sartre and sometime lover of Nelson

Biography

Algren—and the question of her achievements as a writer and thinker. In that sense, this study is truly a literary biography and not just a feminist fable like Francis and Gontier's *Simone de Beauvoir*. Bair's presentation is a sustained and detailed portrait that benefits significantly from a series of interviews with the subject herself as well as numerous friends and relatives. Indeed, Bair had proposed that de Beauvoir herself provide a simultaneous commentary to her own story, but this audacious plan was stilled by de Beauvoir's death in 1986. Even without the presence of de Beauvoir's distinctive voice, however, this book is a superb psychological and literary document that chronicles a life and a career that were by turns notable and notorious. —*John Brosnahan*

Belford, Barbara.
Violet: The Story of the Irrepressible Violet Hunt and Her Circle of Lovers and Friends—Ford Madox Ford, H. G. Wells, Somerset Maugham, and Henry James.
Simon & Schuster, $21.95. 324p.

Violet Hunt's life is remarkable for what she achieved—minor fame as a novelist—but it is more so because of the company she kept: she was friend or lover to many well-known writers and artists, among them, Ford Madox Ford, H. G. Wells, Somerset Maugham, and Henry James. Hunt's conventional but unhappy childhood laid an orthodox foundation for her rebellion against established modes of conduct, a pattern of unconventional behavior that she sustained throughout her life, with emancipation always triumphant over respectability. Belford reconstructs Hunt's life through the use of a series of diaries that Hunt kept, some of which have only just recently been discovered. Making ample use of the documentary material, Belford reveals the full scope of Hunt's professional and personal achievements. —*John Brosnahan*

Beschloss, Michael R.
Eisenhower: A Centennial Life.
Harper, $29.95. 245p.

Those of us who remember Ike tend to favor the image of the beloved war hero and later chief executive who presided over the calm and prosperous America of the 1950s. Of course, Eisenhower's life and legend are a little more complex than that. This attractive, full-bodied volume, published in celebration of Ike's one-hundredth birthday, offers fabulous photos and a text that presents an informed and often insightful overview of one of the great lives of the twentieth century. The humble Abilene, Kansas, roots; the West Point appointment; the years as seemingly the quintessential army bureaucrat; marriage to Mamie Doud; World War II triumphs and travails; the presidential years; the illnesses; the retirement to Gettysburg—all are covered here with a knowing sense of Eisenhower's place in history. Of special interest is the material (both words and pictures) on his role as Supreme Allied Commander and his dealings with the great generals and leaders of the war and following. —*Martin Brady*

Bisnow, Mark.
In the Shadow of the Dome: Chronicles of a Capitol Hill Aide.
Morrow, $19.95. 320p.

Bisnow contracted a political bug in the mid-1970s and permanently decamped for the big time in D.C. Does the fever ever break? Apparently not, if his career is typical. Congressional staffers shift jobs every other year with scant regard for their bosses' party labels or even geographical origins. And why not? Opportunities abound in an institution that by any index has been a growth industry since 1975. Hence the power of unelected assistants, who time and again write lawmakers' speeches and prepare the language and provisions of their bills and astonishingly enough, occasionally cast their votes (albeit by proxy). Bisnow has written an important book that embraces two fundamentally adversarial audiences: denizens of the Hill will love his anecdotal portrayal of their world, and reformers aghast at that description will enjoy his wry reflections on the very same stories. —*Gilbert Taylor*

Boyd, Brian.
Vladimir Nabokov: The Russian Years.
Princeton, $25. 598p.

The first volume of Boyd's biography of the Russian-born writer (the second is scheduled to be published in 1991) takes a close look at the experiences of his childhood and early adult life. Cataclysms, both private and historical, from the revolutionary events in Russia to the writer's eventual exile in Europe and the U.S., expose seeds that would later flower in Nabokov's writings, which are examined from a number of intriguing aesthetic and psychological perspectives. Nabokov's philosophy as well as his noted style is examined extensively in this record of a life and a career, with many references made to both the Russian texts composed in this period and to English works to come. Full discussions of Nabokov's relationships with families and friends, with fellow émigrés and writers, add a revealing personal side to this sympathetic dissection of a notably reclusive and brilliant author. —*John Brosnahan*

Brandon, Ruth.
The New Women and the Old Men.
Norton, $19.95. 286p.

Brandon is a noted scholar of nineteenth-century European cultural history. Her latest work closely examines the personal relationships forged by some of the leading literary lights of the late Victorian Age who were attempting to live as sexual equals despite cultural imperatives to the contrary. Here the reader meets Eleanor Marx (Karl's youngest daughter), famed South African novelist Olive Schreiner, Havelock Ellis, Rebecca West, H. G. Wells, Margaret Sanger, and their partners in love and life. With the precision of a detective (Brandon is also the author of two detective novels), the author unearths the fascinating evidentiary details that disclose to what degree these allegedly enlightened men and women successfully engaged in an equal partnership (the book's title is a clue). This captivating work, accessible to the general

Biography

public, makes an important contribution for its articulate rendering of the shocking truths behind the public personae of some significant historical figures. —*Mary Banas*

Caro, Robert A.
The Years of Lyndon Johnson, V.2: Means of Ascent.
Knopf, $24.95. 506p.

The second volume of Caro's study of Lyndon Johnson delivers on the intimations and insinuations that ended volume one (*The Path to Power*) of this astounding and contentious analysis of presidential character. In the seven years covered in this volume, Caro attempts to show how Johnson went from a loser in the special election of 1941 to a winner in the 1948 election that ultimately, but just barely, placed the former Texas congressman in the U.S. Senate. The author also demonstrates how, during this same period, Johnson consolidated his cunning but often ruthless search for political power and money. Caro's most damning charges rest, first, on the 1948 election and how Johnson may have stolen it at the last minute and, second, on the way Johnson created a private fortune based on an expanding media empire. As Johnson developed his political craft—licking his wounds from his campaign defeat, elaborating on his military record in World War II, cultivating the corrupt functionaries that would help him win higher office, ingratiating himself with his supporters in a two-faced manner—his mature personality began to emerge in a clash of contradictions that the narrative captures so well. While Caro's diligence for detail is evident in his extensive interviews and research, the interpretation of the evidence is frequently so slanted against Johnson that LBJ becomes a tragic figure, sympathetic in a way that Caro never intends. —*John Brosnahan*

Cassady, Carolyn.
Off the Road: My Years with Cassady, Kerouac, and Ginsberg.
Morrow, $22.95. 416p.

Jack Kerouac's 1957 *On the Road* is an American classic, and fascination with life in the fast lane of the Beat movement still runs high. Curiosity about the facts behind the fiction will be fully satisfied by this candid memoir. Cassady illuminates all facets of the complex love triangle between herself, husband Neal, and Kerouac. She chronicles her struggles with Neal, a powerfully charming, manipulative, volatile, and punishing man, who put her through hell. She has covered this territory before in the slender volume *Heart Beat: My Life with Jack and Neal*, but here we get the entire history of the marriage, which began when Neal was still married to another woman (whom he continued to see) and Carolyn was pregnant with the first of their three children; the affair with Jack was a source of comfort and stability. Many excerpts from previously unpublished letters give insight into the thoughts of Kerouac, Cassady, and close friend Allen Ginsberg about love, friendship, art, and spirituality. Cassady re-creates, with fresh surprise, the roller coaster of pain and pleasure she endured, as well as the tremendous discipline she acquired that enabled her to survive and grow, unlike her men, who self-destructed. A moving and unstinting account of potent personalities in pivotal times. —*Donna Seaman*

Chancellor, John.
Peril and Promise: A Commentary on America.
Harper, $17.95. 160p.

Chancellor's vita reads like a political almanac of the last 40 years. His front-line involvement in the major events of our times instills his commentary with depth and passion. This highly readable, essayistic book was written in anger and frustration, yet it offers a determinedly hopeful message—roll up your shirtsleeves and get to work. Chancellor walks us through all that's wrong with our society: debt, rotten educational and political systems, poverty, support of the elderly at the expense of the young, and even cynicism. His information is thorough but presented briskly. He derides industry for its myopic focus on short-term goals and us for our attitude of "entitlement," which makes us expect more than we're willing to pay for. After providing a balanced overview of mediocrity in high places and its results, Chancellor offers some strong, clear, and controversial recommendations including the abolishment of primaries, 12-month school years, a national service corps, and a drive to become technologically literate and competitive. Never mind "kinder and gentler," Chancellor tells us we need to be tougher and smarter. —*Donna Seaman*

Christianson, Gale E.
Fox at the Wood's Edge: A Biography of Loren Eiseley.
Holt, $29.95. 493p.

Archaeologist, professor, and literary naturalist Eiseley was a brilliant poet and writer as well as a cult hero to members of the 1960s counterculture; he was a contemporary and an acquaintance of such notables as Aldous Huxley, Rex Stout, W. H. Auden, and Louis Leakey; and he was a thoughtful, opinionated, and sensitive man, one who suffered what Christianson, author of *In the Presence of the Creator: Isaac Newton and His Times*, called "a chronic case of emotional hemophilia." In the mid-1920s, Nebraska-born Eiseley was hopping trains to see the West; at the same time he was contributing poems and essays to a new literary magazine, *Prairie Schooner*, and participating in archaeological digs throughout the western states. Christianson writes deftly; each chapter is a historical tale unto itself, meshing Eiseley's often sad personal life (his mother was mentally ill) with his turbulent professional career (his early reporting of his discovery of Yuma Indian implements caused a campaign to stop others from "raiding Wyoming's treasures"). Christianson's meticulous and intelligent detailing of Eiseley's life, which should be of interest to both scientists and writers, will undoubtedly draw readers to Eiseley's own works, among them *The Immense Journey*, *Darwin's Century: Evolution and the Men Who Discovered It*, and *The Night Country*. —*Eloise Kinney*

Biography

Citati, Pietro.
Kafka.
Knopf, $22.95. 320p.

The biographer of *Goethe* turns to a later European author who shares the earlier writer's emotional sensitivities, albeit within a much more contemporary framework. Citati doesn't so much review Kafka's life as reconstruct his experiences to telling effect. The book really injects the reader into Kafka's life and career, with Citati no reticent commentator, throwing his judgments and interpretations right into the narrative fray. A brilliant psychobiographical portrait that re-creates Kafka's legendary complexity in detail and with complete sympathy. —*John Brosnahan*

Cofer, Judith Ortiz.
Silent Dancing: A Partial Remembrance of a Puerto Rican Childhood.
Arte Publico, $8.50. 158p.

Through short stories and poems, Cofer relates her earliest memories of a lush Puerto Rican experience—with grandmother telling stories under the mango tree—and shares her feelings about her transient, Catholic adolescence, moving between the island and the States. Her autobiographical sketches develop themes of the immigrant experience ("doing time" in the U.S.): navy life, loss of ethnicity, the battle of the sexes, crossing over into adulthood. Born in 1952, with her father often away on navy leave, Cofer acts as translator for her mother, learning that "English was my weapon and my power," and comes of age during the Cuban missile crisis. Most of the poems reiterate themes developed in the stories, but "Why Providencia Has Babies" can stand on its own. Even for younger readers, this is a delightful, thoughtful assessment of a bicultural, bilingual life, in which Spanish remains the "language of fun, of summertime games." "Cold/hot, English/Spanish; that was our life." —*Kathryn LaBarbera*

Cottell, John E.
Code Name Badger: The True Life Story of a British Secret Agent.
Morrow, $19.95. 384p.

Cottell, serving in the British army in World War II, was recruited into a branch of the secret service known as SOE (Special Operations Executive) and sent by Churchill into occupied Holland in spring 1944 to deliver a coded message to a Dutch resistance leader. It was the beginning of 30 years as a secret agent, often in danger. For example, on one wartime mission he was almost disemboweled by the Nazis. His young Belgian wife, also an SOE agent, was tortured and killed in Ravensbruck on her third sortie into occupied France, and Cottell himself was captured, tortured by the Gestapo, and interned in Buchenwald until American forces freed him. Ironically, he had been set up by the SOE and was expected to break under torture, thereby giving false information to the Germans. Later, during the cold war, he was exposed by a traitor in the secret service and put in Moscow's Lubjanka prison. What with such lurid incidents, his life reads like the wildest of spy novels.

But it's all supposedly true, and the publisher claims it was written in defiance of Britain's Official Secrets Act. —*George Cohen*

Cray, Ed.
General of the Army: George C. Marshall, Soldier and Statesman.
Norton, $29.95. 849p.

An exhaustively detailed but accessible biography of a man who "exemplified in his lifetime all that was America's best—it's sense of mission, of responsibility, of integrity, even nobility." Those are Cray's words, and though they may be tinged in purple, their essential veracity is borne out by the record of Marshall's many impressive accomplishments during his lengthy career of service to the American public. Cray shows us how, as the architect of Allied grand strategy in World War II, Marshall played a crucial role in the defeat of Germany and Japan, and how, as the inventor and implementor of the eponymous Marshall Plan, he played an equally crucial role in the revitalization of postwar Europe. Two key ideas thus impress themselves upon the reader: that Marshall, more than any other individual man or woman, literally made the world safe for democracy; and that a direct line of cause and effect may be drawn from the institution of his policies and programs to the recent toppling of Communist regimes in Eastern Europe and the concurrent diminishment of Soviet power worldwide. Cray's conclusion? Marshall must be counted as one of the greatest men of this, or any, age. As such, he richly deserves the treatment accorded him here. —*Steve Weingartner*

✓ **Cronin, Anthony.**
No Laughing Matter: The Life and Times of Flann O'Brien.
Grafton Books/Trafalgar Square, $39.95. 400p.

One of the foremost modern Irish writers is Flann O'Brien, the persona of Brian O'Nolan (1911–66) when writing some of the most mordant, peculiar comic, or tragicomic novels, or antinovels, or metanovels in English. O'Brien had another pen name, Myles na gCopaleen (Myles of the little horses), under which he wrote in Irish one of the funniest books of this century, *An Béal Bocht* (translated as *The Poor Mouth*), and also, in both Irish and English, a daily column for the *Irish Times* called "Cruiskeen Lawn" (the little brimming jug), which, again, contains some of the greatest humorous and satiric writing in Western literature. He—O'Nolan-O'Brien-Myles—is shockingly little known in the U.S., a situation most previous books about him (scholarly disquisitions and inquests, almost autopsies, of his work) have not helped. This biography, written with genuine literary distinction by a poet and novelist who knew the man, may help bring the writer a wider audience. Cronin mixes biographical reconstruction with critical evaluation, placing both within the context of Irish culture and politics as O'Nolan knew and participated in them. His is a rich portrait and a piece of writing that reminds us that biography as well as the novel can be the medium of literary excellence. —*Ray Olson*

Biography

✓ **Crow Dog, Mary and Erdoes, Richard.**
Lakota Woman.
Grove Weidenfeld, $17.95. 288p.

Born Mary Brave Bird on South Dakota's Rosebud reservation, the author of this compelling autobiography knew all too soon that to be a "woman of the Red Nation, a Sioux Woman," would not be easy. Raped at 14, a drunken shoplifter while more privileged youth were still in school, she finally found herself in the American Indian Movement and began to rebuild her self-esteem. She traveled the trail of broken treaties and gave birth to her first child under fire at besieged Wounded Knee. Now married to the religious leader, Leonard Crow Dog, Mary continues her struggle for native self-determination. Thanks in part to collaborator Richard Erdoes—a prominent writer on Indian issues—this narrative flows from the oral tradition, especially in the deeply moving first chapter in which Mary recites the devastating losses she experienced before even reaching midlife. —*Pat Monaghan*

✓ **Doder, Dusko and Branson, Louise.**
Gorbachev: The Last Tsar.
Viking, $22.95. 442p.

At last, a book equal to the most interesting politician in the world. Doder and Branson, ace Moscow correspondents, trace in satisfying detail and with exemplary clarity the cataclysmic changes that the Soviet leader has been pressing since his 1985 accession to what, as their subtitle implies, continues to be the throne of Mother Russia. They show his successes and failures as alliances have shifted and seethed within the Communist hierarchy and as the peoples of the many separate nations cobbled together by the tsars and Stalin after them have taken to glasnost and perestroika with gusto. Even more impressively, they verify his steadfastness to the twin ideals of creating a thoroughly contemporary nation and keeping its union together. They represent Gorbachev's gut motivations as a dedication to historical, social, and economic truth; a determination to lift the Soviet peoples' level of material and psychological comfort; and an eagerness to be a part of the turning away of the Russian soul from dreams and wishful thinking to pragmatism and hard work. The authors present an almost preternaturally compelling portrait of Gorbachev's leadership by refraining from polemics both pro and con, by sticking to observation and the most modest and impartial interpretation possible. If you read only one book about Gorbachev, let it be this one. —*Ray Olson*

Edwards, Anne.
Royal Sisters: Queen Elizabeth II and Princess Margaret.
Morrow, $22.95. 448p.

Popular biographer Edwards burrows this time into the mutual lives of the reigning British queen and her only sibling. With typical lack of hesitation in assigning thoughts and attitudes and motives to the subjects of her research, Edwards limns the intertwined story of the two daughters of King George VI (who reigned from 1936 to 1952)—Elizabeth, older by four years and reserved, Margaret, always in her shadow, but feisty. That's the theme followed in this dual biography: since childhood, big sister was groomed for glory while little sister had to learn she would forever remain second best. The consequences of this on their relationships to spouses and parents are also examined. Far less than definitive, yet more than simply ladies-magazine fare. —*Brad Hooper*

Farrell, Suzanne and Bentley, Toni.
Holding on to the Air: An Autobiography.
Summit, $19.95. 340p.

American ballerina Farrell spent almost her entire professional career as a member of the New York City Ballet, including a period as chief muse and companion to choreographer George Balanchine. Farrell presents a fairly frank discussion of their relationship, in which their artistic compatibility never meshed with the romantically perilous reality of a May-December attachment. When Farrell fell in love with and married a fellow dancer her own age, she left the NYCB but eventually made a tearful and triumphant return to her home company. The main thrust of this account rests in Farrell's development from a stagestruck girl into one of the most acclaimed performers of her generation. Along the way, Farrell comments on the roles that Balanchine created for her and describes the rigors of rehearsal and performance in convincing terms. She also discusses the persistent injuries that ultimately led to her decision to stop dancing. This memoir also serves as moving tribute to Balanchine, a man who inspired—and who was inspired by—his dancers. —*John Brosnahan*

Fast, Howard.
Being Red.
Houghton, $22.95. 366p.

The late Howard Fast, an acclaimed historical novelist, was also a journalist, a public speaker, a pamphleteer, and, most notably, a martyr to the cause of the American Communist Party. This often intriguing and always well-written memoir tells of Fast's humble New York beginnings, his success as a youthful novelist, his rocky but enduring marriage, his World War II stint with the Office of War Information, and, more prominently, his card-carrying party status—along with his many battles with HUAC, J. Edgar Hoover and the FBI— and the blacklisting mentality of film and publishing executives. Fast never denied his leftward leanings, ultimately causing himself and his family a lot of grief. He served time for "contempt of Congress," traveled and spoke as a symbol of antifascism and socialistic ideals, ran for public office, and endured such snubs from the publishing community that he was forced to self-publish and -promote perhaps his most popular novel, *Spartacus*. Along the red road, he met and mingled with the likes of Pete Seeger, Paul Robeson, Jean-Paul Sartre, H. L. Mencken, John Howard Lawson, and others who expressed their admiration (if not their affection). This is a well-wrought

Biography

and evocative account, which, strange to say, "names many names." —*Martin Brady*

✓ **Fenyvesi, Charles.**
When the World Was Whole.
Viking, $19.95. 218p.

"In these closing years of the twentieth century, the authentic, distinct, historical Jew is turning into a folk memory." Fenyvesi has set out to preserve that memory by sharing his family history. His relatives were landowners in Hungary during the days of the Hapsburg empire, an unusual position for Jews, but one that harks back to biblical times. Fenyvesi's ancestors loved the land and lived generously and devoutly, raising large families and enriching the lives of their villages. This is the world of Issac Bashevis Singer—the realm of ghosts and miracles, dreams and blessings. Fenyvesi's prose sings the magic of long-cherished stories of several generations, particularly that of his grandfather, Karl Schwarcz, a wise and benevolent patriarch, and his "graceful, fragile, and otherworldly" grandmother. Working from his Uncle Shumi's family chronicle, Fenyvesi's retelling includes the collapse of the Schwarcz's "empire" after World War I and the suffering of the Holocaust. A moving and lyrical account of an exalted legacy. —*Donna Seaman*

Forbes, Malcolm.
What Happened to Their Kids? Children of the Rich and Famous.
Simon & Schuster, $19.95. 352p.

When it comes to the children of famous parents, perhaps Jesus was the only true success. Mostly, though, the well-known and well-to-do have produced rotters, and Forbes takes a certain amount of glee in presenting this alphabetically organized rogues gallery. In the *A*'s we learn about the son of Pope Alexander VI (father, apparently, of at least 14 kids), who was said to have scattered chestnuts over the floor while 50 nude prostitutes crawled about to retrieve them. Benjamin Franklin's son, William, wasn't kinky (at least Forbes doesn't know about it if he was), but young Bill dismayed his dad by becoming a leading Tory. And so it goes: Carrie Nation's daughter was an alcoholic, atheist Madalyn Murray O'Hair's son became a preacher. By the time readers get to the *R*'s and learn that the daughter of U.S. Representative Leo Ryan, who died in Jonestown, is a follower of Bhagwan Shree Rajneesh, there are no surprises left. This eminently browsable tale comes complete with Forbes' implicit message for beleaguered parents everywhere: damned if you do, damned if you don't. —*Ilene Cooper*

Gies, Frances and Gies, Joseph.
Life in a Medieval Village.
Harper, $22.95. 272p.

Through archaeological evidence and historical research, the Gieses re-create life in a typical English medieval village. Elton, England, is the focal point of the authors' efforts to portray the everyday life and social structure of the High Middle Ages. After giving a brief summary of Elton's origins and development in the Roman and Anglo-Saxon periods, the book examines just how the residents lived and worked within the feudal structure at the beginning of the fourteenth century. The emphasis is on the conditions of the villagers and peasants and not their masters, and the concentration on routines and events makes for a revealing glimpse of medieval culture at its most elemental level, with all of its religious, economic, and political nuances. Among the specific topics discussed are the justice system, the organization and influence of the church, and the various types of employment. Illustrated with photographs of artifacts from Elton itself and from other sources contemporary to the period. Notes, bibliography, glossary; index. —*John Brosnahan*

Gill, Brendan.
A New York Life: Of Friends and Others.
Poseidon, $19.95. 335p.

Long-term *New Yorker* staff writer and veteran book author Gill presents a series of biographical sketches of individuals, many deceased, with whom he has had some connection or were part of his New York arts-and-letters world. Averaging eight pages, the trenchant profiles demonstrate both exceptional literary dexterity and clear-eyed appraisal. Some of the figures Gill features are of limited note, including public relations man Ben Sonnenberg and art dealer Jay Rousuck, but others will be widely recognized, such as Joseph Campbell, Eleanor Roosevelt, and Dorothy Parker. Each sketch represents an engaging mix of wit and aplomb and will undoubtedly garner an extensive audience. —*Brad Hooper*

Goldman, William.
Hype and Glory.
Random/Villard, $18.95. 320p.

Goldman admits that "for years my two greatest ambitions in life have been to be a judge at the Cannes film festival and a judge at the Miss America contest." Amazingly enough, in 1988 his dreams came true. This memoir of his stints as evaluator of film and flesh does not read like a trip through fantasyland because Goldman is down-to-earth and even insecure around the edges (he's downright paranoid at times). As a screenwriter and novelist (known for *Marathon Man* and *The Princess Bride*), Goldman has seen plenty of movies made, but serving as a juror at Cannes gave him a whole new perspective on the business. (One of the worst elements of his learning experience: fellow juror Nastassja Kinski asking, "Why do you think so much?") Actually, he thought equally hard for the Miss America pageant and reports on the magic and misery he witnessed as a participant in that much-criticized beauty/scholarship competition. Even now he gets the giggles trying to explain the official point system of the 1938 Miss America Pageant ("Fifteen points for head construction? What language is that in?"). Sharp-witted and howlingly funny, this book will appeal to Hollywood fans and those who enjoyed Goldman's *Adventures in the Screen Trade.* —*Denise Perry Donavin*

Biography

✓ **Goodall, Jane.**
Through a Window: My Thirty Years with the Chimpanzees of Gombe.
Houghton, $21.95. 222p.

The author of the celebrated *In the Shadow of Man*, which covered Goodall's first 10 years at Gombe, offers another dynamic, anecdotal science popularization that dovetails with and extends the first book in recognizing and respecting chimpanzees as individuals and as members of a complex society. Readers of *Shadow* will appreciate learning what has happened to some of the chimps met previously, but the focus here is on their progeny and interrelationships, whether between mothers and children or in sexual behavior, power plays, war, and love. Characterizing the research as windows "opened up by science [through which] we can see ever further, ever more clearly, into areas that once lay beyond human knowledge," Goodall describes interactions witnessed by herself and her team, including scientists, students, and Tanzanian field staff members. She states that the study at Gombe has gone beyond providing a base for speculations about prehistoric life: it has opened a window into the way of life of our closest living relatives, giving us not only a better understanding of the chimpanzee's place in nature, but also of humanity's. Goodall also makes a passionate plea for the conservation and welfare of the animals, calling the captivity and abuse of chimpanzees "our shame." An enthralling account. —*Sally Estes*

Greene, A. C.
Taking Heart.
Simon & Schuster, $18.95. 208p.

Greene, a Texas journalist, says his "isn't so much a book about escaping death . . . as it is a book about finding life." In late summer 1987, his doctor and his wife, Betty, agreed he needed a heart transplant and convinced him to accept that fact. Sixty-four and in poor condition, he was turned down by one program but accepted by another; perhaps the most affecting part of his account is the description of waiting for the transplant. His desire to fill in the "lost hours" in the operating room spurred him to write, yet only in the last chapter does he describe the procedure. Among the concerns he raises along the way are the need for more reassurance of the patient while in the recovery area and whether to thank the donor. In a last poignant, personal note, he reveals that Betty died an "easy death" as he was finishing the book. A commonsensical, low-key account that may help potential transplantees and their families. —*William Beatty*

22

✓ **Greer, Germaine.**
Daddy, We Hardly Knew You.
Knopf, $19.95. 311p.

Greer cuts close to the bone with this family memoir that examines her father's life and their relationship. *Troubled* isn't exactly the word for this father-daughter bond; and *nonexistent* applies for only part of their lives together; but *perplexing* would seem to cover the various stages of their lives together and apart. World War II created the initial separation between the two when Greer's father went off to battle and did not see his just-born daughter for the duration. This book, however, represents a total break as Greer discovers that her father had created a chronicle of lies to disguise his common past from other people and from his own family. As Greer journeys around the world in search of the truth, she fearlessly and impressively sorts out her feelings, both those toward her father that have now been hopelessly transformed and revoked by her discoveries and those toward her own later experiences that are presented with so much spirit in this astounding book. —*John Brosnahan*

Grimes, Ann.
Running Mates: The Image and Reality of the First Lady Role.
Morrow, $21.95. 352p.

Is the first lady just the president's wife, or is she his closest political adviser and the person who will set the tone in domestic policy during his term? Is she solely a wife or also a politician? Political reporter Grimes explores these questions in an insightful book. Drawing on interviews (her own and published accounts) with the 1988 presidential candidates' wives, their own and their husbands' advisers, and longtime family friends, Grimes offers a behind-the-scenes look at the role these women played before, during, and, in the case of Barbara Bush, after the election. As might be expected, the majority of material concerns Kitty Dukakis and Barbara Bush; Grimes examines Dukakis' addiction problems in the context of the campaign and Bush's ability to build an image at odds with her true ambition and political astuteness. Also explored are such issues as whether the potential president's wife can have her own career (e.g., Elizabeth Dole's position as secretary of transportation), whether she should speak out on issues, how accessible her private life should be to the press, and whether her religious views represent a threat to her husband's individuality. A thoroughly engaging but altogether serious book. —*Jill Sidoti*

Grutman, Roy and Thomas, Bill.
Lawyers and Thieves.
Simon & Schuster, $19.95. 210p.

Trashing the profession people love to hate, well-known trial attorney Grutman feeds us feisty expert testimony about just how sleazy things get in the legal world. He comes out swinging, accusing lawyers of being greedy, manipulative, and cutthroat, the ultimate chameleons. And he has the

Biography

examples to back up his claims, beginning with the unbelievable but true story about his first boss in the Bronx in the 1950s. From there he takes us through his days in court with Larry Flynt ("the nation's court jester"), Jerry Falwell, and Henry Kissinger and provides an update on today's species of ambulance chasers, private eyes, and merger-acquisition attorneys and their unsavory practices. Rounding out his attack with comments on outrageous fees and incompetent juries and judges, Grutman leaves us laughing and crying. His pugnacity is bound to elicit controversy and plenty of admiration for a gutsy book. —*Donna Seaman*

Gyatso, Tenzin, Dalai Lama.
Freedom in Exile: The Autobiography of the Dalai Lama.
Harper, $22.95. 304p.

The Dalai Lama—born Tenzin Gyatso—has been a monk for 50 years, a leader in exile for more than 30. His story is, in part, a chapter in the 2,500-year history of Buddhism as well as a testament to the "mendacity and barbarity" of Communist China. This extraordinary tale begins in the rarefied mountains of Tibet, when the search party for the reincarnation of the Thirteenth Dalai Lama comes to Gyatso's home. Declared the Fourteenth Dalai Lama, his early years followed the traditions of his predecessors until China invaded Tibet in 1950. The young Dalai Lama tried to negotiate with the Chinese, but finally had to flee for his life in 1959. Taking refuge in India, he guided the settlement of Tibetan refugees and began the long struggle of making the world aware of the atrocities against humanity and the environment that the Chinese continue to commit in Tibet. Writing in careful English, a language he modestly claims not to be comfortable with, the Dalai Lama conveys his spiritualism—his gentleness, honesty, and forbearance. Besides the details of his daily life, he describes, in disarmingly matter-of-fact language, some of the supernatural mysteries of Tibetan Buddhism. Throughout, Gyatso shares his unshakable belief in the basic good of humanity and the necessity for universal responsibility. —*Donna Seaman*

Hartog, Leo de.
Genghis Khan: Conqueror of the World.
St. Martin's, $24.95. 225p.

Hartog's history of the powerful Mongol warrior-chieftain encompasses not only the span of the man's life, but the events that overtook the Mongol empire in the years immediately following his death. As recounted here, the story of Genghis Khan is one of recurrent warfare and the bloody conquest of unimaginably vast territories and the fabled kingdoms that lay within them. It's peopled with characters who are too fantastic not to be real: i.e., the valiant young Jalal al-Din Mangubirdi, last sultan of the doomed Kwarazm empire; Jebe and Subedai, two of the Khan's most brilliant generals; Jochi, Chaghatai, and Ogodei, the Khan's courageous but quarrelsome sons; and, of course, Genghis himself. Those with a general interest in history or a particular interest in military strategy will doubtless be enthralled by this book, which is one of the few that deals with authority on the Mongol's brief but violently dynamic turn on the world stage. —*Steve Weingartner*

✓ **Hayes, Harold T. P.**
The Dark Romance of Dian Fossey.
Simon & Schuster, $21.95. 384p.

This posthumously published, extensively documented biography by the former editor of *Esquire* magazine looks for the private Dian Fossey, the person behind the facade she painted in *Gorillas in the Mist* and that was somewhat carried on in Farley Mowat's *Woman in the Mist*, which drew heavily on Fossey's journals, notes, letters, etc. Hayes, an Africanophile, was galvanized by Fossey's brutal murder to get *Life* magazine to sponsor his three-year research into the zoologist's life. Hayes acknowledges that in trying to ascertain the truth, he often ran up against conflicting testimony—discrepancies between Fossey's memory and the accounts of others who were involved. There is not a lot of gorilla lore here; what emerges, however, is a compassionate, fascinating portrait of a driven woman, a portrayal that does not downplay the ugly side of her nature—her rages, her treatment of Africans, her frequent paranoia about people who worked for her, her drinking, her self-destructiveness, etc.—but still shows her as a woman of great courage and dedication to the mountain gorillas, a woman "who considered them doomed and would employ whatever means, fair or foul, to try to save them." Eventually, the preservation of the gorillas became her obsession, "the expression of all Fossey's deepest emotions and fears." —*Sally Estes*

Hayes, Walter.
Henry: The Man Who Was Henry Ford II.
Grove Weidenfeld, $19.95. 336p.

Both a friend and employee of Henry Ford for more than 20 years, Hayes offers a sympathetic memoir of the man who inherited and ran the American automobile giant founded by his grandfather. Moreover, as a former Ford executive, the author can chart the company's rocky history under Ford's leadership, including discussion of the company's expansion to an international corporation and the elements—Japanese competition, the oil embargo—that began to affect production and sales. Ford becomes in this account more than the man who launched the Edsel; he also brought to his company the tools of modern management that ensured its corporate survival and growth. Henry Ford's family life and three marriages are also charted, but the emphasis is chiefly on his company dealings and on his personality as a business leader. Hayes further offers his view of Lee Iacocca and his departure from Ford after a failed coup; this version of that incident provides a somewhat different account and analysis of these events than does Iacocca's best-selling book. —*John Brosnahan*

✓ **Holmes, Richard.**
Coleridge: Early Visions.
Viking, $19.95. 409p.

There really have been few literary biographies better than this Whitbread winner from England. It deals only with the first half of Coleridge's life, but the tempo is quick and the direction of the narrative focused. While most biographers spend a good deal of time dilly-dallying (showing off and proving their credentials), Holmes works hard to stay with his portrait and conceal the effort that lies behind his craft. And what a rich, lurid, fascinating subject he has. Coleridge was metaphysician, poet, preacher, journalist, opium addict, plagiarizer, scholar, father, and friend. He had a prominent forehead, wild, rolling eyes, sensuous lips, glossy black hair, and a brilliant sense of humor; not surprisingly, he dazzled nearly everyone who met him. His nightmares were terrible, his depressions were deep, his periods of manic energy prolonged. In short, Coleridge was very much the prototype of the romantic poet; like Beethoven, he synthesized in his life the themes and attitudes that would define the age. Holmes chose a point in the middle of Coleridge's life for his caesura; one wonders how the second volume of this work could be better than the first. —*Stuart Whitwell*

✓ **Hutton, Ronald.**
Charles the Second: King of England, Scotland, and Ireland.
Oxford, $29.95. 554p.

The hapless Stuart dynasty featured plenty of colorful though not necessarily superior monarchs during the centuries it held sway over Scotland and, later, the rest of the British Isles. Common historiographical opinion has it that Charles II, son of the deposed and beheaded Charles I, was an affable, even charming individual while only a passably good king. Hutton's biography of this seventeenth-century ruler corroborates the accepted wisdom. Only 18 years old when his father was forced to mount the scaffold and the Cromwellian republic proclaimed, Charles lived precariously in exile for many years. Eventually tiring of puritanical republicanism, the people of England, Scotland, and Ireland opened their doors to a restored monarchy under Charles II. The conclusion Hutton draws of Charles' reign is that he possessed "a set of strongly marked characteristics with a cold void at the center of them." Charles Stuart's life makes for fascinating reading, and Hutton does the story to a luminescent turn. —*Brad Hooper*

✓ **Jeal, Tim.**
The Boy-Man: The Life of Lord Baden-Powell.
Morrow, $29.95. 768p.

Baden-Powell, founder of the scouting movement: altruistic champion of young minds and bodies or fascist closet pederast? Biographer Jeal, the author of *Livingstone*, has another British hero with clay feet to cut down to size—or to restore to prominence. He begins by showing how Baden-Powell was first the recipient of hagiographical tributes, due to the influence of his wife and the scouting establishment, and later the object of wildly sensational rumors that couldn't be solidly documented. With his customary sensitivity and indefatigability, Jeal attempts to determine just where, between these two extremes, the truth lies. As Baden-Powell's early family life is exposed, he emerges as a child of the paradoxes and self-deceptions of late-Victorian society. His famous military exploits in the Boer War are open to question, his marriage late in life was probably a sham, and the real origin of the scouting ideal may have been consciously appropriated from someone else. But the most fascinating thing behind Jeal's assessment of these charges is the psychological detail brought into play as he reconstructs Baden-Powell's life and personality. Dampening without completely quenching the dazzling impression that Baden-Powell made upon the world, Jeal paints a portrait that is both real and agonizing. —*John Brosnahan*

Jeffares, A. Norman.
W. B. Yeats: A New Biography.
Farrar, $30. 374p.

Literary scholar Jeffares opts for an entirely new biography of Yeats rather than a revised version of his 1948 study, *W. B. Yeats: Man and Poet.* With the results of over thirty years of new critical opinion and research of his own and by other people, Jeffares is able to supply a sensitive investigation of the contradictions that Yeats experienced as he developed into one of the world's great poets. Although not intended as a critical study, the book also sheds new light on Yeats' work as Jeffares explores Yeats' flirtation with paranormal and occult phenomena, an interest that appears frequently in his writing. Likewise, Yeats' consciousness of modern Irish politics and his acknowledgment of his own role as a literary figure are skillfully documented. On a more private level, Jeffares re-creates Yeats' family life and education and, without yielding to the temptations of psychobiography, supplies a convincing chronicle of Yeats' life, mind, and art. —*John Brosnahan*

Kean, B. H. and Dahlby, Tracy.
M.D.: One Doctor's Adventures among the Famous and Infamous from the Jungles of Panama to a Park Avenue Practice.
Ballantine, $19.95. 480p.

Now in his late seventies, Kean is a consummate diagnostician and a humane physician who, with journalist Dahlby's help, tells his life story with humor, suspense, and imaginative flair. He began his career in tropical medicine but found himself in the army in Germany right after World War II. Unusual experiences there with penicillin production, a salt mine loaded with medical supplies and live ammo, and the original bust of Nefertiti were topped later in New York City when his patients included Salvador Dali, Gertrude Lawrence, Marcus Wallenberg, and the shah of Iran. His book is not, however, a matter of high-society name-dropping; it is the lively, believable story of a conscientious physician who sees both his patients and himself clearly. —*William Beatty*

Biography

Keith, Slim and Tapert, Annette.
Slim: Memoirs of a Rich and Imperfect Life.
Simon & Schuster, $22.95. 223p.

Imperfect it might have been, but what a life! And rich in both senses of the word. Slim Keith may not be a recognizable name to many, but those familiar with Hollywood in its glory days will remember her as the wife of director Howard Hawks and the model for the cool, elegant gal personified by another Hawks discovery (via Slim), Lauren Bacall. Keith writes rather dispassionately about her life with Hawks. Cold and uncaring, he nevertheless always wanted Slim by his side. That allowed her to be part of the Hollywood scene, associating with such manly types as Clark Gable. Wisely, Keith did not let a bad marriage stand in the way of her happiness; she fashioned a life for herself, then entered another marriage with Broadway producer Leland Hayward. Though Hayward was the love of her life, this marriage was not to last either, nor the succeeding one to Britain's Lord Keith. What makes Keith's life interesting is not so much what she's done, but how she's done it—with an enormous amount of style and savvy. As she writes, "God blessed me with a happy spirit and many other gifts. What I was not blessed with I went out and got. Sometimes the price was too high, but I've never been much of a bargain hunter." Keith's also been blessed with a good co-writer, who manages to transform the ramblings of a society woman into an interesting treatise on the way life should be lived, even if you're not center stage. —*Ilene Cooper*

Kesey, Ken.
The Further Inquiry.
Viking, $24.95. 256p.

Neal Cassady—aka Dean Moriarity in Jack Kerouac's *On the Road* —was king of the 1950s beatniks. A laborer with an eighth-grade education who picked up a lot of fancy learning on his own, he seemed a natural to drive the bus that bore those archetypal hippies, Ken Kesey and his Merry Pranksters, on the 1964 journey immortalized by Tom Wolfe as *The Electric Kool-Aid Acid Test*. His experience bombing back-and-forth cross-country in a state of chemically altered consciousness was invaluable. After all, who else could've been a better attending metaphysician at the birth of hippiedom? In Kesey's latest conceit—a closet docudrama illustrated with 150-plus color photos and a black-and-white "flip book" feature of Cassady in action—ol' Neal's spirit (his drugged body wore out some time ago) is on trial on the astral plane for precisely that midwifery. This is an excuse to rehash the whole trip, including verbatim samples of Cassady's motormouth raps from the driver's seat. The pictures considerably enhance the book's interest, which otherwise may be felt only by hardened high-'60s buffs. —*Ray Olson*

Khrushchev, Sergei.
Khrushchev on Khrushchev: An Inside Account of the Man and His Era.
Little, Brown, $22.95. 480p.

When the Politburo members threw out their mercurial comrade in October 1964, they also consigned him to that then-traditional vale of ex-Soviet leaders—the nonperson. And so Nikita Sergeyevich seemed to the outside world—never named, only denounced as the anonymous author of "harebrained" schemes—until the sensational publication of his memoirs by Little, Brown six years later. How that remarkable document was recorded and safeguarded from the KGB is the centerpiece of son Sergei's own reminiscences, which are inherently fascinating, both for describing the mechanics of getting the project done and for their observations of Khrushchev's life in retirement. Whatever one thinks of Nikita's public career, one must sympathize with the harassment to which the man was subjected by his successors in their effort to suppress the memoirs. If even the former leader of the Soviet Union was not immune to petty indignities like phone taps and bugs (in the bathroom, no less), imagine the lot of the average Ivan during the "era of stagnation," the current euphemism for the sclerotic Brezhnev years. Nikita's resistance to all this, ironically, converted him into a dissident, a status that reverberates beyond his grave—from the son's four-year joust with the authorities to erect a tombstone to his current efforts to retrieve remnants of the memoirs still in their hands. In recollecting his father's fall from power, Sergei makes eye-popping allegations, for example, that Brezhnev at first wanted to assassinate his boss before settling on legal means of removal. A critical piece of historical information, recommended highly. —*Gilbert Taylor*

Kirkland, Gelsey and Lawrence, Greg.
The Shape of Love.
Doubleday, $19.95. 256p.

Ballerina Gelsey Kirkland's previous memoir, *Dancing on My Grave,* was notable for its tell-all attitude toward drugs and sex among the ballet set, but the current installment concentrates less sensationally on her rehabilitation as both a dancer and a personality. After she was fired by the American Ballet Theatre, her career seemingly ended because of disability and drug addiction, Kirkland was invited in 1986 by the Royal Ballet to appear in *Romeo and Juliet* and *The Sleeping Beauty.* With her supportive husband serving as coauthor, Kirkland reveals the struggles she faced in trying to regain her technique and emotional equilibrium just as the spotlight was focused on her both as a dancer and an author. This book shows how Kirkland worked simultaneously on these two roles, and with flairs of temperament and wild mood swings, how she was often frustrated by other people and by herself in the process. This tale of survival against heavy odds, however, is no mere sob story. Kirkland reveals how she found more stability as a dancer and a woman in the turmoil of returning to the stage, if only for a final series of performances. —*John Brosnahan*

✓ **Kisor, Henry.**
What's That Pig Outdoors? A Memoir of Deafness.
Hill & Wang, $18.95. 226p.

Besides being the highly respected book editor of the *Chicago Sun-Times,* Henry Kisor is a fine purveyor of crisp prose in his own right and a well-known advocate of computers and their value in crunching words. He also happens to be deaf—though to hear him tell it, the stumbling blocks posed by any affliction are strictly in the eyes of the beholder. In this forthright memoir, Kisor tells the fascinating story of the hearing loss he suffered at age three (after a bout with meningitis), and how, with the dogged support of his parents, he became a student of the Mirrielees Method, which combines lipreading with visual charts and a knowledge of sentence syntax to allow the intelligent learner to "hear" with the eyes. In effect, Kisor was "mainstreamed" long before such arrogant terminology existed: he attended public school, went on to Hartford's Trinity College, gained a master's in journalism at Northwestern, and cut his teeth as a general editorial type with a Chicago sailing magazine before embarking on a big-time newspaper career. *Candid* is the watchword here, with Kisor relating stories of the practical difficulties of living in the hearing world, the vagaries of lipreading (hence the book's odd title), his constant struggle to improve what speech he does have, the valued role his wife has played in professional and personal situations, and the freedom that has been won for deaf people everywhere by various technical devices. Kisor is also outspoken regarding the current "deaf" agenda—he supports the concept of rights, but he's not sold on the heavy reliance on American Sign Language or the idea of deaf people maintaining their own culture. In addition, there is a uniquely interesting chapter in which Kisor recounts his adventures interviewing some of the great literary minds of our time. A liberating document—and a heck of a good read. —*Martin Brady*

Kuralt, Charles.
A Life on the Road.
Putnam, $19.95. 256p.

Kuralt, the genial, round-faced one so familiar from his CBS "On the Road" shows, relives his journalistic career. Starting as a 12-year-old stringer reporting baseball for the *Charlotte News*, Kuralt made rapid progress to high school then college newspapers and straight to a reporter's desk. From there he was summoned to New York City to write radio news for CBS broadcasters, including Edward R. Murrow. Then, at 23, Kuralt moved swiftly into the role of correspondent. He scooped international news agencies with photographs of a ship hijacking, covered Vietnam, and served as CBS Latin American reporter before he found his calling traveling the back roads of the U.S. The anecdotes from his motor-home days are priceless and fill nearly half the book. Kuralt is able to sum up a situation perfectly, imparting a strong visual image laced with wit. This tour of his own life may be his best human-interest feature yet. —*Denise Perry Donavin*

✓ **Kurth, Peter.**
American Cassandra: The Life of Dorothy Thompson.
Little, Brown, $22.95. 592p.

This exemplary biography not only details the life of one of America's great political journalists, but also admits us to the marvelous circles in which she traveled: from foreign correspondents in Europe between the wars to the literati who surrounded her husband, Sinclair Lewis; from deluded emperors to lesbian playwrights. The book's substantial length barely does justice to a brilliant woman's fascinating life. Arriving in Europe in 1920, all wit and guts, she became the first woman foreign bureau chief, reporting from Vienna and later Berlin. Expelled from Germany by Hitler himself, she began her anti-Fascist campaign in her syndicated column, "On the Record," while enduring the collapse of her marriage and the death of a son. In later years, before her own death in 1961, she became an éminence grise in the worlds of letters and journalism. Kurth's stirring account, which masterfully re-creates a life of substance and drama, should at least partially restore Thompson to the prominence that once was hers. —*Pat Monaghan*

Lambert, Gavin.
Norma Shearer: A Biography.
Knopf, $24.95. 292p.

Queen of MGM in the 1930s, Norma Shearer becomes the subject of an exceptional Hollywood biography, one that is perceptive rather than fawning or carping, soberly rather than sensationally written. The Canadian-born Norma was taken as a teenager by her mother, along with Norma's older sister, to New York so both girls could be involved in the new business of moviemaking. This strategy didn't work out so well initially, but soon Norma was invited to Hollywood. Married in 1927 to Irving Thalberg, the wunderkind head of production at MGM, Norma made smash after smash; but always worried about her beauty, she retired early—in 1942—rather than allow her adoring public to witness the inevitable erosion of her physical charms. Shearer died in 1983, one of those figures from the past about whom most people say, when reading the obituary, "But I assumed she was dead long ago." A generous treatment all the way through. —*Brad Hooper*

Lee, Hermione.
Willa Cather.
Pantheon, $29.95. 409p.

While never falling out of critical favor, the novels of Nebraskan Cather have certainly been enjoying a renaissance of appreciation lately. In British critic Lee's mind, the lucidity of Cather's prose belies the complexity of her sensibilities; other biographies of Cather, in Lee's estimation, too *easily* connect the person and the place—too readily find her writing a mere reflection of pioneer midwestern life and nothing more. To Lee, it is a much deeper situation than that. Her reading of Cather's novels and short stories reveals a series of conflicts between Cather's propensity for realism and her propensity for romance, her coexisting female and male self-identities, her dual sense of the power of raw nature and of civilization, among others. An erudite and graceful critical biography. —*Brad Hooper*

Biography

Li, Kwei.
Golden Lilies.
Viking, $17.95. 158p.

Rescued from dusty entombment by Eileen Goudge, author of *Garden of Lies* (1989) and numerous books for young adults, this collection of letters by a Chinese noblewoman is a treasure. Kwei-Li was born in 1867 and defied tradition by learning to read and write. The book contains two series of letters. The first were written to her new husband while he was away on political business, the second are letters to her mother-in-law, 25 years later, when Kwei-Li's husband was governor of Kiang-su. The early letters are fresh and vivid, scintillating with descriptions of the countryside and the goings-on at her mother-in-law's compound. Kwei-Li is by turns poetic and slyly sarcastic. The letters from Shanghai deftly convey the tremendous turmoil of 1912 when China was beset by Westerners and their customs. Kwei-Li is perceptive, passionate, and eloquent, providing an invaluable view of a pivotal point in history. —*Donna Seaman*

Lingeman, Richard.
Theodore Dreiser: An American Journey, 1908–1945.
Putnam, $39.95. 560p.

In the second volume of his definitive biography of Theodore Dreiser, Lingeman recounts the mature life of a giant of modern American literature. A sympathetic imagination breathes life and meaning into a wealth of facts uncovered through painstaking research. Lingeman deftly weaves his discussion of Dreiser's fiction and poetry into an engaging narrative of the writer's personal life, illuminating the complex interrelationship between art and experience. The writing of *An American Tragedy*, Dreiser's masterpiece, receives particularly thorough and nuanced treatment. Although center stage belongs to Dreiser, the reader catches glimpses of other prominent writers of the day, including H. L. Mencken, John Dos Passos, Sinclair Lewis, and Sherwood Anderson. Generous in his praise of Dreiser, Lingeman honestly depicts the man's failings—including his philandering and his political naïveté—in rendering a complete and balanced portrait. —*Bryce Christensen*

✓ Lisle, Laurie.
Louise Nevelson: A Passionate Life.
Summit, $24.95. 316p.

This biographical study aims to unite the two sides of American sculptor Nevelson's personality: the antic and confident grande dame familiar to her public, and the more reclusive artist who privately nurtured her doubts and conflicts over her role as a creator, mother, and woman. Coming to America from Russia as the daughter of Jewish immigrants, Nevelson never mired herself in memories of this past; instead, she would create herself in her own image. The personal and professional struggles this process involved are detailed in Lisle's sympathetic portrait, which covers both the glamorous social occasions that Nevelson illuminated with her eccentric manner and the bleaker moments when the artist struggled with her muse in her lonely studio. And, of course, there's a full load of outrageous anecdotes for which the ever-outspoken Nevelson has become famous. —*John Brosnahan*

Lovell, Bernard L.
Astronomer by Chance.
Basic Books, $22.95. 320p.

A pioneer of modern astronomy here tells his own story with remarkable insight and candor. Mesmerized as a child by a demonstration of powerful electric arcs, Lovell left the obscure village of his boyhood to become a premier scientist. Originally educated as a physicist, the author found himself in the forefront of radar research during World War II, research that unexpectedly helped open a whole new type of astronomy after the war. Beginning with a few pieces of surplus equipment, Lovell began to map the heavens by measuring the natural radio waves originating in distant stars and galaxies. This work required a radio telescope revolutionary in size and design. The huge telescope that now bears his name stands as a monument to Lovell's single-mindedness in the face of seemingly insuperable financial, legal, and bureaucratic obstacles. Although the book may hold a particular interest for specialists, general readers will find a deeply human narrative, largely unencumbered by technical jargon. Even those not attracted to astronomy will find a rare wisdom in Lovell's reflections on the risks and limits of science. —*Bryce Christensen*

MacAdams, William.
Ben Hecht: A Biography.
Scribner, $22.50. 384p.

The life of one of Hollywood's premier screenwriters is chronicled in this fascinating biography. MacAdams provides a straightforward look less at the events that shaped Hecht's life than at the events Hecht helped shape through his influential, multifarious career as a reporter, novelist, playwright, and scriptwriter. The author admits his infatuation with his subject and, not surprisingly, creates a flattering portrait. The reader does learn, however, some previously undisclosed details about Hecht's costly dealings with the movie industry and gains entry into the inner sanctums of Hecht's other chosen professions. MacAdams places his subject within the framework of cultural history, bringing added dimension to this thoroughly pleasurable work. —*Mary Banas*

Mann, Golo.
Reminiscences and Reflections: A Youth in Germany.
Norton, $25. 324p.

German historian Mann, the son of writer Thomas Mann, has an interesting story to tell of his early life, as would any child of such an important literary

Biography

figure. Add two momentous events—World War I and the rise of Hitler to power in the 1920s and 1930s—that would create tremors in German and world history, and Mann's memoir of growing up in this period assumes an even greater level of importance and resonance. The author's tales of his family place the account squarely in Mann's intellectual tradition (which several of his children, including Golo, have continued to uphold). As a noted historian, the author ingenuously covers the terrors of the first great European war of this century from his viewpoint as a young child awed by military myths but rather removed from the real terrors of the battle. His coverage of the early Nazi period when he was a college student, however, demonstrates how he early learned the bitter truths of the Third Reich and as a result left his country in 1933. The narrative ends with Mann going into exile, with Mann as child and Mann as historian functioning together throughout in a complex unity of unaffected reminiscence and profound scrutiny of the past. —*John Brosnahan*

Mermelstein, Max and others.
The Man Who Made It Snow.
Simon & Schuster, $19.95. 273p.

"I am considered the most valuable witness that the government has ever turned against the cartel. When I first started to talk in 1986, the goverment really didn't have any grasp of the enormity of the cocaine cartels in Colombia." If President Bush ever needed a PR piece to endorse the activities of the U.S. Drug Enforcement Agency, this is it. Mermelstein, a former engineer in a Puerto Rican hotel, became active in the Medellín cartel's drug-running activities through his wife's family. After that, from 1978 to 1985, he had a whale of a time transporting huge amounts of cocaine from Colombia to the U.S.—over land, over sea, in the air—making big dough and running around with a lovely band of free-basing banditos, including the members of the notorious Ochoa family and, more particularly, drug lord Rafael Cardona. Among his other extracurriculars, Mermelstein ran guns in the opposite direction (into Colombia) and was charged at one time with putting the hit on federal witness Barry Seal (he refused). Mermelstein's story is "as told to" writers Robin Moore (*The Green Berets*) and Richard Smitten, the end result being a mostly horrible account of horrible deeds done by horrible people (even the Colombian women come off as either mindless tarts or, in one case, a bloodthirsty dragon lady). Mermelstein concludes by telling us of his time served in prison (where drugs and sex for cash are rampant), the nice little deal he cut with the federal prosecutors (time served in exchange for information), his conversion to Catholicism (honest!), and the bleak life ahead of him as a fugitive from Colombian revenge. To his credit, Mermelstein doesn't really try to evoke any sympathy (perhaps because he knows none would be forthcoming). With drugs seemingly on everyone's minds these days, this book should interest plenty of readers. —*Martin Brady*

Middleton, Harry.
LBJ: The White House Years.
Abrams, $45. 272p.

Through black-and-white documentary news photographs and a short commentary, Middleton offers a more balanced portrait of Lyndon Johnson and his presidency than does the most recent installment in Robert Caro's epic biography, *Means of Ascent.* Middleton, a Johnson staff member and now director of the LBJ Library, has assembled photographs taken by the White House team led by photographer Yoichi Okamoto. This record of life and power in Washington and around the world goes beyond the usual boundaries of photojournalism in capturing a time and a place as the book suggests just what a complicated and compelling personality Johnson could be. Along with a revealing historical picture of the modern presidency, Middleton offers a sympathetic but not uncritical view of a man and his time. —*John Brosnahan*

Modisane, Bloke.
Blame Me on History.
Simon & Schuster, $19.95. 311p.

With fury and sorrow and unsparing analysis of himself and the apartheid system, a brilliant journalist tells what it's like to be black (a *native*) where the law is white. Less graphic and more intellectual than Mathabane's *Kaffir Boy*, Modisane's autobiography was first published in 1963 in South Africa and banned there until his death in exile in Germany in 1986. His focus is the destruction of his home in Sophiatown, the vital, violent, multicultural Johannesburg slum that was razed to make way for whites only. As he walks the broken streets, he remembers his life there—his authoritarian father forced to cringe before white police; the son made to do the same, again and again; the *tsotsi* (gangster) violence; the political protests; his newspaper assignment to try to worship in a white church; his alienation from black politics and white liberalism; his failed marriage; his decision to leave. The writing is sometimes sprawling and repetitive, but few books offer more depth and subtlety about the mind of South Africa, or about the pain of being marginal in any society. Modisane quotes the bitter graffiti writer who changed the segregated railway sign, "Natives cross here," to "Natives *very* cross here." —*Hazel Rochman*

Molesworth, Charles.
Marianne Moore: A Literary Life.
Atheneum, $29.95. 512p.

This biography of poet Marianne Moore examines the life and work of its subject in a vibrant manner, honoring both the spirit and substance of Moore's art. Moore the personality often has received more recognition than Moore the poet, and Molesworth integrates these two aspects of her life through a number of critical readings of her most important works while at the same time covering important steps in Moore's development as a poet. The influences on Moore's poetic style and her friendships with other writers and poets

Biography

are also probed in a revealing fashion. Molesworth affectingly re-creates Moore's life and world in its dazzling achievements and subtle complexities. —*John Brosnahan*

Nixon, Richard.
In the Arena: A Memoir of Victory, Defeat and Renewal.
Simon & Schuster, $21.95. 384p.

Say what you will about him, but Richard Nixon has to be the most indefatigable political character of the modern age. Mistrusted by millions, yet devotedly admired by millions of others, Nixon presses on, his mission to communicate his thoughts and opinions unfettered by time or age (at 77, he's younger than Reagan). This volume serves as a kind of omnibus collection: Nixon on China, Nixon on glasnost, Nixon on the press, Nixon on philosophy of life, Nixon on campaigning, and so on. The 40 chapters (e.g., "Enemies," "Family," "Causes," "Peace," "Illness") come off in typical Nixonese, that is, always conscious of the importance of a high tone, yet occasionally flawed by a suspicious corniness and a sense of ego that can make the reader cringe. The Watergate material is superficially self-effacing without Nixon ever admitting to anything other than poor judgment; the chapter on wife Pat is laudatory yet too brief and reveals nothing of how the first lady has fared recently; and the assault on critics is especially reserved for those mean-spirited ones who have cost Nixon millions in spurious litigation fees over the years. Otherwise, the material expressing Nixon's political world view is rather a rehash of previous, more specific volumes. (Nevertheless, Nixon does have an understanding of, and experience in, foreign affairs that can't be easily matched.) The great political names of the century are, of necessity, dropped freely, leaving the reader to concede that Nixon's done it all—and at a level of commitment that demands respect if nothing else. —*Martin Brady*

Njeri, Itabari.
Every Good-Bye Ain't Gone: Family Portraits and Personal Escapades.
Times Books, $17.95. 226p.

American journalist Njeri's family portraits are sensitive, often funny sketches that convey the complexity of relationships and the bittersweet nature of familial ties. She brings to life her "Jamaican princess" grandmother; an exasperatingly stoical mother and brilliant, flawed father; an outrageous, much-disapproved-of aunt; and assorted cousins and friends. Readers also witness the black experience: women who won't surrender, to relatives or other troubles; families sharing the burden of child rearing; and generations of gifted individuals who flower or are lost to the streets and drugs. Finally, these stories offer a glimpse of the fiercely bright, emotionally fragile child—the author—who was tempered by the fire of this family. Just as "every shut-eye ain't sleep," painful experience doesn't always mean failure. Readers will recognize and respond readily to Njeri's warmth, honesty, and wit. —*Virginia Dwyer*

Ogden, Chris.
Maggie: An Intimate Portrait of a Woman in Power.
Simon & Schuster, $22.95. 384p.

If Margaret Thatcher had not grown up from grocer's daughter to become prime minister, she would have liked to have been Anna, the English governess from *The King and I.* This intriguing account of one of England's most influential politicians expertly synthesizes British political history with a touch of tabloid-style zing, complete with action verbs. Like a brilliant Thatcher campaign, *Maggie* leaves the reader impressed; despite brief examinations of the opposition's view, her strong political sense seems as irrefutable as the dark side of her policies. Thatcher emerges from these pages as a bright, driven political mind, a politician who combines hard work, little sleep, and a particular brand of determination to earn a job she never believed she nor any woman would hold in her lifetime. The leader who directs wars and busts unions admits to shedding a few tears after a hard work day; she believes women's' rights have been won, yet she irons and turns out the airing cupboard for relaxation. Ogden says, finally, "Try to imagine what it would be like today if she had not been around a decade ago." It is as difficult to picture a hypothetically un-Thatchered country as it is to imagine a Britain still governed by consensus and public politeness, carefully considered feelings and the politics of compromise. —*Deanna Larson-Whiterod*

Pinkus, Denny.
A Vase for a Flower: Tales of an Antique Dealer.
St. Martin's, $16.95. 224p.

Throughout his career as an antique dealer in Israel, Pinkus has collected stories as rare and precious as the relics, artwork, and jewelry that he buys and sells. One of his tales is about a woman who refuses to buy some valuable jewelry until the store owner summons up a suitably romantic tale about its origins (in total disregard of the impeccable facts about the item's constitution and provenance). Pinkus reaches back into his childhood in Bolivia (where his parents resided after fleeing Nazi Germany) to tell about Catholic heirlooms that indicated hidden Jewish heritage forsaken during the Spanish Inquisition. Pinkus tells how he has identified priceless items unrecognized by his competitors; he also tells about instances when he has not been as canny. Pinkus has a fine Singer-like touch, and he artfully keeps his stories quite brief (two pages or so). Once begun, this collection is difficult to put down. —*Denise Perry Donavin*

Porter, Katherine Anne.
Letters of Katherine Anne Porter.
Atlantic Monthly Press, $29.95. 744p.

Katherine Anne Porter was one of the finest short-story writers the U.S. has produced. In celebration of the one-hundredth anniversary of her birth, here is a selection of the myriad extant letters penned by her to friends and relatives. Appearing either verbatim or in extract, the letters are definitely worthy of publication in book form, for, obviously investing much time and thought into her correspondence, Porter related scintillating details about her many travels, social behavior, and, of course, her writing; from the latter, the reader appreciates her dedication to her art and, too, what a judicious, discerning critic she was of the writing of others. A life both outwardly and inwardly churning is observable in these letters. —*Brad Hooper*

✓ **Potter, E. B.**
Admiral Arleigh Burke.
Random, $24.95. 512p.

During World War II, Burke was known as "31-knot Burke" for the full-tilt way he managed a destroyer flotilla in sea battles with the Japanese. Though he never received the public acclaim accorded to the Halseys and MacArthurs, Burke did rise to a certain level of fame for a brief span of time. That time is long past; today, his name and reputation have almost faded from public memory. With this sprawling biography, Potter seeks to refocus attention on a bona fide hero and a genuinely interesting man who is now known, probably to his amused displeasure, as "the last living great naval commander of World War II." This is a work of love on Potter's part and was written with the aid and blessing of Burke himself. More than an illuminating biography, it is a stirring account of men and the sea, a world at war, and the modern evolution of the U.S. Navy. —*Steve Weingartner*

Pritchard, William H.
Randall Jarrell: A Literary Life.
Farrar, $25. 352p.

Some members seem to disappear from American literature's hall of fame; others seem to reappear; and still others, like Randall Jarrell, the poet and critic who died a quarter of a century ago, wait outside the portals for canonization. Pritchard's judicious study should carry some weight in the deliberations, wherever and by whomever they are conducted. It is the first comprehensive attempt to read each half of its subject's life—the written part and the lived part—in the context of the other. Readers envious of precosity will follow avidly the literary career of the intimidating undergraduate sponsored by John Crowe Ransom, Allen Tate, Robert Penn Warren, and Yvor Winters. Pritchard's familiarity with the careers of professional poets, his close, no-nonsense readings of poetry, and his appreciation of that lesser genre, the literary review, are authoritative. This book should be of genuine interest to readers indifferent to the eternal pecking order but concerned with Jarrell's unique solutions to the social and aesthetic problems faced by poets. —*Roland Wulbert*

Randall, Willard Sterne.
Benedict Arnold: Patriot and Traitor.
Morrow, $25. 516p.

A figure of ignomiy, Benedict Arnold here receives surprisingly sympathetic and nuanced treatment. Tracing Arnold's life from his high-spirited boyhood in Puritan Connecticut to his contentious final years in London, Randall depicts a complex and fascinating man—brave but vain, magnanimous yet avaricious, patriotic but self-interested. The reader is led not to excuse Arnold's treachery but to admire his battlefield courage before his political apostasy and to sympathize with his sense of injustice when he was repeatedly slandered by jealous Revolutionary rivals. Exploding the prevalent view that Arnold's wife was an innocent bystander during her husband's perfidy, Randall exposes Peggy Arnold as a charming but cunningly active plotter against the security of the U.S. Although the Arnolds command center stage, the narrative offers tantalizing glimpses of George Washington, John Adams, Horatio Gates, and other prominent political and military leaders. This biography deserves serious study from those interested in understanding the perilous struggles that gave birth to the nation. —*Bryce Christensen*

Rhodes, Richard.
A Hole in the World: An American Boyhood.
Simon & Schuster, $19.95. 256p.

Rhodes, the author of *The Making of the Atomic Bomb,* now tells the story of how he grew up as a victim of child abuse. He was barely a year old when his mother killed herself with a gun while he lay sleeping in his crib. Left with three children to raise alone, Rhodes' father struggled to earn a living and care for his family singlehandedly. Enter, at this point, the evil stepmother and the source of the writer's physical and emotional torments—vividly portrayed in concentration-camp language. (He was saved only by being placed in a home for delinquent boys with his older brother.) Rhodes surges from Tom Sawyer antics to Nazi metaphors, with revenge the theme of his story, all told in a blunt yet simple manner. Unfortunately, the scars are so intermingled with lyrical nostalgia that the process of healing that this account celebrates becomes more a laborious work of therapy for Rhodes than a cautionary domestic lesson for his reader. —*John Brosnahan*

Rowan, Carl T.
Breaking Barriers: A Memoir.
Little, Brown, $19.95. 424p.

Despite some stilted and hasty writing, the autobiography of the famous black journalist who personally crashed many ossified whites-only parties is magnetically readable, at times deeply moving for anyone who cares about justice and equality. Rowan was one of the first black naval officers, the first black reporter on a major metropolitan daily, one of few black newsmen covering the major civil rights events of the 1950s, the first black higher-up in the State Department, one of the first black ambassadors, etc. Also, and source of much of his memoir's deepest interest, Rowan advised LBJ, serving as USIA director and National Security Council member during his presidency. The mercurial Texan is arguably the most intriguing Oval Office occupant ever, and Rowan's anecdotes about him tighten his hold upon our imaginations. There were many Johnsons, Rowan says; the one we ought to remember "was the best president that the poor, 'at risk' people of America ever had." After

Biography

his presidential service, Rowan again crossed the Rubicon, becoming the first black syndicated columnist. Now a senior political commentator, he recently came under fire for a shooting incident that he thoroughly explains, as he does nearly everything in the book, without tooting his own horn too much. —*Ray Olson*

Sachs, Albie.
Running to Maputo.
Harper, $18.95. 224p.

Antiapartheid radical Sachs, a white lawyer, made world headlines two years ago when he was nearly killed in a car-bomb assassination attempt in Maputo, Mozambique. He lost an arm and an eye. His account of the explosion and his journey to recovery is intimate, wrenching, and funny, integrating the personal and the political with a poignant self-consciousness and a strong sense of the absurd that in no way diminish his passionate commitment to the African National Congress. "I lost my arm, my watch, my signature, my handshake, the callus on my middle finger where I held my pen," he says. But he also got the chance to start anew. The long months in a London hospital and in physical therapy put him in touch with his body, and he's as candid about his coming to terms with his disability (he refuses to wear a prosthesis) and about his celebration of sensuality (he laughs at himself discussing perestroika with his lover in the bath) as he is about his fervent ascetic self. Previously, Sachs survived years of solitary confinement in a Cape Town prison. Yet his greatest heroism lies in his transcendence of all desire for personal vengeance; he believes his triumph will be his return to a democratic, nonracial South Africa. —*Hazel Rochman*

✓ **Sakharov, Andrei.**
Memoirs.
Knopf, $29.95. 627p.

When Andrei Sakharov died in December 1989, the world mourned. The *New York Times* wrote that he was "widely referred to as the conscience of Soviet society." His memoirs, completed after his release from exile in Gorky, were written both to refute the insidious lies of the KGB and to set down the truth about himself and his beloved and long-suffering activist wife, Elena ("Lusia") Bonner (author of *Alone Together*). An inspired physicist assigned to work on thermonuclear weapons and controlled fission, Sakharov grew concerned about the biological implications of nuclear testing and wrote the first of his many influential and controversial public statements. Often putting his scientific work on hold, the Nobel Peace Prize recipient became a tireless champion for "prisoners of conscience," communicating his convictions about social injustice to the West and to Soviet leaders in spite of constant harassment and threats. His accounts of the famous hunger strikes are chilling—the mistreatment suffered, the strength of such gentle people—and his descriptions of the labor and determination required to create and disseminate his writings are extraordinary. Stupefyingly cruel, the KGB routinely confiscated

Sakharov's manuscripts, diaries, and notes; he had to rewrite his memoirs several times. This record of persecution and perseverance, illuminated by the radiance of Sakharov and Bonner's moral power, reminds us of the importance of the written word. —*Donna Seaman*

Silesky, Barry.
Ferlinghetti: The Artist in His Time.
Warner, $24.95. 320p.

Lawrence Ferlinghetti's *A Coney Island of the Mind* is the best-selling modern book of poetry. Silesky's biography, besides giving us the facts of the poet's life, also features material based on interviews with fellow writers, critics, and acquaintances, who offer insight into the Ferlinghetti oeuvre. Silesky takes a peculiar approach to the coincidences of Ferlinghetti's life: "While Gertrude Stein was telling Hemingway that he was not a good enough writer ... Emily was living with her young charge (Lawrence) some 120 miles east of Paris . . . where Gutenberg may have been when he invented the printing press." (Far out—but so what?) Other coincidences may raise questions about destiny in the minds of the most rational-scientific readers, for example, the 20-year-old armed robber just released from Clinton Prison who lets Allen Ginsberg, recently released from a mental hospital, read his poems in a lesbian bar is Gregory Corso. This book may bring home to many the realization that the Beats are now history. Was it so long ago? —*Roland Wulbert*

✓ **Simon, Kate.**
Etchings in an Hourglass.
Harper, $19.95. 256p.

The third and final volume of Simon's memoirs retains the captivating frankness of *Bronx Primitive* and *A Wider World*, accounts of her childhood and adolescence. Here we read of Kate Simon the talented, persevering adult, finding an outlet for her omnivorous interest in the world in her career as a travel writer. Simon's personality was perfect for this strenuous undertaking; she was adventurous, curious, tolerant, flexible, and sensual, possessing an anchoring yet buoyant sense of self. Travel also helped her cope with a staggering string of tragedies—she lost a husband, her only child, and her younger sister to disease. Simon tells their stories as well as tales about her affairs, friendships, and other entanglements in Mexico, England, Italy, India, and New York. Written in the last years of her life—Simon died in February 1990—this book offers eloquent testimony of a bold, creative, and examined life, fully lived. —*Donna Seaman*

Styron, William.
Darkness Visible: A Memoir of Madness.
Random, $15.95. 83p.

The strange fruit of American novelist Styron's long bout with depression is this memoir of his affliction—and that of other noted writers—with this little-understood psychological phenomenon. Styron first introduces his own case history with a gripping account of the condition's paralyzing climax on a trip to Paris. He then digresses a bit, adding his own name to a list of notable writers and artists who have experienced similar self-doubts and suicidal tendencies. In Styron's instance, alcohol addiction fueled the crisis that landed the writer in the hospital where he made his recovery. For all that Styron admits about his problems, however, much remains unsaid, particularly regarding the ways this depression affected his own writing and working habits. Unfortunately, while Styron poignantly reveals his own suffering, he adds minimal understanding to the overall medical problem, either as to what caused it or how it can be contained and cured. This essay is an expanded version of a speech first given at Johns Hopkins University School of Medicine and later published in *Vanity Fair*. —*John Brosnahan*

Thwaite, Ann.
A. A. Milne: The Man behind Winnie-the-Pooh.
Random, $29.95. 576p.

Milne is known worldwide as the author of *When We Were Very Young,* *Winnie-the-Pooh, Now We Are Six,* and *The House at Pooh Corner*. What many don't realize is that this whimsical children's writer was, in his time, a successful journalist and West End and Broadway playwright. In this insightful biography, Thwaite traces Milne's life from boyhood to death, exploring his complex relationship with his son, Christopher Robin, and brother, Ken, and his equally complex feelings about his writing career: though Pooh brought him fame and fortune, it was his theater work for which Milne wanted to be remembered. In life, as Thwaite shows, Milne rubbed shoulders with the rich and famous—H. G. Wells, P. G. Wodehouse, J. M. Barrie, Leslie Howard, and others. The author also clears up confusion about the origin of Winnie-the-Pooh's name, sheds new light on Milne's collaborations with illustrator Ernest Shephard, and brings a wider understanding to the relationship between father and son. For devotees of Pooh and children's literature, as well as followers of the British literary scene, this portrayal fascinates as it entertains. —*Barbara Elleman*

Trump, Donald J. and Leerhsen, Charles.
Trump: Surviving at the Top.
Random, $21.95. 236p.

Three years after his best-selling *Trump: The Art of the Deal*, in which the New York financial wizard offered sage business advice and shared details of his big spending, comes his testimony on how to remain on top of the heap once you've scrambled to get there. With a senior writer at *Newsweek*, Trump relates the recent ups and downs he's experienced—the former including his purchase and restoration of the Plaza Hotel and his construction of the Taj Mahal casino in Atlantic City, and the latter centered on his marital troubles and the financial overextension that nearly brought his empire down. Written with confidence—naturally—this is a delicious peek at the habits and philosophy of one for whom "the important thing is the getting, not the having." —*Brad Hooper*

✓ **Tucker, Robert C.**
Stalin in Power: The Revolution from Above, 1928–1941.
Norton, $29.95. 672p.

According to Tucker's massive biography, Stalin, by the mid-1920s, had come to fancy himself capable of being a state builder at least on a par with Alexander Nevsky, Ivan the Terrible, Peter the Great, and, especially, the just-deceased Lenin. While the general secretary recognized in the collectivization of agriculture—as prelude to industrialization—the area in which he could realize his historic ambition, he would accomplish his task through a calculated act of terror aimed at the dispossession of the peasants. From his reading of the Russian past, he concluded that such were the means necessary to make his revolution "from above" successful where others had failed. So the deed was done, and in 1934 the 17th Party Congress gathered to praise *de profundis* the genius who pulled it off. Two events belied the obeisance paid to Stalin: a cabal tried to replace him with Sergei Kirov, and 200 delegates actually voted against him. In a brilliant psychological analysis, Tucker treats this episode as the fulcrum, in Stalin's mind, for solving his political problems. Hence, Stalin set up the "judicial" machinery of the Terror in the summer of 1934 and, probably in emulation of Hitler's "blood purge" of the same season, put the guillotine in motion by arranging for Kirov's assassination in December 1934. Tucker makes his case in the manner of a prosecutor ticking off facts in an airtight case; his provocative brief caps effectively robs Stalin of his most fervent wish: to have history remember him as Russia's greatest leader. —*Gilbert Taylor*

Ulrich, Laurel Thatcher.
A Midwife's Tale: The Life of Martha Ballard, Based on Her Diary, 1785–1812.
Knopf, $24.95. 416p.

Scholars, educators, researchers—in fact, anyone seeking a better understanding of how life was lived in New England during the late 1700s will find this richly detailed biography immeasurably useful and appealing. Ulrich, an associate professor of history, has carefully combed the daybooks and interleaved almanacs kept by housewife and midwife Martha Ballard beginning at age 50. From these early diaries Ulrich extracted the telling details of Ballard's life in and around the seaport town of Hallowell, Maine, and pieced together an accurate account, enlarged by the editor's commentary, of "the dailiness" of the average woman's lot. Here we catch a rare glimpse of family events, visits to neighbors, dangerous river crossings, childbirth, weather highlights, public scandals, and ordinary workaday doings in the plain, quaint words of the person who lived or observed them. The seemingly trivial becomes fraught with meaning in the skilled hands of this historian, and what history texts typically make abstract is returned to concrete form here. —*Mary Banas*

Biography

Wallach, Janet and Wallach, John.
Arafat: In the Eyes of the Beholder.
Carol Publishing Group/Lyle Stuart, $19.95. 550p.

He likens himself to the phoenix, arisen from fire, but in the U.S. he is simply a terrorist. However, recent events have spawned questions about the true Yasser Arafat, stubble-cheeked chairman of the PLO. "Is he a terrorist?" "Is he—terrorist or no—in control of his movement?" What the Wallachs, coauthors of *Still Small Voices*, have created to answer such questions is less a biography than an exposé. Exposed in *Arafat* are the details of the chairman's life and early activism; the conflicts of peoples—Israel, the Arab nations, Arafat's Fatah and other Palestinian organizations—grasping for power and land in the Middle East; and the covert, previously undisclosed, negotiations between the U.S. and the PLO. Through their ongoing research and interviews with numerous leaders, from Israel's Yitzhak Shamir to Palestinian radical George Habash to Arafat himself, the authors have molded many verbal descriptions of Middle Eastern history into a resonant, sometimes contradictory, but always compelling study. Arafat appears as the proud, indefatigable leader who, in practice, is pragmatic and political. —*Angus Trimnell*

Business

Akst, Daniel.
Wonder Boy: Barry Minkow—the Kid Who Swindled Wall Street.
Scribner, $19.95. 288p.

People get cheated and conned every day. Only when those whose job it is to know better become victims is it remarkable. Young entrepreneur Minkow fooled auditors and supposedly savvy investors and was a "media darling," the subject of glowing articles and an occasional talk-show guest. Because he made such good copy, the press initially told his story unquestioningly. Minkow was a 15-year-old rug cleaner who went on to create ZZZZ Best, a carpet-cleaning service, and made more than $100 million while still a teenager. His company, though, turned out to be a front for phony loans, money laundering, tax evasion, and credit-card scams; Minkow was convicted on 57 counts of fraud and sentenced to 25 years in jail in March 1989. This story has already been told by Joe Domanick in *Faking It in America*, but reporter Akst was one of the first skeptics and originally broke the story, covering it for more than two years in the *Los Angeles Times* and the *Wall Street Journal*. He tells the tale of what Minkow did—and how he did it—exceptionally well. —*David Rouse*

Band, Richard E.
Contrary Investing for the 1990s: The Insider's Guide to Buying Low and Selling High.
St. Martin's, $18.95. 260p.

One of the more intriguing theories of speculation is that of contrary investing. Espoused in varying forms by several successful investment strategists, the theory says essentially that the key to investment profits is to distrust popular advice, ignore herd psychology, and avoid "fashionable" trends. Instead, the individual must thoughtfully analyze alternative options. Band, editor of the widely read newsletter "Personal Finance," updates his earlier version of the insider's guide to buying low and selling high, *Contrary Investing* (McGraw-Hill, 1985). He advises how best to buck the crowd in stocks, bonds, and real estate and suggests how to cope with the possible return of high inflation rates. For the small investors with the heart of a gambler, this book will have all the appeal of a straight flush. —*David Rouse*

Bernstein, Aaron.
Grounded: Frank Lorenzo and the Destruction of Eastern Airlines.
Simon & Schuster, $19.95. 238p.

Perhaps no CEO is more widely despised than airline manipulator Frank Lorenzo. He is loathed by unions and employees. He lacks the respect of fellow business leaders; Eastern Airlines ranked 301st out of 305 companies in *Fortune*'s 1990 list of most-admired firms. A federal judge declared his management team incompetent. *Business Week* labor writer Bernstein tells the four-year, headline-grabbing tale of Eastern Airlines' tailspin with absorbing detail—right up to this year's ouster of Lorenzo and Eastern's bankruptcy proceedings. Included in the unusual assortment of principals are ex-astronaut Frank Borman, convicted junk-bond dealer Michael Milken, and former baseball commissioner Peter Ueberroth. In itemizing Lorenzo's union-busting campaigns and financial scheming, Bernstein offers an intriguing, instructive story with a cautionary message: American business can no longer arrogantly treat employees as a disposable resource. —*David Rouse*

Bull, Diana and St. James, Elaine.
The Equity Sharing Book: How to Buy a Home Even If You Can't Afford the Down Payment.
Penguin, $8.95. 309p.

Two California realtors introduce the concept of equity sharing ("the way at least two parties—an owner-occupied and nonresident owner—pool their funds to buy a property") in this accessible guide to an innovative method of purchasing real estate. As explained, both owners are listed on the deed and mortgage and when the property is sold, the partners share in the profits of the sale. The authors cover all facets of this unique real estate transaction that promises benefits for both parties. Numerous case histories are peppered throughout the text to augment the discussions of tax considerations, financing, the equity sharing agreement, property maintenance, expenses, and potential problems. Admitting that this is more complex than a conventional

Business

real estate purchase, the savvy realtors do a credible job of introducing and explaining a method of real estate wheeling and dealing often used by first-time buyers lacking sufficient down-payment funds. —*Sue-Ellen Beauregard*

Card, Emily.
The Ms. Money Book: Strategies for Prospering in the Coming Decade.
Dutton, $19.95. 234p.

Even though *Ms.* magazine and the women's movement have both undergone many changes over the last 15 years, each is still primarily concerned with the economic status of women. Card, who was responsible for the drafting of the Equal Credit Opportunity Act, is a *Ms.* contributing editor. On cable television, in the magazine, and now here, she counsels women on financial planning—emphasizing cash flow, tax effect, and future growth. After explaining these concepts, she applies them to eight cases that represent composites of typical women's financial pictures. Card also provides guidelines for adapting her advice to individual situations. Numerous appendixes include tax charts and tables and identify additional resources. —*David Rouse*

Ciullo, Peter A.
Save Big Money on a New Car: A Common Sense Buyers Guide.
Maradia Press, $6.95. 64p.

In fewer than 100 pages, Ciullo exposes the car-buying process for what it is—a negotiated sales transaction. He helps the reader in constructing lists of must-have features, selecting possibilities among the many car models, determining costs incurred by the dealer, and preparing a facts-and-figures sheet with which to meet the salesperson. Using hypothetical couples in typical buying situations for illustration, Ciullo enjoins dealing up from the invoice rather than down from list price, removing the rebate from the sales negotiations, and refusing to pay such manufacturer-reimbursed costs as dealer prep and advertising. Overall, this little guide is easy to read, neither too dry nor overly detailed. —*George Hampton*

The Editors of Entrepreneur.
Entrepreneur Magazine's Complete Guide to Owning a Home-based Business.
Bantam, $12.95. 320p.

Many individuals yearn for the independence that a 9-to-5 job cannot give them. Add to that the fact that more jobs in more industries are becoming less secure. The result is a growing number of persons who want to start their own business. For many who lack start-up capital, though, the dream of owning a business is an elusive one. For these individuals, an attractive alternative is establishing a home-based business. There are already scores of books devoted to starting and running a business out of one's home. A few of them are quite good; many are not. Now comes an excellent, comprehensive guide from the editors of *Entrepreneur* magazine. Publishers of the tremendously popular start-up manual series, they offer expert advice drawn from their monthly magazine. *Entrepreneur*'s material is not normally available in trade book format. *—David Rouse*

Fucini, Joseph J. and Fucini, Suzy.
Working for the Japanese: Inside Mazda's American Auto Plant.
Free Press, $19.95. 252p.

Satoshi Kamata has already suggested that conditions in a Japanese company may not be as harmonious and benevolent as they are often portrayed. In *Japan in the Passing Lane* (Pantheon, 1983) he showed the hardships and dehumanization faced by workers on Toyota's assembly lines. The Fucinis, a husband-wife team who have compiled two previous books profiling notable entrepreneurs, similarly describe conditions at Mazda's Flat Rock, Michigan, auto plant. They suggest that cultural differences between management and workers further complicate problems. Theirs is a disturbing picture. Some employees may have had axes to grind, but even so, the authors interviewed more than 150 employees and managers from the Flat Rock facility. And Mazda backed out of its original agreement to cooperate. The Fucinis provide a stark counterpoint to the many books on Japanese management. *—David Rouse*

✓ Gabor, Andrea.
The Man Who Discovered Quality: How W. E. Deming Brought the Quality Revolution to America.
Times Books, $21.95. 320p.

Only recently have Americans become aware of W. E. Deming, the one individual most often credited with changing "made in Japan" from a synonym for cheap, poorly made merchandise to one for quality. Even though he has been the subject of several books and scores of articles, few are really certain of his specific contributions. Gabor, a *U.S. News & World Report* senior business editor, details how Deming introduced the Japanese to quality control. She then devotes the greater portion of her book to describing how a handful of American companies (Ford, General Motors, Florida Power and Light, Xerox, Procter & Gamble) have adopted Deming's principles and why many more should. Because much of the material about Deming has not been accessible to the general reader and because of Deming's unique importance, this book is a significant addition to the literature of business. *—David Rouse*

✓ Gelsanliter, David.
Jump Start: Japan Comes to the Heartland.
Farrar, $19.95. 214p.

Dedicated to his father, "who would never drive a foreign-made car," Gelsanliter's book charts the evolution of the American automobile industry since the Japanese began building plants in the U.S. Documenting the 1980s and the arrival first of Honda in Ohio, then of Nissan in Tennessee and Toyota in Kentucky, the author focuses on the conflict between U.S. labor practices

Business

and the Japanese insistence on remaining nonunion. The roles of union-busting law firms, newspaper editors, NAACP and AFL-CIO representatives, and the UAW in this controversy make for intriguing and enlightening reading. In addition, discussions of key American managers in the Japanese plants and state government officials who heavily recruited Japanese business to their counties reveal the politics of this industry. Gelsanliter shows us the pros of Japanese investment, teaching the value of competition. With Honda soon to pass Chrysler as the number three U.S. automaker, this chronicle provides a riveting and timely look at how the U.S. and Japan are adapting both to a world economy and to each other. —*Kathryn LaBarbera*

✓ **Goodrum, Charles and Dalrymple, Helen.**
Advertising in America: The First 200 Years.
Abrams, $49.50. 288p.

Advertising both helps set and reflects trends. As a result, it serves as an important barometer of business, culture, and society. Goodrum and Dalrymple have put together this magnificent 200-year history of print advertising in the U.S. They document changes in the way we live, but focus particularly on the role of women in our society. Goodrum's text is filled with fascinating narratives, and the 566 illustrations in the oversize volume are sometimes amusing, sometimes surprising, and always interesting. There is an excellent bibliography, and the detailed index makes this a useful reference book. It's also the ideal Christmas present for those have-everything ad execs. —*David Rouse*

Holstein, William J.
The Japanese Power Game: What It Means for America.
Scribner, $22.95. 256p.

Almost everyone recognizes the names Sony, Minolta, and Honda, but few can identify Nakasone, Takeshita, Hashimoto, or Kato. Holstein, a *Business Week* associate editor and two-time Overseas Press Club award winner, portrays these and other Japanese political figures and shows how American lives are more affected by political decisions made in Japan than they are by products made there. By describing in detail its recent influence-buying scandal, he demonstrates how Japanese business and politics are intertwined. Holstein defines the role power plays in Japanese culture and tells who wields it, reports on the many recent political scandals, predicts how politics will be affected by such trends as nationalism and women's rights, and warns that the U.S. must take the Japanese economic challenge seriously. Holstein's book will make a good companion to such classics as Ruth Benedict's *Chrysanthemum and the Sword* and Ian Buruma's *Behind the Mask*. —*David Rouse*

Irwin, Robert.
Tips and Traps When Buying a Home.
McGraw-Hill, $19.95. 190p.

In easy-to-understand language, Irwin has taken much of the stress and uncertainty out of home buying. A companion to *Tips and Traps When Selling a Home*, this book provides the basic knowledge necessary to make buying a home less of a headache for the average person. The author addresses each stage of the buying process from choosing an agent, to negotiating with the seller, to closing the deal. Drawing on 25 years of experience as a real estate broker, he explains common traps and misconceptions and offers tips on avoiding them—for instance, when the seller might be held liable for concealing defects in the house. This is one of the most accessible and thorough treatments for home buyers available. *—Jill Sidoti*

Kaponya, Paul.
How to Survive Your First 90 Days at a New Company.
Career Press, $12.95. 166p.

One school of advice has it that the first five minutes of an employment interview are the most critical. Kaponya suggests that the second important career hurdle one must face is the first 90 days at any new job. The 90-day time frame is significant because most organizations review performance and end probationary status after this time. Kaponya recommends self-assessment techniques and construction of a personal inventory to help evaluate career, organization, and job choices. He includes survival tips for the first 90 days: how to deal with different types of bosses, how to handle stress, and how to compensate for a lack of training or education for a particular skill. *—David Rouse*

Klott, Gary.
The New York Times Complete Financial Guide to the 1990s.
Times Books, $19.95. 416p.

The new decade makes even last year's advice seem dated. Klott, author of previous, similar guides on taxes and investing, offers one of the first of what surely will be many guidebooks for the 1990s. This book carries the authority of the *New York Times* by virtue of its being published by Times Books, but the *Times* disclaims responsibility for it. Nonetheless, Klott has put together an encyclopedic compendium of practical advice and useful predictions dealing with a generous range of financial matters (with *financial* very broadly interpreted). In his drive to be complete, he covers everything from air travel to video phones in sections devoted to the workplace, real estate, demographic trends, banking, taxes, etc. *—David Rouse*

Kushner, Malcolm L.
The Light Touch: How to Use Humor for Business Success.
Simon & Schuster, $18.95. 231p.

Humor in business can be serious business as demonstrated by Kushner, "America's premier corporate humor consultant." It is generally accepted that humor can be therapeutic, help relieve stress, or serve to defuse a tense situation. Kushner, though, advocates humor as a managerial tool and explains that being humorous is more than telling jokes or being "funny." He shows how humor can be used to handle hostility, resolve conflicts, motivate employees, and improve communication. He also identifies occasions when humor is inappropriate and discusses racist or sexist jokes and advises where to draw the line on practical jokes. It may say something about the state of American business that today's executives need a book to teach them how to be funny, but even the smallest gesture toward eradicating gray-flannel dreariness should be supported. —*David Rouse*

Mackay, Harvey.
Beware the Naked Man Who Offers You His Shirt.
Morrow, $17.95. 395p.

Mackay is a premier Minneapolis envelope entrepreneur, an in-demand public speaker, and the author of the best-selling *Swim with the Sharks without Being Eaten Alive.* Here he offers another "feel-good-about-yourself" business book that promotes certain positive modes of thinking for anyone trying to succeed in the workaday world. "Take This Job and Love It!" says Harvey. "Don't Confuse Charisma with a Loud Voice," says Harvey. "It Takes More Than a Shoeshine and a Smile," says Harvey. In nearly 100 brief "lessons," Mackay covers the business turf on topics such as getting along in the office, initiative, hard work, nepotism, salesmanship, failure, interviewing for a new job, and on and on. Harvey loves to trot out anecdotes involving his favorite sports and business personalities (e.g., Lou Holtz, Warren Buffett, John Y. Brown, etc.), which sometimes lends an air of name-dropping for name-dropping's sake. And his advice is often so flippant and easy that you've no doubt already thought of it yourself. Still, for those who like to be reminded that success requires a reasoned and cool approach to complex sensibilities, responses, and attitudes, Mackay has probably fashioned another winner. —*Martin Brady*

Mann, Jim.
Beijing Jeep: The Short, Unhappy Romance of American Business in China.
Simon & Schuster, $19.95. 314p.

Mann, who spent three years in China as a correspondent for the *Los Angeles Times,* focuses on a joint manufacturing venture between American Motors Corporation and Beijing Automotive Works in an eye-opening examination of American-Chinese business enterprises. When China opened its doors to American companies in the late 1970s, American Motors jumped on the bandwagon. After much hassling and negotiating, AMC and Beijing Automotive Works forged a joint agreement to build the popular Cherokee Jeep vehicle at the Beijing plant. While the partnership seemed successful on the surface, problems plagued AMC's efforts to deal with Chinese officials and workers. Told through the eyes of American executives who lived in China, this book documents the inevitable problems that occur when two companies from different cultures and with differing business philosophies attempt to work together. Chrysler Corporation's buyout of American Motors in 1987 and the 1989 political uprisings in China further affected the already tenuous relationship between the two companies. An engrossing account that paints U.S. businesses in a favorable light. —*Sue-Ellen Beauregard*

Business

✔ **Mayer, Martin.**
The Greatest-Ever Bank Robbery: The Collapse of the Savings and Loan Industry.
Scribner, $22.50. 416p.

The almost daily dose of headlines for the last couple of years warning of the collapse of the savings-and-loan industry seems to have desensitized most Americans to any sense of crisis. This may be in part because of the unthinkable consequences and the unfathomable enormity of the problem. Now best-selling nonfiction juggernaut Mayer chillingly and compellingly chronicles the crisis. He anticipated current events with his *The Bankers* (Norton, 1978) and *The Builders* (Weybright and Talley, 1974); he gained further insight as a member of President Reagan's housing commission. He charges that the industry is a web of self-interest and makes the extraordinary claim that 20 to 50 percent of those in the industry are swindlers! In spite of the inevitable legal and financial detail he piles up, Mayer clearly makes his case and attempts to predict the uncertain future that will certainly affect us all. There have already been several good books detailing S&L troubles, notably Stephen Pizzo's (and others) *Inside Job* (McGraw-Hill, 1989) and Paul Pilzer's *Other People's Money* (Simon & Schuster, 1989), but Mayer's insider's perspective may finally capture our attention. —*David Rouse*

Miller, Peter G.
Buy Your First Home Now: A Practical Guide to Better Deals, Cheaper Mortgages, and Bigger Tax Breaks for the First-Time Home Buyer.
Harper, $17.95. 240p.

One major element of the American dream, owning one's own home, is becoming unattainable for increasing numbers of families and individuals. Over the last 10 years the cost of a house has risen more than 10 times the increase in earnings of the average American. Miller, a Washington, D.C.–based real estate broker, warns the potential first-time home buyer that the time to buy is now because things are only going to get worse. In so doing, he provides a straightforward analysis of the real estate market, useful advice on real estate transactions, information about mortgages, and tax tips. As is the case with these types of books, because of uncertain tax laws and an ever-changing mortgage market, the best book is often the most recent one. —*David Rouse*

Business

Morris, Charles R.
The Coming Global Boom: How to Benefit Now from Tomorrow's Dynamic World Economy.
Bantam, $19.95. 288p.

This latest addition to the already crowded field of "doom-boom" books tells individual investors and companies how to take advantage of the coming worldwide economic growth Morris predicts. A consultant and *Los Angeles Times* columnist, Morris bases his conclusions on several premises: Baby Boomers will fuel a burst of entrepreneurial activity, global competition will cause quality and productivity to improve, a real estate crash will allow the average American a greater percentage of disposable income. Morris divides his book into sections devoted to the opportunities that will be created for companies, people, and governments. He provides many useful examples to illustrate his points, and each chapter concludes with an in-depth case study. —*David Rouse*

Pollan, Stephen M. and Levine, Mark.
The Field Guide to Starting a Business.
Simon & Schuster/Fireside, $9.95. 292p.

Financial consultant Pollan and coauthor Levine, who teamed up on *The Field Guide to Home Buying in America* (Fireside, 1988), have partnered again to produce a first-rate, "play it straight" manual that avoids the cloying enthusiasm and gimmickry of so many entrepreneurial primers. Implying that there is no such thing in a business as status quo ("all businesses are heading either toward success or failure"), the authors present well-reasoned, traditional guidance on how to begin a new or buy an existing enterprise and keep it flourishing. Along with tips on evaluating the feasibility of an idea, securing financing, and identifying a market, they explain what to do if a growth crisis occurs, demonstrate how to draft a loan proposal, and discuss the responsibilities of the outside professionals (accountants, attorneys, bankers, etc.) that most businesses need. With examples of successes and failures scattered throughout, the text is as readable as it is informative. —*Stephanie Zvirin*

Porter, Sylvia.
Sylvia Porter's Your Finances in the 1990s.
Prentice Hall Press, $22.95. 303p.

Reliable stand-by Sylvia Porter has finally updated her much-sought, well-heeded financial advice to cover the 1990s. Although not nearly as substantial as her *New Money Book for the '80s*, this guide will certainly win a role as a dependable, first-place-to-look reference. Porter divides her advice into three sections: acquiring money (jobs, savings, investments), preserving holdings (tax considerations, insurance, retirement security), and trends for the 1990s (financial planning). Numerous charts and worksheets are included. —*David Rouse*

Schreiber, Norman.
Your Home Office.
Harper, $12.95. 336p.

With plenty of firsthand experience with the problems of motivation, loneliness, and anxiety that often accompany working where you live, Schreiber offers home-based businesses an edge up by providing guidelines for better organization and efficiency. He covers the basics—zoning issues, insurance needs, office supplies and furnishings, equipment such as phones, faxes, and copiers—and advises on procuring and working with outside professionals, computer processing, special phone equipment, etc. The microcomputer section is particularly informative on both hardware and software capabilities. Concluding sections address the less mechanical and more serious issues like taxes, debt management, and marketing strategies. An excellent business guide for a solitary work style. —*George Hampton*

Stern, Sydney Ladensohn and Schoenhaus, Ted.
Toyland: The High-Stakes Game of the Toy Industry.
Contemporary, $19.95. 352p.

A fascinating look at the toy industry. The cleverly organized text interweaves the histories and analyses of legendary products and manufacturers with the evolution of the recently successful Dino-Riders. From its inception in the imagination of the inventor to its promotion, production, and marketing, the yearlong saga of Dino-Riders unfolds like any corporate drama. Meanwhile, the authors expose toys and companies you've always wondered about, such as Barbie, G.I. Joe, Twister, Betsy Wetsy, Mattel, and Parker Brothers, as well as others you've more recently heard of, like Coleco, Teddy Ruxpin, Trivial Pursuit, Cabbage Patch Dolls, and Nintendo. They also consider the influential yearly Toy Fair, toy safety, the relationship of war toys to violent behavior, and whether full-length cartoons should serve as advertisements for particular toys. Their observations make the private, often "fly-by-the-seat-of-your-pants" world of toys more familiar to the toy buyers of the world. —*Micaela Sullivan-Fowler*

Sterngold, James.
Burning down the House: How Greed, Deceit, and Bitter Revenge Destroyed E. F. Hutton.
Summit, $19.95. 292p.

This is one more story of 1980s excess. Sterngold tells how greed, deceit, and revenge caused the collapse of the E. F. Hutton brokerage firm. This tale has already been told at least twice before, in Mark Stevens' *Sudden Death* (NAL, 1989) and Donna Carpenter's and John Feloni's *The Fall of the House of Hutton* (Holt, 1989). Sterngold adds his perspective as a journalist who covered the ongoing events for the *New York Times*. He interviewed more than 100 persons for this book, including the principal protagonists. Sterngold writes well and holds the reader's attention, and this is probably the best book of the three—but for some, the plot may be too familiar by now. —*David Rouse*

Business

Tatsuno, Sheridan M.
Created in Japan: From Imitators to World-Class Innovators.
Ballinger, $21.95. 240p.

Japan bashers often like to assert that the Japanese are successful imitators but that they lack creativity and inventiveness. Tatsuno, a California-based high-technology consultant, debunks that conceit on several accounts. In the creative fields of architecture, photography, and fashion, the Japanese have long been noted for their bold innovation. More than 10 percent of all U.S. patents are granted to the Japanese, and three of the top four recipients of patents in 1987 were Japanese firms. Furthermore, Tatsuno explains that the Western and Japanese notions of creativity are at odds. Breakthroughs are achieved *after* a Zen-like contemplation of ideas that have been recycled, examined, nurtured, and refined. He suggests, also, that the Japanese will be the ones to pioneer new products in the categories of high-definition television, new generation computers, and superconductors. *Created in Japan* should attract a lot of attention. —*David Rouse*

Watson, Thomas J. and Petre, Peter.
Father, Son & Co.: My Life at IBM and Beyond.
Bantam, $22.95. 480p.

It may be difficult to imagine the faceless IBM company with personable leaders at the helm; nonetheless, the scrappy Watsons ran the company for six decades. Cowritten by Thomas Watson, Jr., who stepped down as IBM's chairman in 1970 after he suffered a heart attack, this intriguing account traces the Watson family involvement with this behemoth company. Watson's father, Thomas, Sr. (who at one time was the highest paid person in the U.S.), was a premier salesperson before he became manager of the Computer-Tabulating-Recording Co. (later changed to IBM) in 1914. The elder Watson's impact on IBM is duly noted here, while the author places his own experiences within the context of his father's accomplishments. After a less than sterling record in high school and college, the younger Watson seemed an unlikely candidate for staid IBM when he began working on the sales force in 1937. Although he quickly rose within the firm, Watson claims he had to constantly battle his father to achieve "real power." Watson is never hesitant to point out his own flaws and to recount the personal differences he had with his father—who was in his 80s when he retired from IBM. —*Sue-Ellen Beauregard*

✓ Weiss, Robert S.
Staying the Course: The Emotional and Social Lives of Men Who Do Well at Work.
Free Press, $24.95. 302p.

There have been plenty of books about aberrant males—alcoholics, child abusers, con men, etc. But here is a study of average middle-class men who go to work happily and return home contentedly. Of course, no one's life is quite that perfect, but Weiss' study demonstrates that it is possible to achieve financial and domestic harmony without being the man in the gray flannel suit. From an admittedly specialized pool (only 80 men were interviewed in suburban and urban New England areas), Weiss draws general conclusions that hit home. He states that work is a man's means of defining himself and demonstrates, through sample remarks and incidents, the degree to which success and/or stress in the workplace influences a man's self-image, his family life, and his role in the community. There is an old-fashioned cast to the responses here and an almost ominous lack of vision about the effects of feminism (generally, if the wives work, their jobs come off as secondary in terms of economics and importance). Weiss' findings indicate a society that either has regressed or has not altered to accommodate working women as peers. It is an intriguing perspective and certainly one that can give both men and women new insight into the way men feel and think. —*Denise Perry Donavin*

Cookery

Balsey, Betty, ed.
Best Recipes from the Los Angeles Times.
Abrams, $29.95. 304p.

Here are more than 200 carefully selected recipes, with ethnic cuisines well represented and fresh food and healthy eating emphasized. Twelve chapters cover the diversity of California cooking, where food trends often begin but old favorites such as meat loaf (three kinds) always have a place. The newspaper's reliable test kitchens offer up such dishes as tamale pie, chicken and beef fajitas, fresh garlic soup gratinée, peanut noodles and pork, steak salad, and chutney bread. Desserts are rich, featuring high-calorie sweets made with chocolate, butter, and cream. The collection is underscored by sensitivity to ease of preparation, microwave usability, short ingredient lists of easily available items—but no nutritional information provided. —*Iva Freeman*

✔ **Brody, Jane E.**
Jane Brody's Good Food Gourmet: Recipes and Menus for Delicious and Healthful Entertaining.
Norton, $25. 640p.

What Julia Child has been to French cuisine in the U.S., Jane Brody is to the growth of healthful cooking—and eating—in our saturated-fat society. Up to a point, others have tried and succeeded, but Brody's consistently winning recipes and books (*Nutrition Book, Good Food Book*) have advantages far beyond her respected stature as a *New York Times* reporter. First, she's unabashedly borrowed from friends, food magazines, other well-known chef-authors (Pierre Franey and Craig Claiborne, to name two), even Brody fans, modifying all contributions and original recipes with eyes on both the caloric and fat content. Second, her presentations are creative yet down-to-earth. The more than 500 recipes range from string bean pâté and African yam soup

Cookery

to salmon with rhubarb sauce and chicken salad with mango and garlic green beans. Common sense reigns; there are hints and tips on equipment, mail-order sources (for Roquefort cavatelli!), basics, garnishes, yields and measurements, and menu suggestions. Third, she's honest; she admits an occasional yearning for an indulgence in chocolates and fatty foods (sausages), with the final passwords being "all things in moderation." —*Barbara Jacobs*

✓ **Bugialli, Giuliano.**
The Fine Art of Italian Cooking.
Times Books, $24.95. 672p.

In Italian life, as in its cooking, regional customs are more than stylistic differences—they indicate an entirely distinct dialect, background, and culinary approach to native ingredients. In this expanded and updated version of his popular cookbook, Bugialli imparts the pride of a native Tuscan and Florentine as he introduces northern Italian cuisine based on research into ancient and still-used recipes and traditions. With conviction and respect for regional peculiarities and distinctions, Bugialli first introduces the historical background of northern Italian cooking styles, including a fascinating description of the marriage feast of Maria de'Medici. Ingredients indigenous to the region and the inherently light Tuscan cooking approach are explored, including the all-essential Tuscan bread; a wide assortment of recipes follow, which fill courses in a formal or informal Italian meal. Recipe notes are exceptional and lend a rich historical context for ingredients and methods. A robust reintroduction to the gastronomic glory of the northern Italian kitchen. —*Deanna Larson-Whiterod*

Claiborne, Craig.
The New York Times Cook Book.
Harper, $25. 736p.

With many new and updated recipes, Claiborne's culinary compendium reflects changes in cooking trends and transformations of eating habits since it was first published in 1961. In the wake of the food revolution, new gourmet twists are recorded (Buffalo chicken wings, for example), more dishes from various ethnic kitchens are presented (Mexican and Oriental flavors join the French and Italian), and some of the more elaborate creations have been replaced or simplified (galantine of turkey giving way to tuna carpaccio). Health consciousness also raises its head as more fish and less cholesterol are involved. The original illustrations—both the colorplates and the black-and-white demonstration photographs—have disappeared, however. Still, as a basic collection of recipes that covers both the traditional American table as well as more recent culinary diversions and experiments, the latest Claiborne production is well-nigh definitive. (Harper is also reissuing Claiborne's *New York Times International Cook Book* , the original companion volume to *The New York Times Cook Book*. The foreign guide retains its illustrations but has not been revised or updated.) —*John Brosnahan*

Cunningham, Marion.
The Fannie Farmer Cookbook.
Knopf, $22.95. 864p.

In this latest edition of a cookery classic, Cunningham maintains and underlines the basics while keeping up with changes in tastes and methods. The microwave, referred to as "an unperfected appliance" in the twelfth edition, is here given its due along with outdoor cooking and vegetarian recipes. The literary references of the book's previous revision—"Blancmange, a cornstarch pudding, . . . is the dessert that Jo of *Little Women* often carried to Laurie, her frail neighbor, to help restore his health"—remain, but are unpretentiously slipped in amid good, practical instructions on outfitting and working in a modern kitchen. Far better than the Betty Crocker updates and a great preliminary/accompanist to Julia Child's *Way to Cook. —Denise Perry Donavin*

Deighton, Len.
ABC of French Food.
Bantam, $19.95. 256p.

Can a spy novelist write about French cuisine? Why not, when he's as well informed and passionate as Deighton proves to be. This walk through the culinary alphabet is filled with cooking and wine tips. Deighton never misses the opportunity to make fun of nouvelle cuisine while he is explaining, defining, musing, and drawing delightful sketches that enhance the text. He consistently delivers solid information about this changing but fiercely traditional cuisine. (Chefs and food writers, often ignored, are given attention.) An extensive annotated bibliography with original publication dates and sources, footnotes, and an index are all unusual but certainly useful features. Deighton is a professionally trained cook and has produced a work that will be valuable for almost every level of cooking. *—Iva Freeman*

Heatter, Maida.
Maida Heatter's Best Dessert Book Ever.
Random, $24.95. 448p.

The title says it all. Filled to bursting with the most delicious concoctions, this book is for the dietary sinner in all of us. Beginning with recipes for chocolate cakes (rum chocolate truffle roll, white chocolate and banana cake, bishop's bread) and ending with sauces (raspberry, chocolate, clear caramel), and covering pies, refrigerator desserts, tarts, and ice cream in between, Heatter has outdone herself. The introductory sections offer advice on ingredients, equipment, and techniques. The recipes themselves are easy to follow and range from fairly easy cookies to day-long culinary productions. More difficult recipes begin with tips to make them more successful, and many contain helpful notes at the end. Sure to be popular. *—Jill Sidoti*

Cookery

Jackson, Michael.
Michael Jackson's Complete Guide to Single Malt Scotch: A Connoisseur's Guide to the Single Malt Whiskies of Scotland.
Running Press, $18.95. 240p.

The author of the peerless, invaluable *World Guide to Whisky* and the peerless, invaluable *New World Guide to Beer* proffers potables epicures a third peerless, invaluable vade mecum. Tall pocket-book-sized, Jackson's new work describes the making of single malt whiskies and the reasons for their marked differences in color, aroma, and taste. More lusciously, in an alphabet of distilleries, it evaluates more than 100 and their products. Jackson accords each distillery one to five stars, reflecting his assessment of its seriousness as a single malt producer. More provocatively, after remarks on each malt's color, nose, body, palate, and finish, he rates it numerically between 50 and 100. A color reproduction of the malt's label appears with each set of remarks and ratings, so that the whole affair resembles a field guide, which is exactly how connoisseurs will use it, both at home and in the Highlands, the islands, and even the Lowlands. Advice on visiting distilleries, list of further reading, and index appended. —*Ray Olson*

✓ **Jones, Evan.**
Epicurean Delight: The Life and Times of James Beard.
Knopf, $24.95. 352p.

A biography with recipes is unusual, but James Beard is no ordinary subject, as Jones' admiring and sympathetic portrait makes clear. Beard was one of the founders of the American food establishment, and his varied achievements as a cook, teacher, food consultant, and cookbook author are all documented in this informal and appreciative volume. Along with Beard's experiences as a cook, Jones also covers his subject's influential childhood in Oregon and his early efforts as an actor in New York where he first entered the cooking profession as a cocktail party caterer. The book also covers some of the darker currents that flowed through Beard's life as Jones reveals difficult relationships with family members, male lovers, and ungrateful protégés. Jones never probes too deeply into these touchy areas, although some of the intrigues of the food establishment are covered in the final chapters. What ends the book and each chapter, however, is exactly what Beard would have approved of himself: a selection of recipes that are identified with his life and his celebrated taste and that represent his considerable contribution to the American table. —*John Brosnahan*

Koffmann, Pierre and Shaw, Timothy.
Memories of Gascony.
Van Nostrand, $44.95. 256p.

Koffmann is the chef and owner of London's La Tante Claire restaurant, and here he returns to his gastronomic roots in Gascony. This is as much a culinary and family reminiscence as it is a cookbook, with Koffmann recalling visits with his grandparents and describing the landscape, people, and food of this region of France. Koffmann also offers a series of dishes that will bring the taste of Gascony to the reader's homes in the form of *la cuisine du terroir* , the robust peasant tradition in cooking and eating that the region still preserves. Ducks (and especially their fattened livers), rabbit, prunes, confits, and ragouts figure prominently in the Gascon kitchen, and Koffmann deftly interprets these ingredients and dishes in his own establishment and in recipes for his readers. A series of evocative color photographs add further charm to this story of a way of life and a way of eating. List of restaurants in Gascony and wine merchants in London; index. —*John Brosnahan*

✓ **Madison, Deborah.**
The Savory Way.
Bantam, $22.95. 444p.

Madison expands the vegetarian gourmet concept beyond the menu of her acclaimed *Greens Cookbook*, this time with an emphasis on simple home cooking rather than the restaurant-originated recipes of her previous collection. The taste may still be sophisticated, but the ingredients are easy to find, and the techniques are simple to follow. Madison supplies an interesting repertoire of more than 300 dishes covering nearly every element of large and small meals, plus a number of snacking alternatives. The inspiration for these dishes is equally broad, with Italian, French, Oriental, and other cuisines as well as American cooking, old and new, all represented, with many good companion cross-ethnic dishes noted in the text. Some of the recipes incorporate eggs, butter, and other dairy products, but even the strictest vegan should find plenty to love and even share with nonvegan friends. An appendix covers kitchen equipment, pantry staples, suggested menus, and sources. —*John Brosnahan*

Manjon, Maite.
The Gastronomy of Spain and Portugal.
Prentice Hall Press, $35. 320p.

This handsome encyclopedic introduction to the cuisines of Spain and Portugal ranges from *a la brasa* (a cooking method) to *zarzuela de mariscos a la catalana* (shellfish stew, Catalan style). In between is a wealth of information on the history of the two countries' cookery and descriptions of their food, wine, and cooking techniques, as well as a bountiful supply of classic Spanish and Portuguese recipes. One caveat: not all the recipes are easy for cooks not already conversant with the area's food and cookery. The *A*-to-*Z* entries are well cross-referenced for ease of use, and the index is arranged by types of food, cooking methods and terms, kitchen equipment, and wines and spirits, etc. Scattered black-and-white drawings and photos and 10 sections of color photographs enhance the text. A delightful excursion that offers nostalgia for returned travelers and will whet the appetites of those contemplating an Iberian vacation. —*Sally Estes*

Cookery

Neal, Bill.
Biscuits, Spoonbread, and Sweet Potato Pie.
Knopf, $19.95. 312p.

This superlative cookbook beckons with the warmth and gracious hospitality of an Old South tea party. Recipes and notes are shared affectionately, filled with culinary traditions from centuries of southern familial and historical heritages. Chapters for cornmeal, hot biscuits, British rolls (crumpets, scones, baps), breakfast cakes (pancakes and waffles), yeast breads, and whole grain breads are filled with carefully selected recipes giving admirable results. Confections and sauces (pralines, brittle, and divinity), fruit desserts, "delectables" (custards, mousses, and puddings), cookies and small cakes, pies, tarts, frozen desserts, and home-baked cakes (fruit, sponge, and pound cakes) follow with equal satisfaction. Quotes from southern writers and famous southern cookbooks of the past add to the homey, generous feeling that emanates from this baker and his oven. —*Deanna Larson-Whiterod*

Crafts

Barton, Julia.
The Art of Embroidery.
Sterling, $24.95. 144p.

At first blush, the new embroidery often seems like a mishmash of textures and styles, colors and techniques. Through Barton's tutelage, confusion nearly becomes modern symmetry. Instead of teaching basic stitches, she concentrates on the whys and wherefores of design. With a wealth of color photos, she demonstrates the options and combinations to add to traditional embroidery—drawing, painting, quilting, appliqué, machine embroidery, etc. Most exciting is her explanation of embroidered jewelry and ornaments, including gossamerlike yet sturdy fabric beads, hand-stitched cords, necklaces, belts, earrings, and flowers. The occasional ethereal subject notwithstanding, she dispenses practical information, too, on materials and equipment, different stitches, and finishing instructions. —*Barbara Jacobs*

Berman, Jennifer and Lazarus, Carole.
The Glorifilia Needlepoint Collection.
David & Charles, $29.95. 192p.

The London-based Glorifilia shop has been quietly gaining a reputation for fine European stitchery design since its establishment in 1975. Now the secret is out; partners Berman and Lazarus, through an enchantingly personalized text and more than 25 patterns, prove the reasons behind their success. Inspiration ranges from medieval tapestries and Oriental art to the British Museum and Monet. Color photographs, charts, and ample instructions guide beginners as well as professionals. The only drawback is that directions for many of the hundreds of needleworks pictured are not included. —*Barbara Jacobs*

Bliss, Debbie and McTague, Fiona.
Country Knits: With Over 30 Glorious Designs.
Trafalgar Square, $29.95. 142p.

Country style has invaded the world of knitting, which, in this instance, means a new interpretation of such classic techniques as Fair Isle, Guernsey, Tyrolean, and Aran knits. English designers, Bliss and McTague, offer suggestions involving softer patterns, embroidered or knitted-in motifs more contemporary in tone, and a range of muted colors (pastels and heathers). Full-color photographs accompany each of the 30-plus designs; though the focus is on women's apparel, sweaters for men and children are also included. The emphasis on British brand-name yarns (with no American substitutes) may bother some not-so-sure stitchers, as might the lack of basic how-to's. —*Barbara Jacobs*

✓ **Byrd, Byron Keith and Krukowski, Dennis.**
O Christmas Tree.
Rizzoli, $40. 160p.

Christmas tree designer Byrd has compiled a paean to "O Tannenbaum" that reads and looks like holiday decorations of the rich and famous. Whether adorned with cattelya orchids or priceless family heirlooms, Baccarat ornaments or feathers and fluff, the trees of many well-known artists, designers, and Hollywood folks are showcased, from Giorgio Armani to Joan Rivers. The wild and weird are juxtaposed against the traditional and conservative in these designs, mainly drawn from penthouses and cottages on the East Coast—more specifically, New York, Connecticut, and Massachusetts. A collection of breathtaking photographs and ideas that can inspire even the most pragmatic. —*Barbara Jacobs*

Classic Crafts: A Practical Compendium of Traditional Skills.
Simon & Schuster, $35. 223p.

This coffee-table book offers a breathtakingly lovely introduction to 35 old-time crafts now enjoying a renaissance. Each section of the book, divided somewhat arbitrarily into textile, paper, kitchen, and decorative arts, is filled with exquisite *House and Garden* –like photographs and text that romances the craft rather than explains it. Not only are the more usual handiworks (such as quilting and papermaking, dried flowers and stenciled tiles) included, but also some of the more exotic—making goat cheese, smoking fish, stick dressing, and bookbinding. Individual projects are featured; however, elementary how-to's are excluded. —*Barbara Jacobs*

Crafts

The Complete Book of Needlecrafts.
Chilton, $25. 240p.

Amidst literally tons of books published on needlecraft, both generic and specific types, this British import in its first U.S. publication stands out for two reasons. First, every chapter builds on knowledge gained in the previous few pages, reinforcing the confidence of beginning stitchers and spurring them on to more difficult projects. So, for example, the embroidery section starts with the very easy cross stitch, graduates to a combination of techniques in a sampler, and ends with explanations of beadwork. Second, the 70-plus designs are not only for practical, useful projects but they also showcase motifs and patterns unusual to the U.S. Hobbyists who follow instructions for making a cows-in-a-field rug will learn the basics of hooking, while those who construct rag books for their toddlers will pick up the how-to's of appliqué. A good resource for any stitcher. —*Barbara Jacobs*

✓ **Hecht, Ann.**
The Art of the Loom: Weaving, Spinning and Dyeing across the World.
Rizzoli, $35. 208p.

Following a full explanation of the basic principles of weaving, spinning, and dyeing, Hecht focuses on eight areas of the world where outstanding examples of age-old methods of these three interrelated crafts are still practiced today. Visually exceptional (brimming with striking black-and-white and color photographs) as well as informatively superb, her book takes the reader to the American Southwest, the Middle East, West Africa, Indonesia, Japan, Nepal, Guatemala, and Peru; a detailed chapter on each area discusses unique materials and methods found there. Whether the weaver or spinner or dyer be Navaho or bedouin, uncomplicated utensils nonetheless result in dazzling products—a fact certain not only to fascinate, but also to stimulate the craftsperson, who, just as certainly, will adore this book. —*Brad Hooper*

Innes, Miranda.
The Country Home Book: A Practical Guide to Restoring and Decorating in the Country Style.
Simon & Schuster, $29.95. 192p.

English and American country houses are temptingly described and illustrated in Innes' introduction to a popular decorating style. The author takes the reader through the various elements of a room's design—walls, lighting, floor coverings, etc.—and indicates how each part can lend the country look to an entire house or just one room. What makes Innes' advice especially appealing are the instructions she includes for achieving the country look; both in the text itself and in a lengthy appendix she covers numerous projects that are well suited for the do-it-yourself decorator. Color photographs and drawings help to visualize the completed effects and step-by-step restoration procedures. —*John Brosnahan*

Film & Drama

✓ **Belushi, Judith Jacklin.**
Samurai Widow.
Carroll & Graf, $21.95. 442p.

She takes the samurai part of her title from the character her husband, John, made famous on "Saturday Night Live," but Belushi's focus is on the word *widow*. With both humor and melancholy, she allows readers a look at the diaries she's kept in the years since John's death, revealing in the process the pain she has experienced as well as her coping mechanisms—which sometimes involved using alcohol as her crutch. Naturally, John's status as a celebrity altered the usual grieving process. Not only did Belushi have to deal with the manner in which John died, she also had to sort out her feelings about the woman who gave him the lethal injection of heroin. On the other hand, the outpouring of affection she received from his public was a source of comfort. Particularly interesting is Belushi's portrait of Bob Woodward. Initially she saw his biography of John, *Wired*, as a vehicle for vindicating John's name; how it turned in her mind into a betrayal of his memory makes fascinating reading. Belushi is willing to do what many writers can't or won't—let the reader see their pain. That the wife of a well-known man, who died such a public death, can make her story seem like any woman's is a tribute to the honesty of Belushi's writing. —*Ilene Cooper*

Benny, Jack and Benny, Joan.
Sunday Nights at Seven: The Jack Benny Story.
Warner, $19.95. 302p.

As his only child tells it, the most important thing in Jack Benny's life was his famous radio and television show. But you don't have to take it just from Joan. Her part of this book is frequently interrupted by excerpts from an unpublished autobiography Dad worked on a few years before his death in 1974. Hence, the dual author credit. Although Joan tells a bit about her own affairs, the emphasis is first upon Jack, and then upon the dizzying list of fellow clowns, full-time (like Phil Harris, Dennis Day, Eddie "Rochester" Anderson, and Mel Blanc) and "slumming" (like suave matinee idol Ronald Colman), who were the foils for the hilariously reactive Benny comic style. Benny devotees will fervently embrace the book, finding it cozy and gratifying. Those who don't know Benny's work, however, may find it kind of a snooze. (Soften them up with tapes of the show—as funny today as ever.) Illustrated with 32 pages of previously unpublished photos. —*Ray Olson*

Brochu, Jim.
Lucy in the Afternoon.
Morrow, $18.95. 249p.

There seems to be a new category of biography—the friend-to-dead-stars genre. First we had the recent memoir of Bette Davis by her (estranged) pal Roy Moseley, and now this "intimate biography" of Lucille Ball as told through the eyes of a guy who played backgammon with her almost every day for the last eight months of her life. Like Moseley, Brochu was a fan long before he was a friend; he eventually sent Lucy a script, which engendered an invitation to her house, which in turn sealed the relationship. Brochu's technique of relating Lucy's life story as she told it to him across the backgammon board proves both interesting and lively. Unfortunately, he makes the mistake of setting himself up as Lucy's costar, regaling readers with all manner of bon mots that cracked Lucy up over the duration of their sojourn together. He may have been funny at the time, but a Fred Mertz he isn't. Still, there's plenty of Lucy here, as well as lots of amusing insider gossip. (Agnes Moorhead was fun, Orson Welles wasn't.) Since this is the first major biography of Lucille Ball, it's sure to attract attention among those who watch her reruns—and with all those television signals bouncing out into space, that's everyone in the universe, isn't it? —*Ilene Cooper*

Brodsky, Joseph.
Marbles: A Play in Three Acts.
Farrar, $17.95. 87p.

You could probably say that Brodsky is to Yevtushenko what Shostakovitch was to Prokofiev: not merely the artist as wayward, difficult son, but the artist as thorn, troublemaker, heretic . . . sarcastic and dangerously clever. *Marbles*, like Brodsky himself, is restless, ironic, talkative, and brilliant, with everything designed to keep us off balance. Two men sit in a prison cell at the top of a tower one mile high, sometime in the future but also sometime in ancient Rome. Emperor Tiberius (now dead) seems finally to have everything worked out: an unvarying percentage of prisoners, the perfect rationing of water, computers that supply every need, and the social structure to keep his order. Subject and object are one, the dialect has taken its seat in synthesis, history has overcome its tension. But the men are not happy; neither the heavy, superstitious, good-natured fellow preoccupied with his sexual frustration, nor the cynical, dry, quoter of poets. They can escape but see no point; they irritate each other but are really part of the same single being. The drama is all talk, but there isn't a moment when it goes slack. Like all great writers, Brodsky is a master of saying what he means. —*Stuart Whitwell*

Cameron, Judy and Christman, Paul J.
The Art of Gone with the Wind: The Making of a Legend.
Prentice Hall Press, $29.95. 254p.

A wealth of rare photos, many of them never before published, highlight this behind-the-scenes look at what remains one of the most popular motion pictures ever to come out of Hollywood. Of special interest to movie buffs and

GWTW fanatics are photos like the one that shows Vivien Leigh discussing an upcoming scene with Clark Gable and director Victor Fleming, or stills of scenes that were eventually cut from the released version of the film. In the accompanying text, the authors describe the making of *GWTW* in chapters that focus on such topics as preproduction, sets, costumes, and makeup. The by-now-famous story of the search for an actress to play Scarlett O'Hara is recounted, along with anecdotes that provide telling insights into 1930s Hollywood. The introduction by Daniel Selznick pays an amiably affectionate tribute to his father, producer David O. Selznick. —*Steve Weingartner*

Considine, Shaun.
Bette & Joan: The Divine Feud.
Dutton, $18.95. 320p.

Considine dishes the dirt with a ladle—and it's delicious. A book about either Davis or Crawford is bound to contain plenty of pure bitchiness—perhaps even more than the fainthearted could handle—but put these two irrepressible divas together, and what you have is a delectable catfight. Considine has done his homework, with quotes culled from *Modern Screen* and *Photoplay*, from dear Louella and Hedda, and from assorted other Hollywood types. Interviews with the principals and their cadre of husbands, friends, and children add additional flavor. All the anecdotes are organized into a cohesive narrative that alternates between Crawford and Davis, but which also bring the two together when their paths cross, which they did frequently and explosively. Both ladies come across as larger than life, tougher than nails, and obsessed with themselves. There are plenty of naughty secrets revealed here, but the juiciest involve Crawford's overactive libido: there's the rumor that she had an affair with Marilyn Monroe, and best of all, there's this little snippet: "Rock [Hudson] was back in the poolhouse, taking a shower, when the lights went out. Suddenly, he felt the warm, naked body of Joan Crawford beside him. 'Sssh, baby,' she whispered, 'close your eyes and pretend I'm Clark Gable.'" —*Ilene Cooper*

✓ Corman, Roger.
How I Made a Hundred Movies in Hollywood and Never Lost a Dime.
Random, $18.95. 256p.

As maker of western, horror, biker, stewardess, nurse, and women-behind-bars pictures, Roger Corman is internationally respected as a director. In France, where the French make it their business to appreciate neglected aspects of American culture, Corman is considered a true artist. Although he prefers to consider himself a craftsman, on numerous occasions his movies seem to have fallen into art, as if by happy accident. Here Corman reviews his career, shares anecdotes, and gives advice on how to be as successful as he has been in the "corrupt art form" of film. Mixing commerce and art, Corman came up with a surefire formula: "R-rated exploitation genres blending fast-paced action, humor, a touch of sex, and a liberal sociopolitical viewpoint." With an instinctive marketing sense, frugal and efficient direction, and authoritarian control over the product, Corman developed a Midas touch, producing more than 200 low-budget movies, practically all of them profitable. Among his widely recognized cult classics are the original version of *The Little Shop of Horrors*, the Vincent Price/Edgar Allan Poe cycle, and *X—The Man with the X-Ray Eyes*. In addition, he has helped launch the careers of more than a handful of well-known actors, writers, and directors (Jack Nicholson, Peter Fonda, Bruce Dern, Robert DeNiro, Sylvester Stallone, Martin Scorcese, Francis Coppola, Ron Howard, and Jonathan Demme, among others). Anyone interested in the movies can't help but like this book. —*Benjamin Segedin*

✔ **Crisp, Quentin.**
How to Go to the Movies: A Guide for the Perplexed.
St. Martin's, $15.95. 240p.

The man who has styled himself as "one of the stately old homos of England" turns out to be the freshest movie commentator since goddess knows when. He is very much to the point in discussing a film's general look and tenor, its players' physical attributes and thespian capabilities, and its social and moral implications, which he never fails to remark upon wittily, provocatively, and persuasively. To his work he brings seven decades of moviegoing and the attitude that movies should be an antidote to life, which, he notes, is comparatively so badly acted and poorly dressed. Not a carping critic, Crisp prefers to be perplexed rather than offended by a film that disappoints him. Perhaps gay readers, to whose presumed tastes for elegant superficialities and kinky sex he strives to cater (although he says repeatedly that he thinks sex is a mistake in both movies and life), will most readily embrace Crisp the critic. But not to read him because he's gay is to miss lots of laughter, lots of worldly wisdom, and lots of love for the silver screen. —*Ray Olson*

Davidson, Bill.
Jane Fonda: An Intimate Biography.
Dutton, $18.95. 304p.

This responsible and respectful biography traces Jane Fonda's growth from a floundering rich kid to an electrifying actress and savvy businesswoman with an unflinching social conscience. Present are all the trappings of a film-star bio: glamour, love affairs, addiction, conflict, and tragedy—though Fonda defies all cliché. Personal sorrow and physical affliction brought passion and power to her film performances and tireless zeal to her political activities, though in the latter Fonda engaged in some regrettable faux pas, including the infamous footage of "Hanoi Jane" astride a North Vietnamese antiaircraft gun. (But Fonda learned quickly and has paid for her mistakes many times over, enduring death threats and government harassment.) Then there is her personal life—marriages to Roger Vadim and Tom Hayden, motherhood, complex feelings toward her father, the late Henry Fonda—and her artistic career as a fine actress in such movies as *Klute, Coming Home, The China Syndrome*, and *On Golden Pond*. And finally there's Jane Fonda the exercise tycoon, who began her workout enterprise when she overcame bulimia. In conclusion, Davidson lists "key words" to describe his subject: "courage, guts, mettle, steel, and moxie." Jane Fonda connects with the world, and many fans will want to read this well-rounded account. —*Donna Seaman*

Eyman, Scott.
Mary Pickford: America's Sweetheart.
Donald I. Fine, $19.95. 321 p.

Although she's probably no longer a household name, Mary Pickford remains the quintessential screen actress, and as this biography clearly shows, she was a liberated woman far ahead of her time. Eyman combines durable research with a lively writing style as he traces his subject's ground-breaking movie career as well as her checkered personal life. Besides all the delicious gossip (the actress' affairs and relations with other cinema heavyweights are duly recounted), some of the most interesting material here has to do with the founding of United Artists by Pickford, husband Douglas Fairbanks, Charlie Chaplin, and D. W. Griffith. An engaging biography and a fascinating look at an era. —*Ilene Cooper*

Gardner, Ava.
Ava: My Story.
Bantam, $19.95. 320p.

The autobiography of the recently deceased film star. Born and raised in North Carolina, Gardner was a young, shy beauty with a drawl when she caught the eye of an MGM man. In six fast months she went from secretarial school to Hollywood, where she posed for cheesecake stills and married Mickey Rooney (for a year). Gardner describes herself as just a little ol' country gal gaga over her new life, but she was also a hard-drinking party girl, pursued by many, including the eccentric, manipulative Howard Hughes. Her second year-long marriage was to Artie Shaw, whose constant criticism led Ava to take an IQ test to find out if she really was just a dumb broad. Then she married Frank Sinatra, and they battled it out, boozily and violently. Meanwhile, her career progressed in spite of her lack of ambition. She offers gossipy, behind-the-scene accounts of her films, including *The Killers* (1946), *The Snows of Kilimanjaro* (1952), *The Barefoot Contessa* (1954), and *The Night of the Iguana* (1964). Gardner is unabashedly sensual, kooky, and volatile, wrapping up her life story with the declaration: "The truth is, honey, I've enjoyed my life. I've had a hell of a good time." Can't argue with that. —*Donna Seaman*

Gilliatt, Penelope.
To Wit: The Skin and Bones of Comedy.
Scribner, $24.95. 320p.

Gilliatt is one of our best critics, and any collection of hers is worthy of note. However, a bit of confusion obscures the purpose of what its publishers call "a major new work" that categorizes "modes of comedy," shows "how the technique for each of them differs," and tells its readers "what exactly it takes to be funny." In fact, the bulk of the book seems to have been accumulated over the years, and is made up of pieces on the theater (*The Balcony, The Caretaker, A Flea in Her Ear*) and film (*The Pink Panther, A Duchess in New York, An Evening with Eddie Murphy*) along with interviews of comic actors. The comic artists covered range from Buster Keaton to Whoopi Goldberg. Not really anything more than a collection of reviews, but because it's Gilliatt, it's worth reading. —*Roland Wulbert*

Gottfried, Martin.
All His Jazz: The Life & Death of Bob Fosse.
Bantam, $24.95. 460p.

Show-biz legend Bob Fosse always had a taste for the dramatically macabre, and even his death on the opening night in Washington, D.C., of the revival of *Sweet Charity* suggests a desire to leave the audience always astonished. Drama critic Gottfried gives a functional version of Fosse's ride from teenage hoofer in Chicago strip joints to award-winning Broadway/Hollywood choreographer/director and also sketches in his subject's chameleonlike personality, which could switch from passion to insult in a second. Fosse's complicated marital and love lives are also probed, suggesting that the autobiographical turbulence that Fosse put in *All That Jazz* was no exaggeration. While Kevin Grubb's recent *Razzle Dazzle: The Life & Work of Bob Fosse* (St. Martin, 1989) focused more on Fosse's art and illustrates much of his choreographic work in an excellent series of color illustrations, Gottfried's study manages to combine his subject's messy private life with his creative existence to form a very personal and sympathetic portrait. —*John Brosnahan*

✔ **Gurney, A. R.**
The Cocktail Hour and Two Other Plays: Another Antigone and The Perfect Party.
NAL/Plume, $8.95. 251p.

Three newer comedies by one of our most adroit theatrical magicians work marvelously on the mind's as well as the actual stage. *The Cocktail Hour* is set during one, at which a play called *The Cocktail Hour* by the playwright son of a blueblooded family makes havoc of that would-be-civilized domestic ritual. *Another Antigone* concerns the conflict between a conservative classics professor and an iconoclastic female student that eventually boils down to the age-old opposition between the classical Greek and the Jewish weltanschauungs. Then there's the quite mad, but serious, *Perfect Party*, in which a middle-aged man from the old WASP elite throws over his professorship to seek celebrity as the nation's best host; arch and artificial from the outset, this tour de force is the theatrical—hence loftier, less scabrous—equivalent of a John (*Pink Flamingos*) Waters movie. Each is funny, very well crafted, and a genuine contribution to literature. —*Ray Olson*

Helfer, Ralph.
The Beauty of the Beasts: Tales of Hollywood's Wild Animal Stars.
Tarcher, $17.95. 240p.

Helfer is an animal trainer (and former stunt man) whose exotic and domestic animals have performed for television, movies, and commercials, such as "Daktari," "Star Trek," "Gentle Ben," *Journey to the Center of the Earth, Clarence the Cross-eyed Lion*), and Schlitz beer ads. The author is a practitioner of Affection Training, his own nonaggressive method of animal-handling based on "love, patience, understanding, and respect." Helfer will not use whips, guns, or chairs and avoids fear-trained animals ever since, as a stuntman, he was disarmed then chewed on by an angry lion. Reminiscing about starting his own ranch, which became home to 1,500 animals, Helfer reveals many of his secrets, for example, how he trained 5,000 flies, shampooed and permed a lion, and taught an ostrich to use a phone book. Celebrities, including Carol Burnett, Elvis Presley, and Mae West, frequently visited the ranch and even pitched in with the chores. Many of his famous neighbors turned out to help when his ranch was nearly devastated by a flood. Helfer's account of the heroic responses of both the people and the animals during the disaster makes a heart-rending finale to an irresistible book.—
Denise Perry Donavin

Hope, Bob.
Don't Shoot, It's Only Me: Bob Hope's Comedy History of the United States.
Putnam, $19.95. 320p.

Hope, the official comedian of the U.S. armed forces since 1941, tells his own version of American military history. Stories of war, peacetime, and presidents are interspersed with one-liners, gags, and sentimental memories. Hope demonstrates how his comedy routines have changed since World War II, when he told jokes such as, "I've been digging a bomb shelter under my cellar and I can't quit now. The tunnel almost reaches Hedy Lamarr's house." Compare that to these lines delivered to marines stationed aboard the USS *Kennedy* "during the paranoid '80s." Hope said, "Iran is the Disneyland for fanatics. Iran is where Santa makes three lists: who's been naughty, who's been nice, and who's nuts." Hope talks at length about "the last good war" (World War II), then tells about his career at home when he switched from radio to television. The comedian's nostalgic road tour of World War II bases and bunkers, occupied Japan, Korea, Moscow (during the cold war), Vietnam, and the Middle East is a journey his fans won't want to miss. There's not much personal history here (perhaps Hope wasn't home long enough to generate any), though he did write an autobiography in 1955 (*Have Tux, Will Travel*). —*Denise Perry Donavin*

Film & Drama

✓ **Howe, Tina.**
Approaching Zanzibar.
Theatre Communications Group, $8.95. 102p.

The New York Blossoms are on their way out west, to Taos where Charlotte's Aunt Livvie lies dying. They're an unusual family. Wally and Charlotte are creative—he a composer, she a quilter—with two children of their thirties, 12-year-old guitar prodigy Turner and his 9-year-old sister Pony, both as smart and imaginative. Moreover, Livvie, the object of their pilgrimage, is a Christo-like artist who creates huge, impermanent installations in natural settings. The play follows them across the country through a series of typical family scenes: arguing while driving, camping, father and son fly-fishing, visiting relatives along the way, finally arriving to be surprised by Aunt Livvie's condition. Howe fills her play with exquisite comedy tinged throughout by fantasy, producing a virtuoso piece—for ensemble acting and for the stage designer—that is also a deeply resonant depiction of familial love. She is at work adapting it for television, which promises a TV experience as rich as that afforded by her earlier portrayal of a woman and her aging parents, *Painting Churches*. A wonderful, wonder-filled, hilarious, touching, permanent addition to the American theater. —*Ray Olson*

Leff, Leonard J. and Simmons, Jerold L.
The Dame in the Kimono: Hollywood, Censorship and the Production Code from the 1920s to the 1960s.
Weidenfeld & Nicolson, $22.50. 384p.

Film buffs old or historically minded enough to recall the Production Code Administration (nicknamed the "Hays Office" for Will Hays, its hucksterish founder) will be enthralled by Leff and Simmons' history of its nearly 40-year reign as Hollywood's official, in-production censor. The pair highlights influential conflicts between censors and moviemakers over such hot-in-their-time properties as Mae West, *Dead End* (1937), *Gone with the Wind* (1939), *The Outlaw* (1943), *A Streetcar Named Desire* (1951), *The Moon Is Blue* (1953), *Lolita* (1962), and *Who's Afraid of Virginia Woolf?* (1966). Limning these contretemps, they also sketch the personalities of actual code enforcers Joe Breen and Geoffrey Shurlock and disclose their relations with such problematic allies as the Catholic church's Legion of Decency. The code was eventually supplanted by the lettered (*G, PG, R,* and *X*) ratings system, which finally freed the producers to produce and the censors—er, the raters—to merely rate, not hamstring a project with their objections. —*Ray Olson*

Marx, Samuel and Vanderveen, Joyce.
Deadly Illusions: Jean Harlow and the Murder of Paul Bern.
Random, $19.95. 256p.

This spring's second exposé of murder cover-ups in the early years of Hollywood. The first, Robert Giroux's *Deed of Death*, ferreted out the truth about the murder of silent-picture director William Desmond Taylor. Here we get the goods on the death of popular MGM director Paul Bern in 1932. Married to Jean Harlow and known for his kindness, Bern was found shot in their home. His death was ruled a suicide after a motive was established: the studio claimed Bern was impotent and killed himself out of frustration. But Marx, one of MGM's insiders and a friend of Bern's, remained disturbed by this characterization and has now finally revealed the truth, which takes the shape of a tale right out of the melodramas of the time. Marx shares behind-the-scenes trivia about Harlow, Irving Thalberg, and the high-handed machinations of the studios. It's a bit plodding, but it will attract film buffs and fans of true crime. —*Donna Seaman*

Mordden, Ethan.
Medium Cool: The Movies of the 1960s.
Knopf, $24.95. 320p.

In the Golden Age of Hollywood, film prescribed rather than reflected the values of society. Mordden says that "for the first fifty years the movies are about romance. Nothing happens in the 1950s. Then, from 1960 on, the movies are about reality." The end of the McCarthy era heralded the collapse of the studio system, launching a rebellion against the authoritarian control of the moguls. This rebellious spirit spawned the New Cinema, a more daring, mature, sexier, and violent cinema, and an alternative to the tame pictures of a tamer time. In comparing Doris Day and Rock Hudson's *Pillow Talk* (1959) with Jon Voight and Dustin Hoffman's *Midnight Cowboy* (1969), a world of difference can be seen in filmmaking and subject matter. Mordden notes that in "the 1930s, sex registered as wit"; in the 1940s, as crime; "there was no sex in the 1950s"; and in the 1960s, sex was sex. In analyzing dozens of movies, from *The Manchurian Candidate* and *Psycho* to *The Graduate* and *Butch Cassidy and the Sundance Kid*, Mordden offers perceptive critiques of trends and themes in a radically altered and a more socially relevant medium. —*Benjamin Segedin*

Osborn, M. Elizabeth, ed.
The Way We Live Now: American Plays and the AIDS Crisis.
Theatre Communications Group, $24.95. 279p.

No profession has been harder hit by AIDS than the theater, which has responded with myriad benefit performances and a host of plays that, if not all primarily concerned with it, have something trenchant to say about AIDS. This set of 10 pieces, including full-length dramas, one-acts, excerpts, and a story arranged for five readers, attests to the vitality of this body of work. Reprinted from other books are Hoffman's *As Is*; the titular one-act from Fierstein's *Safe Sex*; Lanford Wilson's superb and surprising monologue, "A Poster of the Cosmos," from *Best Short Plays, 1989* (Applause Theatre Books, 1989); and the man's monologue from Durang's *Laughing Wild* (Grove, 1989). Welcome first publications include Terence McNally's sketch, "Andre's Mother," recently expanded into a teleplay starring Sada Thompson and Richard Thomas; David Greenspan's "Jack," a poignant exercise in literary cubism for three women's and one man's voices; and excerpts from two

Film & Drama

as-yet-unstaged plays. Only Harry Kondoleon's punningly titled *Zero Positive* is tiresome on the page. The arranged story, Susan Sontag's "Way We Live Now," lends itself well to the effort. —*Ray Olson*

Pepper, Terence and Kobal, John.
The Man Who Shot Garbo: The Hollywood Photographs of Clarence Sinclair Bull.
Simon & Schuster, $40. 256p.

Clarence Bull (1896–1979) was head of MGM's stills department for nearly 40 years, producing "icons of the age which fixed the studio and its stars in the public's imagination." Following an introductory chapter highlighting the important stages of his career is a 183-plate album of Bull's movie stills and studio portraits featuring the giants of the silver screen during his day (which, interestingly for him and us, corresponded to the golden age of Hollywood). A few faces and names, though famous decades ago, have since been forgotten, but most of those captured in exquisite radiance are actors whose legends live on. The classic series he took of Greta Garbo is arresting, certainly, but the whole collection deserves to be pored over again and again. Captions give pertinent background information on each photo. —*Brad Hooper*

Rawlence, Christopher.
The Missing Reel.
Atheneum, $19.95. 384p.

Who invented movies? Thomas Edison, as he so brashly claimed? Or was it Augustin Le Prince, who mysteriously disappeared en route to file a U.S. patent for his moving-picture camera in 1890? Rawlence, a filmmaker and writer, got hooked on the history of moving pictures after he moved into the inventor's former residence in Leeds. Le Prince had been working on the development of a moving-picture camera and projector in secrecy and isolation for years, separated from his stateside wife and family and fearful of having his discoveries stolen. Rawlence turned detective and retraced the path of Le Prince's life, steeping himself in the inventor's technical reasoning as well as his personality. He hints, suspensefully, at various explanations for Le Prince's disappearance while simultaneously relating a sympathetic account of his wife's ordeal and providing a lively history of the litigious beginnings of the movie industry. A captivating tale of the price of obsession. —*Donna Seaman*

✓ **Rebello, Stephen.**
Alfred Hitchcock and the Making of Psycho.
Dembner Books, $24.95. 256p.

No post–World War II American movie has been more influential than Alfred Hitchcock's *Psycho*—the first, and probably still the best, slasher/splatter movie—now 30 years old. Rebello celebrates the anniversary with a thorough history of the film, from preconception (the crimes of rural sociopath Ed Gein and the novel ace thriller-writer Robert Bloch based upon them) through hammering out a script, casting and shooting (filming the famed shower sequence is the book's centerpiece), to its unprecedented worldwide reception (audiences screamed *and* laughed, totally bewildering Hitchcock and everyone else involved with the picture). Rebello avoids both ponderous critical analysis and fan-mag gossip in what must be reckoned a model single-film study. Especially notable is his recognition that *Psycho* changed not just popular film style, but Hitchcock's life and reputation as a filmmaker, sharply dividing his career into all that led up to and all that unsatisfactorily followed his intentionally low-budget experiment. —*Ray Olson*

Rico, Diana.
Kovacsland: A Biography of Ernie Kovacs.
HBJ, $19.95. 342p.

For some, the end of the postwar American heyday came not with the assassination of JFK, but with the January 13, 1962, car crash that killed Ernie Kovacs. Rico—whose biography is far more lavish and, it must be said, reverent than Walley's slapdash *Ernie Kovacs Phile* —was not among them, coming to the gently outré comic's work as late as 1981. She made up for lost time, interviewing everybody she could find who knew Kovacs and sleuthing down his every word and image. Accordingly, her book is full of descriptions of programs from throughout her subject's incredibly productive 20-year career. She leaves no doubt of his originality, although she concedes the much faster pace of TV nowadays makes Kovacs' unhurried style seem leaden-footed. She partakes of that slowness herself in a book that is nothing if not meandering, but that won't matter to the fans whom Kovacs' work, seen on public and cable channels, continues to win. For them, especially for those who saw his shows the first time around, he remains the absolute flower of TV's golden age. —*Ray Olson*

Shaffer, Peter.
Lettice & Lovage.
Harper, $17.95. 100p.

The newest play from one of Britain's most successful dramatists (*Five Finger Exercise, The Royal Hunt of the Sun, Equus, Amadeus*) is an unmitigated delight. It's about the initially chilly, ultimately warm relationship between two middle-aged women rather bogged down in life. Lettice is the daughter of a female theatrical entrepreneur from whom she imbibed a love of history and histrionics. Lotte, daughter of an art-book publisher, is a former student of architecture with a historical turn of mind herself. They meet when Lotte, as an executive of Britain's Preservation Trust, fires Lettice as a tour guide because of her outrageous embroiderings upon the meager facts she is supposed to relate. Friendship develops afterwards from their shared love of the color and drama of pre-Commonwealth England and detestation of the look of contemporary London. Both women's parts, written for star turns, are

Film & Drama

full of comic invention based upon credible, though eccentric, characterization. —*Ray Olson*

Film & Drama

Sragow, Michael, ed.
Produced and Abandoned: The Best Films You've Never Seen.
Mercury House, $9.95. 384p.

Thanks to video, movies that didn't lend themselves to the promotional blitzes necessary for prolonged box office draw get a second chance. This guide to the "best" of "neglected" films shows that they are more creative, subtle, provocative, unpredictable, and fresh than their commercial siblings. Containing almost 100 reviews from films released in the last 20 years, this selection includes many productions by "A-list" directors at their most personal and daring, including John Huston, Robert Altman, Brian De Palma, Jonathan Demme, and Francis Ford Coppola. Contributing reviewers include Pauline Kael, Judith Crist, Roger Ebert, Richard Schickel, and Stephen Schiff. Fourteen chapters group the films under such headings as "Unseen Truths," "Off the Beaten Laugh Track," and "Shades of Noir." More specialized and in-depth than Leonard Maltin's guides, this is a great tool for connoisseurs of cinema. —*Donna Seaman*

Truffaut, François.
François Truffaut: Correspondence, 1945–1984.
Farrar, $50. 672p.

Like most collections of correspondence, this one has an inclination to render a fragmented picture of the individual's life—often a frustrating portrait that tends to tease rather than define. Truffaut, the great filmmaker who died of a brain tumor in 1984, was a diligent and prolific letter writer who took almost as much pride in his mastery over the written word as he did the moving picture. The auteur behind *The 400 Blows* and *Jules and Jim*, and author of an exemplary interview with Hitchcock, was weaned on cinema, becoming an influential film critic at an early age, before launching the French New Wave. Here are the collected letters to Alfred Hitchcock, for whom Truffaut showed an undeniably sycophantic devotion; Eric Rohmer and Louis Malle, his colleagues at *Cahiers du Cinéma*, and filmmakers in their own right; and Robert Lachenay and Helen Scott, dear comrades, collaborators, and confidants. Of note is an exchange with Jean-Luc Godard, in which Truffaut calls the unpredictable, radical director of *Breathless* a "poseur" and "the Ursula Andress of militancy." (Despite their feud, Godard contributes a brief, but poignant foreword.) Noticeably absent here is much mention of the events of May 1968 and the Langlois affair. Recommended for lovers of film, in general, and lovers of Truffaut, in particular. A volume of personal letters is currently in preparation. —*Benjamin Segedin*

Health & Medicine

Brinker, Nancy and Harris, Catherine McEvily.
The Race Is Run One Step at a Time: My Personal Struggle—and Everywoman's Guide—to Taking Charge of Breast Cancer.
Simon & Schuster, $18.95.

Having lost a favorite aunt and her sister to breast cancer, Brinker was no stranger to its devastating effects. In fact, she fulfilled her sister's dream of helping more women understand and prevent it by creating the Susan G. Komen Foundation for the Advancement of Breast Cancer Research. So when she was diagnosed, she knew more than the average woman about her options and outlook. She believes that all the information available to her helped immensely. Now she wants to share her accumulated knowledge. With Harris' help, she does so beautifully. The tone is that of an ordinary woman; the spirit it bespeaks is extraordinary. Brinker's story forms the framework of the book, within which she includes accurate and easy-to-understand explanations of treatment options, technology, testing, side effects, medical terminology, prognosis, and more. What may be most helpful is frank discussion of how losing a breast affected Brinker's self-image and sex life. A true advocate for others with the disease, Brinker gives them positive reinforcement *and* empowering information. —*Mary Ellen Sullivan*

✓ **Callahan, Daniel.**
What Kind of Life: The Limits of Medical Progress.
Simon & Schuster, $19.95. 303p.

Americans perceive good health as the most important goal in their lives. Callahan asks, "Should it be?" His provocative question is answered within philosophical and practical contexts and with an eloquence and profundity readers have come to expect from the author of *The Tyranny of Survival* and *Setting Limits: Medical Goals in an Aging Society.* Callahan points out that resources are finite and cannot be endlessly poured into an impossible search for perfect health and longevity. He also examines how society must learn to achieve a better quality of life on all levels for everyone. Callahan's is not a utopian scheme but a reasoned readjustment of priorities, with as much thought granted to morality as to economics. —*Denise Perry Donavin*

Gallagher, Hugh Gregory.
By Trust Betrayed.
Holt, $24.95. 352p.

A searing account of how respected, rational, and otherwise decent members of Nazi Germany's medical community proceeded with government approval and in a "careful, orderly, and quite methodical manner" to kill over 200,000 of their permanently disabled patients. In explaining how physicians who were bound by the Hippocratic oath to protect and preserve life could inflict death instead, Gallagher, himself disabled, illuminates the frustration dynamic that always exists to some degree between the physician and a chronic patient. That the German physicians set about eliminating this frustration by eliminating the source was a course of action made possible, Gallagher tells us, by a horrifying concatenation of the murderous Nazi zeitgeist and the fear and loathing of the disabled that seems to be a universal human trait. A valuable contribution to the history of the Nazi era, as well as to the literature on the struggle for the rights of the disabled. —*Steve Weingartner*

Gutkind, Lee.
One Children's Place: A Profile of Pediatric Medicine.
Grove Weidenfeld, $19.95. 288p.

Gutkind offers a colorful picture of activities at the Children's Hospital of Pittsburgh. The personalities he sketches along the way range from nationally known transplant specialist Thomas Starzl and local surgeons, pediatricians, and nurses to the hospital's administrators, chaplain, and staff specialists. As Gutkind depicts it, patients and their families play individualized, not stereotyped, roles in the 24-hour days and 7-day weeks of the hospital's never-resting life. Many incidents typify the diagnostic skills, operative procedures, and thoughtful caring so important in pediatrician-patient and teacher-student relationships. The subtitle aside, this is basically the story of one pediatric hospital, which—thanks to Gutkind's feeling for the place and its people—is a factual document with a warmly human atmosphere. —*William Beatty*

Haas, Scott.
Hearing Voices: The Notes of a Psychology Intern.
Dutton, $18.95. 208p.

A young psychology intern shares his emotional highs and lows during his stint at the Commonwealth Mental Health Institute in Cambridge, Massachusetts. In his thoughtful, honest entries, Haas logs his fears—of physical harm at the hands of patients, of providing inadequate care—and worries about his personal frailties intruding on the therapy he provides. Typical of Haas' wisdom are his words on long hours ("But what we lose by working too hard is some of the capacity to meditate on our patients"); he can also be provocative, challenging the politics of the mental-health community: "Psychiatry's control of the field of mental health is taken for granted. It does not come under scrutiny." Haas' writing reflects the vulnerability of a man new to his profession and expresses feelings of impatience, compassion, and guilt. However, he demonstrates a generous philosophy toward work, as a care provider who always respects his patients and aches to know the answers to the questions he asks. —*Kathryn LaBarbera*

Marion, Robert.
The Boy Who Felt No Pain: Tales from the Pediatric Ward.
Addison-Wesley, $17.95. 224p.

In 14 case histories, pediatric geneticist Marion blends medical facts with the doctor's relationships with patient and family, producing a heart-warming mixture. A particular virtue of his writing is his ability to show how he learned during his years of medical school and practice as he unostentatiously teaches the reader. Two excellent examples of this ability are the stories of Tommy, a victim of amniotic band syndrome, and of Randy, who had von Gierke's disease. Marion describes the unsettling birth and early months of Tommy, "the baby who had no face," with sympathy for the feelings of the parents and medical staff but without sensationalism. The account of Randy, a five-year-old with a faulty liver, emphasizes what Marion learned from the child's predicament. If Marion's memoirs could be converted into a television series without sacrificing his style, they would do much to counter the sensationalism and lack of realism of most medical programs. —*William Beatty*

Miller, Laurence.
Inner Natures: Brain, Self, and Personality.
St. Martin's, $19.95. 304p.

The intricate workings of the brain, the organ of personality, are still not well understood, but progress is steady. This is an attempt to dissect the assumptions of current neuropsychological thought. Miller, trying valiantly not to overwhelm his readers with overly technical or academic language, describes how the brain "represents, facilitates, and determines the cognitive and emotional processes that form our identities." The first half of the book contains a discussion of selfhood and an analysis of the brain's "self-systems." Then Miller tackles the fertile subject of personalities. He relates tales of the curious behavior associated with brain dysfunctions, but typical personality types are Miller's primary focus. These include obsessive-compulsives, paranoiacs, psychosomatics, geniuses, and even nerds. He concludes with a look at healthy personalities and "self-change." A demanding book that will give those who brave it a freshly informed framework for understanding themselves and others. —*Donna Seaman*

Pietropinto, Anthony and Simenauer, Jacqueline.
Not Tonight, Dear: How to Reawaken Your Sexual Desire.
Doubleday, $18.95. 336p.

"I have a headache" may be a funny line for comedians, but for those whose spouses aren't ever up for sex, it apparently rings a little hollow. Almost every form of physical and emotional longing has been covered by self-help books, so it should come as no surprise that what therapists call "sexual desire disorder" is about to have its moment in the limelight. This isn't a book for those who can't, just for those who don't want to. Why don't they want to? All kinds of reasons: fatigue, depression, worries, anger, intimacy conflicts, etc. For those who have trouble pinpointing just which reason fits their case, the authors include numerous self-awareness questionnaires and quizzes. Like

Health & Medicine

most books of its ilk, this one is filled with anecdotal information. For instance: " 'I'm a sexual *klutz*,' Lester moans . . . 'When we finally got down to it, I couldn't give her an orgasm' . . . 'I'm a loser in bed.' " While readers will no doubt get to know more about the Lesters of this world than they wish, they'll also get some practical, useful information. The authors, in fact, offer quite a hopeful prognosis—at least for those with enough desire to read the book. —*Ilene Cooper*

Reinisch, June M. and Beasley, Ruth.
The Kinsey Institute New Report on Sex: What You Must Know to Be Sexually Literate.
St. Martin's, $22.95. 544p.

The famous Kinsey reports were two academic treatises by Dr. Alfred Kinsey: *Sexual Behavior in the Human Male* (1948) and *Sexual Behavior in the Human Female* (1953). Both books became best-sellers and exploded protective myths about "normal" sexual behavior in America. Now the Kinsey Institute has compiled years of research into a comprehensive overview aimed at improving our "sexual literacy." The first chapter, too hot to be released at galley stage, will reveal the results of a survey on what we really know about sex, and if recent findings about our lack of knowledge about world affairs are any indication of our cognizance, we're in trouble. At any rate, this is sex education at its most accessible. Reinisch and Beasley cover as many aspects of sexuality as possible, including sexual anatomy, preferences, contraception, and health and psychological issues from childhood to advanced age. A question-and-answer format covers a lot of territory efficiently and generates an air of immediacy and reassurance. The only value judgment Reinisch makes is that people have the right to choose their forms of sexual expression, but she does support healthy, safe sex, concluding with a sobering section on the many types of sexually transmitted diseases, including AIDS. The demand for practical information about sex has never been higher. —*Donna Seaman*

Sidransky, Ruth.
In Silence: Growing Up in a Hearing World.
St. Martin's, $18.95. 340p.

Because Sidransky's parents were both deaf, she grew up with signing as her first language, fully mastering speech only after her entrance into school. Both Ruth and her younger brother, Freddy, are capable of hearing and often served as the translators for their parents. Stressed over and over again in this autobiography is the rich sense of language and personal history transferred to Ruth by her capable, loving parents. Her father Benny's jocular nature and unquenchable thirst for knowledge is described, and Ruth's discerning tales about—and from—her mother help to further broaden this insightful look at everyday life in a deaf household of the 1940s. Sidransky's loving, cogent story is certain to dispel mistaken notions about the hearing handicapped. —*Denise Perry Donavin*

Smith, Jane S.
Patenting the Sun: Polio, the Salk Vaccine, and the Children of the Baby Boom.
Morrow, $22.95. 320p.

In 1954, Smith's parents requested that their then six-year-old daughter be part of an experimental program to test the Salk polio vaccine. Consider: such a request back then is like asking a parent today to test an AIDS vaccine on their child. Smith's personal involvement in the landmark Polio Pioneers program is perhaps what makes this chronicle of the vaccine's development so utterly fascinating. In a lively narrative that draws on her interviews with Albert Sabin and Jonas Salk, the author richly details the events leading up to the historic moment of discovery and the breathtaking introduction of the vaccine to an anxiously awaiting public. Interwoven throughout are well-chosen anecdotes that perfectly capture the popular culture's reactions to each new stage of the program. This behind-the-scenes record of one of the most important public health measures ever is a vitally important book, especially since it carries an important reminder for today's and future parents about the dangers of not following an immunization program. —*Mary Banas*

✓ **Stone, John.**
In the Country of Hearts: Journeys in the Art of Medicine.
Delacorte, $17.95. 224p.

Stone, a poet and a cardiologist, has written a delightful and informative book. Combining clinical perception with the history of medicine, he tells of patients with "blue baby" and Marfan's syndromes—as might be expected—but he also deals with lesser-known problems. Whether the patient is the elderly Mrs. Corrigan, who needed a new heart valve and later invited Stone to her home outside Atlanta to pick fresh figs, or the young Bryan, whose "heart problem" turned out to be big tonsils and adenoids, they are presented as living, feeling human beings. As their cardiologist, Stone has a special relationship with them that is educational for all involved—including the reader, who learns much about transplants, pacemakers, balloons, and magnetic resonance imaging in these clinical histories that are also good short stories and personal essays. —*William Beatty*

Taylor, Robert L.
Health Fact, Health Fiction: Getting through the Media Maze.
Taylor, $16.95. 174p.

Taylor's book may evoke relieved sighs from those who, because of the ever-increasing barrage of health warnings, have developed a fear of living. His attitude may be characterized by the suggestion that one should take everything one hears or reads with a grain of salt—especially since salt is apparently dangerous only to a very few individuals. His discussions of the actualities of so-called health risks and of the media distortion of medical findings are especially enlightening. The book also commendably teaches wariness of propaganda and slanted journalism as well as the need to

Health & Medicine

occasionally pay more attention to what is *not* said than to what is said; to live, react, and behave moderately; and to remember that sometimes the same statistics can be used to "prove" just about anything. —*Richard Mills*

✓ **Weil, Andrew.**
Natural Health, Natural Medicine: A Comprehensive Manual for Wellness and Self-care.
Houghton, $19.95. 342p.

As a Harvard physician, holistic health advisor Weil has considerable mainstream cachet. He's powerfully persuasive when encouraging consultation of an osteopath or naturopath for persistent problems regular doctors (allopaths) can't solve because he also says, unqualifiedly, that no one should take the traumatic injuries allopaths excel at treating to any other kind of practitioner. Softened by such one-two punches, many a skeptic may follow him everywhere in his guide for self-managed health. Should they, they'll find some extraordinary advice, vended with charm as well as authority (the latter rarely, however, accompanied by citation of specific research). Statements such as "not to worry about protein at all and to eat less of it" and "addiction is not a psychological or pharmacological problem" seem to fly in the face of conventional wisdom, but Weil argues rationally and commonsensically for them. The four parts of his self-care enthusiast's bible are devoted to preventive maintenance; specific measures for warding off cancer, heart attacks, strokes, and immunity failure; self-treatment with vitamins, supplements, and herbs; and home remedies for common complaints. Annotated resource lists on finding holistic practitioners and suppliers of vitamins and herbs are appended. —*Ray Olson*

✓ **Yanker, Gary and others.**
Walking Medicine: The Lifetime Guide to Preventive and Rehabilitative Exercisewalking Programs.
McGraw-Hill, $24.95. 512p.

Authoritative, fact-packed, comprehensive—this is an impressive guide to walking for health and happiness. The text is divided into seven "minibooks," each of which draws on the knowledge of appropriate medical experts to cover a common medical problem and features one or more walking programs, which are divided into five fitness levels, from the most unfit to the professional athlete. The first minibook introduces walking as an activity that can be modified for every age group and provides self-administered tests for readers to determine their fitness levels and physiological ages. From there the guide moves on to walking for arthritis, back, and joints (a section that spells out the basic walking techniques) through cardio-walking (including an in-depth review of the heart, lung, and circulatory system), walk-shaping and weight control, walk-therapy to reduce stress, leg exercises and footwear design and selection, and, finally, a state-by-state directory of more than 400 health professionals, physicians, and researchers. Advice includes special diets and behavioral modification exercises as well as exercise-walking routines. Though they stress that walking is not a panacea, the authors offer it as "a reasonable way of helping you to control, ameliorate, or perhaps prevent health problems." —*Sally Estes*

History

Abel, Elie.
The Shattered Bloc: Behind the Upheaval in Eastern Europe.
Houghton, $20.95. 262p.

Abel won prizes for his coverage of the 1956 Hungarian and the 1968 Czech revolts against communism. In this book, he updates us on not only Hungary and Czechoslovakia but also their neighbors in an Eastern Europe now engaged en masse in smashing the Iron Curtain (he points out, however, that these nations see themselves as Central Europe, as opposed to Russia, to them the true east of their subcontinent). Abel's two-part treatment first examines the peculiar situations of each of the restive nations and the even stranger case of multinational Yugoslavia. He then considers the political, economic, and social challenges these nations face as they strive to democratize and simultaneously maintain relations with Moscow while reaching out for aid to the West and Japan. Although much of what Abel imparts has been widely reported in print and broadcast media, his book is a literate, compellingly readable précis that anyone interested in the momentous events unfolding in the Communist bloc would profit from reading. —*Ray Olson*

Adelson, Alan and Lapides, Robert.
Lodz Ghetto: Inside a Community under Seige.
Viking, $29.95. 402p.

In the process of eradicating the Lodz ghetto, the Nazis put a murderous end to the existence of more than 200,000 Jews. That end did not come overnight but gradually, in horrible increments, as the ghetto inhabitants were sent to Auschwitz in groups of 20,000 or more. It was a process that lasted nearly five years (1939–44), and in that time many of those doomed Jews managed to create a substantial written record of what it was like to live in a community that had been collectively condemned to death. They did so in diaries, notebooks, poems, and other writings, many of which are excerpted in this book. Those bearing witness include schoolchildren, a journalist, a theologian, a doctor, and a girl who shall remain forever anonymous—and eloquent. The testimony of these cruelly stilled voices is certain to evoke powerful emotions in most readers. It is just as certain to raise those gallingly unanswerable questions that ask why and how the Holocaust could have ever happened. —*Steve Weingartner*

History

Atwan, Robert and Vinokurov, Valeri, eds.
Openings: Original Essays by Contemporary Soviet and American Writers.
Univ. of Washington, $40. 319p.

A unique international collaboration of outstanding writers from the U.S. and the USSR featuring original essays revolving around seven themes: history, geography, art, literature, science, sports, and ways of life. Among the estimable contributors are Geoffrey C. Ward, Eleanor Munro, Joyce Carol Oates, and Barry Lopez on the American side, and Yuri Nagibin, Viktor Astafyev, and Viktor Potanin for Mother Russia. Essayists from both nations refer glancingly to perestroika but never celebrate it explicitly. The collection's joyousness emanates contextually, perhaps from the trust that follows suspicion, or maybe merely from the presence of the other nation's readers. Excellent Glasnost reading. —*Roland Wulbert*

✓ Barnet, Richard J.
The Rockets' Red Glare: When America Goes to War Two Hundred Years.
Simon & Schuster, $24.45. 450p.

Stand on that crumbling wall in Germany and ponder this: in the era of the nation-state, a major war arises approximately every 50 years. Will the decade of democracy help bring that to a halt? One thing this study of America makes plain is that the people are hard to manage. They have no stomach for war, and try as they might, governments can manipulate and deceive them for only so long. But can nations get along without making war? Barnet doesn't conclude so, though well he might: America goes to war a lot, as do all powerful nations. Yet people generally find war repugnant; they can rouse themselves for a fight, but their hearts seldom remain in it. Why, then, do they so often find themselves toiling under its yoke? Because the *idea of nationhood* traps them. Dripping like lead on the wings of democracy and its vision of man, it makes of a people something defensive, proud, vengeful, and self-righteous. Yet although this fair, balanced, sober and sobering history of the nation's ministers and their struggle with the people leads us to conclude that nationhood and democracy do not happily mix, after looking back across 200 years, Barnet draws some suprisingly upbeat conclusions and centers them on a simple but powerful idea: American governments have not proven wiser than the people. —*Stuart Whitwell*

✓ Beckwith, Carol and Fisher, Angela.
African Ark: People and Ancient Cultures of Ethiopia and the Horn of Africa.
Abrams, $65. 328p.

A beautiful, monumental work. The "Ark" is the Horn of Africa, a region encompassing Ethiopia, Somalia, and parts of Kenya and the Sudan. Free of the stamp of colonialism, "vast and remote, the Horn of Africa . . . shelters an astonishing variety of human societies: from the ancient and highly sophisticated to the remote, simple and untouched." This is a collection of unexpected and stirring portraits accompanied by Graham Hancock's vivid prose.

Photographers Beckwith and Fisher have recorded people at play and in prayer, decked out in elaborate finery, proud, graceful and seemingly outside of time. The Christians of Lalibela worship in 800-year-old churches "hewn directly out of the solid red volcanic rock." The Falashas practice an ancient, pre-Talmudic Judaism, while the Surma women wear lip plates and the Karo paint their bodies, transforming themselves into otherwordly creatures. The photographs are stupendous, radiating the energy of lives ordered by tradition and strong cultural identities. —*Donna Seaman*

Beesley, Earl A. and Gibbons, Garry.
The Treasure Houses of England: A View of Eight Great Country Estates.
Abrams, $67.50. 152p.

Eight of the brightest and best known of England's stately homes are highlighted, nay lionized, in this album of 67 breathtaking panoramic color photos that are generally two feet wide, and even wider in the book's eight gatefolds. The personal introductions by the eight current owners (Beesley and Gibbons are the photographers) are refreshingly brief, the entry for each house consisting primarily of an architectural sketch preceding the opulent photographs. Demonstrating the architectural and decorative riches of Britain's aristocracy, the pictures display stunning formal gardens and broad sweeping lawns punctuated by classical statuary and elaborate fountains, all evoking the aura of a distant time and place. A splendid book not just for tourists and Anglophiles, but for anyone with a love of domestic grandeur as only the English could conceive it. —*Robert Seid*

Brother against Brother: Time-Life Books History of the Civil War.
Prentice Hall Press, $39.95. 431p.

Another single-volume, illustrated history of the American Civil War? Don't we have enough of these already? Perhaps, but this one is first-rate nonetheless. Condensed from the splendid 28-volume series on the Civil War, this book bears all the hallmarks of a Time-Life publication: excellent writing, wonderful illustrations, and top-notch production values. It even carries the imprimatur of James McPherson, who has written a single-volume Civil War history of his own (the Pulitzer Prize–winning *Battle Cry of Freedom*), and who here contributes some typically lucid and on-the-mark introductory comments. Deserving of special mention are the photographs, many of them—particularly those of Grant and Sherman—so rare as to impart a thrill to the reader who encounters them for the first time. —*Steve Weingartner*

Burgess, Alan.
The Longest Tunnel: The True Story of World War II's Great Escape.
Weidenfeld & Nicolson, $19.95. 320p.

Burgess reenacts the escape of Allied POWs from Stalag Luft III during World War II. Only 3 of the 76 escapees reached safety, and 50 of the recaptured POWs were murdered by the Gestapo (in deliberate violation of the Geneva convention) under orders from Hitler. Burgess reconstructs the search for the guilty parties by Allied special investigators, spelling out the fate of the Nazis

History

as clearly as he has reported the activities of the POWs in their struggle to return home. Burgess delineates the tunnel digging and the elaborate creation of costumes, identity papers, compasses, and other escape necessities—stories that are familiar from Paul Brickhill's classic *The Great Escape*, and the many movie and television take-offs that it spawned. This story has been told before, of course, yet Burgess, who was an RAF pilot, explains that his approach is a more personal one bolstered by previously unavailable details of survivor testimony as well as newly uncovered military documents. — *Denise Perry Donavin*

Chafets, Ze'ev.
Devil's Night and Other True Tales of Detroit.
Random, $19.95. 241p.

Does anybody really care about Detroit? Chafets is counting on America at least being interested, although he contends suburbanites and even some Detroiters have purged themselves of any feeling for the once-great Motor City. An expatriate who left Pontiac, Michigan, for Tel Aviv, Israel, at the age of 20 in 1967, Chafets returned in 1988 to write this book, which is one man's impression rather than an informed "study." His is a poignant portrait of a city that once believed in opportunities for blacks and whites in high-paying factory jobs and in the glittering world of the music business. But when the auto industry skidded, and Motown moved to LA, dreams gave way to desperation. Detroit and its suburbs have become segregated and polarized, and the Motor City is viewed by many as Crime City, a depopulated wasteland. There are, however, those who see Detroit as a unique study in black self-governance, struggling but in some ways ahead of its time. Despite some naive perceptions, Chafets manages to convey convincing concern as he neatly strings together the pieces that make his book interesting and graceful. —*Deb Robertson*

Cooper, William J. and Terrill, Thomas E.
The American South: A History.
Knopf, $50. 800p.

Two professors address the nonacademic reader in a sensitive but not defensive narration of the history of the southern portion of the U.S. from colonial times to the present. The account incorporates, as should a good comprehensive historical survey, the economic, social, political, and cultural factors involved in the evolution of the region. Cooper and Terrill chronicle the engendering and maintenance of a "southern" consciousness, which gave to residents of the lower half of the country a sense of separateness; furthermore, they delineate the elements in southern life that distinguish the region from the North, East, and West. Though these differences have lessened in intensity in recent years, the authors see on the part of southerners an insistence that the South retain its old-line identity. —*Brad Hooper*

Cortázar, Julio.
Nicaraguan Sketches.
Norton, $15.95. 142p.

Argentine novelist Cortázar places his political convictions upfront in these essays, which offer a firsthand account of the Sandinista revolution and government and a defense of the regime. Cortázar's dedication to the cause of Nicaraguan liberation is formidable, and his voice is raised in support of both the Sandinistas' aims and actions. The writer is no mere apologist, however; he remains fully convinced of the rightness of Nicaragua's course while recognizing the perils that may block that path to progress. Cortázar's experiences as a writer who lived and worked in Europe and who has traveled throughout Latin America in the last decade—and who returned to his Argentine homeland from exile just before his death—lend extra meaning and poignancy to the highly provocative political content of the pieces. —*John Brosnahan*

Delano, Jack.
Puerto Rico Mio: Four Decades of Change.
Smithsonian Institution, $24.95. 224p.

Jack Delano, one of the now-famous photographers who participated in the Farm Security Administration's landmark documentary photo project begun in the 1930s, traveled extensively throughout the country to shoot every facet of (mostly) rural life. Sent to Puerto Rico, he documented the lives of a poor but proud and gentle agrarian people. He returned often, finally to reside there, and this volume contrasts his 1940s depiction with that of the developing yet still largely impoverished Puerto Rico of the 1980s. Delano's strong black-and-white photos reflect the Puerto Rican people's dignity and humanity and his respect for them. Essays on the people, the island's history, and Delano's achievements preface the photos in side-by-side columns of English and Spanish; comments from some of the persons in the photos follow them. Strongly recommended for its historical, sociological, and anthropological as well as photographic interest. —*John Alderson*

✓ Donleavy, J. P.
A Singular Country.
Norton, $18.95. 198p.

"Now you would betimes in the homeland of the shamrock itself be forgiven for expressing an observation as to where can you see your real ordinary down to earth and less blessed Irishman who isn't still standing there at the door of his thatched cottage owning a bit of land and smoking his clay pipe and day dreaming as he looked over the hedgerow and down the road into the infinity." What novelist-playwright Donleavy is really saying, after you extract the brogue from his long-winded, idiomatic, "St. Bridget Be Praised" prose, is that the Ireland most of us like to think we know—the popular image of, say, John Ford's classic film *The Quiet Man* —is no more. Oh, yes, the verdant pastures still exist (where the developers haven't broken ground, that is), and the charming seacoast castles can still be viewed (though you can bet Harry and Mabel of Dayton, Ohio, will be there with their Nikon), and you can still observe people quaintly riding bicycles on occasion (when a Ferrari doesn't threaten to run them down). Otherwise, the land of saints and scholars struggles with things that have probably made Barry Fitzgerald turn over in his grave many times. Video porn is now imported, for instance, wealthy foreigners have infiltrated the land, women have nodded toward liberation, religion is in a precarious state, and the Irish young head to England for abortions and jobs. And yet, through all the satiric jabs and sarcasm and the sometimes riotous old-sod humor, Donleavy's colorful, even poetic portrait of a hard-up kingdom finally evidences what we've known about the Irishman all along: "Beneath all his aesthetic ineptitudes he is a genius in dealing with the vicissitudes of life." —*Martin Brady*

Edelstein, Andrew and McDonough, Kevin.
The Seventies: From Hotpants to Hot Tubs.
Dutton, $12.95. 224p.

We've "done" the 1960s, now it's time for the diverse 1970s, the decade that realized the gospel of the sixties and ushered in the Me syndrome. The year 1973 was every bit as intense as 1968. Edelstein and McDonough have great fun recounting and ridiculing the events, trends, and attitudes of the time. Happily glib, but right on target, the authors frolic through witty analyses of movies, music, fashion, and TV. Politics is a rich vein from Nixon, Agnew, and Kissinger to Jerry Brown ("the missing link between the hippie and the yuppie") and Jimmy Carter. The seventies revolutionized the lives of women and gays and inspired an "explosion of spiritualism," including cults and TM. Doing drugs was de rigueur; the authors trace the shift from the culture of pot to that of cocaine, noting the attendant change from introspection to the obsession with money and status. Lots of photos and time lines help to make this a browser's delight. —*Donna Seaman*

Egan, Timothy.
The Good Rain: An Exploration of the Pacific Northwest.
Knopf, $19.95. 254p.

Although Egan's nature adventures in the Pacific Northwest begin with the ecologically dubious sprinkling of his grandfather's cremated ashes into a mountain stream, the pace and the environmental concerns of his story soon regroup after this hilariously maudlin introduction. *New York Times* correspondent Egan aims to follow the tracks of the region's earlier explorers as he tries to reexperience their journeys and exploits in our own time. In particular, Egan follows the example of Theodore Winthrop, whose wilderness stay in the Pacific Northwest in the mid-nineteenth century revealed for Egan both the mystery and the possibility of the region. Egan manages deftly to balance between the past and the present on his own trip, as he assesses the historical record and also focuses in on the present-day conditions that have not completely erased the Pacific Northwest's unique character as a place where humans and the natural world can meet and interact on not-quite-equal terms. —*John Brosnahan*

✓ **Ehrenreich, Barbara.**
The Worst Years of Our Lives: An Outsider's View of the Eighties.
Pantheon, $18.95. 251p.

Liberals have become so meek and retiring lately that most of them don't dare anything as attention-getting as political satire. Happily for the state of the art, Ehrenreich—a traditional liberal who has kept the progressive indignation of her working-class family's humanism burning brightly—isn't so timid. In this collection of squibs for the likes of the *New York Times*, *New Republic*, and *Mother Jones*, she rounds on such targets as "Fleece U." (the high cost of college), "Automating Politics" (i.e., getting the people out of it), and the many varieties of smugness conservatives in power are guilty of. What's funny about her comments is their bold sarcasm, their unfair but truthful exaggerations, and such deliciously partisan pronouncements as, "I was raised . . . with a stern set of moral principles: Never lie, cheat, steal, or knowingly spread a venereal disease . . . [and] never, ever . . . vote Republican." Occasionally, however, as in the piece on a suburbanite consumed by the well-founded fear that public knowledge of her son's AIDS will stigmatize her, there is no room for humor, only for the intelligent moral indignation that is a constant throughout the book. —*Ray Olson*

Engelmann, Larry.
Tears before the Rain: An Oral History of the Last Days of the Fall of South Vietnam.
Oxford, $22.95. 400p.

Reading what the eyewitnesses have to say in this book about the last weeks, days, and hours of South Vietnam can be an excruciating experience. Of course, being painful, their stories are also thoroughly compelling. Among the 70 Americans and Vietnamese who share their memories with Engelmann are Graham Martin (the American ambassador to South Vietnam when it fell), newsman Ed Bradley, ex-CIA station chief Tom Polgar, and numerous individuals who were, at the time, government officials, soldiers, nurses, or simply civilians trying to get out of the country before the communist takeover. Their narratives paint a grim picture of what must certainly be regarded as a kind of nadir in the fortunes of the people of South Vietnam and America. Yet they also reveal a great deal of heroism, humor, wisdom, and sheer wide-eyed wonder at having been present for the enactment of a watershed event in history. —*Steve Weingartner*

History

Foner, Eric and Mahoney, Olivia.
A House Divided: America in the Age of Lincoln.
Norton, $35. 179p.

This companion to a well-received Chicago Historical Society exhibit is a warm and lovingly produced work. Columbia University's Eric Foner provides the text, which gives a graceful, informed overview of the antebellum U.S., the Civil War years, and the great conflict's aftermath. Best of all are the portrayed exhibit pieces, including clean reproductions of paintings, archival photos, and lithographs of famous people, places, and events as well as contemporary artifacts, including furniture, posters, armaments, sheet music, and dishware. Foner's text and much of the graphic material focus specifically on the slavery question and its impact on social, governmental, and military policies and the general conduct of the war. Not surprisingly, notable pictures are of pieces from the historical society's excellent collection of Lincolniana. Among the other great names of the era pictured are Stephen A. Douglas, Robert E. Lee, Ulysses Grant, John Brown, and Frederick Douglass. —*Martin Brady*

Gray, Francine du Plessix.
Soviet Women: Walking the Tightrope.
Doubleday, $19.95. 224p.

American novelist and journalist Gray traveled throughout the Soviet Union to see what effect glasnost has had on women's lives. What she discovered will confound, amaze, and inspire her readers, especially when she cuts through the more stilted images of that country's society and culture. While women are, theoretically, accorded equal rights under Marxist theory, Gray found that stereotypes and chauvinism die hard and that real liberation is just as difficult to achieve as in any Western country. Moreover, the odd juxtaposition of puritanism and sexual freedom in the USSR has often made relationships between men and women edgy and unfulfilling. (Many of the women Gray talked to are single mothers with careers who prefer, in fact, to raise their children alone.) But careerism is only part of the story here, and the book documents the conditions of medical care, education, and employment as well as considers the worlds of fashion, art, and literature, where women play important roles. Most of the people Gray met travel in well-educated intellectual circles, yet their views and observations are amplified through the author's personal involvement and insights. —*John Brosnahan*

✓ **Green, Martin.**
The Mount Vernon Street Women: A Boston Story, 1860–1910.
Scribner, $24.95. 320p.

Green has a talent for investigating the uncharted byways of intellectual and artistic history—see his studies of *The Von Richtofen Sisters* and of post–World War I English aesthetes in *Children of the Sun* —and again he comes up with a surprising winner in this account of an American family at the turn of the century. The Warrens of Boston first made their mark and fortune in the business, but the second generation extended their interests to social work, philanthropy, and, in the case of Ned Warren, to art collecting on such an enthusiastic level that his holdings formed the basis for the classical antiquities collection of the Boston Museum of Fine Arts. The Warren children also played out their roles in a family tragedy that used greed and sexual passion as the catalysts for sibling rivalry on a grand scale. Ned is the key character in this drama, and his flamboyant homosexuality touched off the spark that would produce an inferno ending suicide and dynastic decline. As in most of Green's investigations, the characters who have minor roles in the story—here, Oscar Wilde, Henry Adams, and Bernard Bernenson, among others— will be better known to the reader than the featured players. But the author persuasively makes us care about the lesser-known figures who dominate the action in this evocative re-creation of a particular place and time in social history. —*John Brosnahan*

Harden, Blaine.
Africa: Dispatches from a Fragile Continent.
Norton, $22.50. 384p.

Four demanding years as the *Washington Post* bureau chief in the sub-Sahara gave Harden X-ray vision; he can see through the confusing surface of African politics into the cultural conflicts at the center of the continent's myriad problems. His introductory overview recognizes Africa's scourges of famine, disease, poverty, and corrupt rulers. He then zooms in on individuals to "try to make the world's poorest continent more understandable—and less piteous—by making it more human." He witnesses the conflict between "the rural old and the urban young" and the burden of supporting an extended family. In another chapter, a famous Kenyan court case involving the burial of a man who married outside his tribe pits tribal beliefs against modern values. Harden exposes the wasteful bureaucracy and ignorance of foreign aid projects and describes various dictators, or "Big Men," who make themselves rich and keep their countries poor. Forceful, knowledgeable, and eloquent, Harden brings Africa into focus. —*Donna Seaman*

Hibbert, Christopher.
The American Revolution through British Eyes: The War for America, 1770–1781.
Norton, $29.95. 375p.

With vivid narration and analytical poise, veteran popular historian Hibbert revisits the American Revolution from a British perspective. Beginning with the Stamp Act of 1765, which the British saw as not only perfectly legal but also morally defensible—but which colonials saw as an outrageously inappropriate piece of legislation—the author interprets the War for Independence as viewed by the mother country: more a dirty insurrection than the sacred pursuit of liberty. Hibbert makes sure the reader not only sees the "other" side but also sees "our" side more lucidly and more realistically.

History

Hibbert's books are always a joy to read and learn from, and this one is certainly no exception. —*Brad Hooper*

Hobhouse, Henry.
Forces of Change: An Unorthodox History.
Arcade, $22.95. 272p.

One might reasonably assert that the success of the germ theory of disease paved the way for the disease theory of history. The latter is the subject of one of five thoroughly enjoyable chapters that comprise this sweeping survey of human demography since Columbus, et al., exchanged smallpox for maize. The other chapters smoothly explain the other side of the population equation, the food supply, and how that has been affected by agricultural technology, the nutritional value of newly discovered plants and animals, and their interaction with the physical geography of the U.S., the USSR, Japan, and elsewhere. With the inexorable workings of these processes, buttressed by the relative disappearance of pandemics, giving the earth its highest population ever, the author's resurrection of the specter of Thomas Malthus takes on a timely imperative. Hobhouse's ready and versatile command of his sources supports this fine example of the material view of historical change, which, the subtitle notwithstanding, is now part of mainstream historiography. An inexpensive alternative to Fernand Braudel's epic trilogy, *Civilization and Capitalism.* —*Gilbert Taylor*

Human Rights in China.
Children of the Dragon: The Story of Tiananmen Square.
Macmillan/Collier, $19.95. 224p.

Excepting official Chinese opinion and fallen hard-line Communists like Honecker and Ceausescu, the universal emotional reaction to the violent termination of 1989's democracy movement was sputtering vituperation. The majority opinion will undoubtedly be encouraged to sputter a little less by this compendium of photos and dozens of eyewitness accounts. Their vehement impact imparts the feeling that the suppression of the "counterrevolutionary rebellion" is temporary—the spirit of freedom was not completely flattened under tank treads. Appropriately enough, the book opens with a summary of Tiananmen Square's symbolic place in Chinese political culture and proceeds to short testimonials by those who encamped on its pavement last spring. These convey the pulse of the developing maelstrom: some speak of organizing demonstrations, others of dodging bullets. In particular, Fang Lizhi speaks eloquently through the postcrackdown gloom of the eventual futility of repressing visceral yearnings for freedom. —*Gilbert Taylor*

Hyland, William G.
The Cold War Is Over.
Times Books, $18.95. 240p.

A former CIA analyst and expert on Soviet affairs, Hyland has written an admirably succinct and well-thought-out book that surveys the history of the cold war, its immediate aftermath, and its possible impact on the future. His most important conclusion on this subject is stated in the book's unequivocal title. The cold war is over, he tells us, and not only that: America and its allies have won it. And we won because the Western alliance was stronger than the Soviet empire, and because the Soviet-Communist system was inherently and fatally flawed. Ideologically, economically, morally, communism didn't stand a chance against the West. Unfortunately, though, it was able to generate a great deal of misery and death before its demise. The cold war, Hyland contends, was therefore a necessary war that we did not seek, but had to fight. —*Steve Weingartner*

Kempe, Frederick.
Divorcing the Dictator: America's Bungled Affair with Noriega.
Putnam, $24.95. 469p.

Kempe, the well-regarded reporter for the *Wall Street Journal*, draws on his sources covert and overt to chronicle Manuel Noriega's rise from barrio-born bastard to the most demonized caudillo in recent memory. A more loathsome character is hardly to be found in fiction, and Kempe characterizes Noriega as a Frankenstein monster, Richard III, and the Wizard of Oz all rolled into one. In the second guise he epitomized the cunning, utterly amoral opportunist who knew precisely how to manipulate the rivalries among Washington's foreign policy bureacracies. The factors in the mishandling of the popular and political clamor for the ouster of the drug-running murderous dictator is the centerpiece of this story. Until early 1988, Noriega remained a relatively minor irritant. But then an ambitious prosecutor irrupted indictments into presidential politics, and cautious candidate Bush could not countenance quashing them, which was then Noriega's price for resignation. So U.S. policy, if that be the word, was, Micawberlike, to wait for something to turn up. It did in May 1989, unfortunately in the form of Noriega's native brutality in stealing an election. After the U.S. blew a low-risk chance to support a coup—which the U.S. had publicly encouraged—Noriega's declared policy became "Clubbings for the undecided, bullets for the enemies, and money for friends." Kempe's investigative retrospective is sure to spark reassessments of sledgehammer solutions to foreign policy problems. A riveting book that will be in certain demand as Prisoner #41586 drags out his defense in Miami. —*Gilbert Taylor*

Kessler, Lauren.
After All These Years: A New Look at the Sixties Generation.
Thunder's Mouth, $13.95. 240p.

While advertisers trivialize the more faddish aspects of the 1960s, the underlying beliefs in social justice and responsibility, peace, and respect for the Earth are alive and well. Using a "then and now" approach, Kessler traces the lives of 51 people who still practice the values they preached 20 years ago. The combination of oral history and essays establishes context and continuity. Interviewees include such notables as Angela Davis, Tom Hayden, Gloria Steinem, and Arlo Guthrie, as well as a civil rights attorney, a teacher, health-care coordinators, a Baptist minister, an investigative journalist, a psychiatric social worker, a screenwriter, and even the mayor of Eureka Springs, Arkansas. People are candid about the evolution of their expectations and the choices they've made and are proud of their convictions. Free of clichés and stereotypes, this is vital and affirmative social history. —*Donna Seaman*

Le Guin, Magnolia Wynn.
A Home-Concealed Woman: The Diaries of Magnolia Wynn Le Guin, 1901-1903.
Univ. of Georgia, $24.95. 400p.

This fine historical work shows us life in the early part of the century for a rural Georgian woman who, despite coming from one of the regions' wealthier families, nonetheless spent her life "home-concealed," birthing nine children while nursing her aging and sick parents. For more than a decade in her prime, she kept a series of diaries: sewing in October 1905, wondering if she can finish four dresses, three coats and six pairs of pants by the New Year; delighting in little Maggie's emerging speech in December 1906, having deciphered "an me" as "hand it to me"; seeing 12-year-old Askew off on a visit to town in June 1908. Through such intimate mundanity, we understand how love has been experienced by eons of mothers. Personal history at its most moving. —*Pat Monaghan*

Lincoln, W. Bruce.
Red Victory: A History of the Russian Civil War.
Simon & Schuster, $24.95. 626p.

With this book, Lincoln completes a trilogy on modern Russian history that includes *In War's Dark Shadow* and *Passage through Armageddon*. Like the previous two titles, it's a monumental work that manages to incorporate serious scholarship with all the best and most readable aspects of a popular history. After setting the stage with a look at the roots of the conflict, Lincoln gets to the meat of his subject with a lengthy but well-paced narrative that traces in exhaustive detail the military and political course of the civil war from its beginnings, shortly after the two revolutions of 1917, through the Kronstadt sailors' revolt of 1921. A final chapter on the civil war's aftermath and enduringly bitter legacy ends with Trotsky's assassination in Mexico in 1940. Throughout this endeavor, Lincoln remains scrupulously objective, an approach that serves to underscore the atrocious savagery that normally characterized the way Red and White factions alike dealt with each other. A more cynical appraisal of the Bolsheviks and their motivations could have been made—but, as portrayed here, their actions are damning enough. And that being the case, we are able to understand why some of the eastern European inheritors of the political system that the red victory made possible are currently engaged in its dismantlement. —*Steve Weingartner*

Lord, Bette Bao.
Legacies: A Chinese Mosaic.
Knopf, $19.95. 242p.

Lord was born in China but left with her family in 1946 for the U.S., only to return in 1979 as the wife of the American ambassador. Lord's book *Spring Moon* (1981), an affecting fictional memoir, evoked a family's ties to the country in early twentieth-century China, and now the author updates that account with a nonfictional study of the lives of the Chinese people—and of her own experiences—in the China of today. Lord begins her story in April 1989, at the moment when, as she and her husband were preparing to leave Beijing for a new post, the prodemocracy demonstrations started in Tiananmen Square. To her own reminiscences of China in this period she adds the portraits of the people she met and talked to—other voices, as she calls them. The resulting mosaic links the clear images of the past with some equally vivid impressions of the present. —*John Brosnahan*

Malkin, Peter Z. and Stein, Harry.
Eichmann in My Hands.
Warner, $22.95. 288p.

In May 1960, a team of Israeli secret agents ended a 12-year search by capturing the notorious SS leader Adolf Eichmann in Buenos Aires and flying him to Israel to stand trial for his part in the destruction of six million Jews. During the chaotic days after World War II, Eichmann—using a false name— had escaped from a U.S. prisoner-of-war camp in Germany. In 1950, with the help of the Nazi underground and a Franciscan monk, Eichmann had fled to Buenos Aires aboard an Italian ship. Malkin, one of the Israeli agents, aided by coauthor Stein, gives a firsthand account of the thousands of details involved in the Nazi's capture: false passports, forged papers, safe houses, physical training of the agents, cars rented, cover stories, disguises, places to hide Eichmann between abduction and deportation. Although everyone knows the ending, this is a gripping and suspense-filled story told well. —*George Cohen*

Miller, Judith.
One, by One, by One: Facing the Holocaust.
Simon & Schuster, $22.95. 464p.

Miller traveled through six countries—Germany, Austria, the Netherlands, France, the USSR, and the U.S.—in an effort to perceive how the Holocaust is remembered. She writes about the discomfiting struggle between repression of the memories of that horrible time and the necessity of never allowing its horror to be forgotten. Miller found that rationalization and relativization are the most common and insidious forms of memory suppression, and she concludes, "We must remind ourselves that the Holocaust was not six million. It was one, plus one, plus one. Only in understanding that civilized people must defend the one, by one, by one can the Holocaust, the incomprehensible, be given meaning." Miller's book delivers a powerful message. —*George Cohen*

History

Oakes, James.
Slavery and Freedom: An Interpretation of the Old South.
Knopf, $22.95. 288p.

While there have been countless books on slavery in America, Oakes' volume takes a significantly different approach in its discussion of the issue within political and economic contexts. Traditionally, history has been written from the perspective of those in power—the power that emanates from financial and political status—Oakes reminds us, and the reason "emancipation did not settle the meaning of the Civil War" is that, after it, land ownership remained the most significant factor in the economy and labor market. Hence, freed slaves and sharecroppers lacked the financial wherewithal to forge political bases. Within his analysis of slavery and liberal capitalism, Oakes offers critical judgment of earlier studies, showing how the power of landowners and merchants altered the course of history and affected the views of historians. He also points out that some Southern writers were simply intent on whitewashing the truth. A relatively brief yet erudite volume, packed with provocative thoughts on the writing of history. —*Denise Perry Donavin*

✓ **Overy, Richard and Wheatcroft, Andrew.**
The Road to War.
Random, $24.95. 364p.

This panoramic survey (published as a companion volume to a BBC series of the same name) explores the ever-fascinating subject of how World War II came to pass. The authors are scrupulous in their attempt to tell this exceedingly complex story without the benefit of hindsight—as if the outbreak and the conclusion of the war was not a foregone conclusion. This approach is at once the book's strength and weakness. On the one hand, it results in an objectivity that shades at times into a rather grayish sort of relativism. Certain truths are not illuminated, but obscured: Stalin and Hitler, for example, come across more as individuals who are swept along by history, rather than the ones who are doing the sweeping. The evil that these men personify is thus somewhat watered down. On the other hand, the authors' approach just naturally adds drama to their narrative. It also showcases their considerable literary skills. This cannot be overemphasized: Overy and Wheatcroft are cracking good writers, as well as first-rate historians. —*Steve Weingartner*

Pellegrino, Charles.
Unearthing Atlantis: An Archaeological Odyssey.
Random, $22.95. 320p.

If he had titled it *The Excavation at Thera* —or some similarly forthright title—only those few enthusiasts who know of the stupendous archeological finds on that Greek island would be drawn to this compelling work. But Pellegrino links Thera to the famed disappeared islands of Atlantis, thus assuring it the larger audience it deserves. In fact, Thera may have been Atlantis, if you believe speculation that it was a massive volcanic eruption there which, obliterating Minoan civilization, gave rise to Plato's legend. Or it may have been Crete's Pompeii. Bringing together archeology, literature, paleontology, geology, and luscious description, Pellegrino creates a work that draws us beyond Thera, beyond Atlantis, to considerations of time and morality. —*Pat Monaghan*

Perrot, Michelle, ed.
History of Private Life, Volume IV: From the Fires of Revolution to the Great War.
Harvard, $39.95. 736p.

The fourth volume in a series devoted to the development of the concept of individualism in Western civilization focuses on the nineteenth century, when the debate of private versus public life reached its climax. Between the proclamations of the French Revolution and the grim realities of World War I, the home and family assumed new importance, with the domestic ideal championed as a necessary refuge from political, economic, and social upheaval. The contributing authors examine various topics—architecture, sexuality, medical care, feminism—through multidisciplinary approaches that reveal the increasing individualism that society permitted and often unwittingly encouraged, thus paving the way for modern life. These essays are accompanied by an excellent series of illustrations that will help the reader to visualize the issues and points that this study discusses so provocatively. —*John Brosnahan*

✔ **Pipes, Richard.**
The Russian Revolution.
Knopf, $40. 976p.

Russian history is not an easy subject for the generalist to tackle; particularly difficult to sort out are the circumstances of the 1917 revolution. Pipes, Harvard professor and author of the highly respected *Russia under the Czars*, provides an exhaustive but limpid history of great turmoil, from the last decade of the nineteenth century, when student ferment reached troublesome proportions, to the Bolshevik takeover in October 1917 and the party's subsequent establishment of its own authoritarian regime. It is Pipes' conviction that the Russian Revolution is "arguably the most important event of the century"; displaying both wide-ranging knowledge and well-balanced interpretation, he defends his assertion by portraying the event and its ramifications in various contexts: political, economic, social, and cultural. The serious general reader will gain vast information painlessly and pleasurably. —*Brad Hooper*

Pollard, Sidney, ed.
Wealth & Poverty: An Economic History of the Twentieth Century.
Oxford, $29.95. 256p.

Pollard, a University of Beilefeld (West Germany) economic history professor, has edited this profile of economic events that have helped shape the last

History

century. The book is international in scope, with advisory and contributing editors representing Harvard, Berkeley, and the Universities of Bremen, Hull, and Leicester. It is divided into sections covering approximately 15-year segments. Each section is preceded by a time line overlaying developments in industry, technology, finance, economic policy, and international relations and followed with well-written, readable text. An eclectic collection of nearly 100 biographical sketches ranging from frozen food innovator Clarence Birdseye to Chinese Communist leader Deng Xiaoping is included. *Wealth and Poverty* is quite remarkable, however, for its outstanding collection of photographs and charts. Nearly every one of the several hundred photographs is memorable, and the collection makes the book a pleasure to browse. While the coverage may not be comprehensive, a detailed index makes this book a helpful reference supplement as well as interesting reading. —*David Rouse*

Robbins, Lawrence H.
Stones, Bones, and Ancient Cities.
St. Martin's, $18.95. 254p.

A modern-day Indiana Jones, archaeologist Robbins has compiled facts, theories, and personal experience into seven chapters exploring missing links to human ancestors, cave art, burial practices, the discovery of lost cities, underwater archaeology, archaeoastronomy (the study of "ancient monuments of an astronomical nature"), and the origin of writing. Using a combination of firsthand narrative and straight exposition, which only rarely lapses into a professorial tone, Robbins describes the excitement and speculative nature of archaeology, "the frontier that lies beneath the earth," and the women and men who shaped and continue to shape our understanding of the past. He focuses not just on the big names, but on the lesser-known contributors to the field: the nonscientists and rebel thinkers who dared believe what they saw instead of what was popular and without whom we wouldn't have the information, "sealed by the dust and decay of time," that we have today. A fascinating, highly readable, and informative excursion into the richness of the past and the secrets it still holds. —*Eloise Kinney*

✓ Sale, Kirkpatrick.
The Conquest of Paradise: Christopher Columbus and the Columbian Legacy.
Knopf, $24.95. 384p.

The five hundredth anniversary of 1492 is drawing close, and Sale offers a revisionist examination of how Christopher Columbus made history and what history has made of his discoveries. Among the nuggets of information Sale has unearthed is the the fact that not even the familiar names of the three ships on the adventurer's first expedition to the New World have been quite accurately reported, to say nothing of the different versions of Columbus' own name. Sale organizes his material into two sequences: first, a long digression that reconstructs the state of Europe at the time of Columbus, with many points of reference to contemporary events; second, a journal of Columbus' individual voyages as his discoveries remade the European map—and view—

of the world. In drawing together the historical and social implications of his research, Sale has produced a provocative historical study. —*John Brosnahan*

Schaeffer, Robert.
Warpaths: The Politics of Partition.
Hill & Wang, $25. 400p.

The sanguinary, post–World War II history of Europe's overseas empire demands some sort of explanation—so, says Schaeffer, why not heap the blame on the Great Powers? Whether on India, Palestine, Ireland, or Korea, the author discredits them, along with the solution often used to mediate competing claimants to power: simply divide a territory and leave the rest to chance. Any group that wants to make its claim to state and territory is sorely tempted to use violence in the attempt, according to Schaeffer. The strife perpetrated in several British colonies in the late 1940s typified the situation created by appeals to the sword, so should one wonder why a nearly prostrate Britain, unable to control combatants, simply said, "Good luck, chaps," packed, and left? Schaeffer disapproves of partition, but he does not discuss alternatives to this expedient. He dismisses, or rather denounces as "deeply cynical and historically inaccurate," another explanation of the chaos: these feuds are so ancient, elemental, and intractable as to be impervious to permanent solutions imposed by world powers. A well-researched treatise on thorny historical issues. —*Gilbert Taylor*

✓ **Seidensticker, Edward.**
Tokyo Rising: The City since the Great Earthquake.
Knopf, $24.95. 351p.

A sequel to the intriguing *Low City, High City*, in which Seidensticker portrayed the culture of Tokyo from the 1860s, when the Emperor Meiji restored the supreme authority of the monarchy and moved the Japanese capital from Kyoto to Tokyo, to the 1923 earthquake that devastated the new capital city. Seidensticker now carries the story of Tokyo's growth from the point of its recovery from the earthquake, through the even worse havoc wrought by World War II, to the present day. As in the previous volume, what the citizens did for a living and for entertainment is splendidly detailed as Tokyo, twice the phoenix, rose from the ashes of mayhem to become even stronger, not only as a national social and political force but also as an international economic one. A deep, richly expressed evocation of a vital city's constantly renewed personality. —*Brad Hooper*

Simmons, James C.
We Americans: The View from Abroad.
Harmony, $15.95. 224p.

Alexis de Tocqueville's assertion that "there are certain truths that Americans can learn only from strangers" provides the introduction to Simmons' exploration of America as others see it. Quoting immigrants, illegal aliens, and Japanese entrepreneurs; notables such as Alistair Cooke, Mikhail Gorbachev, and Desmond M. Tutu; and folks like Akira Baba (who runs a sushi bar in Tokyo), Simmons discovers a nation still in its infancy that symbolizes, for many, the future of the rest of the world. From the Ayatollah Khomeini's definition of America as "the Great Satan" to Yakov Smirnoff's exclamation, "What a country!" Simmons has amassed a fascinating collage of commentary extracted from essays, letters, interviews, and conversations that scrutinizes America from the outside in: the landscape and rural communities, the cities, American politics and foreign policy, french fries, and the proliferation of gourmet ice creams that can be found only in America. —*Ivy Burrowes*

Simon, Roger.
Road Show: In America, Anyone Can Become President.
Farrar, $19.95. 331 p.

The election of 1988 was a choice between ideology and competence, conservative and liberal, and divergent positions on the issues. Right? Get real. That year-long marathon of pork-rind eating, flag waving, tank riding, speechifying, damage controlling, and media manipulating was about *campaigning*. Simon, who reported the extravaganza for the *Baltimore Sun*, brings a brand of bemused journalistic detachment to the vicissitudes of what, on the level of pure entertainment, had to be one of the best circuses ever. Under this big top, we can relive all the memorable ripostes, or "sound bites," in hip argot (Bentsen belittling Quayle as "no Jack Kennedy"), self-immolations (Hart's amorous contretemps, Biden's plagiarism), and most importantly, the use of television. Take Willie Horton, whom Simon dubs the Republicans' "most valuable player" for helping Bush overcome a 17-point deficit to win. The conventional wisdom is that the use of Horton's brooding image was a calculated act of race baiting. But it was effective, ranking up there with LBJ's classic 1964 "daisy" ad. The Dukakis camp found itself helpless, while Bush's entourage managed to successfully portray their candidate as a regular guy with a message Joe Six-pack could understand. With an often curmudgeonly wit, Simon also gives a running commentary on the caravans that followed the fizzled fortunes of Jesse Jackson and Bob Dole. (And just in time, too. The next marathoners are already in line.) —*Gilbert Taylor*

Spence, Jonathan D.
The Search for Modern China.
Norton, $29.95. 749p.

Traveling back in time four centuries, Spence views the vast, cataclysmic cycles of modern Chinese history. The author's *Death of Woman Wang* brilliantly depicted a single episode in seventeenth-century Chinese history, and now, on a much grander scale, he considers the political revolutions that have characterized China's evolution in the modern era. Beginning with the decline of the Ming dynasty and ending with the Tiananmen Square massacre, Spence chronicles the cultural and social transformations of the country, concentrating on the many wars and rebellions. At each stage in this process, he expertly considers causes and effects, charting not only historical and political upheaval, but also the subtle mutation of ideas that alternates with the bursts of radical change. —*John Brosnahan*

Stengel, Richard.
January Sun: One Day, Three Lives, a South African Town.
Simon & Schuster, $19.95. 256p.

The mass confrontations of apartheid aren't Stengel's subject: he writes about daily life in Brits, a small town in the eastern Transvaal, far from Johannesburg's power and Soweto's militancy and sorrow. And yet not that far. By focusing on three Brits men whose lives never touch—a prosperous Afrikaans farmer-veterinarian; a black driver, caught up in his community's resistance to their forced removal; and an Indian businessman, once detained without trial—Stengel (a New York contributing editor for *Time*) shows with subtlety and depth how the political system affects ordinary people and their view of themselves. Like Crapanzano in *Waiting*, Stengel combines his commentary, which includes history and political analysis, with his subjects' own words. The pace may be slow for readers wanting more sensationalized coverage, and the organization of the vignettes over a single day seems somewhat arbitrary. However, the style is direct and vivid, and in their candid talk the three men emerge both as complex individuals and as representatives of their country's struggle. —*Hazel Rochman*

Strickland, Ron.
Whistlepunks & Geoducks: Oral Histories from the Pacific Northwest.
Paragon House, $24.95. 320p.

This collection of oral histories is wonderful for many reasons, not the least of which is the way a certain recollection suddenly snaps a particular person, in a particular place and time, into focus. There's Hu ("Scoop") Blonk, former managing editor of the *Wenatchee Daily World* —the man on the scene during the construction of Grand Coulee Dam, a guy who hung out with what he calls "American construction stiff[s]"—making mention of his beautiful hair ("I had a beautiful natural marcel") and his shy ways with women. There's also Dave Beck—born 1894, tenth-grade dropout, lifelong union organizer, eventual president of the Board of Regents of the University of Washington—recalling hard times as a paper boy, duking it out for the best street corners in downtown Seattle. And there is South Burn, literary log cabin builder from Waldron Island, Washington (where people apparently still do without electricity and telephones), building a last log cabin for his terminally ill brother, North Burn. Strickland has assembled a remarkable group of storytellers to relay the history of Washington State. His presence is felt—the stories flow into one another wonderfully—but gently, and each person seems to be telling her or his own tale. This book has an appeal that should extend well beyond the state's borders. —*Frances Woods*

Timerman, Jacobo.
Cuba: A Journey.
Knopf, $18.95. 125p.

In the haunting and still-read *Prisoner without a Name, Cell without a Number*, the Argentine journalist told of his incarceration and torture at the hands of the Argentine military junta in the 1970s. Subsequently in *Chile: Death in the South*, Timerman passionately discussed the repressive dictatorship of General Augusto Pinochet (who has since been replaced by a democratically elected government). Now, he ferrets out the truth on what's going on in another sensitive spot in Latin America. With the collapse of Communist regimes in Eastern Europe and the winds of freedom blowing even across the Soviet landscape, Castro's Cuba stands more and more in isolation in the world. In the summer of 1987, Timerman spent considerable time traveling around the island, talking to all levels of Cubans, from writers to officials to prostitutes. Beneath the tattered exterior of Cuban life, so he discovered, lie even shabbier underpinnings. Aiming to be equable, Timerman nonetheless could not help but conclude that the Castro regime is bankrupt, both spiritually and economically. Details of his journey add up to a gutsy, eloquent account. —*Brad Hooper*

Todd, Oliver.
Cruel April: 1975—the Fall of Saigon.
Norton, $24.95. 451p.

Todd's account of the fall of Saigon to North Vietnamese forces is written in the present tense, which gives it an almost melodramatic immediacy that strikes one as being, somehow, very French. (It will be no surprise, then, to learn that Todd is a Frenchman.) He offers his American audience a perspective of the Vietnam War one rarely encounters on these shores—that of an ex-leftist journalist who became disabused of his pro-Communist sympathies once he saw what the Hanoi regime was really all about. This book, then, is less a chronicle of the war's final, tragic month—although it *is* that—than it is a recounting of the reasons behind one man's ideological passage from the political Left to the Right. It is also something of an embittered, and compellingly argued, jeremiad against a Western media that refused to tell the truth about North Vietnam, and against the European nations that could not see their way clear to aid democracy's cause in South Vietnam. —*Steve Weingartner*

Turner, Frederick.
Of Chiles, Cacti, and Fighting Cocks: Notes on the American West.
North Point, $19.95. 211p.

The West "has been a striking and seductive phenomenon in the American imagination," states Turner, enamored of the land of cowboys and Indians since childhood. Author of *Spirit of Place: The Making of an American Literary Landscape*, Turner's forte is cultural history with a literary and naturalist bent. This stirring set of essays explores the paradoxes of life in the West, the dream versus the reality. He investigates the wild horses controversy, the inventive history behind the myth of Billy the Kid, and the now-clandestine traditions of cockfighting. Chile peppers are praised for their healing powers, and the majestic saguaro cacti are revered for their survival in the harsh desert. Turner captures the intimidating, thrilling beauty of the desert in precise, cantering prose. An insightful and reflective look at the mystique of the land of wide open spaces. —*Donna Seaman*

✓ **Ward, Geoffrey C. and others.**
The Civil War: An Illustrated History.
Knopf, $50. 450p.

The world may not require another one-volume, illustrated history of the Civil War—unless, of course, it's extremely well done, and in this case, tied in with a long-overdue major TV series about the great conflict. This elegant study, based on the PBS script by Geoffrey Ward, Ric Burns, and Ken Burns, offers an authoritative general text covering the war's beginnings, progress, conclusion, and aftermath. The book also presents colorful excerpts from diaries and other contemporary writings, illustrative anecdotes concerning key figures as well as rank-and-file citizens, and special contributions by important historians Don Fehrenbacher, Barbara Fields, Shelby Foote, James McPherson, and C. Vann Woodward. And then there are the photos, paintings, battle maps, engravings, newspaper and poster reproductions—approximately 500 in all, beautifully printed, with some seeing publication for the first time. The credits for the television film are appended, stirring even more interest for the tube version: stars include narrator David McCullough and notables such as Sam Waterston, Julie Harris, Jason Robards, Morgan Freeman, Garrison Keillor, Jody Powell, Colleen Dewhurst, Studs Terkel, and many others as the voices of the movers and shakers of the era. But make no mistake: the buffs will be clamoring for this impressive tome long after the video recorder has shut off. —*Martin Brady*

✓ **The Warsaw Ghetto.**
Hippocrene, $29.95. 195p.

This truly remarkable book, produced in Poland to commemorate the forty-fifth anniversary of the Warsaw Ghetto uprising, contains 122 pages of black-and-white photographs, many of them published here for the first time. They were culled from the Central Commission for the Investigation of Nazi War Crimes in Poland, the Jewish Historical Institute, and the Documentary Film Studio in Warsaw. The photographs, both horrifying and poignant, portray life and death in the ghetto more vividly than words; most have no captions. The segment on children is perhaps the most heartrending—young boys and girls in rags standing in freezing cold, some already dead in the streets. Other photos graphically show Jews arriving in the ghetto with their meager belongings, Jews being rounded up for forced labor or deportation, bodies (nothing more than skin and bones) being carted away in wagons, and remarkable scenes of the uprising itself. Six chilling accounts of the ghetto life, including one by a leader of the uprising, precede the photographs. One of the most exceptional books to come out of the Holocaust. —*George Cohen*

Whelan, Richard.
Drawing the Line: The Korean War, 1950–1953.
Little, Brown, $24.95. 448p.

Once known as the "forgotten war" for the precipitous way it seemed to have faded from public memory, the Korean War has in recent years received a fair amount of long-overdue attention from scholars and writers of military history (see *The Korean War*, by Max Hastings, and Russell Spurr's *Enter the Dragon*). Whelan's book focuses primarily on the political, or rather, geopolitical aspects of that conflict. (Readers seeking a detailed narrative of Korean War campaigns and combat will have to go elsewhere.) Thoughtful readers won't be disappointed with this effort, however—it's at least as absorbing and stimulating as any blood-and-thunder account. The author's approach is thematically driven by the notions that the Korean War was essentially a world war in miniature and that, for all its casualities and inconclusiveness, it should be judged a victory by the anti-Communist coalition that fought it. —*Steve Weingartner*

Wilson, A. N.
Eminent Victorians.
Norton, $25. 240p.

There can be no doubt that our view of Victorian England has changed dramatically since 1918, when Lytton Strachey wrote *Eminent Victorians*, a series of satirical biographies designed to expose the humbug of the era. With Laura Ashley wallpaper decorating trendy homes on both sides of the Atlantic, novelist Wilson concludes it is time for another look at the Victorians. In uniformly perceptive essays that are tough-minded yet reveal a generous spirit, he examines the lives of Prince Albert, William Gladstone, Charlotte Brontë, Josephine Butler, Cardinal Newman, and Julia Margaret Cameron. Whether discussing Prince Albert's role in defining the modern British monarchy, the effect of Brontë's work on women's education, or Newman's historic conversion to Catholicism, Wilson captures the dichotomies of Victorian life, the energizing tension between "spirit and matter, morality and desire, money and romance." Better able than Strachey and his fellow Bloomsburians to place the humbug in its historical context, Wilson is finally won over by the "size and self-confidence of the Victorian achievement." In a doubting age still prone to Prufrockian timidity, he finds the sheer vigor of the Victorians a source of wonder. —*Bill Ott*

Yahil, Leni.
The Holocaust: The Fate of European Jewry, 1932–1945.
Oxford, $39.95. 816p.

An Israeli historian's reassessment of the condition of European Jews before and during World War II. Yahil addresses many of the problems and enigmas of the Holocaust—the continuing historical debate over the real impetus behind the German plan to destroy the country's Jewish population, the initial response of the Jewish population to the first steps of the tragedy, the ultimate opposition mounted within the Jewish community. Yet he integrates his own scholarly responses into a comprehensive narrative of what happened at each stage of the Nazi's genocidal mission throughout Europe. The book also examines anti-Semitism both before and after World War II and recounts the rescue efforts mounted by various organizations and individuals. While Yahil's style can be a bit dry, his treatment is highly effective both in its historical circumspection and in its detailed research. —*John Brosnahan*

Zee, A.
Swallowing Clouds.
Simon & Schuster, $24.95. 316p.

A book to relish! Take the premise that Americans only see Chinese pictographs on menus; follow with the fact that Americans like Chinese food and thus are inclined to read about it; now assume that Americans would also like chatty anecdotes about Asian life. Blend, and you've got Zee's book: a stockpot of cuisine, history, poetry, etymology, linguistics, and personal experience. Each chapter teaches you a pictograph—three flowing lines for water, for instance, which eventually are rotated into three short horizontal dashes that appear in names of recipes involving soup stock. Along the way, you also learn the background of Chinese folkways and manners, the history of foods (Did pandas teach the eating of bamboo shoots?), and even basic Confucian philosophy. Zee, a theoretical physicist and author of *Fearful Symmetry*, has created a wonderful hybrid form here. —*Pat Monaghan*

Humor

Adamson, Joe.
The Bugs Bunny Golden Jubilee: 50 Years of America's Favorite Rabbit.
Holt, $35. 192p.

By traditional Chinese reckoning, it may be the year of the horse, but for Americans, it's the year of the bunny. Bugs, that is, who, incredibly enough, is now 50 years old. Movie journalist Adamson uses the text for this oversize tribute to tell once again the tale of the wascally wabbit's birth, development into the movies' second (after Mr. Mouse, of course) big cartoon star, and subsequent career. Adamson cheerfully and skillfully blends testimony from the mounds of earlier writings on the great hare with his own lucubrations to produce a just-thoughtful-enough appreciation of perhaps the most durable Hollywood luminary of them all. This book is just one element in a multimillion-dollar blitz of publicity and merchandising intended to make sure no one doesn't notice Bugs' birthday. Includes some 200 pictures, most of them in color. —*Ray Olson*

Humor

Amory, Cleveland.
The Cat and the Curmudgeon.
Little, Brown, $17.95. 306p.

The Cat Who Came for Christmas—Amory's previous entry about his cat, Polar Bear—having met with hysterical popularity, the ostensibly curmudgeonly author has decided to run out his luck with a sequel. He takes up where the success of the first book left Polar Bear, as a new feline star in the firmament of American celebrity. In fact, the first chapter is about how Polar Bear manages his fame. The second's about Polar Bear's fan mail. The third's about Polar Bear's curmudgeonliness, his encounter with a sheep dog, Amory's adventures at chess, and some other things. And so it goes for four more chapters and an envoi imparting Amory's acquisition of a younger cat, one Polar Star, who is PB's "kitten image." Written in Amory's characteristically literate, mildly facetious tone, the book will probably suit its predecessor's fans to a (C-A-) T. Those who aren't amused by self-indulgence over pets, however, may want to bury it in the litter. —*Ray Olson*

Garmaise, Freda.
Tough Girls Don't Knit and Other Tales of Stylish Subversion.
Little, Brown, $17.95. 256p.

While Garmaise is neither as well known nor as funny as Fran Lebowitz, she strikes a few familiar and amusing chords as she recounts her sundry attempts to find some harmony in an unharmonious world. It isn't easy. Shoppers don't get enough respect, and her children are ready to disavow her at the drop of a parking ticket. The only thing that's easier today than it was yesterday is coloring your hair. Garmaise speaks authoritatively on the terrors of the open dressing room, the appeal of being an older other woman, and the quandary of what to do with one's ashes (the after-death variety, not the cigarette kind). At their best, these quirky vignettes leave us pondering such unexplained mysteries as why the inventor of nylon killed himself 20 days after the patent was granted. —*Ilene Cooper*

Grizzard, Lewis.
If I Ever Get Back to Georgia, I'm Gonna Nail My Feet to the Ground.
Villard, $17.95. 308p.

Lewis Grizzard has published a string of widely popular books of light southern humor, among them, *Chili Dawgs Always Bark at Night* and *Don't Bend Over in the Garden, Granny, You Know Them Taters Got Eyes*. This memoir of his life and times as a proud Georgia boy smack dab in the middle of the manic newspaper business certainly contains its share of laughs, but it's more a tale of many trials and tribulations. Grizzard knew early on that he wanted to cover big-time sports. From hometown Moreland, Georgia, he made his way to the journalism school at the University of Georgia in Athens, eventually attaining the position of executive sports editor of the *Atlanta Journal* at the ripe old age of 23. Proving to be an editorial whiz, with an eye for innovative layout and journalistic approaches, he later served in nonsport editorial capacities at the *Journal* before serving as editor of the *Chicago*

Sun-Times' sports section, a two-year stint that Grizzard would just as soon forget. Leaving his snow-ruined Weejuns behind in the Windy City, he joined the *Atlanta Constitution*, briefly as a sports columnist and then as humorist-at-large, a job he still holds today. Grizzard did it all in the sports journalism arena—covered big-time football, baseball, golf, etc.—but more than that, his book is about the wacky characters he's known in the newspaper game, the stressed-out, never-a-dull-minute existence of the big-time editor (his three marriages were utter failures), and his devotion to the red clay of Georgia. In addition, Grizzard's accounts of how a newspaper was published before the computer revolution are charmingly fascinating. This surprisingly multi-dimensional account will appeal to more than just a regional audience. —*Martin Brady*

Koren, Edward.
What about Me? Cartoons from the New Yorker.
Pantheon, $9.95. 128p.

Koren's fuzzy people and other creatures, so familiar from the pages of the *New Yorker* magazine, appear in this collection of his droll cartoons. In one scene, Koren has drawn a construction site at which the familiar diamond-shaped Men Working sign bears a more accurate message: Men Drinking Coffee. In other cartoons, Koren squares off frazzled parents and their far-more-assertive preschoolers in hilarious confrontations. The foibles of the middle-class middle-aged are trenchantly depicted in these clever scenarios. —*Denise Perry Donavin*

Leno, Jay, ed.
Headlines: Real but Ridiculous Samplings from America's Newspapers.
Warner, $7.95. 188p.

A regular feature of Leno's appearances as substitute host on Johnny Carson's "Tonight Show" involves the reading of real but inadvertently daffy headlines from the nation's newspapers. Here he has compiled more than 400 such headlines, newspaper photos, and ads, most of which are accompanied by an expressive photo of Leno and his appropriately ironic commentary. A sampling: "Researchers call murder a threat to public health"; "Condom week starts with a cautious bang"; "Drought turns coyotes to watermelons"; and "Death row inmates no longer allowed day off after execution, official says" (prompting a bemused Leno to observe, "Boy, you thought the other warden was tough!"). Leno's popularity and the often hilarious content of this material should attract an avid audience for this book. —*Steve Weingartner*

✓ **Letterman, David.**
The Late Night with David Letterman Book of Top Ten Lists.
Pocket, $8.95. 192p.

Top Ten Reasons Reading Letterman's Top Ten Lists Is Better Than Watching Them on TV
10.   Easier than lugging around a television set

9. Don't have to look at Dave's bad haircuts while enjoying lists
8. The Romance of the Written Word
7. Can get right to the funny stuff without waiting for Tony Randall interview.
6. Enjoy three from one list, two from another
5. Can listen to Mantovani in the background, rather than drum rolls
4. May be passed around at family gatherings
3. People will see you reading it and will think you're cool
2. The book is always better than the TV show
1. Don't need to know how to set your VCR; just need to know how to turn a page.

—Ilene Cooper

✓ **Trillin, Calvin.**
Enough's Enough: And Other Rules of Life.
Ticknor & Fields, $19.95. 251p.

Enough is never enough from the humorist regularly seen in the *New Yorker*. Whether Trillin is writing about politics, ordinary people, or current events, he definitely puts a new slant on those time-honored topics. These 77 essays culled from his syndicated column, "Uncivil Liberties," offer insight into "Noriega's Undies," great recyclers who are despised by lesser mortals, and even fruitcake. The self-described "jackal of the press" can take any topic and spin from it fun, thought-provoking prose. It's easy to see why Trillin was mentioned by William Zinsser (*On Writing Well*) as a model for writers.
—Denise Perry Donavin

Wasserstein, Wendy.
Bachelor Girls.
Knopf, $16.95. 192p.

Wasserstein is best known as a playwright, the author of *The Heidi Chronicles*, but she is also the other side of Fran Lebowitz—a single, funny, New York Jewish humorist, yes, but one whose wit is gently filtered rather than raw and rough like a lung full of Camel smoke. That doesn't mean she pulls her punches. Whether re-creating her own little *Bonfire of the Vanities* escapades or describing the hassle of dealing with body hair, Wasserstein always strikes a responsive chord. Most of the 30 essays here were originally published as magazine pieces, but one has the feeling they will stand up pretty well even under a second or third reading. You don't have to be Jewish, single, or even a woman to like Wasserstein (though it may help). *—Ilene Cooper*

Literature & Language

Baron, Dennis.
The English-Only Question: An Official Language for Americans?
Yale, $22.50. 236p.

Many Americans think that English is the official language of the U.S. Others are urging passage of an English language amendment to the Constitution to make English our nation's officially recognized language. Baron, a noted professor of linguistics and rhetoric and an expert on the subject, closely examines both sides of the complex controversy surrounding whether minority-based languages should in effect be outlawed by making English the country's only legally accepted language. He traces the history of the English-only debate, whose roots, he says, are as old as the U.S., and shows how and why non-English speakers are viewed by many Americans as subhuman or unpatriotic. The basic premise behind this intriguing study is that the debate is essentially pointless because English already functions as the official language of U.S. courts, laws, businesses, schools, and government. Legislation cannot force people to use English, argues Baron; only changing social forces can. Objective, thoroughly researched, and clearly presented—a real eye-opener. —*Mary Banas*

Bradbury, Ray.
Zen in the Art of Writing.
Capra, $18.95. 152p.

Referring to his writing habit, the prolific Bradbury says, "I have learned, on my journeys, that if I let a day go by, I grow uneasy. Two days and I am in tremor. Three and I suspect lunacy. Four and I might as well be a hog, suffering the flux in a wallow." In the series of essays he presents here, the mental attitudes and physical disciplines that are part and parcel of his writing career—more specifically, of his *love* and *need* for writing—are discussed in various contexts. Bradbury reflects, he recollects; in essence, he offers a paean to the grace the muse has bestowed upon him. Bradbury's style in these essays is at once elegant and spicy, providing by example the best possible advice to other writers. A warm book for the author's many admirers. —*Brad Hooper*

Bryson, Bill.
The Mother Tongue: English in the World Today.
Morrow, $18.95. 288p.

Bryson approaches his subject with verve. Opening gleefully by quoting nonsensical directions translated from Japanese into English, he goes on to discuss how English, in spite of its many baffling traits, has become the

Literature & Language

international language of business and science. Bryson glides from a historical summary of linguistics to discussions of quirky names, swearing, dialects, meaning shifts, and how people tend to "compress and mangle words." He reports on attempts at creating artificial languages such as Esperanto and notes that translation is a costly and error-prone industry. Never technical and always entertaining, Bryson, a true word lover, offers a cascade of examples of the vagaries of language. A fascinating subject, deftly handled. —*Donna Seaman*

✓ **Capek, Karel.**
Toward the Radical Center: A Karel Capek Reader.
Catbird Press, $23.95. 382p.

Imagine discovering the rich, warm humanity of a Dickens or a Gogol, and you have some idea of the impact of this selection from the work of Czechoslovakia's foremost twentieth-century writer. Barely known in this country, Capek yet contributed to our language the word *robot* —given its English meaning in *R. U. R. (Rossum's Universal Robots)*, an exciting, though talky, melodrama about the nature of intelligent life. The play is one of three here presented in new or revised translations, as are the volume's many short stories, feuilletons (i.e., mini-essays on familiar subjects such as "Cats," "A Cold," "Inventions,"), and essays. To a piece, the selections are delightful, compassionate, and modernly conscious of the mysteriousness of everyday life; indeed, most of the stories are little mysteries that have less to do with crime than with coincidence. Capek was, as the anthology's title suggests, a man of no party other than humanity's, a man for whom the routines of normal life were infinitely more important and valuable than the agendas of any nation or hero. He is a writer it is hard not to love. —*Ray Olson*

Cmiel, Kenneth.
Democratic Eloquence: The Fight over Popular Speech in Nineteenth-Century America.
Morrow, $22.95. 416p.

Sure to surprise readers who suppose grammar to be nothing more than a dull collection of rules, Cmiel recounts the great cultural struggle over correct speech in the late eighteenth and nineteenth centuries. After the American Revolution, traditional standards of verbal refinement seemed inappropriate for the new republic. Yet during the next century, the growth of public education reinforced the linguistic decorum eroded by newly democratic politics. As technical jargon acquired prestige and as journalists captured large audiences, heated disputes erupted over new dictionaries, grammars, and translations of the Bible. Not merely a quarrel among pedants, the fight over language created a battlefield for average citizens and prominent leaders such as Abraham Lincoln, Horace Greeley, and Theodore Roosevelt. Cmiel tells a fascinating story that removes the veil of familiarity from everyday speech. —*Bryce Christensen*

Codrescu, Andrei.
The Disappearance of the Outside: A Manifesto for Escape.
Addison-Wesley, $17.95. 224p.

Codrescu, justifiably lionized by the National Public Radio audience for his commentaries on "All Things Considered" and by the alternative press world for his surrealist journal, *Exquisite Corpse*, and his poetry, fiction, and essays, will today also attract those of us who want to learn something from police-state exiles who are not only courageous—they've always been that—but who've won! Codrescu writes with authority about the literature of exile and surrealism in all its metamorphoses. "The new magical surrealist hero is someone who goes about doing the same kinds of things you and I do, the only difference being that the hero's doings have enormous consequences that reverberate." Politics, philosophy, memoir, and literary criticism all commingle here with a peculiarly Eastern European sense of humor. —*Roland Wulbert*

Ellison, Harlan.
The Harlan Ellison Hornbook.
Penzler Books, $22.95. 448p.

Redoubtable is one word that might describe Harlan Ellison, but even at that, it all depends on which *Webster's* definition you gravitate toward: "1: causing fear or alarm: FORMIDABLE"; or "2: inspiring or worthy of awe or reverence: ILLUSTRIOUS." This collection of Ellison essays, reviews, and articles—most of them originally published more than 15 years ago—proves either point. Whether he bathetically rails against Jesus ("a scrawny prophet") in "No Offense Intended But Fuck Christmas!" tells us of his trashy girlfriends, vindictively (almost childishly) opines on old Ohio State (as if it were *their* fault he was a lousy student), attacks TV's hold on the American psyche, or staunchly defends the plight of writers who get stiffed by sharpy publishers, Ellison is always provocative. (Sort of like Bart Simpson grown up.) Besides the older pieces—each preceded by a brief, updating "interim memo" that adds context—this collection features a handful of more recent work first published in *Playboy* and *Los Angeles* magazine and one previously un-published. Best taken in small doses, this manic collection does prove one thing: the man can write. —*Martin Brady*

✓ Goldberg, Natalie.
Wild Mind: Living the Writer's Life.
Bantam, $8.95. 256p.

Start writing, Natalie Goldberg says, then keep doing it for five years. It'll take you that long to get the bugs out of the system and be ready to really write. Five years, then, after the immensely popular *Writing Down the Bones* comes this book, perfectly timed for would-be writers who have reached the point where, for instance, they're aware of the complications of juxtaposition within a paragraph or the fine line between waiting expectantly and procras-tinating. This is arguably a better book, because the message of *Bones* was,

Literature & Language

over and over, to just keep writing. Here is a more expansive Goldberg. In addition to excellent tips on writing and lots of intriguing exercises, there is a fuller explanation of the Zen of writing. Particularly clear and important is her distinction between "monkey mind," the bean-counter within, ready to agitate us with needless worry, and the "wild mind" of the title, that vast space that includes our unconscious as well as "mountains, rivers, Cadillacs, humidity, plains, emerald, poverty, old streets in London, snow and moon." An inspiring, inspired work. —*Pat Monaghan*

✓ **Goytisolo, Juan.**
Realms of Strife: The Memoirs of Juan Goytisolo 1957–1982.
North Point, $19.95. 266p.

The first part of Goytisolo's memoirs (*Forbidden Territory* North Point, 1988) was lavishly praised, and no doubt this second part will be equally well regarded. Most striking is its self-effacing honesty: rarely does one see equivocation scrubbed from the truth so vigorously one hurts for the very pinkness of the skin exposed. And while, from the very first, the narrative makes for compelling reading, Goytisolo by no means has a life ravaged by melodrama to fall back on: disillusionment, exile, and a confusion of sexual identity have been balanced by the stability of his relationship with his wife and his unchallenged success as one of Spain's most admired writers. Duras, Genet, Vargas Llosa, and many others make their way into these pages, but the significance of their appearance is slight. What moves one so profoundly is the austere wisdom made beautiful by the resilience and durability of Goytisolo's ideals. —*Stuart Whitwell*

Heilbrun, Carolyn G.
Hamlet's Mother and Other Women.
Columbia Univ., $29.50. 324p.

Critic (and, as Amanda Cross, mystery writer) Heilbrun here collects some of the important essays that, over the past 20 years, have helped forge the pattern of feminist discourse on literature. From her first published paper— when she argued against the conventional notion that Hamlet's mother was a sorry excuse for a queen, seeing her instead as a vital woman of great good sense—Heilbrun has taken on some of criticism's shibboleths. She dares to position Virginia Woolf with James Joyce as head of the family of twentieth-century writers; she sees women's studies as a fresh breeze to stir literature out of the "doldrums" that afflict the discipline. She constantly dares speak secrets in a wonderfully aphoristic style: "All women who have ever read a classic have imagined themselves as men," she says, and "feminist criticism is another way of knowing." —*Pat Monaghan*

Hofmann, Paul.
That Fine Italian Hand.
Holt, $18.95. 224p.

As *The New York Times* bureau chief in Rome, Hofmann offers an unromantic look at a divided Italy. While the north becomes more "European," southern Italy is deluged by red tape, long lines, shady dealings, mishandled funds, family politics, and the still-dominant power of the Mafia. Hofmann's thesis—that the Italy tourists see covers up the social, political and economic problems of the country—reveals the conflicting feelings of a non-Italian living in Italy for most of his adult life. No matter how bad things get, the food and wine remain terrific. —*Kathryn LaBarbera*

Isherwood, Christopher.
Where Joy Resides: A Christopher Isherwood Reader.
Farrar, $19.95. 408p.

No better fulfiller of Emerson's prediction that the literature of the twentieth century would be predominantly autobiographical exists than Christopher Isherwood. This selection from the 50 years of his fiction-, memoir-, and essay-writing career features fine work of all three kinds that all adopt the point of view of either "I" or a character (not the principal protagonist) named Christopher. They are alive with the active, but hardly doctrinaire, social conscience and transparent vision connoted by the famous sentence from *Goodbye to Berlin*: "I am a camera." They include "Sally Bowles," source of both the play *I Am a Camera* and its musical adaptation, *Cabaret*; excerpts from three volumes of recollections and the novel *Down There on a Visit*; essays on writers and the vicissitudes of religious conversion (Isherwood converted to Vedanta); and the short novels *Prater Violet* and *A Single Man*. Gore Vidal contributes an appreciative, personal introduction on his friend's life and work. —*Ray Olson*

Lerner, Andrea, ed.
Dancing on the Rim of the World: An Anthology of Contemporary Northwest Native American Writing.
Univ. of Arizona, $37.50. 175p.

The native American Northwest is defined not by state lines but by geography, language, and sense of place. This vision of a region existing beyond the boundaries imposed by whites is a key to the spirit of this anthology of poetry and short prose. The contributors live in an America within America—the old world of native American culture and its frictional interface with modern mainstream society. The mix of established and emerging writers also supports the claim that this literary tradition is vibrant and healthy. The "elders" include Mary Tall Mountain, Duane Niatum, Gladys Cardiff, James Welch, and Janet Campbell Hale. Some notable newcomers are Crystos, Dian Millon, Jim Barnes, and Robert Davis. Nature is full of secrets, and the past is very much alive in many of the poems and stories while the voices are truth-seeking, haunted, intro-

Literature & Language

spective, and angry. Brief biographies and photographs of the writers add a personal dimension to this eye-opening selection. —*Donna Seaman*

✓ **Lurie, Alison.**
Don't Tell the Grown-ups: Subversive Children's Literature.
Little, Brown, $22.95. 224p.

Here's the book for everyone who always thought all those cute kids and cuddly bears populating the pages of children's books were up to more than they seemed. According to novelist Lurie, the best children's literature is always subversive in that it presents the world from the child's point of view, and since children are inevitably the underdogs in an adult world, that view usually goes against the grain. Looking at the world from below, in other words, allows a fine view of its less respectable aspects, "just as little children playing on the floor can see the chewing gum stuck to the underside of polished mahogany tables. . . ." In a series of essays that cover most of the giants of nineteenth- and early-twentieth-century children's writing, Lurie shows us the many forms that chewing gum can take—from Kate Greenaway's "greeting card version of Wordsworthian innocence" shielding a "sentimental sensuality about childhood that was one of the darker secrets of the Victorian Age," through the concealed moral behind Beatrix Potter's revered *Peter Rabbit*, which argues that "disobedience and exploration are much more fun than good behavior and not really all that dangerous, whatever Mother may say." In addition to eye-opening critical exegesis, Lurie gives us some wonderful bits of psychobiography, including the kinky saga of John Ruskin's infatuation with Greenaway's "nymphet charm" and the tangled web of neuroses that led to boy-child James M. Barrie's creation of *Peter Pan*. Think of this liberating study as a kind of literary salvage operation in which Lurie has rescued children's literature from the winding-sheets of piety. There might even be a good children's story in it: a gang of New Wave dead-end kids go on an Indiana Jonesish adventure leading to a booby-trapped tomb where a phalanx of prim schoolmarms of party-line librarians are holding Peter Rabbit and his pals hostage. The good guys win. —*Bill Ott*

Mairs, Nancy.
Carnal Acts.
Harper, $18.95. 161p.

An outspoken feminist, a Catholic Worker, crippled by multiple sclerosis, Mairs is a tough, careful, moving, intelligent writer whose very personal observations will illuminate the lives of readers who have nothing (apparently) in common with her. She writes about fleeting celebrity, public confessions, civil disobedience, a child leaving college, fear, and, throughout it all, as she calls it, embodiment and language. Unlike her earlier works, *Remembering the Bone House*, for example, these fugitive essays are not meant to be read consecutively. Each one introduces its author and her concerns to its readers. Although each essay dwells both on the degenerative disease that disables her body and on her gender, Mairs never repeats herself. She deserves the widest possible audience. —*Roland Wulbert*

✓ **Meyers, Jeffrey.**
D. H. Lawrence: A Biography.
Knopf, $24.95. 384p.

The story of D. H. Lawrence's life, though it has been told many times, remains one of the saddest and at the same time most hopeful chapters in literary history. Lawrence had much to overcome—his mother's suffocating love; the horror of a world war; the persecution of a society that couldn't accept the intensity and the passion of his art; the debilitating effects of tuberculosis— yet he continued to write books that changed the face of modern literature and to embrace what he called "the insurgent naked throb of the instant moment." The significance of this new biography will be hotly debated among scholars: Meyers sheds new light on Lawrence's tempestuous dealings with such writers as Ford Madox Ford, John Middleton Murry, and Katherine Mansfield, and he offers evidence that he believes proves Lawrence had a homosexual relationship with Cornish farmer William Hocking. But questions of what Lawrence did or didn't do with whom are finally academic in more than one sense; Meyers stakes his scholarly claim, but, fortunately, he knows enough to stay out of the way as much as possible. The triumph of this book is not what it says that others haven't, but that it showcases for a new generation the unquenchable passion of a man who spent 44 years wrestling with the question of how to be fully *alive*. There was much standing in the way of Lawrence's crusade to live, but he never forgot his belief in real courage, which allows one "to face facts and live beyond them." —*Bill Ott*

Noble, William.
Bookbanning in America: Who Bans Books?—And Why.
Paul S. Eriksson, $21.95. 349p.

The endpapers of this cogent and fluid history of bookbanning are covered with unexpected titles of banned books such as *Moll Flanders, The Call of the Wild, A Farewell to Arms,* and *I, Claudius*. Noble, an attorney and author of many books including writers' guides, states that there are "more than one thousand bookbanning incidents in America each year." And those are only the ones that get reported. Noble quotes from transcripts of trials and school board meetings, interviews with librarians, educators, and parents. Striving for balance, he presents both sides of the censorship issue by describing the allegedly offensive content of banned books and analyzing the motives of bookbanners and the role of religion, politics, and fear in well-known cases. From the earliest American libel suit to the uproar over Salman Rushdie, Noble sees bookbanning as a "hardy virus" that must be "confronted consistently." An important book for anyone who reads. —*Donna Seaman*

Literature & Language

✓ **Peterson, Brenda.**
Living by Water: Essays on Life, Land and Spirit.
Alaska Northwest, $15.95. 144p.

A new breed of essayist is aborning in America, especially in the American West. Writing about nature, they write of spirit; writing about humanity, they give voice to the animal in us all. Their work attempts to breach the Cartesian mind-body split by joining us more fully with the world around us. Brenda Peterson exemplifies this new essayist. In her fine book, she brings to the reader her sense of reverence about the natural world, but she is never simplistic: her essay on eating game, for instance, shows us how honoring animals does not necessarily mean not eating them. Swimming with dolphins, waiting for whales, writing ecological tracts, confronting rape and murder: Peterson can write of them all without flinching or becoming sentimental.
—*Pat Monaghan*

Plimpton, George, ed.
The Paris Review Anthology.
Norton, $25. 645p.

If, as William Styron states in his prefatory letter written in 1953 to the editor of the *Paris Review*, "the times get precisely the literature that they deserve," then the past 40 years have been time on its best behavior. Conceived in a Parisian café in 1953, the magazine was intended to reflect its founders' generation; it promoted creative work and demoted the criticism of literature—which filled literary magazines of the time—to the back of the magazine. This anthology gathers, from the over 400 fiction and 1,000 poetry pieces published in the magazine, the most representative of its history. Now-famous writers, such as Beckett, Calvino, Roth, Borges, Carver, Updike, Gilliatt, and Larkin, are represented with early works and join some lesser-known but substantial talents. These selections glow from the pages, the summation of a magazine equal in worth to all of its talented parts. —*Deanna Larson-Whiterod*

Plimpton, George.
The Best of Plimpton.
Atlantic Monthly Press, $19.95. 367p.

As the founder of the *Paris Review*, George Plimpton is an international literary figure. Most Americans, however, know him best as the chief promulgator of a unique mode of sportswriting, the so-called participatory journalism. With Walter Mitty–like derring-do, Plimpton has, among other things, stepped into the ring with boxer Archie Moore, played quarterback for the Detroit Lions, tried to throw a fastball past Willie Mays—then lived to tell about his experiences gracefully and with rare insight. This worthy volume collects Plimpton pieces from the last 35 years. Included are the articles that served as the basis for his well-known books—e.g., *Paper Lion, The Bogey Man* —and a wealth of other sport and nonsport accounts. Plimpton watches a World Series game with poet Marianne Moore; probes the engima that was football legend Vince Lombardi; profiles actor Warren Beatty, novelist William Styron, and big-time agent Irving ("Swifty") Lazar; and even provides portraits of places he's known and loved (Newport Beach, Elaine's Restaurant in New York, Norfolk, Nebraska). (It might be said that Plimpton invented the highfalutin' style of nouveau sports journalism—Roger Angell, Thomas Boswell, et al.—though somehow the idea of Muhammad Ali evincing a "chorus of approbation" from his dressing-room entourage can seem like overkill.) Plimpton prefaces each piece with some words that set it into fresh context. —*Martin Brady*

Safire, William.
Fumblerules: A Lighthearted Guide to Grammar and Good Usage.
Doubleday, $15. 128p.

A *fumblerule* is "a mistake that calls attention to the rule." For example: "No sentence fragments." Each chapter is headlined by a separate example that is followed by a brief explanatory passage illuminating the grammatical rules that have been so cavalierly broken. Miraculously, Safire has created this little book out of a single *New York Times* column and the ensuing barrage of mail he received. A clever and enjoyable language guide. —*Denise Perry Donavin*

Shapiro, Karl.
Reports of My Death.
Algonquin, $20.95. 277p.

The American poet continues his impressive third-person autobiography with the second and concluding volume of what was originally intended to be a three-volume work (*Poet: An Autobiography in Three Parts, Volume I: The Younger Son*). When Shapiro returned from military service in World War II, he came back to the U.S. as a well-known writer and an eventual Pulitzer Prize winner. Although his subsequent career didn't keep up with literary fashions, he has remained a force in the poetry world, both for his own work and his influential roles as a teacher and one-time editor of *Poetry* magazine. This book again combines items of personal and professional interest—ambivalence to the writings and personality of Ezra Pound, the suicide of Shapiro's wife—to intimately telling effect. While the story here isn't quite as vividly told as in the first volume, Shapiro's struggle with life and his muse makes for fascinating reading. —*John Brosnahan*

Sheed, Wilfrid.
Essays in Disguise.
Knopf, $19.95. 264p.

The essay, according to Wilfrid Sheed, is not a literary form in favor, which means that the would-be essayist must disguise his work as book reviews, or news reporting, or whatever sells. Sheed, of course, is very much an essayist— a writer who can set forth "an interpretative literary composition . . . from a personal point of view"—and given such subjects as Robert Lowell, Jean Stafford, A. J. Liebling, John Updike, even Jack Nicklaus, he expounds in an

Literature & Language

amusing, insightful fashion. In his lengthy, enlightening introduction ("Program Notes"), Sheed expresses his regret that these essays originally appeared as testimonial speeches, record liner copy, etc. Yet his readers will be terribly grateful that they have resurfaced in this delightful collection. —*Denise Perry Donavin*

Showalter, Elaine.
Sexual Anarchy: Gender and Culture at the Fin de Siècle.
Viking, $19.95. 218p.

Although the chapters in this interpretation of nonconforming women at the fin de siècle can be read in any order, they are united by the reappearance of the odd woman, a role that originally defined superfluous women—single, hysterical, "sexually unemployed," a threat to the institution of marriage—but came to encompass emerging characteristics of the new woman. Showalter's historiography, cultural analysis, literary hermeneutics, and political commentary are masterful and, oddly enough for a work on irremediably repulsive practices, compelling. The prejudices and fears of Victorian/Edwardian men appear to emerge from science fiction and at the same time to speak for the repressions of men today. Showalter's readings of contemporary culture are no less rewarding than her history. Her interpretation of David Cronenberg's film *Dead Ringer* is a model of its kind. One cavil: she writes without irony that the clitoris was "discovered by an anatomist appropriately named Columbus in the 16th century." Nobody noticed it until then? —*Roland Wulbert*

Sinclair, Andrew.
War Like a Wasp: The Lost Decade of the Forties.
Viking, $24.95. 352p.

"A little island of civilization surrounded by burning churches—that was how the arts felt during the war." So said poet Stephen Spender, describing what it was like for an artist in the Britain of the 1940s. Critic Sinclair re-creates that tempestuous period, analyzing its too easily dismissed literary and artistic output and evoking its unique milieu. His arguments for the lasting contributions of such writers and editors as Cyril Connolly, John Lehmann, Laurie Lee, Julian Maclaren-Ross, and Cecil Day Lewis are convincing and well presented, but it is his colorful, almost novelistic depiction of wartime London that will most engage general readers. Pints of bitter consumed at a prodigious pace as Blitz-wracked literati gathered in the pubs and nightclubs of Fitzrovia—heir to Bloomsbury as the seat of London's Bohemia—helped establish the carpe diem tone of the time and later produced numerous recollections of an era that Sinclair characterizes as having "almost Proustian reverberation—*Remembrances of Times Pissed.*" It was more than that, of course, both historically and literarily, but Sinclair wisely chooses to paint the Big Picture by concentrating on the small details. —*Bill Ott*

✓ **Skal, David J.**
Hollywood Gothic: The Tangled Web of Dracula from Novel to Stage to Screen.
Norton, $39.95. 235p.

With a novelist's flair for vivid scene-setting and characterization, Skal writes the biography of one of the hottest dramatic properties of the century, the quintessential vampire yarn, *Dracula.* So doing, he necessarily writes chapters in the lives of the many remarkable people crucial to the story's near century-long development: Bram Stoker, the theatrical manager who wrote the novel; his widow Florence, who had to fight doggedly for her rights and royalties in it; Albin Grau, the "ardent spiritualist" artist who produced the first, illicit screen version of it, *Nosferatu* (1922); Hamilton Deane, the touring British actor-manager who first dramatized it; Horace Liveright, the legendary publisher who saw a hit in Deane's hackwork, had John Balderston doctor it, and launched it on Broadway; Liveright's "discovery," Bela Lugosi, of course; and others. Perhaps the most fascinating chapter in an enthralling chronicle concerns the Spanish-language version (for Latin American exhibition) of the classic but clunky Lugosi vehicle; made with the same sets, it is, according to Skal, a much better film. Satisfyingly illustrated on nearly every page, this is an outstanding entry in the copious literature about the most popular boogeyman ever imagined. —*Ray Olson*

Thomas, Lewis.
Et Cetera, Et Cetera: Notes of a Word-Watcher.
Little, Brown, $17.95. 192p.

A revered essayist on science has sojourned into the world of etymology. Forty families of words occasion the meditations that comprise this slim volume. Lewis uses no original sources; he is openly indifferent to the field's scholarly literature. Standard etymological dictionaries stimulate his imagination. He is always poetic, even when the *F* -word goads him. *Delight*, for example, "seems, for reasons that are obvious on the face of it, one of the lightest words in the language, an airy breath of a word, all pleasure, luminous, lit from within." *Nude* and *naked* come from "nogw," which, he believes, "had its first meaning as hairless, clothes or no clothes," and served to discriminate us from *bhers* and our other competitors in the Indo-European forests. A bit precious for some, this volume will delight fans of Thomas' *Lives of a Cell* (1975) and *Late Night Thoughts on Listening to Mahler's Ninth Symphony* (1983). —*Roland Wulbert*

Toth, Emily.
Kate Chopin.
Morrow, $24.95. 480p.

A member of a socially prominent family in St. Louis, novelist and story writer Kate Chopin married a Louisiana cotton broker and plantation owner. Left a widow early, she returned to St. Louis and there began a writing career. Her most famous novel, *The Awakening*, was published in 1899, its frank sensuality vilified in many quarters. But recently this splendid work has been recognized as a masterpiece and is being taught in the college classroom. Chopin's fiction is set in the Louisiana she came to know as a married woman; and her novels and stories deal with women's wants and needs inside and outside of marriage. Reflective of much research and careful consideration, Toth's biography paints a rich portrait of a woman who, at the turn of the century, held firm convictions often at variance with the conventions of her time. "Kate Chopin despised rules," Toth asserts, and in a sensitive rendition, she reconstructs all facets of her subject's uniqueness. —*Brad Hooper*

Weatherby, W. J.
Salman Rushdie: Sentenced to Death.
Carroll & Graf, $19.95. 243p.

At this writing, Salman Rushdie is still alive, although the writer and his work are caught in a literary limbo—his life still under Iranian fundamentalist death threat and his *Satanic Verses* held hostage by the publisher's reluctance to issue a paperback edition of the controversial novel. Weatherby sees Rushdie as a test case in the cultural clash that seems an inevitable result of contemporary social history, where religions, civilizations, and ideas come into conflict. Weatherby's study goes over Rushdie's biography before exploring the political turmoil his book has created. Definitely not an apology either for Rushdie, his prickly personality, or his opponents, this book cogently explores the many complex issues raised by *The Satanic Verses* and by its hostile and violent reception throughout the world. —*John Brosnahan*

White, E. B.
Writings from the New Yorker, 1927–1976.
Harper, $20. 288p.

An invigorating collection of White's short pieces for the *New Yorker* 's "Notes and Comments" and "Talk of the Town" sections. White, a consummate essayist and children's author (*Charlotte's Web* and *Stuart Little*), had the twin gifts of firm opinions and limber, poised prose. His sentences are perfect pitches with the snap of a fastball or the surprise of a curve. White takes on McCarthyism and all forms of censorship, advertising, politicking, and faddism. He believes in protecting the environment and articulates the paradox of hawking the "unspoiled wilderness" to people who will then spoil it. An ardent admirer of Thoreau, White savors the world around him; he is funny, compassionate, and aware. Not previously published in book form, these short essays are a delightful addition to the White canon. —*Donna Seaman*

Winkel, Lois and Kimmel, Sue.
Mother Goose Comes First: An Annotated Guide to the Best Books and Recordings for Your Preschool Child.
Holt, $14.95. 174p.

As editor and former bibliographer of *The Elementary School Library Collection*, Winkel and Kimmel know their stuff, as their practical book- and record-finders guide seems to prove. Divided into general topics of interest to preschoolers (concept books, Mother Goose, stories about growing up and families, nonfiction, etc.), their handbook includes a generally solid assortment of titles, emphasizing those with proven kid appeal—from Kunhardt's venerable *Pat the Bunny* to Brian Barton's *Dinosaurs, Dinosaurs* (published in 1989). Annotations are short but lively; grade levels (0–5) are noted. Chapters on lullabies, music, and songs list recordings and books alphabetically, a somewhat confusing arrangement despite the use of symbols to indicate format. Otherwise, books take precedence, with symbols noting their availability in phonorecord format or as part of a read-along kit. The authors' selection of holiday titles is disappointing, but otherwise, the book is a handy quick reference for parents and others who work with the young. —*Stephanie Zvirin*

Woolf, Virginia.
Congenial Spirits: The Selected Letters of Virginia Woolf.
HBJ, $24.95. 472p.

Editor Joanne Trautmann Banks, drawing from the six volumes of Woolf's collected *Letters* (which she coedited with Nigel Nicolson), offers these highly witty, telling, and poignant samples of the novelist's correspondence with friends, relatives, and professional contacts. Woolf wrote vibrantly about books and people, and this condensation increases her dynamism through elimination of the more prosaic missives. Twelve new letters appear here (including five from six-year-old Virginia), and Banks has written a simple introduction to each chapter, highlighting significant moments in the year. In addition, footnotes clarify obscure names and events. Woolf's letters contain descriptions of her practical jokes and feminist activism and evidence of her strong ties with the Bloomsbury circle. —*Denise Perry Donavin*

Woolf, Virginia.
A Moment's Liberty: The Shorter Diary of Virginia Woolf.
HBJ, $24.95. 516p.

A compilation featuring excerpts from the five volumes of Virginia Woolf's diaries, written from 1915 to 1941 and published between 1977 and 1984. Editor Bell has sought Woolf's most arresting comments and private reflections, keeping the focus on personal and social matters, in juxtaposition to Leonard Woolf's 1954 *A Writer's Diary*, which contained Woolf's "preoccupations" with her work. This collection will be greeted by Woolf's fans with the same enthusiasm that was evoked by the abridged collection of Woolf's letters (*Congenial Spirits*). A fine opportunity to experience Woolf's biting wit and scathing depictions of her contemporaries. —*Denise Perry Donavin*

Zinsser, William.
On Writing Well: An Informal Guide to Writing Nonfiction.
Harper, $19.95. 304p.

Zinsser outdoes himself in this fourth edition of his exemplary writing manual. One of the significant improvements is the inclusion of far more samples by women writers; another is simply the evidence of Zinsser's own

Music

growth as a writer and teacher over the past 15 years. He cares about the sound of words, the clutter of sentences, and the veracity of research and makes the reader/writer care just as deeply. Specific instruction on writing humor, business, critical, sports, science, technology, and nature pieces are furnished. Zinsser ably blends both personal and literary anecdotes into a text that is both instructive and entertaining. —*Denise Perry Donavin*

Music

Adler, Richard and David, Lee.
"You Gotta Have Heart."
Donald I. Fine, $19.95. 342p.

Adler's usually remembered as half of the team that wrote the songs in the dazzling 1950s musicals *The Pajama Game* and *Damn Yankees*. The big first chapter of his glitzy, cliché-ridden, wonderfully entertaining autobiography is about the short collaboration with Jerry Ross, who died at 29 from tuberculosis, and it starts the book out with a winning make-'em-laugh, make-'em-cry scenario right out of the movies. Succeeding chapters about events fore and aft of Ross are no less appealing. Son of a concert pianist who couldn't get his son to learn the keyboard, Adler met and melded with a lot of famous names in a variety of capacities. He married Sally Ann Howes, staged JFK's forty-fifth birthday bash in Madison Square Garden, and trysted with a panoply of big-deal ladies. Illness in the family as well as friends has brought plenty of pathos into his life, and his recent, miraculous recovery from cancer through the spiritual discipline of Siddha Yoga gives his self-chronicle an inspirational ending. The only grating thing about his narrative is all the sexual boasting. Adler's not crude or graphic, but to hear him tell it, he's been boffing every babe who came to hand since age eight. —*Ray Olson*

Bergreen, Laurence.
As Thousands Cheer: The Life of Irving Berlin.
Viking, $24.95. 636p.

Evasive about himself throughout his life, and reclusive to the point of hostility in his extreme age, Irving Berlin is not the ideal subject for a big biography. But he crossed paths with so many mouthier show-biz celebs that Bergreen has quite a bit to report, after all. And because Berlin's career paralleled the explosive growth of the modern entertainment industry, no one's going to object when, as often happens, Bergreen digresses to consider tangential figures and developments. His willingness to fill in background is in fact the book's greatest virtue. The extra material makes a rich pop-cultural epic of Berlin's 101 years. The man himself is finally rather unattractive. His enduring traits seem to have been a foul temper and extremely jealous proprietorship: he sued *Mad* magazine when it printed parodies of some of his lyrics, and no one—but no one—was allowed to reprint a Berlin song to which he still owned copyright. He was, however, a devoted husband to the high-society daughter he won from her starchy, bigoted father in a famous elopement. And he did write all those fabulously good-humored songs, whose fans will probably all love this book. —*Ray Olson*

Brandelius, Jerilyn Lee.
Greatful Dead Family Album.
Warner, $29.95, 249p.

"What a long, strange trip it's been," the members of the Grateful Dead observe in one of their songs, and in their case especially, truer words were never spoken. Once upon a time in the late 1960s they were the epitome of the weirdo hippie freak pot-jammin' rock band. Now they're pillars of the rock music establishment. Strange indeed. How they made that transition is not so much the subject of this book as it is the underlying theme. Hundreds of photographs of Grateful Dead members and associates accompany text that traces the band's history from its beginnings through the recent tour with Bob Dylan. The whole thing has been assembled with the kind of playful and deceptively anarchic flair that characterizes the group's concerts. The result is not only a chronicle of the Grateful Dead, but also an absolutely captivating, even charming retrospective of the hippie era. "Deadheads" will love it, of course, but anyone interested in the social milieu of that time will get a kick out of it, too. —*Steve Weingartner*

Büchmann-Moller, Frank.
You Just Fight for Your Life: The Story of Lester Young.
Praeger, $24.95. 298p.

It's not a graceful book, but this is the first thoroughgoing biography of one of America's greatest musicians; its fascination for at least jazz aficionados is magnetic. With the tenor saxophonist 30 years gone and the majority of his peers and valuable eyewitnesses to his life dead, too, Büchmann-Moller pored over interviews with and about Young, gleaning liberally from them as well as interviewing quite a clutch of Young's still-living associates. The portrait that emerges is of the intelligent, introverted, instinctively musical man, sensitive as a new burn, that everyone's always said Young was. But here is the most detailed account of the brief army stint that according to legend ruined Young psychologically, plus more information about his very early career as a member of his father's touring band than appears in any other single place. Along with Porter's magisterial work of musical analysis, *Lester Young*, this is the book to have on the most influential jazzman between Armstrong and Parker. —*Ray Olson*

Christgau, Robert.
Christgau's Record Guide: Rock Albums of the '80's.
Pantheon, $16.95. 513p.

Music critic Christgau makes a living being a fan; he is one of the rare and aging (almost 50) breed of intellectuals who still believe that a life can be saved by rock 'n' roll. Since the 1970s, Christgau has discovered the South Bronx and South Africa; rap has succeeded punk; and CDs have replaced vinyl. In this *A-to-Z* guide to the albums of the past decade, Christgau includes more than 3,000 reviews, giving each a grade. He is selective in his choices, but covers 10 albums of Al Green, 11 each by Merle Haggard, UB40, and the Mekons. The Eurythmics are a solid *B*-level band, according to Christgau, and the Beastie Boys get an *A+* for "Licenced to Ill." Many readers may disagree with the choices, but Christgau's guide is heartfelt. *—Benjamin Segedin*

Densmore, John.
Riders on the Storm: My Life with Jim Morrison and the Doors.
Delacorte, $18.95. 352p.

Densmore spent five energy-charged years of his life as the drummer for the rock group The Doors—"Light My Fire," "Hello I Love You," "People Are Strange," etc.—led by the drugged-out, manic, Nietzschian, superlunged superstar Jim Morrison. This is Densmore's story—of his middle-class Catholic upbringing, of his love for jazz, of his involvement in the 1960s L.A. music scene, of his two marriages and divorces, of fatherhood (and one abortion), of fame and fortune, of his current attempts to make it as an actor—but it is, of necessity, mostly the story of The Doors. How the band met, their struggle to get recorded, playing the bar scene, finding the groove through Morrison's pained lyrical imagery, hitting the concert road, taking lots of acid—these are covered in detail in a peculiar blend of retrospective diary entries in which Densmore tries to recapture the emotions and perceptions of the golden age of rock. Morrison's bizarre on- and off-stage antics—he *never* exposed himself, though, says the author—play an important role here, as Densmore struggles to come to grips with his confused feelings about the group's long-dead lead singer via a series of "open letters." Densmore also relates the sad tale of his brother Jim, whose emotional illness eventually led to suicide. Revelatory and readable. *—Martin Brady*

✓ Friedwald, Will.
Jazz Singing: America's Great Voices from Bessie Smith to Bebop and Beyond.
Scribner, $29.95. 416p.

Talk about filling a gap. There's darn near nothing about jazz singing except for an essay here and there in collections mostly concerned with instrumental music. Sure, there's Gene Lees' marvelous *Singers and the Song*, but it's a set of unrelated articles, not a critical history of an entire field of musical endeavor. So this magisterial, lively, catholic, enthusiastic overview of jazz and jazz-influenced pop singers couldn't be more welcome. Nor could it be more fascinating, as Friedwald not only discusses the major figures—Armstrong, Crosby, Holiday, Fitzgerald, Sinatra, Eckstine, Vaughan, Tormé, Bennett, etc.—in depth, but tantalizingly describes the contributions of secondary and forgotten talents, such as Al Bowlly. Nor could it be more frustrating, for evocative as Friedwald's descriptions of a singer's performance get, some printed musical examples would make it all more concrete for musically literate readers. But fascination outweighs frustration by a ton. This is an absolutely essential book for anybody who cares in the slightest about adult popular music (as opposed to, as Friedwald calls it, "kiddie-pop," i.e., rock 'n' roll). A delightfully, provocatively annotated discography is appended. —*Ray Olson*

✓ **Furia, Philip.**
The Poets of Tin Pan Alley: A History of America's Great Lyricists.
Oxford, $19.95. 304p.

They really don't make songs like the standards of Tin Pan Alley any more, you know. The 32-bar "ballad" is the thing of an era that began with ragtime and ended with rock 'n' roll. It spawned myriad distinctive melodies *and* a body of sophisticated, vernacular verse as striking as the songs of Burns and (Thomas) Moore, as prosodically diverse as the effusions of cummings (e.e.) and (Marianne) Moore. Furia refers to both those modernist icons—implying pop-song influence upon them as he does—while analyzing the felicities of rhyme and diction in lyrics by Berlin, Hart, Gershwin, Porter, Mercer, and an array of lesser lights who collectively transformed the sentimental popular song of the fin de siècle into a form full of verbal and tonal wit. Taking their cue quite literally from ragtime syncopation, these lyricists "ragged" words for surprising and delightful effects that Furia takes equal delight in disclosing. The author's love and enthusiasm for his subject, and also the fact that you can't help humming while reading, make this the rare book of literary criticism that is downright enjoyable. Truly, "the age of miracles ha[s]n't passed." —*Ray Olson*

Giuliano, Geoffrey.
Dark Horse: The Secret Life of George Harrison.
Dutton, $18.95. 288p.

George was always the rather mysterious Beatle: quiet, playing his guitar off to the side, discovering the sitar and Krishna consciousness, seemingly unflappable. This biography by music journalist Giuliano gives us the straightforward dope on Harrison's life, from humble beginnings as a bus driver's son, through the tumultuous Beatles years, and on to his various careers as solo artist, as a member of the Traveling Wilburys, and as record and movie producer. George certainly comes across as a nice guy, and though he has always maintained the image of the seeker of mystic revelation, the facts are, according to the author (who knows his subject well), that George could slug back the booze and do a little drugs with the best of 'em, and he

Music

wasn't always the completely faithful husband we might have suspected him to be. He also enjoys fast cars, gardening, and the much-deserved seclusion of his Henley estate. Most of all, says Giuliano, Harrison will prove to be a survivor. This informative bio helps to fill in the blank spaces—especially of the more recent years—in the life of one of the pivotal sidemen in contemporary pop history. —*Martin Brady*

Green, Stephen and Hyman, Laurence J.
Going to Chicago: A Year on the Chicago Blues Scene.
Woodford Publishing, $19.95. 128p.

It's Maxwell Street, it's the Checkerboard Lounge, it's 500,000 in attendance at Grant Park: it's Chicago and it's the blues. Green spent two years shooting more than 230 duotone photos throughout the city that houses and hosts all the greatest blues artists of our time. Though there are 18 pages of text (comprising Hyman's brief blues lesson and commentary by 10 familiar blues players), this is primarily a photo book. The high-quality pictures document the personalities of the players: Etta James' playful sexuality, Albert Collins' excruciating intensity, Lefty Dizz's poise, Koko Taylor's power, and the smiles and styles of more than 60 other artists. Though it doesn't really have the "reference" value that its publishers claim, this is a browsers' delight. —*Angus Trimnell*

Guthrie, Woody.
Pastures of Plenty: A Self-Portrait.
Harper, $29.95. 288p.

From the dust-bowl country of Oklahoma, Woody Guthrie roamed and rambled to New York City in the 1940s and is remembered today as one of the most articulate voices of the radical, pro-labor folk music movement of the time. The man who wrote the anthem "This Land Is Your Land" and toted a guitar labeled "This Machine Kills Fascists" was also a prolific writer of prose and verse. *Pastures of Plenty* is a small sampling of letters, articles, and notes collected in the Woody Guthrie archives. As in earlier such collections—*Born to Win* and *Woody Sez*—the ordering of the writings can only follow Guthrie's manic creative pace, and thematic organization is impossible. In *Pastures*, however, an attempt is made to present the works in chronological order (from 1936 to the early 1950s), and more attention is paid, and editorial guidance is lent, to the everyday progression of Guthrie's creation. *Pastures* reveals, through Guthrie's sprawling, colloquial style, the common man's visionary with an unfailing belief in music, love, and a planned society. His ideas are not intellectually refined but are based on experience and observation. His recollections of the movement and its players (e.g., Pete Seeger, Leadbelly, Paul Robeson) present a view invaluable to those interested in folk music and social protest. —*Angus Trimnell*

Horowitz, Joseph.
The Ivory Trade: Music and the Business of Music at the Van Cliburn International Piano Competition.
Summit, $19.95. 276p.

Hardly anyone speaks highly of piano competitions today, so one opens with skepticism a book that is advertised as a "riveting exposé" of one of the most famous. Yet this turns out to be quite a pleasing account of a strange and controversial ritual no one seems able to put out to pasture. Frankly, too much is made of the virtues and evils of musical competition. Are the competitions themselves really to blame for a certain uniform style of playing that exists today? Because so many of the finest pianists today won midcentury competitions, and no major career has been launched by a competition since 1975, does it mean that a competition win makes or breaks a pianist? Hardly. The place where composer, performer, and audience meet is bound to be characterized by conflict, brilliance, banality, confusion, and insight, and the success of a book like this is the degree to which it can flesh these elements out. Horowitz does so without sensationalism and reminds us that the value of music is the insight it gives us into people. —*Stuart Whitwell*

Hotchner, A. E.
Blown Away: The Rolling Stones and the Death of the Sixties.
Simon & Schuster, $21.95. 349p.

A hostile and sensationalized look at the career of the Rolling Stones and the death of band member Brian Jones. Hotchner, author of notorious treatments of Sophia Loren, Doris Day, and Ernest Hemingway, is not known for insightful, sensitive writing, but this may be a new low. Why a former air force major and correspondent for *Air Force* magazine would want to write a book about the Stones is one question; another is why the publisher has seen fit to exclude an entire chapter from the review galleys because of its "sensitive information." Are we talking state secrets here? Apparently Hotchner believes that Jones was murdered, rather than drowned accidentally on his estate (not a brand new concept). Aside from that allegation, Hotchner works hard at portraying Mick Jagger as evil, weak, money-mad, and not especially talented except in his bisexual appeal. The book opens with a lurid account of the violence at Altamont and ends with petty sniping at Jagger. To Hotchner's credit, the core of the book does contain dozens of interesting and revealing interviews with all sorts of people, including former manager Andrew Oldham, Marianne Faithfull, and Anita Pallenberg. The stories feature the usual nasty accounts of drugs, sexual excess, and violence (Jones' proclivity) as well as some fey references to witchcraft. Hotchner seems to subscribe to the old notion that rock 'n' roll is responsible for all that's wrong with society, and, even more absurdly, that somehow Jagger is the devil behind it all. A mean-spirited and reactionary book, but bound to appeal to readers who like sordid details and exhumations. —*Donna Seaman*

Leonard, Herman.
The Eye of Jazz.
Viking, $29.95. 155p.

A project undertaken more than 30 years ago eventuates in an oversize album of photo-portraits made from 1948 to 1960 of the period's jazz stars. Much about the book is a bit weird, such as the presentation of the pictures in an alphabet of Leonard's personal nicknames for his subjects. (Some of Leonard's comments are a mite odd, too, for example, the one involving Fats Navarro dying "in a car accident." Wasn't that Clifford Brown?) But the pictures are wonderful, and unlike other, very effective jazz photography, generally sharply focused and more studiedly composed. Jazz players are arguably the most photogenic of musicians, but perhaps that's because they attract the most gifted photo-portraitists. At any rate, they have attracted one here. —*Ray Olson*

✓ McGovern, Dennis and Winer, Deborah Grace.
I Remember Too Much: Backstage with the World's Greatest Opera Singers.
Morrow, $24.95. 388p.

McGovern and Winer set for themselves an enviable task: sitting down with as many of the world's opera stars, past and present, as would talk with them about their careers, and, particularly, their favorite roles. And rather than simply playing back the interviews as given, the authors have arranged the singers' comments by opera; in chapters entitled *La Traviata, Aida, Madama Butterfly,* and others, the likes of Mirella Freni, Anna Moffo, Renata Scotto, Luciano Pavarotti, and—giving her last interview—the late and legendary Met star, Zinka Milanov, disclose not only personal opinions about vocal technique and character portrayal, but also facets of their own indiosyncratic personalities. Charm and commitment come to the fore as these sopranos and tenors discuss likes and dislikes, proud moments, and moments they'd just as soon forget. Luscious reading for the opera fan. —*Brad Hooper*

Merrill, Hugh.
The Blues Route.
Morrow, $17.95. 224p.

Setting out to take the pulse of America's great indigenous music, the blues, journalist Merrill traveled to its four major stations: the Mississippi Delta, Chicago, New Orleans, and California. An informative—and often pleasantly quirky—narrative is interspersed with long passages from interviews with performers, recording agents, instrument makers, and DJs. Merrill affirms the strength of pure blues despite the passing of most of its masters. Replete with enjoyable stories and the opinions of the people who love this powerful, healing, and often undervalued music. Recommended for anyone with an interest in blues and American folk music. —*Angus Trimnell*

Monk, Noel E. and Guterman, Jimmy.
12 Days on the Road: The Sex Pistols and America.
Morrow, $19.95. 256p.

The Sex Pistols' brief but ballistic career shook up the insipid music world of the late 1970s. Spawned by England's hypocritical politics—and incited by entrepreneur Malcolm McLaren—Johnny Rotten, Sid Vicious, Paul Cook, and Steve Jones played raw, fast, loud, and anarchistic rock 'n' roll. This is the chronicle of their notorious 1978 American tour told by tour manager Noel Monk. The Sex Pistols needed a lot of management; Monk discovered that keeping junkie Sid Vicious in line was a 24-hour gig. Vicious was violent and gross—punk to the point of puke. The record company people acted like the Sex Pistols were an infection; no one wanted to get near them. It's amazing that the band actually performed, riling up the crowds who threw full beer cans and pig's snouts at the stage while Vicious spat in return. An explosive chapter in the history of rock. —*Donna Seaman*

Murray, Charles Shaar.
Crosstown Traffic: Jimi Hendrix and the Post-war Rock 'n' Roll Revolution.
St. Martin's, $18.95. 256p.

Coming from an African American musical background to have his music embraced, primarily, by white Britons and Americans, Jimi Hendrix exemplified the musical collisions and contradictions of the 1960s. Murray, a British music journalist, forms this onion of Hendrix's life from the skins of his many influences, predecessors, experiences, and coworkers. Essentially, Murray evaluates Hendrix as a musician-lyricist while using him as a touchstone for an exploration of twentieth-century popular music. In a critical voice, he crafts a dense, ricocheting evaluation of artists from Robert Johnson and Son House to Living Color and Prince. This informed, textured account will be irresistible to devotees of Hendrix and psychedelic rock as well as fans of blues, funk, jazz, and rock 'n' roll. Murray's use of musical terminology may discourage some, but for pop-music collections in which critical accounts circulate, this "not a biography of Jimi Hendrix" will be greatly appreciated. —*Angus Trimnell*

Near, Holly and Richardson, Derk.
Fire in the Rain.
Morrow, $19.95. 384p.

Leftist singer-songwriter Near's autobiography is really an oral document, reading like a string of between-numbers raps, full of breaks in continuity where, by the tone of what's said, it's easy to imagine Near bursting into song. It also hops all over the place chronologically, relating now a childhood incident, now a recent concert-tour tale, now a reminiscence of early stabs at conventional showbiz success. Still, it basically proceeds from her rural northern California beginnings through her Hollywood days and on to her subsequent long career as activist-entertainer on behalf of the radical causes of her time—opposition to the Vietnam War, to U.S. meddling in Latin America, to apartheid, and to U.S. cultural imperialism; advocacy for feminism, pacifism, democratic socialism, and lesbian feminism. Near does a lot of earnest preaching for her politics, which she shows intricately and stressfully intertwining with her everyday life, never more so than when, as a declared lesbian, she subsequently did not behave as an exclusive lesbian. She's the Pete Seeger of her generation, and she resembles him in that if her sweetness sometimes cloys, her dedication inspires. —*Ray Olson*

✓ **Palmer, Christopher.**
The Composer in Hollywood.
Marion Boyars, $39.95. 336p.

"Film music is, and always has been, a minority interest," Palmer introductorily observes. Perhaps that fact dictated the steep price of this wonderful book. Pay up anyway, if you're a music nut. Palmer, himself an orchestral arranger for films, appreciates both dramatic functionality and musicality as he critically examines, sans musical examples but with admirable concreteness, the work of eight titans of Hollywood composing: Max Steiner, Erich Wolfgang Korngold, Alfred Newman, Franz Waxman, Dimitri Tiomkin, Roy Webb, Miklós Rósza, and Bernard Herrmann. Each appreciation includes a little biography and lots of close analysis of how music fits film in each composer's best and most characteristic achievements. It's more than enough to make movie-music maniacs chase all over town to rent copies of the many old flickers whose scores Palmer enticingly scrutinizes, or alternatively, to plunder the soundtrack record bins. Besides the single-composer chapters, a ninth notes 1950s scores by Alex North, Elmer Bernstein, and Leonard Rosenman that broke romanticism's hold on movie music. Surely each of that trio, and several others, deserve individual treatment in a sequel. What do you say, Mr. Palmer? —*Ray Olson*

Pawlowski, Gareth L.
How They Became the Beatles: A Definitive History of the Early Years, 1960–1964.
Dutton, $24.95. 208p.

This book certainly treads familiar Fab Four ground, but it *is* a very nice book. It's unclear just who Gareth Pawlowski is, besides an obvious Beatles freak. And yet, while many of the pictures he's assembled have been seen before, many have not. Focusing on the formative years, Pawlowski blends a straightforward chronological account of the Beatles' personal and professional doings with photos of the band in action, rare record labels and jackets, concert ticket stubs and programs, newspaper items (including the obituary of ex-Beatle Stuart Sutcliffe), and other collectible snippets. Some of the pix here are valuable history, Pawlowski having included outtakes from sessions that produced photos we *do* know (e.g., Albert Marrion's famous "leather" set), as well as private snapshots of the early band (with Pete Best as drummer) in performance or rehearsal. All the photos are black and white except five color prints (never before published) of the group at Hamburg's Star Club in December 1962. Definitely a fave-rave for the many loyal fans. —*Martin Brady*

Picardie, Justine and Wade, Dorothy.
Music Man: Ahmet Ertegun, Atlantic Records, and the Triumph of Rock 'n' Roll.
Norton, $18.95. 263p.

This may look like a biography of the only founder of Atlantic Records who's still with the company, but it's actually an anecdotal romp through the 40 years of the pop-record biz that the label's survived. Son of an early ambassador to the U.S. from Kemal's Turkey, Ertegun is an interesting guy, but so are former Atlantic associates Herb and Miriam Abramson, Jerry Wexler, and Tom Dowd. So are his counterparts at other labels, especially the outrageous Syd Nathan of Cincinnati's legendary King Records (the country-music outfit that discovered James Brown). So are the Atlantic singing and songwriting stars—Ray Charles, Ruth Brown, the Drifters, Leiber and Stoller (the Rodgers and Hart of rock 'n' roll), etc., and later Led Zeppelin, Foreigner, the Rolling Stones, etc.—who also walk through this book. In fact, Ahmet's pretty constantly being upstaged. Rock history buffs won't mind that situation at all. —*Ray Olson*

Seeger, Pete and Reiser, Bob.
Everybody Says Freedom.
Norton, $29.95. 266p.

Seeger and Reiser present a vivid overview of the Christian, nonviolent civil-rights movement of the 1950s and 1960s and the various roles that music played in it. Using primarily the words of activists—mostly students—they follow the campaigns of SNCC, SCLC, and CORE to desegregate the southern states and bring blacks to the voting booth. They have collected, and present throughout the text, the songs—some original movement songs, some adapted traditionals—in musical notation including the vocal line(s) and guitar chords. Music sections, set in a gray background, accent the expressive pictures and stories of shared struggle, violence, and disillusionment. Hope is held high, and one can see that this is written to succeeding generations, for the speakers encourage the children of today to engage in protests and to sing and live their beliefs. —*Angus Trimnell*

Selvin, Joel.
Ricky Nelson: Idol for a Generation.
Contemporary, $18.95, 256p.

There can be nary a Baby Boomer out there who doesn't remember Ricky Nelson—youngest of the show-biz Nelson clan, smart-mouthed enfant terrible of TV's "Adventures of Ozzie and Harriet," and child actor turned pop singer/teen heartthrob. While Ricky crooned such mellow rockabilly tunes as "Travelin Man" and "Hello Mary Lou," dad Ozzie set up a considerable trust fund for his doe-eyed son, more prosaic brother David tried to keep his cool (and find his niche in life), and mom Harriet pretty much stuck to the script of the artificial domestic Eden that was portrayed each week on ABC. Alas, for the last 20 years of his life, Ricky tried mightily to recapture his recorded charm. He had record deals aplenty, but aside from his 1971 hit (sort of) "Garden Party," it was for Rick mostly an endles string of two-bit TV appearances and one-night stands in small towns and county fairs. Sure he made some bucks, but when he died in his private plane on New Year's Eve 1985, he was $1 million in debt, his marriage to Kris Harmon (daughter of football's Tom and sister of actor Mark) was in bitter shambles, his children didn't know him, he'd been hit with a paternity suit, and rumors of drug abuse abounded. Perhaps what comes across most lucidly in Selvin's readable biography is the fact of Rick's personality: apparently, an absolute cipher. A nostalgic, ultimately pathetic look at a lost American pop icon. —*Martin Brady*

Story, Rosalyn M.
And So I Sing.
Warner, $24.95. 256p.

Story profiles the careers of notable African American women whose musical talents broke racial barriers. The earlier sections of the book are the most successful, as Story delves into the lives and personalities of Sissieretta Jones and Elizabeth Greenfield, nineteenth-century divas who paved the road for those who followed. The middle section focuses on mezzo soprano Marian Anderson, the first black to sing at the Metropolitan Opera, while the final chapters feature interviews with Leontyne Price, Shirley Verrett, and Grace Bumbry, along with short clips on recent and current stars. These later sections capably address such current problems for black singers as vocal and visual ethnicity, but the real revelations and surprises come when Story deals with the turmoil and trauma that pioneer divas faced and overcame. —*John Brosnahan*

✔ **White, Timothy.**
Rock Lives: Profiles & Interviews.
Holt, $19.95. 512p.

White, perhaps America's premier rock critic, offers an anecdotal history of rock 'n' roll in the form of profiles of and interviews with the music's biggest names. He begins with fresh examinations of the prototype rockers: classic rowdies like Chuck Berry and Jerry Lee Lewis, playing hard and living harder; neglected stylists like Professor Longhair; shy oddballs like Buddy Holly; and maybe the godfather of them all, delta blues guitarist Robert Johnson, whose skills (legend has it) were acquired in a deal with the devil. White's narrative follows the beaten track: up the Mississippi Delta, extended stays in New Orleans and Memphis, and on to the stockyards of Chicago. White starts with the noble intention of providing some slight semblance of plot, the suggestion of a linear pattern extending from Robert Johnson to Keith Richards to Jon Bon Jovi. Does it really exist? Nah. Rock thrives on its nonlinear tangents, and, despite White's doomed attempt at narrative logic, it's those tangents, the sense of sprawling discontinuity, that give the music, and this book, its energy.

Guitar gods Eric Clapton and Jimmy Page; singer-songwriters Joni Mitchell and Paul Simon; the unclassifiable, pixified dandy Prince; dead souls (Jimi Hendrix), troubled souls (Brian Wilson), and ubiquitous souls (the Grateful Dead)—they're all here, and they're all captured on the page, in White's words and their own, with an immediacy rare in rock journalism. Music books don't make many best-seller lists, but this one just might. —*Peter Robertson*

Occult

Brown, Sylvia and May, Antoinette.
My Guide, Myself: The Psychic Odyssey of Sylvia Brown.
NAL, $18.95. 256p.

Even New Agers may not know the name Sylvia Brown, but she has an interesting story to tell. The granddaughter of a psychic, Sylvia was only a child when she first felt the presence of the Indian woman who became her spirit guide. Sylvia's experiences with her guide, whom she christened Francine, led eventually to the formation of the Nirvana Foundation for Psychic Research, which reveals God's word according to New Age tenets. But it's not the philosophy that's of most interest here. Readers will be caught up in the story of an earthy, amusing woman who has her full share of ups and downs in the course of discerning the most incredible things about other people. Perhaps due to the presence of cowriter May, the book is eminently readable—even those who think the whole cosmic thing is mumbo jumbo may enjoy this peek into another dimension. —*Ilene Cooper*

✓ Cabot, Laurie and Cowan, Tom.
Power of the Witch: The Earth, the Moon, and the Magical Path to Enlightenment.
Delacorte, $17.95. 320p.

What's in a name? A lot, especially if it's *witch*; authors Cabot (known as the "Official Witch of Salem") and Cowan trace the derivation of the word to roots meaning "bend or shape," "wit," and "wise ones." And, in discussing the misconceptions of witches as evil and destructive, the authors feel that the time is right to speak "openly and clearly" about what witches do. Moving from a sound history of witchery, in which the phenomenon is traced back to the shift from matriarchy to patriarchy in pagan times, they provide the steps for achieving the "alpha mental state"; definitions of the laws of witch science; recipes for a variety of "magical spells for health, prosperity, protection, and love"; milestones in a witch's life (including ceremonies for different stages, such as birth or death); and an optimistic look into the future of life on this planet. The highly readable prose and multiple tips for employing magic in one's own life make this a valuable handbook for those interested in this controversial, misunderstood religion. —*Eloise Kinney*

Markides, Kyriacos C.
Fire in the Heart: Healers, Sages, and Mystics.
Paragon House, $18.95. 224p.

The third part of a trilogy, continuing the ideas developed in *The Magus of Strovolos* and *Homage to the Sun*. Presenting Greek Cypriot spiritual wisdom to the English readership, Markides, a political sociologist, takes a phenomenological approach to the mystical cosmology that he describes. Spiros Sathi (aka Daskalos) and Kostas, Sathi's most advanced disciple and successor, are the two spiritual masters who become the key characters in this conversational work; their ideas about and reports of their experiences with "the worlds that lie beyond the reach of our ordinary senses" form the main substance of the book. Expressing a traditional Greek philosophic notion of the human person as composed of three modalities of being—the material, the psychic, and the noetic—Markides centers much of the discussion on their mastery and the subsequent abilities to engage in out-of-body travel and to transcend karma. This book will appeal to readers interested in paranormal phenomena. —*Sheila McGinn-Moorer*

Quigley, Joan.
"What Does Joan Say?": My Seven Years as White House Astrologer to Nancy and Ronald Reagan.
Birch Lane Press, $17.95. 173p.

Astrologers should maintain at least the same amount of confidentiality as a lawyer, but don't try to sell Joan Quigley on client privilege. Ron and Nancy's astrologer, of course, has her reasons for telling all: she was offended by Nancy's book, *My Turn*: "It reads like fiction, and much of it is evasive." Well, *ex-c-use me*, as Nancy might or might not say. Is that reason enough, the former first lady might wonder, for her once-loyal employee to reveal such secrets (or make such claims, depending on your point of view) as, "I was responsible for timing all the press conferences . . . delayed President Reagan's first operation . . . chose the time for Nancy's mastectomy." Her influence, though, spread far beyond planning the calendar—or so she says, claiming to have "re-created Nancy's image" and "defused Bitburg." It is difficult to know how Quigley thought she would come across in this book, but the fact is she seems like a megalomaniac (and one who calls the president "Ronnie"). If Quigley was as powerful as she says (and she says it over and over), it's pretty scary. If Nancy is the witch that Quigley makes her out to be, no wonder she keeps alienating friends and family (except Ronnie, of course). This book is exploitive, gossipy, and leaves a terrible taste in your mouth. It's also riveting—just like the aftermath of a car accident. —*Ilene Cooper*

Snow, Chet B.
Mass Dreams of the Future.
McGraw-Hill, $19.95. 352p.

Worried that you'll be ill in your later years? Wondering if social security will be around in the year 2,000? Don't bother speculating; there's not going to be a year 2,000. Well, there will be, but according to Snow, who has hypnotically "progressed" subjects to a future life, the earth will be sparsely populated at the turn of the century, courtesy of a cataclysmic event that will alter the planet. Of course, none of this is news to New Agers familiar with the writings of Edgar Cayce and Ruth Montgomery, among others. Snow first got into the progression business when he began his own past-life regressions with noted researcher Helen Wambach. Author of *Life before Life* (Bantam, 1979), Wambach thought it would be interesting to study the future as well, but, as she began progressing people, she discovered that hardly anyone seemed to be alive at the turn of the century. When Wambach became ill, Snow carried on her work, trying to determine what's going to happen to all of us in the next 10 years. His sobering conclusions are certain to prompt heated discussion. Snow makes the usual disclaimers about free will altering events, but if what he predicts comes true, there's only one thing to do: buy lots of stuff with charge cards long about 1997. —*Ilene Cooper*

Parenting

Ashner, Laurie and Meyerson, Mitch.
When Parents Love Too Much: What Happens When Parents Won't Let Go.
Morrow, $19.95. 352p.

The title of this excellent book is misleading, for as healthy parents know, parents can never love their children too much. What this work discusses instead are parents caught up in obsessive and/or controlling "love" that seeks to meet the parents', rather than the children's, unfulfilled needs. Written by two therapists, one a specialist in family dynamics, this highly readable guide is packed with insights gleaned from real-life cases, many of them vividly detailed here. Readers will also find expert advice on ways to cope with or avoid this particular widespread family dysfunction. And adult children seeking to better understand and cope with the legacy of being overparented will greatly benefit, too. —*Mary Banas*

Goldstein, Robin.
Everyday Parenting: The First Five Years.
Penguin, $6.95. 256p.

Parents of infants, toddlers, and young children will appreciate this guide to the intricacies of child rearing. Crossing over from 1987 small-press publication to the mass-market big time in this edition, Goldstein shows that occurrences like tantrums, hitting, not sharing, and sibling rivalry are universal and can be handled within a consistent framework of offering love and establishing discipline. Her many short chapters appear in large sections on dependency; sleeping; eating; independence; setting limits; children's thinking; fears and imagination; toys, play, and socializing; being nice; and caretakers and preschools, respectively. Each chapter addresses the kind of concern that seems too mundane to broach with a pediatrician, too emotion-

Parenting

ally loaded to discuss with over-zealous relatives, or too embarrassing or personal to share with acquaintances—things like weaning, age-appropriate play, whether to spank, and switching from crib to bed. —*Micaela Sullivan-Fowler*

Newman, Susan.
Parenting an Only Child: The Joys and Challenges of Raising Your One and Only.
Doubleday, $19.95. 256p.

Newman, herself the parent of an only child (by a second marriage), assesses the nature of the single-child family and provides both reassurance and guidance to adults in a quandary about only-child parenting. Using a generous infusion of comments by parents, teachers, and only children (both adult and teenage), she refutes the stereotypic image of the single child as a spoiled brat, socially inept and dependent, replacing it with a vision of children who are highly motivated, creative, and intelligent. While she is encouraging about single-child families, she is also realistic about dilemmas involved in raising an only child—maintaining balance within a small family, dealing with situations when there is no "sibling sounding board" to diffuse frustration, coping with disapproval from outsiders, pulling back when it is time to let an only child grow up. What she strives for is practical parenting, and her advice makes good common sense. —*Stephanie Zvirin*

✓ **Schwartzman, Michael and Sachs, Judith.**
The Anxious Parent.
Simon & Schuster, $19.95. 324p.

"Anxiety *does* have a place in our lives, and it's a drastic mistake to ignore it or hope that it will just go away," writes psychologist Schwartzman, who, with Judith Sachs, offers some practical, positive advice mindful of the function worry plays in parenting. Aiming counsel at the overprotective parents of infants, toddlers, and preschoolers, Schwartzman considers how feelings about being inadequate and losing control, often rooted in past experience, trigger destructive parenting responses in the present. Deliberately structured high-stress scenarios set the tone for follow-up discussion about parent-child conflicts over developmental activities, including sleeping, eating, cleanliness, safety, and social skills. For each area of concern, the authors suggest implementation of a multistep, self-help plan incorporating behavioral fact-finding, parental history, and careful discussion of the problem with the child to help parents evaluate their actions in a new light and undertake sensible, systematic changes beneficial to all concerned. —*Stephanie Zvirin*

Sullivan, Michael and Schultz, Susan.
Adopt the Baby You Want.
Simon & Schuster, $18.95. 192p.

Sullivan brings 15 years of experience as an adoption lawyer to this extremely useful handbook of basic information on U.S. adoption practices and procedures. Although there's a smattering of annoying self-promotion here (Sullivan owns three adoption agencies in different parts of the country), the author's insider view results in a no-nonsense, shoot-from-the-hip style that leaves readers assured of the accuracy of his advice. Included in this very informative, well-organized guidebook are a personal inventory to help couples determine their readiness to adopt, summaries of the advantages and disadvantages—as well as the costs—of adoption types (e.g., open, closed, cooperative) and sources (e.g., for-profit and nonprofit agencies, independents such as doctors and lawyers), advice on how to proceed and what red flags to watch for, details on foreign and special-needs adoptions, and an overview of current and prospective trends in adoption practices. Appended are a sample home study, a well-detailed glossary, and an information guide that lists books on all phases of adoption, including how to explain adoption to children, as well as U.S. state adoption sources and the adoption coordinators in each of Canada's 12 provinces. A clear-eyed primer that's "must" reading for all prospective adoptive parents. —*Mary Banas*

Philosophy & Psychology

✔ **Ackerman, Diane.**
A Natural History of the Senses.
Random, $19.95. 352p.

A marvelous celebration of the senses—their evolution, function, cultural values and roles, folklore, and idioms. Ackerman, an award-winning poet and author (*On Extended Wings*), is a natural student of the senses, combining the discoveries of an inspired scholar with the lyricism of a poet. In the section on smell, Ackerman explores perfumes and the types of scents different cultures find attractive. Touch is shown to be essential to life; its therapeutic aspects as well as forms of pain are described. Taste leads to an examination of the social importance of food; vision includes an analysis of beauty. Ackerman compares people to animals to point out the fact that different beings sense different worlds. While her discourse is encyclopedic, it is also personal, allowing us glimpses of her lively and creative life. Ackerman writes wisely about the profound emotional responses senses trigger, and she invites us to think about the fact that we have more than five of them. (The unknown beckons!) A beautiful, stimulating book. —*Donna Seaman*

Philosophy & Psychology

Adler, Mortimer J.
Intellect: Mind over Matter.
Macmillan/Collier, $16.95. 224p.

Our premier popular philosopher here argues the continued usefulness of the now commonly disparaged term *mind*. It is a useful concept, he avers, because neither psychological behaviorism nor the varieties of existential philosophy have successfully shown that the brain and brain activities are sufficient to account for what we call thought. Something that as yet must be regarded as immaterial is involved in intellection, the peculiar activity of intelligence that distinguishes humans from all other creatures. Readers unacquainted with modern philosophy will be astonished to learn of its shortcomings in common sense that Adler then proceeds to point up and excoriate. He is ever on the side of common sense, provided that it is genuinely sensible, i.e., informed by observable data. If sometimes even he becomes tiringly abstract and stiff, that's the trouble with philosophy. No one writes it more accessibly, not in our time. —*Ray Olson*

Bepko, Claudia and Krestan, Jo-Ann.
Too Good for Her Own Good: Breaking Free from the Burden of Female Responsibility.
Harper, $17.95. 272p.

Women's lives are often defined, limited, and controlled by the code of "goodness"—being available to others at the expense of their own sense of purpose and well-being. Women tend to live their lives in service to others, including taking complete responsibility for maintaining relationships, internalizing anger, and always being visually attractive. The costs of "goodness" are devastating, often masking a real sense of "female shame," i.e., the resistance to thoughts of being a separate person with her own strengths and weaknesses. These costs include a poor self-image, feelings of inadequacy, insecurity, and overwork. The authors offer suggestions to women on how they can learn to be independent, to begin caring for themselves, to give up feeling guilty about their lives, and to formulate new rules for living. Highly recommended. —*Jane Jurgens*

✓ **Berry, Wendell.**
What Are People For?
North Point, $19.95. 192p.

Wendell Berry is our Thoreau and our Ruskin, our William Morris and even our Paul Goodman. Like all of them, he speaks about how we live and how we might live, measuring both against the standard of "nature" by which he means all of nonhuman creation plus the abilities, habits, and proprieties inherent to us as creatures inextricably interdependent with that non-humanity. In the essays of this new collection, his overarching concern is never far from sight, whether he is discussing a book, an admired person's career, or the great issues of the day. He advances stewardship, physical involvement in work and the pleasure it affords, diversity in agriculture and in human skills, and the spiritual responsibililties of marriage and community as the elementary duties and rewards of worthy human life. At the same time, he decries the money economy, industrialization, mechanization, agribusiness, and very cogently, the cultural shortsightedness of many feminists and conservationists as ultimately inimical to a life worthy of humans. Ever thought provoking and always gracefully and powerfully expressive, Berry, in these essays, proves himself to be arguably the most essential social and cultural critic of our day. —*Ray Olson*

✓ **Bettelheim, Bruno.**
Freud's Vienna and Other Essays.
Knopf, $22.95. 271p.

Reading any one of the 18 essays in this collection can affect the reader like an especially productive session with a psychotherapist. Invariably, one comes away from them feeling enlightened, invigorated, somehow strengthened. This is altogether appropriate: Bettelheim is a preeminent psychoanalytic theorist and practitioner. He is also an accomplished man of letters, as he has demonstrated repeatedly in such past outings as *The Uses of Enchantment* and *Surviving and Other Essays*. Here, he once again succeeds in communicating complex ideas in the eloquent yet unpretentious prose that distinguished his previous works. It's a prose filled with unimpeachably sound thinking, whether he's discussing how the ambience of Vienna helped shape Freud's thinking on the nature of neurosis; what we can do to stimulate a sense of wonder and mystery in our children's lives; or how the ghetto mentality of pre–World War II European Jews fostered a willful ignorance of Nazi intentions as well as an almost total disinclination to defend themselves. This is the kind of book that you read once and then return to again and again to more thoroughly assimilate—and enjoy—all the wisdom that is found between its covers. —*Steve Weingartner*

Bloom, Allan.
Giants and Dwarfs: Essays: 1960–1990.
Simon & Schuster, $22.95. 376p.

Bloom, author of the highly controversial *Closing of the American Mind*, challenges readers with yet another volume of his often difficult but exceedingly stimulating philosophical ruminations. These collected essays explore with much wit, wisdom, and admirably restrained fervency such topics as the crisis in modern education, the thinking of Leo Strauss and Raymond Aron, the flaws in liberal theories of justice, the works of Shakespeare, Rousseau, Swift, and Plato, and, most importantly, the reason why we should read those works. Some of this gets to be pretty heavy going, but that's good: Bloom shows his respect for us, as well as the whole philosophical endeavor, by not dumbing down his writing. The chances of this book taking off like Bloom's previous surprise best-seller are slim, but the author's name should spur serious interest. —*Steve Weingartner*

Philosophy & Psychology

Dreher, Diane.
The Tao of Peace: A Guide to Inner and Outer Peace.
Donald I. Fine, $18.95. 320p.

This book seeks to guide an environmental revitalization of the earth by holistically healing and focusing the energies of all people. Dreher, child of the 1960s and specialist in developmental psychology, uses the ancient nature philosophy of Lao-tzu—as handed down in his *Tao Te Ching*—and various true-life stories to build in the reader a respect for the self, natural cycles, and the environment. Especially important are her examples of individual action and her many annotations listing books and organizations that are involved in spiritual growth and activism. Her unabashed advocacy of ancient Chinese beliefs such as *chi* energy and yin/yang properties will cause some to dismiss her, but her lessons are quite useful. This is an important subject for the 1990s and one that promises to bring a renewal of environmental consciousness. —*Angus Trimnell*

Gay, Peter.
Reading Freud: Explorations & Entertainments.
Yale, $24.95. 240p.

A front-rank Freud scholar exhibits a taste for fun in a collection of essays ranging from "Freud and the Man from Stratford" (wherein Gay explores Freud's acceptance of an oft-published theory that Shakespeare's works were really written by the earl of Oxford, Edward de Vere) to "Serious Jests" (in which Gay cites various Jewish jokes often told by Freud, and offers an insightful glimpse of the anti-Semitism rampant in Freud's Vienna). Other essays analyze Freud's choices of names for his six children (which demonstrate a loosening of old familial ties and a forging of new scientific ones, as in his naming of one son, Ernst, after a respected scientist-friend), examine Freud's own choice of ten books for good reading, and look at free will in Freud's work. Gay succeeds grandly in his effort to "reduce the blank spots on the map we now have of Freud's mind." —*Allen Weakland*

Gaylin, Willard.
Adam and Eve and Pinocchio: On Being and Becoming Human.
Viking, $18.95. 267p.

In a strong rebuttal to current theories of animal rights, Gaylin asserts the primacy of human beings over all other life on Earth. A leading psychiatrist and ethicist, he fears the consequences of a diminished sense of our species' uniqueness. The classic story of Pinocchio—enriched with analogies drawn from biology, anthropology, religion, and psychology—here serves as a parable illustrating the process through which humans make themselves the most wonderful, yet distinctively unnatural, of creatures. In morality, imagination, intelligence, and family life, humans demonstrate godlike powers not found even in our highest primate relatives. Recent developments in biotechnology represent the most remarkable evidence that a great gulf separates humankind from the animal kingdom. Gaylin defends biotechnology against its critics, yet he urges prudence and restraint in its development. Engaging and provocative, this book will stir thought and controversy. —*Bryce Christensen*

Grudin, Robert.
The Grace of Great Things: Creativity and Innovation.
Ticknor & Fields, $20.95. 288p.

Grudin refers to "insight . . . that fills us with unspeakable delight and seems to renew the world." Readers will have this experience as they follow his investigation into the nature of creativity and innovation. In discussing the origins of creative expression, the ethics of creativity, and the politics of innovation, Grudin attempts to describe processes we rarely examine: inspiration, discovery, analysis, and imagination. These are not divine gifts, he says, but the results of acquired habits of work, practice, focus, and skill. Grudin assures us that work has aesthetic possibilities: "Jobs can be elegantly conceived and gracefully done." He encourages us to live the drama of inner life more fully and to develop a "sense of wholeness." An eloquent and challenging volume that emphasizes the need to be more open to creative thought, both individually and as a civilization. —*Donna Seaman*

Karpinski, Gloria.
Where Two Worlds Touch: Spiritual Rites of Passage.
Ballantine, $10.95. 336p.

A discussion of crises as opportunities, from the perspective of the effects of reincarnation on one's current life. Karpinski offers practical suggestions for dealing with life changes such as birth, death, accidents, and job loss. Outlining her "Seven Steps of Conscious Change"—the form, the challenge, the resistance, the awakening, the commitment, the purification, the surrender—Karpinski argues that following such a process allows one to move from personal impotence in the face of crisis to personal power. —*Sheila McGinn-Moorer*

Kinder, Melvyn.
Going Nowhere Fast: Step off Life's Treadmills and Find Peace of Mind.
Prentice Hall Press, $19.95. 288p.

Kinder, coauthor of *Smart Women, Foolish Choices* (Crown, 1985), tackles the drive for self-improvement that dominates many people's lives. Kinder says "when we attempt to find happiness in this way we engage in a never-ending quest that subtly and inevitably makes us even more unhappy." The result is the treadmill mentality in which people pursue goals that are unobtainable and not truly desirable. The drive to be the perfect spouse, sex partner, parent, wage earner, or physical specimen is driving people way out of line, Kinder says. It is his hope that this book can act as a "Stop" sign for those aboard such treadmills. Kinder does not encourage inertia, just moderation and a realistic setting of goals, since "any change built on self-loathing is doomed to be fragile and short-lived." Choice anecdotes, dire warnings, and comforting reassurances enrich this how-to-shape-up-your-psyche manual. —*Denise Perry Donavin*

Philosophy & Psychology

Philosophy & Psychology

Kotre, John and Hall, Elizabeth.
Seasons of Life: Our Dramatic Journey from Birth to Death.
Little, Brown, $24.95. 450p.

Based on a PBS series, this tie-in title traces human development and growth through three "clocks"—biological, social, and psychological. Using case studies to illustrate its points, the book begins with the addition of a new generation to an established Pennsylvania farm family. Also profiled are a grade-school unwed mother, a young adult punker, a middle-aged baby boomer, an active retiree, and an elderly widow in a senior group-living arrangement. In between these profiles are the analysis and explanations that present information on the periods of life and the steps of development on the physical, mental, and social levels. The book sympathetically charts these life journeys and is especially effective when it concentrates on the concrete examples it provides. —*John Brosnahan*

Kuriansky, Judy.
How to Love a Nice Guy: Marrying "Down" and End Up with It All.
Doubleday, $17.95. 256p.

It should be just as easy to find a nice guy to love as a jerk, right? Though the experience of thousands of women screams "No," Kuriansky, the host of a cable TV advice show called "Money & Emotions," says "Yes! Yes! Yes!" The problem, as Kuriansky sees it, is that many career women are still looking for someone successful or socially prominent. The answer may be a taxi cab driver. Although her point—that women today may need different kinds of fulfillment than they did in the past—is valid, she strings what could be a one-page essay into a very long book, filled with—what else?—anecdotes "based on real people." So we have the story about Linda who dumps her date, Sam, for sexy Henri (names *have* been changed, but perhaps you guessed that). It's a mistake: Henri takes a powder. Also filling space are a number of quizzes to help women determine what they really want out of life, as well as the 10-step program to finding love where you least expect it. Plumbers and construction workers look out—the time of your time may be near. —*Ilene Cooper*

Lightner, Candy and Hathaway, Nancy.
Giving Sorrow Words: How to Cope with Grief and Get on with Your Life.
Warner, $19.95. 272p.

Lightner, famous for founding Mothers Against Drunk Driving (MADD), says in the autobiographical first chapter of this comprehensive adviser for the bereaved that it took her the five years she was involved in MADD to reach the point at which she could fully acknowledge and deal with her grief for the 13-year-old daughter whose hit-and-run death spurred her activism. Lightner's testimony is the first of many she and Hathaway use to make their points on a panoply of topics, from the cyclical nature of grieving and the customs of mourning, through the impacts different circumstances of death have upon the grief-stricken, to methods of helping children who are grieving and of taking care of oneself during the transition from "the person you used to be" before the death you are grieving "to the person you will become." Quite a considerable literature on grief has arisen, especially during the 1980s, but perhaps nothing in it speaks to as broad a prospective audience as carefully and practically as this book. —*Ray Olson*

Pennebaker, James W.
Opening Up: The Healing Power of Confiding in Others.
Morrow, $18.95. 256p.

Pennebaker argues that we literally worry ourselves sick. Bulimia, insomnia, and substance abuse can all be linked with repressing the natural urge to confess. He believes that talking about the horrors in our lives—be it childhood trauma, infidelity, failure, death, or the fear of natural disasters—is a healthier way of coping than "becoming stupid" (i.e., fixating on the superficial details of everyday life). This latter type of avoidance-behavior causes undue physiological stress, which in turn makes us more miserable (our "self-constructed paradox"). Pennebaker endorses prayer, therapy, support groups, writing, and talking into a tape recorder as valid methods of coping. In fact, his experiments show that, over time, people who confess in one form or another lead happier lives, with less frequent visits to the doctor. Interestingly enough, Pennebaker points out that intense negative and positive emotions produce identical physiological stress responses. Which means we should also admit our feelings of euphoria, instead of feeling guilty about gloating. So talk about it, and if it seems no one is listening, then write it down. It's such a relief. —*Kathryn LaBarbera*

Pibum, Sidney, ed.
The Dalai Lama, a Policy of Kindness: An Anthology of Writings by and about the Dalai Lama.
Snow Lion, $4.95. 152p.

"If we each selfishly pursue only what we believe to be in our own interest, without caring about the needs of others, we not only may end up harming others but also ourselves." So said the Fourteenth Dalai Lama (Tenzin Gyatso) in accepting the Nobel Peace Prize. That speech and various essays, interviews, and excerpts from selected writings make up this useful collection that provides a brief overview of His Holiness' life, personal growth, and philosophy. Other pieces discuss the man's daily routine, review current events in Tibet—whose cultural heritage and political freedom the Dalai Lama seeks to preserve from the vantage point of his Tibetan government-in-exile in India—and capture the Dalai Lama's words on such topics as kindness, compassion, reason, science, meditation, living sanely, etc. Clear, concise, interweaving practical discussion with things of a more ethereal nature, this offers a revealing look at one of the century's most remarkable individuals. —*Martin Brady*

Philosophy & Psychology

✓ **Signell, Karen A.**
Wisdom of the Heart: Working with Women's Dreams.
Bantam, $12.95. 336p.

Into a marketplace filled with self-help books that peddle little more than common sense comes this excellent introduction to dream analysis for women interested in using their dreams for personal growth. Those with no previous experience in such analysis receive foundational instruction on how to capture dreams and understand Jungian vocabulary. But even experts in dream symbolism will gain from Signell's provocative analyses of the dreams that betoken the traumas of one's life and help confront aggression, transform anger, and explore sexuality. Especially memorable are the dreams themselves, which, though briefly told, are resonant with symbolism: of the woman who, constantly needled by her siblings, dreamed of actually swallowing a sewing needle; or the woman who, in her dream of a Dolly Parton carnival ride, struggled to come to terms with her feminine fullness. —*Pat Monaghan*

Simon, Sidney B. and Simon, Suzanne.
Forgiveness: How to Make Peace with Your Past and Get On with Your Life.
Warner, $19.95. 240p.

A tough approach to resolving the disastrous effects of childhood trauma is given in the Simons' knowledgeable, dispassionate look at the process of truly letting go. Suzanne Simon was sexually abused by her father, and the calm certainty of a survivor—about what is true and necessary—is felt throughout the text, which seeks, with clarity and sympathy, to penetrate the shields that all victims must develop in order to move past fear, denial, self-blame, and anger. Other case histories recounted here are unfailingly convincing, as are the analysis and advice. —*Virginia Dwyer*

✓ **Solomon, Robert C.**
A Passion for Justice: Emotion and the Origins of the Social Contract.
Addison-Wesley, $22.95. 352p.

A much-needed book for general readers who have despaired of ethical philosophy as an intellectual game played by academic specialists. Justice, Solomon cogently insists, is not primarily a matter of abstract theorizing. Rather, it is an expression of personal character, rooted in emotions felt by ordinary people. The author indicts his professional colleagues for defining justice in the bloodless terms of politics and economics, while neglecting those sympathies and attributes of the heart that enable people to recognize and oppose injustice. In their hypotheses about the "social contract" and the "state of nature," modern intellectuals obscure rather than clarify the ethical demands of everyday life. Some readers will protest that Solomon listens too much to sociobiologists, others that his emphasis is too visceral, too unreflective. But most will welcome the critique of desiccated notions of justice and the appeal for compassion that motivates action. —*Bryce Christensen*

Tannen, Deborah.
You Just Don't Understand: Talk between the Sexes.
Morrow, $18.95. 324p.

You'll recognize yourself in Tannen's many entertaining examples of skewed conversations between men and women. Why do women feel offended when men offer advice instead of commiseration? Why do men sometimes think of women as nags? Tannen, a sociolinguist and author of both popular and scholarly books about communication, claims that males and females grow up in different cultures, even within the same family. While she's aware of the pitfalls of generalization, Tannen can still make a good case for gender categorization, and no one will deny that women and men frequently find themselves arguing over how things are said rather than the substance of the statement. Culling examples from her personal experiences, studies of communication of all age groups, even fiction and films, Tannen describes many situations in which people talk at cross-purposes. She suggests that understanding these ingrained habits of conversation will improve relationships. Free of jargon, this is a successful hybrid of psychology, sociology, and self-help. —*Donna Seaman*

Plants & Gardening

✓ **Anderson, Frank J.**
A Treasury of Flowers: Rare Illustrations from the Collection of the New York Botanical Garden.
Little, Brown/Bulfinch Press, $60. 176p.

A selection of 80 exquisite, rare, color prints from the "golden age of botanical illustration." Anderson, honorary curator of rare books and manuscripts at the New York Botanical Garden and author of a half-dozen previous books about plants, has chosen prints from 16 outstanding illustrated botany books published in Europe and Russia between 1675 and 1883. A great spectrum of plants is embraced, everything from jimsonweed to mountain laurel, rhubarb to blue waterlilies. Each of the original books and artists is described, and each full-page print (10-by-14) is accompanied by a pithy summary of the illustrated plant's lore including medicinal uses. Anderson is a cultured and fastidious narrator, not above slipping in cutting remarks on current affairs and their effect on the environment. A celebration of nature's floral wonders, as well as artistic triumph. —*Donna Seaman*

Brown, Jane.
Sissinghurst: Portrait of a Garden.
Abrams, $39.95. 136p.

Brown's previous book, *Vita's Other World: A Gardening Biography*, studied Vita Sackville-West's landscaping schemes at Knole and Long Barn. Now the author turns to Sissinghurst, the last and greatest of the gardens created by Sackville-West and her husband, Harold Nicolson. Actually, Brown goes back to Sissinghurst's medieval origins and documents the estate's development and decline over four centuries until it was reclaimed by Sackville-West as a country home in 1930. The book then records the planning and development of the garden over the next few decades and also credits the work of the people who helped the Nicolsons with their grand scheme as the property eventually became the responsibility of the National Trust. The other notable point in this book is a series of photographs taken by John Miller, which date from 1988 and 1989 after the great gales of 1987 uprooted much of the surrounding landscape; these photographs not only show the opening of splendid new vistas but also illustrate the current condition of the gardens. Notes, bibliography; index. —*John Brosnahan*

Ferguson, J. Barry and Cowan, Tom.
Living with Flowers.
Rizzoli, $40. 207p.

With the aging of the baby boomers has come a concomitant increase in interest in gardening and all things green and living. Three well-known experts—Ferguson as horticultural consultant, Cowan as free-lance writer, and Mehling as accomplished photographer—capitalize on this trend by combining their talents to create a floral travelogue. The text meanders through a variety of topics, touching on sources, settings, seasonal arrangements, gifts and special occasions, as well as technical details. Occasional sidebars, from using baby's breath to forcing bulbs, add a sense of structure to the narrative. This beautifully designed and illustrated book brings a world of wonder to gardeners and appreciators alike. Appended are listings of reputable mail-order catalog companies and nurseries, botanical and plant societies, and recommended readings. —*Barbara Jacobs*

Heriteau, Jacqueline and Cathey, H. Marc.
The National Arboretum Book of Outstanding Garden Plants: The Authoritative Guide to Selecting and Growing the Most Beautiful, Durable and Care-free Garden Plants in North America.
Simon & Schuster/Stonesong Press, $39.95. 292p.

An excellent reference guide listing 1,700 flowers, herbs, shrubs, trees, ground covers, vines, ornamental grasses, and aquatics—plants that Heriteau and Cathey call "carefree." The description of each plant gives information on growth rate and light, soil, and moisture requirements, as well as a rundown of its appearance. The book is an essential guide for serious gardeners. —*George Cohen*

✓ **Keen, Mary.**
The Glory of the English Garden.
Little, Brown/Bulfinch Press, $50. 256p.

If gardens of the past represent thoughts and aspirations and not merely horticultural technique, then this book's photographs alone will transport those weary of hedge clippers and hybrids back to this loftier gardening plane. Visually stunning, the work is equally impressive for its history of gardens and gardening. The photographs of unfamiliar English locations are incomparable in artful use of light and angle, while a readable and comprehensive text documents the history of inspired gardens and gardeners whose influences and abilities are evidenced throughout. From the chapter "Knots, Herbs & Flowery Meads," which begins with medieval gardens in Chaucer's day, to the concluding "Pottage, Peas, Peaches & Pineapples," a warm entreaty for a return to the kitchen garden, the photographs, illustrations, and words entwine with each other, providing a living space in which gardeners or gardeners-at-heart can be enveloped. *—Deanna Larson-Whiterod*

Lennox-Boyd, Arabella.
Private Gardens of London.
Rizzoli, $50. 224p.

Here are 39 of London's most beautiful private gardens, some of which the author designed herself. Lennox-Boyd describes their history, designs (some include black-and-white layouts), and types of plants. And there are 225 photographs, 80 in color. These lovely gardens include one surrounding a Victorian villa, another that is a strip 139 feet long and 25 feet wide sloping gradually down to the Thames, yet another that is six floors up on the roof of a building on Kensington High Street—a Spanish garden complete with Moorish pergolas, fountains and palm trees, an Elizabethan herb garden, ancient stone arches wreathed with wisteria, a grove of nut trees, and a stream filled with ducks and flamingos. These treasures are captured in Lennox-Boyd's lucid prose and John Miller's stunning photographs. *—George Cohen*

Lloyd, Christopher and Bird, Richard.
The Cottage Garden.
Prentice Hall Press, $29.95. 192p.

British authors/gardeners Lloyd and Bird look back in horticultural history to the English cottage garden of the Victorian period. Here in the charming profusion of old-fashioned flowers and in the informal sprawl of plants, they see an inspiration for modern garden landscapes. The authors interpret the cottage garden to include both flowers and vegetables, often in conjunction with one another in the same plot; they also show how to re-create such authentic plantings in a number of examples geared to specific purposes and effects. Appropriate species, garden features and accessories, and general details on garden planning and upkeep are illustrated with a large number of tempting color photographs that evoke the attractions that these gardens

Plants & Gardening

hold for gardeners, past and present. An appendix gives recipes and instructions for using garden produce and flowers. —*John Brosnahan*

Olwell, Carol.
Gardening from the Heart: Why Gardeners Garden.
Antelope Island Press, $24.95. 240p.

Olwell interviewed 21 men and women "who live to garden and garden to live." These diverse gardeners include a self-proclaimed "horticultural thrill seeker" in Berkeley, California, who combines odd plant forms with sculptures; a couple in their seventies who transformed windswept dunes into a desert garden on a three-quarter acre lot in Santa Clara, Utah; a Billings, Montana, gardener who raises vegetables and ornamentals despite a growing season that averages 134 days; and a gardener in Alaska who complains that "the biggest animal pests in our garden are moose: fortunately, the snowshoe hare haven't discovered our garden yet." Olwell divides her book into chapters on " The Garden as Paradise," " The Garden as Provider," " The Garden as Teacher," and " The Garden as Healer," and concludes with a 41-page appendix of information about pesticides and a glossary of gardening terms. Full-color photos of the eccentric gardeners enliven the pages of what is certainly the year's quirkiest gardening book. —*George Cohen*

Reddell, Rayford Clayton and Galyean, Robert.
Growing Fragrant Plants.
Harper, $35.95. 176p.

Encyclopedic in scope, this guide to the current trendy approach to home gardening—mixing scented flora—is richly illustrated and chock-full of advice for buying, growing, and harvesting different kinds of plants. The oversize volume features annuals and perennials, bulbs, herbs, vines, and even trees and shrubs. Practical tips abound, including preferred soil cultures and factors determining hardiness. Anecdotal accounts of working with the plants as well as plant histories add spice to a useful package. While the layout does nothing to accent the color and black-and-white photos, the pictures' clarity and attractiveness compensate. —*Robert Seid*

✓ **Tanner, Ogden.**
Gardening America: Regional and Historical Influences in the Contemporary Garden.
Viking/Studio, $40. 255p.

Lavishly illustrated with full-color photographs arranged in an attractive layout, this volume is more than the brief history of American gardening outlined in the first chapter. Moving geographically from the lush seaside herb and perennial gardens of the Northeast, through the sprawling azalea walks of southern plantations, to the windblown evergreens and rockeries of the Pacific Northwest, the book chronicles the diverse landscape of America in rich and vivid detail. Native prairies of the Midwest, desert oases of the Southwest, rose and water gardens of the Middle Atlantic states—in all, 50 gardens, both public and private, are examined from a historic as well as a horticultural point of view. Special gardens and techniques are featured, and there is even a section listing garden and estate tours open to the public with a short description of each. A book as varied and interesting as the many vistas it depicts. —*Robert Seid*

Poetry

Bell, Marvin.
Iris of Creation.
Copper Canyon, $17. 85p.

Bell's tenth collection follows closely on the heels of his *New and Selected Poems*. Reading these poems, one is immediately struck by the poet's range of styles and themes, by his unique view of the world, by the depth of emotion gracefully, effortlessly conveyed. In "Not Joining the War," for instance, Bell informs us almost offhandedly, "Lots of things sound like applause: / the dead hands of leaves in October, / or the slapping of tank treads in parade." He is as skilled with prose poetry as with the lyric, the genre he most often employs. His themes run the gamut from birth to death and love to loneliness, often presented with a surrealistic tinge or a Zen-like slant. In "Darts," we read, "The way the feathers follow the tip of the dart / is the way we can be when the wind's up," reminding us of a Western version of a koan. A major new collection by one of our finest and most acclaimed poets. —*Jim Elledge*

Booth, Philip.
Selves.
Viking, $16.95. 74p.

In his eighth collection, Booth offers a crystalline view of a landscape and a people—rural New England and its residents—that become, in the course of the book, representative not only of Booth and *his* part of the country but of all Americans and the entire U.S. Booth's chief talents are his ability to observe objectively and to capture on the page the cadences of contemporary speech. In "Game," for example, a hockey game and the between-period comments by "boys at the urinals" work in tandem to reveal subtly and occasionally humorously the poet's disgust over "our innate violence." Similarly, in "Old," the theme of aging unfolds, then folds back onto itself, only to unfold over and over in the manner of dialogue. What is revealed, finally, is the irony of aging: "they have aged again / to be children: / beyond control, they have gained / control. —*Jim Elledge*

Poetry

✓ **Clampitt, Amy.**
Westward.
Knopf, $18.95. 128p.

Clampitt ranges across the U.S. landscape—California, Kansas, Georgia—observing "the round earth's numbly imagined rim" ("John Donne in California"), "refineries, trellised and turreted illusory cities" ("Iola, Kansas"), and "thicketings / of juniper, bull brier / and yaupon" ("Savannah"). In characteristically lush, though at times impenetrable, language, she views the terrain metaphorically, reporting that the human spirit somehow survives, despite the hardships it encounters—the lack of love, the violence, the poverty. Nowhere in the book is this idea more succinctly expressed than in "Vacant Lot with Pokeweed": "notwithstanding . . . / . . . wholesale upheaval and dismemberment, weeds do not hesitate." Clampitt's fans will be delighted by her fourth collection. —*Jim Elledge*

Erdrich, Louise.
Baptism of Desire.
Harper, $16.95. 96p.

Most poems in this book were written between two and four a.m., "a period of insomnia brought on by pregnancy," and Erdrich provides brief notes on "scraps of the night's reading," including religion, myth, and science, as well as the Shoppers' Cable Network. Some lines do need the notes to "shed slant light," especially those tied to Catholic doctrine, but the best poems combine the domestic and the metaphysical—the light of the refrigerator and the bowl of the night sky—with a startling clarity and a sense of painful struggle sometimes reminiscent of Dickinson: "And the spirit in the sinking light / holding its own sharp elbows." The exquisite poem "The Flood" moves from humdrum basement appliances to images of birth, nature, and leaving home ("it was as if I could escape only by abandoning / everything"); in the "aftermath," the wires are still "alive and dangerous." Erdrich's poetry is a "snake of the double helix," as well as of "the orange rind"; it's of "the long reach, the margin"; of contained rage. Those times awake, alone, are "hard hours." —*Hazel Rochman*

Hall, Donald.
Old and New Poems.
Ticknor & Fields, $24.95. 244p.

Hall has gotten steadily better, as this selection of 40 years' work attests. The later the poem, the more lucid in syntax and diction it is likely to be, and the more like good prose it reads. The subject matter—death, personal memories, and the delights of the rural places Hall has lived in—hasn't changed much over the years. Still, there has been some change, evidenced by several fine dramatic monologues in the latter half of this volume that, along with some prayers and the occasional wry squib (humor does not come easily for Hall), are the most impressive things in the book. In many other poems, however, although always a good, solid craftsman, Hall is plagued by an inability to know when and how to end the poem, so that the reader either flags in attention or is ultimately disappointed. But the good's definitely good, and there's more of it than even-more-respected contemporaries such as Richard Wilbur and Maxine Kumin afford. —*Ray Olson*

✓ **Laux, Dorianne.**
Awake.
BOA Editions, $16. 63p.

Now this is what poetry's supposed to be! Take the first poem, "Ghosts," in which the poet describes herself watching a young man, inside a neighboring house, paint his kitchen. A woman joins him, and their obvious love makes Laux suddenly feel that "I'm getting too old / to sit on the porch in the rain." At this poignant realization many poets would have stopped. But Laux brings us inside, where she mourns that she's also " Too old to dance / circles in dirty bars." And too old for love: "too old for that, the foreign tongues / loose in my mouth." She remembers all the girls she was, the lovers she could have followed, and takes us into the bedroom, where she nests with "a man who sleeps in fits, / his suits hung stiff in the closet . . . When he rolls his body against mine, I know / he feels someone else. There's no blame." In poem after poem, Laux takes us on journeys into a particular life so specifically realized that she finds the common ground of all lives. —*Pat Monaghan*

Levertov, Denise.
A Door in the Hive.
New Directions, $16.95. 96p.

If *A Door in the Hive* is a lesser collection than its predecessor, *Breathing the Water*, it is only because the longest piece in it, "El Salvador: Requiem and Invocation," is the libretto of an oratorio and incomplete without music. Full of political, as well as humane, passion, it is less polished than the shorter poems that make up the rest of the book. Of these, the most immediately impressive—including luminous revisionings of the Annunciation, the Nativity, the harrowing of Hell, and the dubiousness of St. Thomas—are overtly religious, full of both mature wisdom and the profound ingenuousness that is the finest innocence. Many other poems—reactions to art, to nature, to the physical evidence of history (e.g., "A Stone from Iona," "The Past (II)")—are as well crafted, as inviting to repeated reading as any this truly invaluable poet has ever written. —*Ray Olson*

Morgan, Robin.
Upstairs in the Garden: Selected and New Poems, 1968–1988.
Norton, $19.95. 242p.

It's hard for feminists of a certain age to read some words of Morgan's without weeping: "I want a woman's revolution like a lover / I lust for it, I want so much this freedom . . . that I could die just / with the passionate uttering of that desire." Those are the heady words of a movement's youth—of the youth of a generation of women. This collection brings together some of those early famous works with later, less passionate utterances. Overall, it shows Morgan to be an uncannily accurate transmitter of the zeitgeist. If her prosiness is sometimes irksome, the propulsive quality of her work more than compensates. —*Pat Monaghan*

✓ **Sadoff, Ira.**
Emotional Traffic.
Godine, $15.95. 81p.

Sadoff's fifth collection relies heavily on memory—the poet's and his reader's—or, as he tells us in "In the House of the Child," the volume's introductory poem, "nothing's been discarded here, / though the cabinets have been emptied out, / and the closet's scent is purely cedar." Nostalgic but never sentimental, emotional but never weepy, Sadoff explores the rooms of the house of memory top to bottom, its lawn, its driveway. His is a quiet but dramatic poetry in which the small things and events of this world are shown to be fraught with meanings beyond the obvious, in which battles are waged between the seen and the unseen, between light and darkness—sometimes without a clear-cut victor. Early in the book, Sadoff states, "A world without predators: the parent's dream," with the word *dream* suggesting not only a goal but a fantasy, neither of which the parent will ever obtain. The predators that life engenders—real or imagined, beyond our control or easily vanquished—are his targets. His aim is always true: a bull's-eye time and time again. —*Jim Elledge*

Seth, Vikram.
All You Who Sleep Tonight.
Knopf, $18.95. 64p.

Coming cold to the poetry of Vikram Seth can be a shock. For here are rhyme, meter, formal stanzas as precise and well managed as those of a nineteenth-century versifier. Moreover, Seth is not afraid to express commonplace feelings with utter lucidity. He would be cloying and sentimental were he not also carefully contemporary in his diction and fully capable of the learned allusion. He is, unsurprisingly, neither American nor English, but Indian, although well acquainted with California, England, and China, in addition to his homeland. His internationalism seems to have freed him from belaboring strictly personal experience—a habit that makes so many poets so tiresomely obscure and hermetic—and freed him to express the emotional tenors of such common matters as love lost and love remembered, observing landmarks as a traveler, and thinking deeply about everyday things and events. At any rate, the emotions and cogitations no less than the language and formal qualities of his poems are surprisingly accessible, even more surprisingly intelligent and humane (the latter especially in six exemplary dramatic monologues). —*Ray Olson*

✓ **Soto, Gary.**
Who Will Know Us?
Chronicle, $8.95. 69p.

In his fifth collection, Soto turns his attention and sharply honed skill on childhood, religion, family life, and his travels, among other topics. His style is straightforward and down-to-earth, his manner genuine and relaxed, his voice quiet but assured, even when, as at the conclusion of the volume's title poem, he ruminates, "The train. Red coal of evil. / We are its passengers, the old and young alike. / Who will know us when we breathe through the grass?" Soto's work entices because of the ease with which it approaches, then deals with the most basic yet complex human experiences. In "Inventory of a Vacant Lot," for example, he speaks succinctly of the life force, simultaneously mysterious and frightening, benign yet aggressive: "The grass, once cornered by cement, / Now itches for life and feeds on the tiniest cracks." A master at discovering in ordinary, common, sometimes trite or comical situations the soul's struggle with the world, and with itself, Soto has few rivals on today's poetry scene. A must read. —*Jim Elledge*

✓ **Stern, Gerald.**
Leaving Another Kingdom.
Harper, $19.95. 256p.

There are several reasons why Gerald Stern is one of the most admired of contemporary American poets, and this selection of his work over 20 years bears testimony to them. Item: his biblical verse form—long unenjambed lines filled with repetition. Instance: "I will give you Sappho / preparing herself for the wind; / I will give you Voltaire / walking in the snow." Item: his incredible ability to capture fiercely emotional states without being maudlin. Instance: "I am going to be unappeased at the opossum's death / I am not going to stand in a wet ditch / with the Toyotas and the Chevies passing over me / at sixty miles an hour / and praise the beauty and the balance / and lose myself in the immortal lifestream." Item: his vast arrogance tempered with real humility. Instance: "I am studying paradise and the hereafter, / a life beyond compare, / a great log thrown up for my own pleasure, / an unbelievably large and cold and beneficent sun." How can you resist a poet like this? Don't try. —*Pat Monaghan*

Williams, Miller.
Living on the Surface: New and Selected Poems.
Louisiana State Univ., $24.95. 184p.

Covering 30 years, Williams' new collection is culled from eight previous books, to which is added a generous portion of new poems. These are sharply honed observations of the day-to-day—the depths to which we fall, the ruts in which we find ourselves, and the edges to which we're often pushed. In "On the Death of a Middle-Aged Man," for example, Williams defines a life of boredom and pathos succinctly and gracefully: "Beverly who wished his mother wanting a girl again / had called him something at best ambiguous,

Popular Culture

like Francis or Marion." Wit and humor flow in and out of the collection, at times counteracting, at other times emphasizing, the despair of the lives being observed. In "Fly Me to the Moon," two people find no love in their relationship and, lacking it, resign themselves to something else: "This is not what he thought it would be, but nothing else is, either. She would agree." Pain and despair, portrayed honestly and never sentimentally, characterize much of this must-buy collection. A sobering look at contemporary life. —*Jim Elledge*

Popular Culture

Baker, Russell.
There's a Country in My Cellar: The Best of Russell Baker.
Morrow, $20.95. 360p.

Arranged in a topical fashion, Baker's collected essays (his "greatest hits") offer a review of recent American history, fads, and politics. In 1962 Baker began to write "a casual column without anything urgent to tell humanity." He even called himself the "nothing columnist" because he was told to write about nothing too serious. Having written in the 1960s and 1970s, Baker couldn't avoid serious topics, however, considering all the social upheaval that marked those decades. But here he keys in on a range of lighter subjects as well. He reports the results of a family-style Charles Kuralt mission—traveling around the U.S. looking for colorful stories in quaint places. He talks about how vacations have changed— "from the old motels where you backed the station wagon up to a door and shoveled children, turtles, cats, luggage and Grandmother into the room" to the new ones that look "larger than Kennedy Airport." Baker's columns reveal the times in all their richness and idiosyncrasy. —*Denise Perry Donavin*

Dengrove, Ida Libby and Martin, Frank W.
My Days in Court: Unique Views of the Famous and Infamous by a Court Artist.
Morrow, $18.95. 256p.

Court artist and two-time Emmy winner Dengrove makes observations on criminal behavior and capital punishment while word sketching the great and near-great who passed through the courts of New York and New Jersey during her 15 years on assignment for NBC. Here, Dengrove describes how she prepared herself as an artist, how she got her start at the network, and what the working conditions are like. Tidbits are featured throughout on the famous and the infamous, from Yoko Ono to Son of Sam. More fun than a year's subscription to the *Enquirer*. Includes twoscore of the artist's illustrations. —*Cynthia Ogorek*

Dodson, Bert.
Nuke II: Another Book of Cartoons.
McFarland, $13.95. 128p.

A second helping (after *Nuke*) of the most trenchant, forthright, liberal-left strip cartoonist going. Nuke ("the world's cutest doomsday weapon," says Paul Ehrlich in the introduction) is still the star here, but other characters also take center stage. Those include the immediately fetching Bitsy and Barney, a homeless boy and his dog; Captain Billy and the Immune System Squadron, tirelessly fighting off interior pollution ("Red alert in the gastric sector— Heavy ingestion of donuts and fries"); Mr. Brain, a walking example of his namesake; and of course, every good political cartoonist's stock company of the leaders of the day. Usually leftist cartoonists are so heavy-handedly ideological they might as well be illustrating the *Communist Manifesto*. Not Dodson, who may be a Marxist, but of the Groucho variety: take, for example, Nuke on the shutting down of unsafe tritium plants—"Hey, this is no time for safety! Our *security* is at risk!" —*Ray Olson*

Feldman, David.
Why Do Dogs Have Wet Noses? And Other Imponderables of Everyday Life.
Harper, $17.95. 272p.

Whoever he is, Feldman, "formerly in the programming department of NBC-TV," is making hay with the reading public through his collections of "imponderables." With the assistance of his devoted readers, Feldman poses such questions as, "Why Are Racquetballs Blue?" "How Did the Football Get Its Strange Shape?" "Is There Any Meaning to the Numbers in Men's Hat Sizes?" and "Why Do Male Dogs Lift Their Legs to Urinate?" The answers are supplied with the consultation of experts. Feldman concludes the proceedings discussing "frustables . . . mysteries that have defied our frequent efforts to answer them." He offers 10 new frustables for his readers to respond to, and provides a "frustables update" based on his previous volumes, e.g., *When Do Fish Sleep?* The humorous questions and their interesting answers add up to a volume of guaranteed popularity and fun. —*Martin Brady*

✓ **Gerber, Ernst and Gerber, Mary.**
The Photo Journal Guide to Comic Books.
Gerber Publishing/Quality Books, $145. 856p.

Ernst Gerber may be the consummate comic book collector. An engineer, he invented the Mylar bags that are the preferred preservative container for individual issues of his passion. In the two 10-by-14-inch volumes at hand, he now spills out the accumulated wisdom and record of his career, and in apple-pie order. On the vast preponderance of the pages are row upon row of comic book covers, filed as sets by most familiar titles (or in rare cases, such as 3-D comics, most distinctive common attributes). Earlier and later titles of the same publication appear under the famous one (e.g., *New Comics* and *New Adventure Comics* are with their renowned third title, *Adventure Comics*). Each cover is reproduced in color as rich and convincing as in the

Popular Culture

finest art book. Nearly all covers for each title-set are shown, and each title-set is followed by a table of information for each issue, pictured or not. The far fewer pages of text contain, in three-column format and Gerber's personal voice and style, his memoirs of his obsession, his advice on all aspects of collecting, a thorough key to using the work as a reference and price guide, and his assessment of the social and historical significance of comic books. Overall coverage is 1933–65. In affording an exhaustive gallery of pop-cultural artwork, Gerber's achievement is invaluable, let alone its nonpareil importance as a collectibles tool. It's stunning, simply stunning. Title, artist, and character indexes. —*Ray Olson*

Groth, Gary and others, eds.
The Best Comics of the Decade, 1980–1990: Vol.1.
Fantagraphics Books, $35. 128p.

The editors have chosen a dangerous name for their anthology, at least from the vantage point of widely read adult comics fans, who'll surely feel that they've overlooked many stories that are a lot better. Nevertheless, this is a fine selection with a scope broad enough to encompass examples of syndicated features such as Jules Feiffer's weekly strip and Matt Groening's "Life in Hell" as well as the panoply of subject matter and styles to be found in such comics magazines as *Weirdo, Raw,* and *Prime Cuts.* There's another bit of Texan colonial history from Jack Jackson, author of *Secret of Santa Saba*; a story about the vicissitudes of the daily strip artist's life from Bill Griffith, creator of "Zippy"; some impassioned political advocacy on behalf of Canadian Japanese interned during World War II; and "Pictopia," a lush bit of comics noir from mainstream comics writer Alan Moore, author of, among others, *Watchmen*. With 28 selections in all, an outstanding anthology. —*Ray Olson*

Kane, Bob and Andrae, Tom.
Batman & Me.
Eclipse Books, $39.95. 155p.

The Caped Crusader's dad, so to speak, tells all—at least about his association with "Batman" and other comics—in an ingenuous memoir that's as naive and speedy as . . . well, as a comic book. Kane, whose flair for cartoon action made him one of the most admired and imitated comics artists, surprises with some of his attitudes. He says he'd really rather have drawn funny comics all these years (but the examples of his humorous efforts reproduced herein raise nary a smile). Further, he resents 1960s pop artists' comics-style paintings, although they brought overdue respectful attention to his medium. And he's forthrightly, however innocently, male-chauvinist (but then, isn't it right that the guy who gave us Batman and Robin feels "I've had better relationships with male friends than women"?). Still, Kane's recollections make sunny reading that no serious fan of his famous creation will want to miss. Appropriately, the text is lavishly illustrated, with a drawing or photo on virtually every page and a hefty color section consisting of three early Batman adventures and newer Batman lithographs and paintings. "A Batman Chronology" is appended. —*Ray Olson*

Kohn, Alfie.
You Know What They Say.
Harper, $17.95. 256p.

You know what they say about swimming right after a meal? Well, it isn't true, according to Kohn, who has researched the "fact quotient" of 81 truisms. Is necessity the mother of invention? Do blonds have more fun? Is a woman's work never done? Is laughter the best medicine? Does grouping students by ability allow them to learn better? Find the answers here. As the questions imply, Kohn focuses on an interesting mix of clichés, popular myths, and common practices. The responses are backed by an extensive array of references. An ideal browsing book. —*Denise Perry Donavin*

Stern, Jane and Stern, Michael.
Sixties People.
Knopf, $24.95. 251p.

In their introduction the Sterns comment that, in retrospect, the 1960s "were as laughable as they were profound." What made them laughable were people—the type of people that so many tried to be. These types, or archetypes, are the focus here. They include perky girls, playboys, folkniks, hippies, rebels, young vulgarians, surfers, English mods, and, last but not least, "Mr. and Mrs. Average American." In analyzing and explicating these characters, the authors have produced an astonishingly perceptive, wonderfully funny book that's guaranteed to produce flashes of recognition and elicit laughter from just about any individual who came of age in that decade. And though at times their writing style and thematic approach may strike readers as a bit too derivative of Tom Wolfe's efforts, they (unlike Wolfe) communicate a kind of ironic fondness for their subjects that nicely complements the bitingly critical tone that informs many of their observations. Thankfully, though, the Sterns pull the whole thing off without any tiresome displays of nostalgia: they seem to be having too much fun with the era and its people to wax sentimental. Most readers will respond in kind. —*Steve Weingartner*

✓ **Stern, Jane and Stern, Michael.**
The Encyclopedia of Bad Taste.
Harper, $29.95. 384p.

It's so bad, it's great! The Sterns, the authors of such kitsch classics as *Elvis World*, now explore the whole, weird wonderful world of bad taste. Definitions of bad taste are a very subjective thing, and the Sterns are nothing if not subjective. Still, you can't say they don't know their *hazarye* (Yiddish for "junk"). It's all here—polyester, Jell-O, fuzzy dice, and a few items you might not have expected: "Breasts, Enormous," Hummel ware, and panty-hose crafts. As the Sterns so eloquently put it, "Could there be any less likely inspiration of creativity than a used pair of panty hose? Panty hose aren't all that lovely even fresh out of the box, with their shriveled nylon legs hanging from a baggy, cloth-crotched panty. As for old, smelly, torn ones: Well, it takes a certain type of genius to find beauty in them waiting to be released." And it takes a certain type of genius to catalog all the world's absurdities and explain how they have shaped pop culture. It also takes writers with just the right amount of wit, irreverence, and style to make us truly appreciate the power of such neglected art forms as, say, velvet painting: "The reputation of velvet painting does not come from bravura technique alone." The Sterns are good–so good they make you want to have a Spam sandwich and watch a telethon. —*Ilene Cooper*

Sudjic, Deyan.
Cult Heroes: How to Be Famous for More Than Fifteen Minutes.
Norton, $10.95. 160p.

British writer Sudjic cheerfully exposes the greed and calculation behind the invented cult status of today's celebrities. Business people cull cult heroes from a variety of mass arenas: sports, movies, music, fashion, art, even architecture. Corporate identities are developed and star products sold. Consumers buy Elizabeth Taylor perfume, Porsche sunglasses, and over-priced designer clothes because they crave reassurance—they're acquiring part of the aura of approval. While it's commonplace to bemoan the style-over-substance attitude, it's fun to get the inside dope on just how vacuous it all is. Sudjic describes name licensing, discusses the "signature" products of Pierre Cardin, Giorgio Armani, Calvin Klein, and Ralph Lauren, and sniggers at the new artist celebrities such as Julian Schnabel, who are more concerned with making the pages of *Vanity Fair* than *Artforum*. Even architects are getting a piece of the action: Michael Graves designs teakettles. Generously illustrated, the captions make for additional good reading. This reasonably priced paperback is not serious criticism but a lighthearted reality check that will attract readers because of the very lures it discusses. —*Donna Seaman*

Religion

Adler, Mortimer J.
Truth in Religion: The Plurality of Religions and the Unity of Truth.
Macmillan, $18.95. 156p.

Adler employs the principle of the unity of truth to attempt to discover, amidst the plurality of the world's religions, where the diverse aspects of a single truth may be found. His essay is divided into five parts: a discussion of the restrictions to be placed upon pluralism when concerning matters of truth; the logical considerations underlying the pursuit of truth and the distinguishing of matters of truth from matters of taste; the task of the philosophy of religion, as distinguished from mythology; the logic of truth and a discrediting of dualism; and further miscellaneous issues to be resolved in regard to the question of truth among the religions. A clearly written essay on a timely and controversial topic. —*Sheila McGinn-Moorer*

Alnor, William M.
Soothsayers of the Second Advent.
Revell, $7.95. 222p.

For almost as long as he's been gone, people have been wondering when Jesus would come back. Turn on much of today's religious broadcasting, and it's apparent this question is still on a lot of minds. Some have devised elaborate methods to pinpoint the moment. Alnor, a religious writer, believes Christ is returning, but unlike his more vocal brethren, he knows neither the date nor the hour and thinks that speculating on these matters only delays the event. Naming various preachers, he lists bad predictions, chapter and verse, and offers quotes from the Bible to prove that the time of the Second Coming is no one's business but God's—despite the great profits made by many who sell books and pamphlets on the topic. Of course, the money only comes in while the predicted date is in the future. *88 Reasons Why the Rapture Will Be in 1988* has probably been remaindered by now. —*Ilene Cooper*

Andrews, Lynn V.
The Woman of Wyrrd.
Harper, $17.95. 214p.

Andrews has acquired quite a following since writing her first women of power adventure, *Medicine Woman*, in 1983. Seven books later, she has traveled the world with her teachers Agnes Whistling Elk and Ruby. Here Andrews travels in Dreamtime to medieval England. She witnesses a previous life in which she is Catherine, a young student of the teachings of Wyrrd, "the study of power and magic in ancient Europe." Her mentor is Grandmother, by turns a kindly old woman or a young beauty accompanied by a giant falcon. Catherine is initiated into various mysteries and falls in love with a dashing wizard. The narrative has all the elements of a romance, yet is infused with spiritualism. While Andrews' books can be read as fantasies, almost as the Nancy Drew stories of the New Age, she claims that her tales are chronicles of actual experiences, and indeed, her accounts mirror many other tales of shamanistic encounters. Intriguingly good reading. —*Donna Seaman*

✓ Black Elk, Wallace and Lyon, William S.
Black Elk Speaks Again: The Sacred Ways of a Lakota Shaman.
Harper, $16.95. 160p.

Lakota shaman Wallace Black Elk, adoptive grandson of the famous Nicholas (author of *Black Elk Speaks*), was persecuted as a young man for practicing his traditional native American religion. But he endured. Now no one calls him "devil worshiper," or says he is possessed. Instead, he is a pipe-bearing elder and repository of sacred knowledge. He is also a mystic whose knowledge of other realities is difficult to capture in the restrictive grammar of English. We can thank anthropologist William Lyon for not over-Englishing Black Elk's words; the shaman could have become a Lakota Shirley Maclaine had his loopy digressions and hypnotic repetitions been smoothed into conventionality. This is the real thing. It should become a classic of its kind. —*Pat Monaghan*

Religion

Fricke, Weddig.
The Court-Martial of Jesus: A Defense of the Jews against the Charge of Deicide.
Grove Weidenfeld, $18.95. 288p.

Though Fricke offers no new evidence in his examination of who killed Jesus, his defense of the Jews is particularly solid. He examines the Gospels in great detail, pointing out their inconsistencies and using them to show how little can actually be known about Jesus from the canonical accounts. After a fine-tuned look at the events surrounding the Crucifixion, he concludes that Jesus was tried, sentenced, and executed by the Romans and that there was no trial before the Sanhendrin. Fricke, a German trial lawyer, served as the court-appointed defense counsel for a Nazi war criminal. This experience led him to search out the biblical roots of anti-Semitism. Unlike other, overly dense books on the same topic, this one is both well reasoned and readable. Though the trial of Jesus is the book's centerpiece, many other theories, such as the controversy surrounding Jesus' marital status, supply additional intrigue. —*Ilene Cooper*

Greeley, Andrew M.
The Catholic Myth: The Behavior and Beliefs of American Catholics.
Scribner, $21.95. 320p.

Greeley debunks the popular myth that American Catholicism is virtually moribund. Employing an impressive array of concrete sociological data to support his thesis, he asserts that Catholicism is thriving in the U.S. Though many American Catholics have lost faith in the institutionalized hierarchy of the Church, they remain assiduously devoted to the essential poetry of their religion. According to the author, these seemingly paradoxical truths are compatible when considered in terms of the intriguing concept of the sacramental imagination. An insightful analysis of the current state of the American Catholic community. As always, Father Greeley's fact fares better than his fiction. —*Margaret Flanagan*

Greeley, Andrew M. and Neusner, Jacob.
The Bible and Us: A Priest and a Rabbi Read Scripture Together.
Warner, $24.95. 320p.

The readers of this provocative book come away with three points: First, the Bible is particularly interesting when looked at as a whole. Second, all those who read the Bible interpret it from the standpoint of who they are and who or what guides them. Third, *all* people can approach, read, and interpret Scripture whether they hold advanced degrees in religion or not. Thus, Greeley and Neusner begin a journey that promises to enlighten not only them, but the readers who accompany them, as well. After an introduction ("Reading Scriptures Together"), the authors alternate chapters, sometimes agreeing with, sometimes arguing against, sometimes criticizing or confronting the other. They cover both the Hebrew Scriptures and the Christian New Testament. In the course of the conversation, each tries to understand the things most cherished by the other. Finally, they talk about the possibility of dialogue between Judaism and Christianity, with Neusner denying it and Greeley confirming it. —*Mary Deeley*

Keizan.
Transmission of Light: Zen in the Art of Enlightenment.
North Point, $29.95. 256p.

"Once Zen master Yunju said, 'If you want to realize such a thing, you must be such a person; once you are such a person, why worry about such a thing?' Hearing this, Daopi was spontaneously enlightened." Attributed to the fourteenth-century master Keizan, *Transmission of Light* is one of the major writings of the Japanese Soto school of Zen Buddhism—a collection of stories about the "awakening" of 53 successive generations of Zen masters. Each tale begins with a short story much like the one above, includes explanation of its meaning and the need for *satori* (i.e., enlightenment), and ends with a short verse, sometimes a veritable pearl, which best conveys the master's principal teaching. Satori, seen as only the beginning and not the end, is attained after many years of searching along the Way that everyone, regardless of race, creed, or gender may, perhaps should, follow. Excellent reading for a clearer understanding of Zen, especially given translator Cleary's choice, insightful introduction to the Soto school. —*Jerry Alber*

Minerbi, Sergio I.
The Vatican and Zionism: Conflict in the Holy Land, 1895–1925.
Oxford, $24.95. 272p.

This addition to Oxford's Studies in Jewish History series was first published in Hebrew in 1985, then in Italian in 1988, and is now translated into English. Minerbi examines the Holy See's policy toward Zionism as a political movement, eschewing analysis of the broader subject of relations between Christianity and Judaism. Part I describes the complex relations between the Holy See and the major powers concerning Palestine from the end of the nineteenth century to the mid-1920s. Part II concerns the evolution of the Vatican's position on Zionism during the same time period, a position that included the premise that a Jewish government for the Palestine region was intolerable to Catholic interests. Although a bit esoteric, this book is nevertheless an engrossing and balanced history of a troubled time. —*George Cohen*

Myers, Kenneth A.
All God's Children and Blue Suede Shoes: Christians & Popular Culture.
Good News/Crossway, $8.95. 213p.

The discussion of the relationship between Christianity and culture is not new, but Myers takes a different tack. Whereas his predecessors have compared the message of popular culture with the content of the Christian faith, Myers follows the more Niebuhrian strategy of comparing structures. Myers attempts to discern the message of popular culture, which is conveyed by its forms (e.g., rock 'n' roll, soap operas) and makes a twofold comparison—first, of the popular message with the Christian message; and second, of the popular secular forms with the popular Christian forms. Myers suggests that Christians have made a serious mistake by shaping the popular forms of Christian culture after the popular secular forms. Insisting that form is content, that it conveys an ethos, Myers argues that many aspects of popular

Christian culture are self-contradictory, saying one thing in words and yet another via form. Myers' obvious evangelical Protestant standpoint may narrow his potential audience a bit, and yet his honest critique certainly encourages broader participation in the discussion among thoughtful people. —*Sheila McGinn-Moorer*

✓ **Pelikan, Jaroslav, ed.**
The World Treasury of Modern Religious Thought.
Little, Brown, $29.95. 615p.

In this remarkable anthology, Pelikan, a formidable religious historian in his own right, brings together a rich selection of religious ideas that will provoke and enlighten readers. His choice of writers is nothing if not eclectic. The book begins with Dostoevsky's intriguing parable from *The Brothers Karamazov*, "The Grand Inquisitor," in which a Spanish cardinal argues to a returned Christ that the freedom God granted humanity is its most unbearable burden. The book is then divided into eight sections: "The Unbeliever," " The Will to Believe," "The Grandeur of God," "Reverence for Life," "The Reconstruction of Tradition," "Love Abides," "Visions of the Other World," and "Faith and Freedom." Among the writers who step forward to state their case within these parameters are Camus, Nietzsche, Buber, Jung, Kant, Einstein, Schweitzer, Emerson, Tillich, Bonhoeffer, Black Elk, and Scholem, as well as various representatives of the Buddhist, Hindu, and Moslem traditions. The book's strength is that it contains no answers (or perhaps too many). Thus, the freedom to believe what one must about religious matters is sustained as a wonderful, terrible burden. —*Ilene Cooper*

Wiesel, Elie and O'Connor, John.
A Journey of Faith.
Donald I. Fine, $18.95. 92p.

A conversation between Wiesel and New York City's Cardinal O'Connor, initiated by the former and moderated by public television host Gabe Pressman. The subjects of the four hours of taped dialogue (later reduced to one hour of television programming) between these two eminent religious leaders range from the Holocaust to childhood memories of revered parents. Wiesel recalls intoning his daily prayers while imprisoned in Auschwitz, where his father died; O'Connor offers no defense when Wiesel criticizes Pope Pius XII for not issuing a plea to aid the Jews. The discourse is intellectual yet informal. Prejudices are aired and common ground is uncovered. An accessible volume, filled with the words of warm, caring men whose experiences and viewpoints are of universal significance. —*Denise Perry Donavin*

✓ **Wills, Garry.**
Under God: Religion and American Politics.
Simon & Schuster, $22.95. 402p.

Frustrated by other reporters' lack of understanding of religious influences upon the 1988 presidential campaign, the scholarly American political journalist has written what may be the definitive study of religion and American politics. Anchoring his argument that understanding Protestantism—especially evangelical Protestantism—is crucial to understanding American politics, Wills recovers much fascinating lost, suppressed, and misunderstood history while accounting for the varying fortunes and foibles of five candidates: the official evangelicals Robertson, Jackson, and Bush; the apostate evangelical Hart; and the rigid secularist Dukakis. He demonstrates how the famous Scopes "Monkey Trial" of 1925 was *not* the legitimating victory for Darwinian evolutionary theory it's thought to have been. Wills explains the fundamentalist "premillenial dispensationalist" theology embraced to great political effect by Ronald Reagan and Dan Quayle. He traces how the apocalyptic sensibility that later animated the "premils" was forged by African American slaves into a communitarian theology that, before it empowered Martin Luther King, Jr., Jackson, and Andrew Young, informed the unusually compassionate, humble leadership of Abraham Lincoln. Moving beyond the religious motives and motivators of particular politicians, Wills devotes the last three sections of his study to the controversies over pornography, abortion and sexism, and separation of church and state. Throughout, he writes with magisterial authority and unsimplistic clarity, and he is not afraid to render the occasional adjudicating interpretation. Easily the most engrossing and informative— and far and away the best written—book on American politics in many, many moons. —*Ray Olson*

✓ **Wolpe, David J.**
The Healer of Shattered Hearts: A Jewish View of God.
Holt, $18.95. 185p.

Wolpe's reflective essay should be of interest to anyone who is grappling with the larger, bewildering spiritual issues that beset most of us at one time or another. It is not so much that Wolpe uncovers something new in humanity's attempt to forge a relationship with God. As a conservative rabbi, he dutifully touches upon the importance of finding the friendship that God can offer, and he contemplates the place of the deity in an evil world. What elevates this treatise, though, is not necessarily what Wolpe says, but how he says it. Using the Torah as well as rabbinic teachings and legends to frame his questions, he leads readers into their own inner explorations. Whether making a point—"With the consciousness of the Divine, the chance to mitigate our savagery is better"—or musing on the longings of a people—"For millennia, Jews have followed [a] tightrope of infuriated faith"—Wolpe's writing, both its style and its substance, ignites the inquiring mind and, thus, turns his book into a meditation of the highest order. As with the best religious writers, Wolpe doesn't always offer answers, but he gently yet persistently asks the right questions. —*Ilene Cooper*

Science & Nature

✓ **Bailey, George.**
Galileo's Children: Scientific Discovery vs. the Power of the State.
Arcade, $24.95.464p.

In a work both timely and profound, Bailey depicts the scientist as heretic in three different but complementary incarnations: Galileo, Robert Oppenheimer, and Andrei Sakharov. Although the comparisons between these three geniuses sometimes lapse into false analogies, the overall synthesis represents a remarkable feat of imagination and intelligence. The author generally sides with the scientists in their confrontations with inquisitorial authorities, yet he resists the simplifications of melodrama. Indeed, he traces a troubling line of influence leading from Galileo to the Communist leaders who persecuted Sakharov, the book's culminating figure. Because of the breakneck pace of events in the Eastern bloc, some of Bailey's comments about communism are already passé, but his fundamental analysis remains convincing and urgent. Challenging for general readers, this volume nonetheless deserves widespread attention among those trying to fathom the cultural contradictions of the modern world. —*Bryce Christensen*

Bishop, Jerry E. and Waldholz, Michael.
Genome: The Story of the Most Astonishing Scientific Adventure of Our Time—the Attempt to Map All the Genes in the Human Body.
Simon & Schuster, $21.95. 351p.

The lengthy subtitle identifies the scope and theme of this fascinating book. Two reporters for the *Wall Street Journal* permit general readers to share in the high intellectual excitement of mapping unknown terrain—the genes of the human body. Remarkably lucid explanations (together with helpful diagrams) dispel much of the mystery surrounding the new technologies permitting scientists to decode the genetic basis for heredity. But the forays into laboratories do not obscure the human motives and personalities of the biological pioneers trying to understand (and eventually to prevent) the suffering caused by Huntington's disease, muscular dystrophy, cystic fibrosis, and other genetic diseases. Yet new possibilities for unraveling human genes raise troubling questions—explored in the final chapters—about abortion, insurance policies, and eugenic ambitions. The authors provide timely insights into scientific questions that are rapidly becoming social and political dilemmas. —*Bryce Christensen*

Book of North American Birds.
Reader's Digest, $32.95. 576p.

An uncommonly sensible approach to the field guide from America's most determinedly popular magazine: a gallery of color paintings of some 600 U.S. and Canadian species arranged—and this is its genius—by rockbottom common-language, rather than scientific, sorting terms. So the chapters are entitled "Birds of Prey," "Large Land Birds," "Ducklike Birds," "Gull-like Birds," etc. Besides its portrait, each bird is represented by scientific name, a map of its distribution, summary physical and behavioral information, and a descriptive-anecdotal note written in complete sentences. A final chapter, "Special Collection," presents rare species three-to-a-page, and a "Traveler's Guide to Birding Sites in North America" concludes. —*Ray Olson*

Brown, Michael H.
The Search for Eve.
Harper, $22.50. 368p.

You've probably heard the story: Berkeley scientists have looked at mtDNA and concluded that all people today are descended from a sub-Saharan African woman who lived about 200,000 years ago. Eve *vincet omnia*, one might say. Of course, this isn't really *Eve*. There were no doubt lots of other bonny lasses running around at the time—indeed, whole populations of them. And quite frankly, paleoanthropologists found this suspicious. Berkeley said that Eve's kids came out of Africa and, *without interbreeding*, socked it to all native hominids in Asia and Europe. But what about all those bones that suggested gene flow, transition, and . . . well, something less violent? Then there were technical questions. Mitochondrial DNA is matrilineally inherited so is never mixed up with Daddy's genes. But what is its relation to nuclear DNA (which makes us what we are)? What is its real rate of mutation? (Two percent wrong and we're several hundred thousand years off on the date.) In telling the story of this riveting debate, Brown simplifies the terms, repeats himself too often, sometimes gets too cute, but almost accidentally captures the rich dynamics of scientific dispute. —*Stuart Whitwell*

✓ **Burroughs, John.**
Deep Woods.
Gibbs Smith/Peregrine Smith, $9.95. 224p.

An affordable and thoroughly delightful collection of John Burroughs' famous essays. The selection is gleaned from seven of his best-known books beginning with an essay on the Adirondacks from *Wake-Robin* (1871) and concluding with a piece about Yosemite from *Time and Change* (1912). While some readers may find his style a bit romantic and quaint—and Burroughs *is* unabashedly poetic—his enthusiasm and warmth lift his prose beyond sentimentality. Burroughs is generous with his observations and delight in the natural world, whether reflecting on how the change of seasons affects people's moods as much as the landscape, or describing "wild and desolate" scenery where "mountains [look] as if they had been swept by a tornado of stone," or a "stream cradled in rocks, detained lovingly by them, held and fondled in a rocky lap or tossed in rocky arms." A timely compilation of the works of one of our most influential naturalists. —*Donna Seaman*

Science & Nature

Science & Nature

Carson, Rob.
Mount St. Helens: The Eruption and Recovery of a Volcano.
Sasquatch Books, $28. 160p.

Carson recounts the May 18, 1980, eruption of Mount St. Helens and the decade of geological events in its wake. Surrounded by stunning photos, his newspaperly accessible prose tots up lives lost, describes scientific efforts to predict and analyze the eruption, and chronicles the herculean effort to clear rubble from waterways and roads. Both praising and criticizing the work of agencies such as the U.S. Geological Survey, the Army Corps of Engineers, and the U.S. Forest Service, Carson drives home the point that fighting nature is often a losing battle. He examines the wonderful natural rebirth of the area through the eyes and comments of prominent geologists, biologists, and foresters, hinting at the underlying conflicts between the interests and financial priorities of science, business, and tourism in disaster areas. A resplendent popular survey of one of the nation's most compelling recent events. —*George Hampton*

Cowell, Adrian.
The Decade of Destruction: The Crusade to Save the Amazon Rain Forest.
Holt, $19.95. 400p.

Irish filmmaker Cowell first came to Amazonia, as a student, in 1957. *The Decade of Destruction* is the record of his experiences in and impressions of this region, which he has filmed up to the present. Publication of this book coincides with release of his films as a five-hour PBS "Frontline" special, but the diary itself merits acquisition. Cowell has seen firsthand the encroachment of the government of Brazil and private developers on this great rain forest, and his keen descriptive abilities and straightforward approach afford his readers a good view as well. A common strain to his varied adventures (with forest indigents, rubber tappers, gold miners, etc.) is his concern with the *social* environment. Throughout his adventures with activists—the brothers Villas-Boas, Jose Lutzenberger, and Chico Mendes—and people of the forest, he characterizes Amazonia as a place of transformation. Those who invade the forest for exploitation soon become those who would save it. At times the coverage seems dull and less pointed, but this should not severely restrict accessibility. —*Angus Trimnell*

DiSilvestro, Roger L.
Fight for Survival.
Wiley, $29.95. 304p.

The companion volume for the series of eight Audubon television specials aired on PBS and TBS in the summer of 1990. The goal is to provide sound ecological knowledge about endangered species and environments in the popular nature show/book format, à la "Life on Earth." The topics are wolves, sharks, sea turtles, dolphins, and cranes, as well as ancient forests, an arctic wildlife refuge, and poaching. Narrators include such luminaries as Paul Newman, Robert Redford, Michael Douglas, and Meryl Streep. The book captures the visual beauty of the series through its photographs and provides additional context and information within its well-written, anecdotal, and observation-filled text. —*Donna Seaman*

✓ **Dorsey, Gary.**
The Fullness of Wings: The Making of a New Daedalus.
Viking, $19.95. 342p.

Basically, this book is a documentary of human-powered flight and the culmination of a team's effort to build and fly such a plane over the Aegean Sea from Crete to Santorini, the same route as the mythical Daedalus. What makes this special are the personalities of the people involved, among them, John Langford, who grew up building model rockets and at MIT found he was able to shift between the world of engineering "hackers" and government bureaucrats. Then there are "Guppy" and "Parky," Langford's buddies who formed the core group for the Daedalus project. There's more to this story than a little aeronautics history, however. It's the thrill of human-powered flight accompanied by practical solutions for the improbable and tinged by the enchantment of engineering. Magical and exciting (like the original Daedalus flight must have been). —*Cynthia Ogorek*

Flegg, Jim and others.
Poles Apart: The Natural Worlds of the Arctic and Antarctic.
Stephen Greene, $29.95. 192p.

The "others" assisting zoologist Flegg are ace wildlife photographers Eric and David Hosking, so prepare to be dazzled. For here—in well-matched two-page spreads, on full pages, and in a profusion of smaller sizes often laid out on pastel pages or inset on larger photos—the colorful products of their cameras appear as resplendent as ever. They illustrate exemplary short reviews not just of the flora and fauna of both poles and their seas, but also of both regions' geological and cultural development, their exploration by Europeans, and their gross similarities and dissimilarities. In all, a gratifyingly gorgeous overview of the earth's extremities. —*Ray Olson*

✓ **Gribbin, John.**
Hothouse Earth: The Greenhouse Effect and Gaia.
Grove Weidenfeld, $18.95. 272p.

The terms *greenhouse effect* and *Gaia* are bandied about a lot but aren't always well defined. Gribbin, respected author of *The Hole in the Sky* and *In Search of Schrödinger's Cat*, among others, goes beyond mere definitions to provide a comprehensive explanation of the mechanics and implications of global warming within a compelling review of earth science, including discussion of the carbon cycle, weather patterns, and the role of oceans and forests. *Gaia* is used to express the concept that "the living systems of Earth can be regarded as a single unit which regulates the environment in such a way as to maintain conditions suitable for life." The term *life* does not necessarily include human life. In other words, the earth will adapt to the changes we have made in ways that we will find unpleasant, perhaps even fatal. For

Science & Nature

people who dismiss this as alarmist, Gribbin provides detailed scientific evidence, including the methodology used, proving that the earth is indeed heating up. Gribbin hopes that if we act now, we can slow down the pace of change and work toward adaptation—the key to survival. Lucid and blunt, this is a must-read for anyone interested in the essential literature of ecology. —*Donna Seaman*

Gormley, Gerard.
Orcas of the Gulf: A Natural History.
Sierra Club, $24.95. 216p.

Gormley's observation of orcas, the killer whales, is an engrossing feat of natural history reporting. The lives and habits of these sea creatures are vividly described as the writer covers their existence from a whale's point of view as a family group or pod moves through the Gulf of Maine off the New England coast. The book details both relationships and conditions within the pod from birth to death and also examines the orcas as hunters who live off prey of all sorts, from small fish to other species of whales larger than themselves. While the reputed savagery of the orcas is placed within the context of their environment, some of the descriptions are quite bloody and harrowing. Human observation of the orcas is also chronicled, as the author re-creates such events as the great tuna massacre in Provincetown harbor and describes various aspects of cetacean research. —*John Brosnahan*

✓ **Hiss, Tony.**
The Experience of Place.
Knopf, $19.95. 214p.

Add Tony Hiss to the list of influential *New Yorker* staff members, including Bill McKibben and John McPhee, who write impeccably about nature and humanity. Hiss has approached the topic of land use, both urban and rural, through a lucid and well-researched study of our inherent relationship with landscape. He believes that heightened awareness of our experience of place will stimulate environmental sensitivity. Beginning with a discussion of simultaneous perception, the complex and subtle way our brain-body systems respond to our surroundings, Hiss leads up to descriptive analyses of how different environments affect our physical and mental well-being. The theme is developed into a bid for regional growth management and the permanent maintenance of rural areas. An observer par excellence, Hiss expresses and elevates our subconscious feelings about where we live and work and arouses our instinct to protect the type of places we need—landscapes that exhilarate us. —*Donna Seaman*

✓ **Kline, David.**
Great Possessions: An Amish Farmer's Journal.
North Point, $16.95. 235p.

The little essays of this delightful collection originally appeared in the Amish magazine *Family Life.* They are observations of creatures, mostly birds, and intriguing plants from ginseng to the American chestnut that Kline and his family have made on and near their farm. They are arranged into four seasonal sections and one more, and they are prefaced with a talk Kline gave at a conference on Christianity and ecology, a talk about the pleasures of farming in the Amish way, i.e., the pleasures of plowing, sowing, reaping, shocking, but overarchingly, of "nurturing and supporting all our community—and that includes people as well as land and wildlife"; in short, of being proper stewards of God's creation. Interwoven with these working pleasures (more than once, Kline speaks of sighting a bird while plowing, while mowing) are the recreational pleasures of wildlife appreciation that the rest of the book's contents memorialize. No one has written this kind of keenly observed, personal, reverent, and wondrous natural history better than Kline. His little book may well become a quiet classic in the manner of *The Compleat Angler* and *The Natural History of Selbourne.* —*Ray Olson*

✓ **LaBastille, Anne.**
Mama Poc: An Eyewitness Account of the Extinction of a Species.
Norton, $19.95. 281p.

Global overviews of environmental conditions are staggering in scope—but there's nothing like sustained observation of one habitat to bring home the hard truth about ecological damage. Well known for her experiences in the Adirondacks, as chronicled in her popular *Woodswoman* and *Beyond Black Bear Lake,* LaBastille has a second identity: Guatemala's Mama Poc, protector of a unique flightless water fowl, the giant grebe, or poc. LaBastille first noticed the birds on a trip to volcano-ringed Lake Atitlan in 1960. She returned five years later, ostensibly for a month or so, to photograph the birds and write an article, but ended up spending over 20 years studying pocs and trying to halt their decline. Amid a life in Guatemala that was filled with adventure, revelation, and love, LaBastille created the country's first national wildlife refuge, and became the first female game warden in the Western Hemisphere. She recounts the challenges and hardships of field work, the joy and productivity of empathic friendships, and the thorniness of the politics of ecology. Sadly, Mama Poc also has the distinction of being the first ecologist to "document the entire process of an extraordinary extinction of a species." While this is a remarkable ecological history, it is also a record of the personal evolution of a resolute, courageous and passionate human being. —*Donna Seaman*

Medawar, P. B.
The Threat and the Glory: Reflections on Science and Scientists.
Harper, $22.50. 204p.

A posthumous collection of essays, lectures, and book reviews, this volume brings together short expressions of the curiosity and wisdom that won so many admirers for Medawar during his lifetime. A Nobel laureate with rare gifts as a writer, Medawar illuminates not only the findings of modern biologists, but also the very nature of scientific discovery. A number of the pieces effectively challenge the notion that mere collection of facts will

Science & Nature

Science & Nature

uncover natural laws; rather, Medawar argues that scientific breakthroughs come in flashes of imaginative insight, mysterious and not altogether unlike the inspiration of poets and artists. In the longest work here—the Reith Lectures of 1959—Medawar anticipates "the future of man" with remarkable timeliness, outlining many of the very issues ethicists now struggle with in deploying new genetic technology. Some unevenness and repetition are inevitable in a work of this sort, but readers trying to understand the cultural significance of science will welcome its publication. —*Bryce Christensen*

Mitchell, John Hanson.
Living at the End of Time.
Houghton, $18.95. 223p.

Mitchell's *Ceremonial Time: Fifteen Thousand Years on One Square Mile of Land* drew praise for its extensive research and unusual conception of time. Mitchell again explores the links between past and present in this account of living in a cabin in the woods. When he and his wife separate, Mitchell builds a rustic cabin—no running water or electricity—on their land. He states that "the woods were the only place I could afford to live," but it is actually a deep attachment to his small parcel of wilderness that keeps him in the woods outside of Boston. (This is Thoreau country, just 16 miles from Walden Pond.) Mitchell enjoys the simple life of gardening, scything, hiking, and visiting with his eccentric neighbors. In addition, he reads a lot, particularly Thoreau's journals and those kept by Mitchell's father, who lived in Shanghai from 1914 to 1917 and traveled to Japan where he climbed Mt. Fuji. Dreams are an important element in the journals and in Mitchell's account, as are experiences that have a mystical aura. The author's immersion in the past and intimacy with the land blurs time, and history manifests itself mysteriously in the present. Mitchell reports the extraordinary with reticence, leaving things open to interpretation. His insight into Thoreau adds new dimensions to our understanding of that legendary figure and to our complex relationship with nature. —*Donna Seaman*

Newman, Arnold.
The Tropical Rainforest: A World Survey of Our Most Valuable Endangered Habitat—with a Blueprint for Its Survival.
Facts On File, $40. 256p.

A 25-year veteran of tropical rain forest research and field work, Newman deftly defines the dynamics of rain forests and their contribution to the environment. He calls the forests "living cathedrals," the "lungs of the planet," and "our planet's most astounding expression of life, the very womb of creation." His prose is, fittingly, lush and passionate, describing the diversity, complexity, and wealth of these unique and essential biomasses. Newman explains, sympathetically, the reasons the rain forests are cut down but makes it clear that the forests provide far more benefits alive and well than cut down for short-term gains. He covers all aspects of the consequences of destroying the forests, including the primary problem—the increase in global warming— as well as the damage done to cancer research when as yet unanalyzed botanicals with medicinal potentials are obliterated. A bit more sophisticated than John Nichol's *The Mighty Rainforest*, this volume also boasts numerous photographs and charts. —*Donna Seaman*

✓ **Rachels, James.**
Created from Animals: The Moral Implications of Darwinism.
Oxford, $19.95. 256p.

Intellectual honesty is perhaps the rarest and subtlest of virtues. Yet the humility it demands is so great that when it is embodied in a person like Charles Darwin, the disciples are few and scattered. Darwinians, of course, abound: his theory of descent by modification uncovered the most fascinating fact of all (we are all descended from a common species), and the whole of modern biology rests upon it. But what about the moral and intellectual implications of this perception? What can we learn from the man's patience, his honesty, his sweet reasonableness? Rachels' book goes only a little way toward answering these questions, but it is a fair beginning; its shortcomings only point out how much remaining work there is to do. One implication of Darwin's work is that our attitude toward *all* life must change: claims of human dignity and the sacredness of human life are meaningless if they cannot be extended to *all* species. In Rachels' hands, this argument is turned into a strong and effective plea for animal rights, but this by no means fleshes out the "moral implications" of Darwinism. Still, the book contains an excellent summary of Darwin's life and work and starts us off on the right track. Every student of the humanities should read it. —*Stuart Whitwell*

The Reader's Digest Illustrated Book of Dogs.
Reader's Digest, $21.95. 384p.

A comprehensive, handsomely illustrated volume on the subject of man's best friend, revised and updated from a 1982 edition. Included are sections on dogs and civilization, identifying dogs, the purebreds, care and feeding, and kennel clubs. Within these sections are chapters that touch on a wide range of dog-related topics, such as the prehistory of dogs, canine psychology, the socialization of dogs, and education and training. All in all, an excellent "everything you need to know" compendium, though the chapters dealing with health and medical problems are especially interesting and informative. —*Steve Weingartner*

Regis, Ed.
Great Mambo Chicken and the Transhuman Condition: Science Slightly over the Edge.
Addison-Wesley, $18.95. 320p.

Regis, author of *Who Got Einstein's Office?* (Addison-Wesley, 1987), strikes just the right note of skepticism in this look at the latest in science's fringe communities. This is the stuff of B-movies. A guy "surgically removes" his mother's head from her body so that she can be reanimated in the future. Others babble about the potential of nanotechnology and the "downloading" of people's minds into computers so they can live forever (plenty of backup copies), free of the constraints of a body. You can even travel via fax. Or perhaps you'd rather be a

Science & Nature

transhuman? Regis feels that we are in the "bold days of fin de siècle hubristic mania," cocky enough to think we can improve on nature. But while we're snickering at these mind-twisting concepts, we have to remind ourselves how impossible things we now take for granted seemed 50 years ago. Science fiction has a way of becoming fact, like it or not. *—Donna Seaman*

Revkin, Andrew.
The Burning Season: The Murder of Chico Mendes and the Fight for the Amazon Rain Forest.
Houghton, $19.95. 317p.

Revkin's book is an impersonal, thorough-going, and adulatory account of the life and assassination of Chico Mendes, Brazil's Lech Walesa, written by a knowledgeable environmental journalist. From humble origins in an obscure corner of Brazil, Mendes learned how to read, then became a labor organizer whose *empates*—occasionally confrontational demonstrations by rubber tappers against ranchers and developers—slowed down the rain forest's rapid destruction and won international support. With lush descriptions of the forests, historical backgrounds of the rubber trade and the governmental efforts to settle the Amazon, numerous interviews with key players, investigative reporting on the alleged assassins and on the environmental effects of deforestation, Revkin successfully depicts the lawlessness, violence, and striking beauty of the Amazon. *—Benjamin Segedin*

Ross, Anne and Robins, Don.
The Life and Death of a Druid Prince: The Story of Lindow Man, an Archaeological Sensation.
Summit, $19.95. 173p.

Lindow Man is the name given to remains found in an English peat bog of a corpse that has been proven to be at least 1,800 years old. Celtic scholar Ross and archaeobotanist Robins met as contributors to the official British Museum publication on this archaeological discovery (*The Body in the Bog*). Using evidence gathered from stomach contents (Robins' specialty) and the body's physical appearance, as well as known events in Celtic history, the two authors surmise that this person was a Druid prince from Ireland who was sacrificed to help turn the tide in the Roman invasion of England. As the authors delve further into the Lindow Man's bizarre death, they speculate on just what his origins were and the meaning of his apparent triple execution. Conjecture vies with documentation in this fascinating volume, which will best suit those with a strong stomach (Ross is quite explicit in detailing her research). Whether or not this discovery is *the* breakthrough in providing insights into Celtic and Druidic history, the authors' story is a fascinating one. *—Denise Perry Donavin*

Savage, Candace.
Wolves.
Sierra Club, $29.95. 159p.

Ninety-seven color photographs of North American wolves in the wild high-light this attractive, fascinating book. Among its many striking images are those showing wolves at play, wolves on the hunt, wolves courting, and a pack of wolves howling in a group sing-along. Savage's accompanying captions and text are amiable in tone and highly informative in content. She informs us that wolves and humans are alike in their social organization; that wolves often howl simply for the pure joy of expressing themselves; that wolves love to play, and will take time to do so even while engaged in such activities as the hunt for food. We also learn the good news of how wolves, once nearly extinct over a wide range, are making a comeback both in their habitats and in the estimation of humankind. —*Steve Weingartner*

Scott, Jonathan.
The Great Migration.
Rodale, $35. 159p.

The sine qua non of the world's largest wildlife preserve (the Serengeti-Masai Mara complex of Tanzania and Kenya) is the nomadic wildebeest upon which the great predators synonymous with Africa subsist. Scott here applies his triple skills as writer, artist, and photographer to this undomesticated cattle's life cycle. Regular readers of African wildlife literature will find nothing much new in the text yet should appreciate its grace and clarity. But as they were with those in *The Marsh Lions*, they'll be blown away by the photos. Big, dramatic, brilliant colored visions of the wildebeest, their stalkers, and fellow herbivores—both still and in vibrant, almost audible action—these pictures are displayed generously on nearly foot-high pages and marred only by some one- eighth-inch mismatchings in across-the-gutter images. A wonder-inducing natural history essay. —*Ray Olson*

Shoumatoff, Alex.
The World Is Burning.
Little, Brown, $18.95. 400p.

While Andrew Revkin, in *The Burning Season*, is invisible and reserved in his coverage of Chico Mendes, Brazilian rubber tapper and defender of the rain forests, Shoumatoff becomes a character interacting with his subjects, asking more probing questions, and presenting a more complex picture of the events surrounding the murder of Mendes and the environmental crisis facing the Amazon region. Supportive of Mendes and his position, though not uncritical, Shoumatoff interviews friend and foe alike, including Mendes' alleged killers, the reputedly murderous Alves da Silva family, and comes up with a different kind of story. Not only do we have the tale of Mendes' life and death, but we have a picture of the aftermath: Brazil and the world's reaction to Mendes' murder, Hollywood's battle for the rights to the story, and Brazil's chronic failure to prosecute the alleged killers. (A film is now in development

Science & Nature

based on a Shoumatoff piece in *Vanity Fair*, to be produced by Robert Redford and directed by Steven Spielberg.) —*Benjamin Segedin*

Young, Louise B.
Sowing the Wind: Reflections on the Earth's Atmosphere.
Prentice Hall Press, $17.95. 224p.

Young has brought the grace of expertise and an appreciation of natural beauty to this sensitive study. The first section describes the structure of the "fragile envelope" that surrounds our planet. Young recounts tales of early and dangerous explorations of the upper atmosphere and explains, in general, the relationship of weather systems to the sun and life on earth. The second section covers three major threats to the atmosphere: the warming of the earth, the destruction of the ozone layer, and acid rain. Young's explanations are comprehensible and imaginative. No alarmist, she bemoans the crisis mentality that clouds the issues and encourages a balanced approach, embracing both sustained research, to learn more about what we don't know, and rapid action based on what we do know, such as the fact that CFCs do destroy the ozone layer. —*Donna Seaman*

Social Issues

Brenneman, Richard J.
Deadly Blessings: Faith Healing on Trial.
Prometheus, $21.95. 375p.

Brenneman takes a dramatic journalistic approach to a question of current popular (and legal) concern: Does the state have the right and/or responsibility to intervene in medical matters if a decision is based on religious belief? Such cases have arisen time and again involving Christian Scientists, but Brenneman shows that the frequency of such incidents is increasing and the scope broadening to include New Age types of psychotherapy and "psychic surgery." By examining three controversial court cases, Brenneman illuminates the difficult issues connected with such faith-healing attempts. Brenneman presents a detailed and readable survey of the legal history of such cases, showing the intricacies of the unavoidable conflict between parental or familial rights to act upon religious beliefs and the state's responsibility to afford the weak the full protection of the law. Highly recommended. —*Sheila McGinn-Moorer*

Buckley, William F.
Gratitude: Reflections on What We Owe to Our Country.
Random, $16.95. 192p.

Mr. Conservatism revives one of the *Four Reforms* he proposed a while back, namely, a term of humanitarian service by every young citizen. As Buckley envisions it, one's stint as, say, a nursing-home orderly, teacher's assistant, or park maintainer, would ideally be undertaken between high school and college. Essentially voluntary, service would be encouraged by both incentives—especially financial assistance with further schooling—and sanctions, such as driver's-license suspension. The scheme would succeed, Buckley argues, if administered by the states, if it is not made part of a war on poverty or some other package of political nostrums, and if military service is *not* an alternative to it. Its intent would be, more than to benefit those receiving services, to foster camaraderie among the service givers and to provide them an organized way to repay the debt they owe society for their nurturance. Although befogged by his characteristic fustian, Buckley's ideas this time are considerably more attractive than outrageous—so much so that liberals may well warm, rather than burn, to them. —*Ray Olson*

✓ **Callen, Michael.**
Surviving AIDS.
Harper, $18.95. 243p.

Good things come in threes: witness the third excellent AIDS dissenter's book this year. Like Michael Fumento (*The Myth of Heterosexual AIDS*), Callen believes the media and officialdom have distorted the epidemic. Like John Lauritsen (*Poison by Prescription*), he believes AZT, the only approved AIDS drug, is dangerous and ineffective. His central thesis, however, is that AIDS is, as Kidd and Huber (*Living with the AIDS Virus*) say, "a *treatable* chronic disease." He ought to know; he is alive and active more than eight years after his own AIDS diagnosis. He bolsters his own testimony with compelling, frequently entertaining interviews with a dozen other long-term survivors (four have died since summer 1989, but even they lived two or more years after Callen interviewed them). He precedes these stories with a first section decrying "the propaganda of doom" promulgated by AIDS bureaucrats, ignorant journalists, and even some activists more anxious about political leverage than the needs of persons with AIDS. He follows them with a section of general and specific survival advice gleaned from his own and others' experiences. For those directly affected by AIDS, this is the book of the year. For everyone else, it's a rich learning experience, uncommonly well and personably written. —*Ray Olson*

Chiras, Daniel D.
Beyond the Fray: Reshaping America's Environmental Response.
Johnson Books, $17.95. 210p.

Chiras teaches environmental science and has written three college textbooks on the subject. His educational skills serve him well in this clearly stated assessment of the environmental movement. Chiras feels that the public is beginning to recognize the problems, and what is now needed is a proactive approach, beyond reactive legal actions and protests. Deep change in our way of thinking can lead to the creation of a "sustainable society" patterned after nature, says Chiras, who offers practical recommendations for bringing environmentalism into the mainstream on a permanent basis. His sympathetic criticism of the environmental movement is refreshing and right on target as he berates the large organizations for their wasteful use of direct mail and argues for more unified and strengthened tactics. Carefully considered and well researched, this is a constructive contribution to environmental thought. —*Donna Seaman*

✔ **Commoner, Barry.**
Making Peace with the Planet.
Pantheon, $19.95. 239p.

In the 20 years since the first Earth Day, much has been said about the environment, but little has really been done about it. While emissions of lead, DDT, and PCBs have been reduced, present dioxin levels are increasing the incidence of cancer, CFCs are destroying the ozone layer, synthetic pesticides and fertilizers are contaminating water and poisoning our food and wildlife, and our garbage is overrunning our landfills. While agencies like the EPA and old-line environmental groups opt for a Band-Aid approach—cooperating with industry, seeking compromise, and treating symptoms—Commoner and grass roots organizations such as Greenpeace attack the problem at its core. Aware that the path to survival is complete elimination of pollution sources, Commoner doesn't mince words. He's blunt and thorough in his analysis, critical of the shortsightedness of industry, the risk-benefit game and the notion of "acceptable risk," and George Bush's proposal of selling pollution rights on the free market. Laying down guidelines, Commoner makes plausible the transition to organic farming, recycling, solar power, and other alternatives to ecologically unsound practices (even suggesting a price tag for this conversion at $470 billion a year for 10 or more years). Commoner injects his commentary with a streak of optimism; he is no naive soapboxer, but a learned, reasonable man of science, aware of market considerations and the urgency of this mission. Sources; index. —*Benjamin Segedin*

Crowley, Patricia.
Not My Child: A Mother Confronts Her Child's Sexual Abuse.
Doubleday, $19.95. 320p.

While the names and a few details have been changed to protect the innocent, this is the true story surrounding the revelations about the Wee Care Preschool, located in a comfortable upper-middle-class New Jersey suburb. Describing the same incidences of child-molestation that Manshel covered in *Nap Time*, Crowley—a newspaper editor and the mother of one of the children involved—examines the emotional and behavioral problems that cropped up in both the children and their families as a result of the abuse. (It took three years to bring the case to trial, but the accused teacher was convicted on 115 counts.) Writing this book was apparently therapeutic for Crowley; it will also be helpful to other parents and service agencies who must deal with similar problems. —*Maurine Hoffmann*

DeMott, Benjamin.
The Imperial Middle: Why Americans Can't Think Straight about Class.
Morrow, $18.95. 256p.

DeMott deserves credit for his deceptively simple thesis: Americans live in a class society but believe deeply in equality. And so we promulgate "the rationalizations that help us suppress consciousness of social differences," according to the accomplished cultural critic, who here offers the fruits of his close readings of entertainment, news, history, and the institutions of education and politics. The inequalities that Paul Fussell views with transcendent irony in his commendable *Class* (Summit, 1983) envelop the author as well as the readers of *The Imperial Middle.* This is a fascinating portrait of our nation in the modern age. —*Roland Wulbert*

Elkington, John and others.
The Green Consumer.
Penguin, $8.95. 374p.

America's present pollution problems and ideas for an improved environment give context to the confusing options facing concerned consumers. (For example, more than 500 disposable diapers are dumped per second into America's limited landfills—and those dumped today will only begin to decompose by the year 2300.) This book raises a "green" consciousness by listing products and services that work toward environmental preservation. The consumption of products—from cars, groceries, personal care items, and home energy and furnishings to gardening, gifts, and traveling—and the purchase of environmentally sound substitutes are pursuasively presented. Here is an effective antidote to environmental scares, placing the power of choice and responsibility for the earth in the hands and pocketbook of each consumer. —*Deanna Larson-Whiterod*

✓ **Faux, Marian.**
Crusaders: Voices from the Abortion Front.
Birch Lane Press, $19.95. 246p.

Faux profiles six activists—four pro-choice, two pro-life—in the hottest national policy debate going, including the attorney who argued against Missouri's abortion restrictions before the Supreme Court in *Webster* v. *Reproductive Health Services*; the director of the St. Louis clinic that brought the suit; Randall Terry of the radical pro-life organization, Operation Rescue; one of Terry's disciples, a born-again Christian single mother who once had an abortion; a black woman striving to bring pro-choice women and women of color together; and the thoughtful president of Catholics for a Free Choice. Faux treats them in as much depth as they would allow her (Terry was too suspicious to talk much) or she could otherwise plumb, homing in on their most important abortion-related experiences and activities, past and present. She labors to be fair and impartial to all, despite her own pro-choice sympathies. Still, some will think she hasn't found attractive enough pro-lifers to balance her four exceptionally competent, knowledgeable, and intelligent

Social Issues

advocates of choice. Regardless, her effort is one of two outstanding recent books—Tribe's *Abortion* is the other—that bring significantly more light than heat to the abortion imbroglio. —*Ray Olson*

Feather, Frank.
G-Forces: Reinventing the World: The 35 Global Forces Restructuring Our Future.
Morrow, $21.95. 454p.

As one recent song proclaimed, "The future's so bright I gotta wear shades." Perhaps Feather listened to it while composing this optimistic preview of events for the next half-century. The crystal ball used for the task is an impressively marshaled welter of data on present social, technological, economic, and political trends, an approach he styles as the "4-STEP" method for thinking about the future of humanity. The author is certainly ambitious, if not audaciously certain, about his predictions on subjects ranging from agronomy to world governance. The only thing impeding the transformation of today's trends into tomorrow's prosperous and equitable reality is obtuse human thought. Thus this impassioned exhortation: "The barrier to a harmonic global future is our purely mental and parochial thinking about a whole host of issues." And indeed, challenges to parochial orthodoxies permeate the book. Environmentalists steamed at atmospheric warming, for instance, or Luddites terrified by biotechnology, will not be amused by Feather's tickling them for their axiomatic faiths. But one must admit that he is an ecumenical iconoclast: since sacred American cows like individualism and capitalism are on the wane, they must be replaced by something called "socialistic entrepreneurialism." One proposal Feather makes to achieve this blissful oxymoronicism is the levy of a global equalization tax (one almost shudders to think of the means that would be necessary to impose it). Clearly there is plenty between these covers to inspire or offend any socially cognizant person, so this Feather should be put in most caps. Bibliography; index. —*Gilbert Taylor*

Fox, Michael.
Inhumane Society: The American Way of Exploiting Animals.
St. Martin's, $18.95. 259p.

Fox, a well-known veterinarian and syndicated columnist, minces no words in a thoughtful look at the way society inhumanely treats animals. It seems that no one is immune from Fox's attack as he even rails against the cruel practices in the agriculture industry, where piglets have their tails amputated to prevent tail biting and poultry are debeaked and declawed. This harsh treatment of farm animals and the deplorable conditions under which laboratory animals are kept is symptomatic of a "lack of ethical awareness," according to Fox. Pet owners are urged to obtain animals from animal shelters and to refrain from buying genetically altered "designer" cats and dogs. A searing, sobering, one-sided viewpoint offering workable suggestions and ideas for saving animals and improving the environment. —*Sue-Ellen Beauregard*

Kinsella, James.
Covering the Plague: AIDS and the American Media.
Rutgers Univ., $22.95. 299p.

Journalist-scholar Kinsella surveys how America's news media have reported AIDS and generally finds them wanting. Too few competent scientific and medical reporters were in place when the epidemic began. Too many editors were wary of AIDS because they felt its predominantly gay victims came from a negligible minority. Too many newspersons—especially TV anchors—were squeamish about using sexually and anatomically explicit language and thus misrepresented the malady's communicability and fostered hysteria and prejudice. Often a combination of all these factors rendered major news providers (*New York Times*, Associated Press, TV networks) ineffective, while smaller outlets (*San Francisco Chronicle*; the gay community paper *New York Native*; National Public Radio) became the authoritative information sources for the general public. The big boys dropped the ball on AIDS, Kinsella concludes, mostly because they weren't personally affected by it; whereas the minor-leaguers performed well because of reporters who were gay or had AIDS-stricken friends or family members. This situation constitutes a telling critique of the Fourth Estate's commitment to its vaunted ideal of objectivity. Cleanly and clearly written sociology as fascinating as it gets. —*Ray Olson*

MacDonald, J. Fred.
One Nation under Television: The Rise and Decline of Network TV.
Pantheon, $24.95. 335p.

A fluid and fact-filled history of television—"the most important social and cultural force in the U.S. during the past four decades." MacDonald starts with the early days and shows how the original broadcast standards dictated TV's format and paved the way for domination by the powerful networks. He examines network programming trends and issues, including commercials, within a social context, decade by decade, discussing such touchstones as race, violence, sex, and profanity. Different types of shows—comedy, crime, sports, and televangelism—are analyzed, as are the implications of political reporting. The author also tracks the policies of the FCC and the effects of deregulation and multimedia conglomerates. Noting how ill-prepared the networks were for the rapid growth of cable and the ramifications of VCR use, MacDonald concludes with a question: Will free television survive? A discerning overview. —*Donna Seaman*

Manes, Christopher.
Green Rage: Radical Environmentalism and the Unmaking of Civilization.
Little, Brown, $18.95. 304p.

Manes is a member of a radical environmentalist group called Earth First!—named in honor of Edward Abbey's *Monkeywrench Gang*. Radical environmentalists engage in "ecotage," actions such as tree-spiking, blockades, and "siltation" (pouring abrasives into bulldozer crankcases). Manes has written a cogent, in-depth explanation of the philosophy and sense of urgency behind ecotage, and a report of its effects. His fluid, logical, and informed approach

Social Issues

establishes the legitimacy of these bold actions. (One aim of Earth First! is to be so extreme that the moderate goals of groups such as the Sierra Club become attractive and attainable.) Ecotage disturbs even the most committed environmentalists; this elucidation of the beliefs held by "ecowarriors" puts their actions in the proper perspective. An important book. —*Donna Seaman*

Naar, Jon.
Design for a Livable Planet.
Harper, $25.95. 320p.

Naar's book offers practical, positive information in an accessible, call-to-action format. The pages are invitingly busy and designed for emphasis. Chapters cover the primary forms of pollution: solid waste, toxic chemicals, water pollution, air pollution and acid rain, deforestation, global warming, and radiation. Glossaries define terms, charts clarify statistics, and the resource sections provide referrals to relevant organizations with addresses and phone numbers. Headings that begin with "What You Can Do..." abound as do a multitude of tips about what to buy, how to save energy, how to have a healthful home, and how to influence legislation. A nation of practicing environmentalists will ensure policies of "positive ecology" from its government. This book provides a blueprint for achieving these goals. —*Donna Seaman*

Neville, Kathleen.
Corporate Attractions: An Inside Account of Sexual Harassment with the New Sexual Rules for Men and Women on the Job.
Acropolis, $19.95. 297p.

In 1981 Neville was a rising star at a Buffalo, New York, television station where she worked as a sales account executive and on-air consumer reporter. The former beauty-pageant entrant was stunned when her married, newly promoted male supervisor made overt sexual advances and indicated that unless Neville complied with his wishes, career advancement was impossible. Neville handled the matter in a professional manner by informing the general sales manager, who took no action. Ultimately, after another complaint by Neville, she was fired. She took her case to district court, where after six years of legal hassling, the judge ruled against Neville in what had become a termination issue rather than one of sexual harassment. Not surprisingly, Neville learned much about corporate politics and the judicial process through her legal ordeal, and in this involving reflection, she not only relates her experiences but offers enlightenment and guidelines for others facing similar situations. As both a reflective memoir and a handbook for dealing with sexual harassment in the workplace, this is a timely, absorbing account. —*Sue-Ellen Beauregard*

Smith, Page.
Killing the Spirit: Higher Education in America.
Viking, $19.95. 288p.

Watch out, Allan Bloom! Pace, William Bennett! The latest jeremiad on the state of American education comes from historian and teacher Smith, who is certainly a provocative and literate critic of his colleagues and the educational establishment. His approach is familiar—a lament for the decline of educational standards and the death of the humanist tradition, particularly at the university level. The best part of the book is the author's informal yet pointed chronicle of American education's historical development; here Smith cogently and wittily summarizes what he views as questionable progress and unambiguous regression in a number of areas: the triumph of research over teaching, the emerging preeminence of science, the publish-or-perish debate, the revision of the reading lists, the student revolts of the 1960s, and even the overemphasis on sports programs. In most of these issues, the author hews to the middle ground, aiming for a position of reason and compromise buttressed by philosophical conviction. Unfortunately, while these questions are easy to ask, the answers are decidedly more difficult to arrive at (but then this seems a problem that is endemic to the alarmist mode of investigation). Smith observes a by-now-familiar path to intellectual dissolution, yet he offers some striking views of, and fresh opinions on, what he sees as the current debacle in the country's universities and colleges. —*John Brosnahan*

Spencer, Page.
White Silk and Black Tar: A Journal of the Alaska Oil Spill.
Bergamot Books, $9.95. 200p.

The daughter of Alaskan homesteaders, Spencer learned about beauty exploring the sights and sounds of Alaska. The Exxon oil spill happened just as she returned from a honeymoon in the back country. A land reclamation specialist for the Alaskan Park Service, she plunged into combating the catastrophic effects of the spilled crude. During 12- to 14-hour days in oil-saturated environments and chaotic park offices besieged by experts and reporters seeking information, she tried to hold her new life and her old love together. Through her personal report, we gain a more immediate sense of what the *Exxon Valdez* disaster did to the people as well as the land: how their lives changed and what they must now do to live with the catastrophe's effects. —*Virginia Dwyer*

✓ **Steele, Shelby.**
The Content of Our Character: A New Vision of Race in America.
St. Martin's, $15.95. 175p.

This must have been a hard book to write, speaking as it does such unpopular truths. It may well be a hard book to read, especially for those deeply invested in a vision of black oppression and white guilt. Steele strikes out at the racism that disguises itself as liberalism or even radicalism but permits blacks to be only blacks and not fully human. He questions why black students call for segregated departments while decrying apartheid, damns those who'd blame all inner-city crime on poor policing, and attacks those who reject successful blacks as abandoning their heritage. He gives names to behaviors: "race-holding," for blaming every discomfort on racism; "grandiosity," for compensatory excellence in permitted areas like entertainment and sports; "subjective correlatives," for the recasting of problems (drugs, teenage pregnancy) as symbols of black oppression; "integration shock," for the self-doubt that comes with access to groups and experiences previously forbidden. Because this brave book stands so far outside the patterns of current discourse—for instance, he isn't certain affirmative action works—the easy reaction will be to accuse Steele of Uncle Tomism. But is that fair? Expect controversy, but read this book and talk about it. —*Pat Monaghan*

Toffler, Alvin.
Powershift: Knowledge, Wealth, and Violence at the Edge of the 21st Century.
Bantam, $22.95. 553p.

There are three elemental tools for the exercise of power, Toffler says: violence, wealth, and knowledge. Of these three, knowledge has become the most important, as telecommunications and computers have become ubiquitous. Indeed, Toffler argues that both violence and wealth are becoming increasingly dependent upon knowledge in order to be meaningfully used or amassed. Moreover, changes in the means of exercising power wrought by technological advances are removing power from nations and putting it into the hands of extranational forces, including huge corporations, organized religions like Shiite Islam and Roman Catholicism, criminal networks like the drug cartels, and ethnic groups (like those of the Soviet Union) long subsumed by nation-states. In short, we're in the midst of great upheaval, and whether anything—the international economy, the world political order, democracy, totalitarianism—will survive is uncertain. (Toffler does reassuringly argue that the U.S. is still best positioned to wind up on top of the heap, but there may be no heap.) This volume concludes a futurist trilogy begun by the mega-selling *Future Shock* and continued by the mega-selling *Third Wave*. It's as prolix as its predecessors but also as compelling. —*Ray Olson*

✓ **Tribe, Laurence H.**
Abortion: The Clash of Absolutes.
Norton, $18.95. 409p.

Harvard legal scholar Tribe gives a magisterial overview of the abortion debate that is hard to summarize, hard to put down. It's the former because Tribe rehearses the legal and moral arguments, pro and con, anent the several changes in U.S. abortion law and politics from the nation's birth right up to cases now before the Supreme Court. It's the latter because Tribe's a darn good popular writer—clear, concise but not clipped, and not above using the congenial vernacularism (e.g., capping a series of mutually exclusive options with the slangy, "or what"). More importantly, perhaps, he spells out what is constitutionally possible in abortion policy, such as an overriding federal statute (despite the recent *Webster* decision's apparent tossing of the abortion ball to the states) or a thorough reversal of *Roe v. Wade* only at the expense of women's rights in toto. In concluding chapters, and very provocatively, he turns to the impact developments in medical technology may have on the fracas and, very trenchantly, to the ultimate morality of anti-abortion absolutists and the class arrogance of many pro-choice advocates. He seems to believe compromise is inevitable if unpredictable. His fine book well may hasten it. —*Ray Olson*

Ulrich, Hugh.
Losing Ground: Agricultural Policy and the Decline of the American Farm.
Chicago Review Press, $18.95. 289p.

According to Ulrich, federal price supports for the farmer, now around $30 billion annually, have been a ruinous failure and ought to be drastically overhauled, even abolished. Since their enactment during the New Deal in the name of saving the family farm and guaranteeing "fair" prices, our rural population has nearly vanished, the number of farms has plummetted, and average farm size has skyrocketed. These policies have virtually created a new latifundia, huge concentrations of land in a few hands, which naturally get the lion's share of Uncle Sam's largesse. And does anybody sense the more pernicious idiocy that subsidies wreaked upon our soybean industry? In the early 1980s the U.S. controlled about 75 percent of the world market. Now, instead of exporting the wonder bean, we have practically exported the whole industry to Brazil and Argentina. Why? Federal price supports make it more profitable to sow wheat rather than soybeans. With humorous bluntness amid its straight-talking position, Ulrich's book is an interesting call to alarm. —*Gilbert Taylor*

White, Robert H.
Tribal Assets: The Rebirth of Native America.
Holt, $19.95. 288p.

Too many of the approximately two million native Americans live in extreme poverty, with low life expectancy, high suicide and fetal alcohol syndrome rates, and a pervasive hopelessness. But there are a growing number of success stories about tribes who have parlayed their landownership into profitable business ventures, creating employment opportunities and revitalizing Indian communities. White covers the development of tribal businesses owned by the Passamaquoddy in Maine, the Mississippi Choctaw, the Ak-Chin of Arizona, and Oregon's Warm Springs tribe. The Passamaquoddy fought a 10-year legal battle, pitting the feds against the state, and won a $40 million land-claim settlement. Smart investments, acquired "bureaucratic savvy," and some bold entrepreneurship paved the way for the establishment of thriving businesses. White portrays the major players in this "quiet revolution" and rejoices in the optimism he perceives in native Americans who are reasserting their rights. —*Donna Seaman*

Will, George F.
Suddenly: The American Idea Abroad and at Home, 1986-1990.
Free Press, $22.50. 409p.

If George Will is America's premier conservative essayist, then he is by dint not necessarily of his conservatism but by the sheer communicability of his words. This collection of nearly 200 of Will's syndicated columns of the past five years is more than ample proof of the man's deft ability to combine fluid, incisive writing with measured conservative—if indeed that is only what it is—opinion. As expected, the topical range is a mile wide, Will focusing on such diverse issues as fetal ethics, the Bork nomination, China, capital punishment, the popularity of Stephen King, the U.S. tax structure, the achievements of Asian Americans, urban change in Chicago, New York, and Houston, and a variety of contemporary politicos (Thatcher, Cuomo, Bush, Reagan, Jackson, Quayle, Dukakis, etc.). Will also stops along the way to talk a little about his special passion: baseball. As a chronicle of our recent times, and as an example of foremost contemporary op-ed journalism, this compendium is second to none. —*Martin Brady*

Sports & Recreation

Abt, Samuel.
LeMond: The Incredible Comeback of an American Hero.
Random, $18.95. 224p.

It seems as though everyone, even those who know nothing about bicycle racing, watched Greg LeMond win the ultimate race, the grueling Tour de France in 1986. LeMond was the first American to win that race, and he was subjected to much scrutiny by the European press, criticized for his choice of food, playing golf, being savvy about the business aspect of bicycling, even for being "too nice" and too loyal to his family. In this seamless blend of LeMond's own words and Abt's energetic narrative, all the machinations of team politics are dissected, with LeMond's intensity portrayed. His struggle to break into European racing and become a champion is impressive enough, but his comeback after a hunting accident is extraordinary. LeMond's injuries were extensive and painful, but Greg is blessed with tremendous recuperative powers, a high tolerance for pain, and strong conviction. (He went from being ranked number 2 to 345 and suffered through dozens of races to rebuild his strength.) In 1989 his dedication paid off—he won the Tour de France for the second time. Cycling is, according to LeMond, "not a healthy sport; it's too difficult." But that won't stop him. Named Sportsman of the Year by *Sports Illustrated*, LeMond will continue to make sports history and attract admirers (as will this volume). —*Donna Seaman*

Anderson, Sparky and Ewald, Dan.
Sparky!
Prentice Hall Press, $18.95. 240p.

George ("Sparky") Anderson is probably the most successful baseball manager of his time. He piloted the Cincinnati Reds' "Big Red Machine" through the 1970s and then moved over to Detroit where, until last season, he continued his winning ways. This is a typical sports biography with lots of compliments and hardly a discouraging word, with Anderson recalling his minor league days as a player and manager, his salad years with the Reds, and his recent stint with the Tigers. He offers plenty of opinions along with personal all-time lists. This perfectly acceptable bio is gummed up a bit with Sparky's account of his struggle as a (gulp!) "winaholic." (Yes, he was addicted to winning . . . and no, he's not kidding.) He's overcome his affliction now, though it may or may not be good news for Tiger fans. If Sparky wins one, will he go on an uncontrollable bender of victories? (Maybe he needs to dry out with a week at the White Sox Victory Abuse Clinic on Chicago's South Side.) A crusty, likable book (just like Sparky). —*Wes Lukowsky*

✓ **Ashley, John Denny and Reed, Billy.**
Thoroughbred: A Celebration of the Breed.
Simon & Schuster, $50. 191p.

"Once again, in a young horse, the long path to glory lay revealed," writes Billy Reed of the emergence of Forty Niner, the colt who resurrected hope at storied Claiborne Farm after the tragic death of Swale. He might as aptly have been referring to any number of talented colts at any number of farms or tracks across the country, for horsemen constantly dream of glory. Ashley documents the journey to that goal through breeding farms to sales rings to training centers and tracks and finally to the classic races that represent the pinnacle of the thoroughbred sport in 150 pages of often stunning photographs. The farm scenes, frequently shot through morning mists or the half-light of evening, are simply gorgeous. Ashley is at his most arresting in capturing racing action, freezing the horses with preternatural clarity in poses and compositions that seem utterly new, though they have been repeated countless times. Rarely has the excitement of thoroughbred racing been communicated so forcefully. —*Dennis Dodge*

Bayless, Skip.
God's Coach: The Hymns, Hype, and Hypocrisy of Tom Landry's Cowboys.
Simon & Schuster, $19.95. 316p.

Bayless, a controversial, award-winning Dallas newspaper columnist since 1978, has written an excellent counterpoint to Dallas Cowboy ex–head coach Tom Landry's recent autobiography. One wouldn't be stretching a point to refer to Landry's book as "the company line." Bayless, on the other hand, basically tries to determine whether Landry and the other two-thirds of the Cowboy trinity, Tex Schramm and Gil Brandt, were the football geniuses they were thought to be or whether they were merely the right three guys at the

Sports & Recreation

right time. Using interviews with former players and coaches as well as his own insight and analytical ability, Bayless draws some surprising conclusions. Top-notch sports journalism. —*Wes Lukowsky*

Bissinger, H. G.
Friday Night Lights: A Town, a Team, and a Dream.
Addison-Wesley, $19.95. 355p.

Pulitzer Prize–winner Bissinger left his job with the *Philadelphia Inquirer* in 1988 and moved to Odessa, Texas. There he began to shadow the Permian Panthers football team. To characterize his book as a study of high school football in football-crazy Texas is misleading and limiting. Is *All the President's Men* about robbery? Bissinger's memorable account is about people: players, coaches, teachers, parents, cheerleaders, and fans. For example, star player Brian Chavez developed an interest in senior English that delighted his teacher, his parents, and added depth to an already admirable young man. Bissinger also explores the generally sorry state of education, the boom-bust economy of Texas, and the curious politics of blue-collar conservatism. High school football is probably *too* important in Odessa, at least to those of us looking in from the outside. From the insider's view Bissinger so carefully provides, Friday night and football makes perfect sense. —*Wes Lukowsky*

Bosco, Joseph A.
The Boys Who Would Be Cubs: A Year in the Heart of Baseball's Minor Leagues.
Morrow, $18.95. 338p.

For every major league baseball player drawing a million per year there are a dozen young men dreaming the dream on six-dollars-a-day meal money in towns called Appleton, Burlington, Pawtucket, and Peoria. Bosco, who began this insider's glimpse into minor league ball as background work for a novel, spent the 1988 season with the Peoria Chiefs, a farm team for the Chicago Cubs. The most memorable player he encountered in the Class A drama was manager Jim Tracy, a former major league player who's equal parts counselor, teacher, motivator, and standup comic. Tracy's wry wisdom, humanity, and ability to assess both ballplayers and human beings keep the disparate young men he manages focused on their careers and reasonably happy in a life-style that encourages ennui. Baseball fans will relish the grass-roots machinations of a major league organization, and non-fans will enjoy the humorous examination of a minute subphyla: the *ballplayus bushleagus*. A wonderful baseball book, filled with exhilaration and despair. —*Wes Lukowsky*

Collins, Nigel.
Boxing Babylon.
Citadel, $18.95. 224p.

Collins' life in boxing includes stints as first a fighter, then as manager, and, most notably, as a member of the press. For several years he was the editor of *Ring* magazine, the most respected publication in the sport. The 15 pieces here focus on some of the fight game's most intriguing personalities, including one-time middleweight champion Carlos Monzon, who today is serving a murder sentence in Argentina, and Tony Ayala, who is serving a lengthy sentence for rape in New Jersey. Collins also explores the mysterious death of former heavyweight champ Sonny Liston, the mental illness that dogged Joe Louis, and the tragedy of one-eyed fighter Gypsy Joe Harris. Fine reading for boxing fans, supplemented with 16 pages of photographs. —*Wes Lukowsky*

Drysdale, Don and Verdi, Bob.
Once a Bum, Always a Dodger.
St. Martin's, $18.95. 256p.

Hall of Fame pitcher Drysdale was the last of the "Boys of Summer" Brooklyn Dodgers to retire, and it's interesting to note that although most of his success came after the team moved to Los Angeles, it's the Brooklyn years he remembers with fondness. Drysdale reminisces at length on the special relationship Brooklynites had with their beloved Bums and the legendary players—Reese, Hodges, Jackie Robinson, etc.—who made up the team. He also recounts the Los Angeles years, including his record-setting scoreless streak of 58⅔ innings. Since his retirement in 1969, Drysdale has been a broadcaster, currently with the Dodgers, and he relates a number of anecdotes from his life behind the mike. There are no bombshells here, no headlines waiting to happen, but Drysdale has led an interesting life, and—with the able assistance of coauthor Verdi—he writes with candor and humor. —*Wes Lukowsky*

Feinstein, John.
Forever's Team: One Extraordinary Team's Journey through the Triumphs and Tragedies of College.
Villard, $18.95. 370p.

In 1978, an unheralded Duke basketball team made up completely of under-classmen got hot at the right time and advanced to the NCAA final game, where the Blue Devils lost to a veteran Kentucky team. Because of the team's youth, the press—with its bandwagon mentality—virtually conceded Duke's unbridled success the next few years. It didn't work out that way, however. Though successful by any reasonable standard, Duke never met the extraordinary expectations with which it had been burdened. Feinstein, the best-selling author of *A Season on the Brink*, tracks the lives of the Duke coaches and players following that magical 1978 season. Though Feinstein tries to inject the melancholy tone of *The Boys of Summer* into his manuscript, it doesn't work. (Basically the coaches and players have all lived full, relatively healthy, and successful lives.) But what he *does* do is reveal the fragile chemistry so critical to team sports, especially basketball. This may not capture the high drama Feinstein would have liked, but it is definitely a fascinating look into college basketball that should drum up plenty of readers. —*Wes Lukowsky*

Sports & Recreation

Ford, Norman D.
Keep on Pedaling: The Complete Guide to Adult Bicycling.
Countryman, $12.95. 212p.

Bicycling as a sport, as recreation, and as exercise is advocated by Ford as just the thing for adult riders. With cycling's growing popularity, this guide shows how adults of different ages and differing degrees of physical conditioning can join the throngs of pedalers on the country's roads and paths. Although some of Ford's advice is geared to an older age group, most of his suggestions apply to riders across the years, making his book a fine general introduction to cycling as well. Equipment, riding techniques, maintenance and repair, and safety considerations are all covered, as are competitive racing and bicycle touring. —*John Brosnahan*

Gregg, Eric and Appel, Marty.
Working the Plate: The Eric Gregg Story.
Morrow, $14.95. 192p.

Gregg was the National League's first black umpire when he arrived in the late 1970s. He was also the biggest, topping out at some 360 pounds. The titular pun provides readers with a clue to what's inside. This isn't as much a humorous book—à la funnyman ex-ump Ron Luciano's memoirs—as it is a good-natured one. Gregg's inspirational rise from one of Philadelphia's worst ghettos was accomplished through hard work, desire, and the heartily appreciated help of many friends. Gregg doesn't duck the tough issues—his weight, racism in baseball, and the umpire's strike of a few years back—and he also relates those "insider" anecdotes fans expect when reading a jock biography. Not an earthshaking volume, but one in which an intelligent participant provides a unique perspective on the national pastime. —*Wes Lukowsky*

Grossinger, Richard and Kerrane, Kevin, eds.
Into the Temple of Baseball.
Celestial Arts, $17.95. 280p.

Never has there been a more enjoyably eclectic collection of baseball literature. The editors unearthed many lesser-known but high-quality essays and poems. Consider for a moment a partial list of the contributors: late baseball commissioner Bart Giamatti, Jack Kerouac, Stephen King, former Cleveland mayor Dennis Kucinich, filmmaker John Sayles, Garrison Keillor, Willie Morris, and poet Richard Hugo. Trying to categorize such a broad selection is impossible, but it's safe to say that for each author, baseball has become a passion rather than a pastime. A special experience for baseball fans. —*Wes Lukowsky*

Heiman, Lee and others.
When the Cheering Stops: Ex–Major Leaguers Talk about Their Game and Their Lives.
Macmillan, $18.95. 310p.

A collection of self-profiles by 22 former major league ballplayers, whose careers spanned from the 1940s, through the golden age of 1950s and 1960s baseball, and (for a few) on into the 1970s. These old hands, most of whom had thriving careers but none of whom reached baseball immortality—e.g., Jake Gibbs, Al Smith, Bob Veale, Roy Sievers, Elroy Face, Chuck Stobbs, Bobby Thomson—discuss, often in poignant terms, the long journey from the sandlots to the "bigs." Interviewees emphasize their lives in the minors, the big breaks that catapulted them to the majors, their teammates, worthy opponents, managers, stingy front-office types (as well as the more generous ones), the big plays in which they were involved, and, finally, their descent from the majors (sadly, more often than not, into oblivion). —*Martin Brady*

✓ **Izenberg, Jerry.**
No Medals for Trying: A Week in the Life of a Pro Football Team.
Macmillan, $18.95. 266p.

The detailed examination of one game has been done for baseball by Daniel Okrent in *Nine Innings* and for basketball by Terry Pluto and Bob Ryan in *Forty-eight Minutes.* Veteran national columnist and sportswriter Izenberg provides the same kind of insight for football with this seven-day dissection of the New York Giants' preparation for a late-season game with the Philadelphia Eagles. Head coach Bill Parcells is the key player in this drama, but Izenberg also profiles assistant coaches, trainers, equipment managers, groundskeepers, and, of course, players to record their activities and thoughts regarding the upcoming game. A thoughtful, humanizing look at a sport that is often categorized as dehumanizing and brutal. This is a must-read for every pro football fan. —*Wes Lukowsky*

James, Bill.
The Baseball Book, 1990.
Random/Villard, $12.95. 341p.

James' *Abstract* changed the way a lot of fans looked at baseball, at least in the statistical sense. (It also spawned so many imitators that he decided to stop writing that seminal guide.) His new annual is less focused—disorganized comes to mind—but at times even more compelling. Included are profiles of current players, thumbnail biographies of baseball figures whose names start with *A* (more letters to come in the future), an analysis of the season past, and a fascinating draft guide for those who participate in fantasy or rotisserie leagues. James is back, and that is good news for baseball fans. —*Wes Lukowsky*

Sports & Recreation

Jennings, Kenneth M.
Balls and Strikes: The Money Game in Professional Baseball.
Praeger, $24.95. 288p.

Despite the thousands of column inches the daily press devotes to labor relations in major league baseball, it's very difficult for the average fan to understand the issues, especially since little historical perspective finds its way into print. Jennings, a management professor, presents the complex financial history of baseball in a readable, richly detailed, and enlightening book. He tackles such issues as free agency, arbitration, pensions, discrimination, player representation, and television revenue. Each topic is carefully explained in a historical perspective and related to the overall financial picture. Of great interest to both baseball fans and those concerned with business and management. —*Wes Lukowsky*

Kirk, Troy.
Collector's Guide to Baseball Cards.
Chilton, $16.95. 224p.

An excellent introductory guide to the burgeoning hobby of baseball-card collecting. Kirk, who began collecting as a child in the 1960s, begins with a brief history of cards and their transformation from kids' stuff to serious collectibles. He then discusses various card manufacturers and their significance to collectors; provides a sampling of very valuable cards with logical analyses of the value basis; and offers tips on building a varied and valuable collection. Other topics include grading card quality (from mint to poor) and collecting cards as an investment. Bound to be a popular item among both seasoned and novice collectors. —*Wes Lukowsky*

✓ Levine, David.
Life on the Rim: A Year in the Continental Basketball Association.
Macmillan, $17.95. 317p.

The CBA is to the National Basketball Association what off-Broadway is to Broadway. The talent is there ofttimes, but for one reason or another the door to the big time is at least temporarily closed. Levine, a former editor for *Sport* magazine, spent a year with the Albany Patroons of the CBA. Though he covers much of the same ground as Heller in *Obsession*, the latter is more the story of a driven coach, whereas this is the players' story. Readers will not forget Vince Askew, who doesn't know if he should accept an offer from a European team because he doesn't know where Europe is; or Kelvin Upshaw, who tangled early and often with coach George Karl but eventually signed a lucrative contract with the Boston Celtics. Levine re-creates a gritty, sometimes cruel world of endless van rides, heartbreaking roster cuts, and tough practices followed by cold showers. But he balances that with humor, humanity, and a tenacious hold on a tenuous dream. Memorable sports reading. —*Wes Lukowsky*

Liebling, A. J.

A Neutral Corner: Uncollected Boxing Essays by A. J. Liebling.
North Point, $18.95. 238p.

Liebling is generally regarded as the paragon of boxing journalists. These 15 previously uncollected essays, mostly from the *New Yorker*, are illustrative of his talent and craft. Arranged chronologically, the essays extend from the early 1950s through the beginning of the Ali years in the 1960s. Among the highlights is a wonderful account of Ali, then known as Cassius Clay, at New York's Madison Square Garden. Clay's prefight posturing and penchant for poetic predictions turned the crowd against him. Liebling's strength was his broad literary background and his ability to apply it to boxing without condescension or the pretense that boxing was anything more than an improbable profession populated by a unique cross section of human beings. —*Wes Lukowsky*

McGuane, Thomas.

An Outside Chance: Classic and New Essays on Sport.
Houghton, $19.95. 294p.

From a critically acclaimed novelist, a newly revised and enlarged collection of essays previously published in 1980—and including an excellent new introduction by Geoffrey Wolff. McGuane is a master of language, possessing pinpoint reasoning, an expansive humanity, and an ability to conjure either tears or cheers (and sometimes both) within the space of one paragraph. Among the highlights here is an essay on noted naturalist-author Roderick Haig-Brown and a hilarious romp through the wild with McGuane's irrepressible hound, Molly. He also examines the motorcycle mystic, bonefishing, and the capriciousness of the gods who conspired to make one fishing trip a rod-and-reel version of "I Love Lucy." McGuane has something for nearly everyone. —*Wes Lukowsky*

✔ Micheli, Lyle J. and Jenkins, Mark D.

Sportswise: An Essential Guide for Young Adult Athletes, Parents, and Coaches.
Houghton, $19.95. 287p.

Micheli's credentials are extraordinary: he's an M.D. and director of sports medicine at Boston Children's Hospital, an associate professor at Harvard Medical School, and the president of the American College of Sports Medicine. Here, he combines his professional expertise with the concerns of a parent to write an informative, readable, and well-organized book that will ultimately benefit many young athletes. Among his major concerns are the fitness levels of young people as they begin competing: don't assume a child is fit enough for intensive, organized sports. He also discusses sports injuries, psychological aspects of youth sports, and nutrition. Chapters are also devoted to the specific concerns of females, handicapped youngsters, and the chronically ill. An important book that can help make sports more enjoyable for both parent and child. —*Wes Lukowsky*

Nadel, Eric.
The Night Wilt Scored 100: Tales from Basketball's Past.
Taylor, $9.95. 143p.

This pleasant collection of basketball anecdotes focuses on the unusual or ironic. For example, in the account of Wilt Chamberlain's record-setting 100-point game, Nadel states that Chamberlain, usually a poor free-throw-shooter, connected on a spectacular 28 of 32 from the line. (Also, the next night, Wilt's same opponents got a standing ovation for "holding" him to 54 points.) These stories will stimulate the memories of older fans or help give new ones a sense of the game's colorful history. Either way, it's a winning selection. Sixty photographs—unavailable for review—will complement the text. —*Wes Lukowsky*

Pallone, Dave and Steinberg, Alan.
Behind the Mask: My Double Life in Baseball.
Viking, $18.95. 313p.

Pallone was a National League baseball umpire for 10 years. After a series of incidents—including a nasty spat with Reds manager Pete Rose and a rumor of sexual scandal—Pallone was not rehired after the 1988 season. He contends he was not rehired because he's gay. It's a moot point; he reached a financial settlement with baseball and will never umpire again. Pallone's professional life was never easy. He was promoted to the major leagues during an umpire's strike and was forever ostracized by his coworkers. The treatment was brutal, and even went so far as to compromise the umpires' on-field integrity. While he was enduring this daily emotional pummeling he was also trying desperately to define his own sexuality. Unable to relate physically with women and unsure of entering the gay world, he remained celibate—and very lonely—for many years. Then when he was able to establish a relationship, the young man he was involved with was killed in a car accident. Often, celebrity tell-alls are suspect, but Pallone's story is too painful and too anguished to have been done only for money. A sad tale brightened only by Pallone's unbreakable determination and ultimate optimism. —*Wes Lukowsky*

Peary, Danny, ed.
Cult Baseball Players: The Greats, the Flakes, the Weird, and the Wonderful.
Simon & Schuster/Fireside, $9.95. 376p.

This collection offers a "tribute to 59 of those special former players . . . whose distinct play (good and bad) and colorful personalities provided us with instant pleasures and precious memories." So be it. It's still hard to see why Mickey Mantle, Willie Mays, Ernie Banks, Lou Gehrig, Roberto Clemente, Sandy Koufax, and the other mainstream, all-time greats profiled here are accorded "cult" status. On the other hand, there are entries that fit the bill terrifically: Vic Power, former first baseman whose flashy fielding was as singular as his batting stance; Bo Belinsky, bad-boy Angels pitcher who hurled a no-hitter, caroused with actress Mamie Van Doren, and did little else; Steve

Dalkowski, flame-throwing Oriole *phee*-nom, who probably threw a baseball faster than anyone before or since but never made it to the majors; Moe Berg, the multilingual, Princeton-educated, Washington Senators catcher who served as a World War II spy; and so forth. The authors of the individual pieces include radio host Larry King, *Bull Durham* author Ron Shelton, actor John Lithgow, film critic Andrew Sarris, scientist Stephen Jay Gould, and various sportwriters and broadcasters. Whether read straight through or browsed at leisure, this is a sure winner for baseball fans. —*Martin Brady*

Peterson, Robert W.
Cages to Jump Shots: Pro Basketball's Early Years.
Oxford, $22.95. 212p.

Peterson's first foray into sports history was the acclaimed *Only the Ball Was White*, a pre-1948 history of the Negro basketball leagues. Here he tackles an equally formidable subject: professional basketball before the advent of the NBA in 1948. He begins with an amusing, detailed version of James Naismith's invention of the game, charts the fledgling leagues' successes and failures, notes the presence of memorable players in the leagues, and, most importantly, tracks the changes in the game itself. Especially interesting is the increasing importance of tall players through the 1930s and 1940s. The author's use of participant quotes and excerpts from old newspaper articles provides a context and an identification with the pioneering spirit of the early professionals. A necessary work of sports history and an enjoyable one. —*Wes Lukowsky*

Pluto, Terry.
Loose Balls: The Short, Wild Life of the American Basketball Association.
Simon & Schuster, $21.95. 477p.

The American Basketball Association had its first jump ball in 1967 and continued through nine tumultuous years, later merging with the established NBA for the 1976–77 season. Despite the great players who began their careers in the ABA—Julius Erving and Moses Malone among them—the league itself has faded into obscurity. But it was fun while it lasted. In this oral history of the league, veteran journalist Pluto relates the memories of dozens of players, coaches, referees, owners, journalists, and broadcasters. Many of the stories revolve around eccentrics such as tough-guy players Wendell Ladner and Warren Jabali or the screwy maneuverings of nouveau riche—heading toward nouveau poor—owners. Beyond the laughs is a sense of camaraderie and an appreciation of great basketball. A must read for hoop fans. —*Wes Lukowsky*

✓ Riffenburgh, Beau and Boss, David.
Great Ones: NFL Quarterbacks from Baugh to Montana.
Viking, $22.95. 192p.

This handsome cavalcade of knowing words and elegant pictures profiles the exploits of NFL quarterbacks, from the league's formative years to the present day. Riffenburgh and Boss' text discusses the QBs' personalities, styles of play, and on-the-field achievements, and the pictures that go along with it are thoroughly appealing, whether it's a shot of an intense Dan Marino fading back to pass or a vintage black-and-white of Bobby Layne barking out the signals. Happily, most of the photos are in vivid color—Bernie Kosar throwing over a leaping linebacker, Jim Plunkett heaving a long one, Randall Cunningham taking off on a scramble, etc.—and the authors' coverage includes not only the all-time greats but also the very competent back-up quarterbacks, those who may have been the subject of controversy, or those who weren't first-rate talents and yet still made careers for themselves at what is the most physically and mentally demanding position in the game. —*Martin Brady*

Robinson, Ray.
Iron Horse: Lou Gehrig in His Time.
Norton, $22.95. 267p.

One of baseball's all-time great players, Gehrig would be a Hall-of-Famer under any circumstances, but the feat that secured his status as a legend was his 2,130-game playing streak. He didn't miss a game during more than 13 seasons and may never have missed one if he hadn't developed the disease that would kill him before he reached 38. Only death could get Larrupin' Lou out of the lineup. This carefully researched biography succumbs occasionally to statistical re-creations of Gehrig's exploits but still reveals much of his quiet, dignified personality. It affords insights into, among other matters, his difficult relationship with a loving but domineering mother, his shabby treatment at the hands of the Yankees when he could no longer play, and the role he played in the rehabilitation of a young tough who would become famous, Rocky Graziano. In all, a solid biography of a genuine hero. —*Wes Lukowsky*

✔ **Sperber, Murray.**
College Sports Inc.: The Athletic Department vs the University.
Holt, $19.95. 382p.

Face it—as big a hold as big-time college sports has on the American psyche, all but the most naive fans realize that there's trouble in paradise. Miserable graduation rates, astronomical financial packages for coaches, illegal payments to athletes, and charges of fixed games have all tainted the mix. Books addressing the problems have proliferated in the last year or so. Is another catalog of collegiate athletic crime really necessary? In this case, yes. While most of the prior literature focused on a specific school or a specific sport, this volume, by an Indiana University professor and former sportswriter, provides an overview of the entire problem. Gathering facts from across the country, Sperber paints a portrait of an industry as prone to graft and thievery as the deregulated savings and loans. Plus, he clearly illustrates how the largesse is pilfered at the expense of taxpayers. An excellent, meticulously researched exposé that deserves a large audience. —*Wes Lukowsky*

✓ **Stauth, Cameron.**
The Franchise: Building a Winner with Basketball's Bad Boys, the World Champion Detroit Pistons.
Morrow, $19.95. 288p.

Stauth spent the 1989–90 NBA season monitoring the world-champion Detroit Pistons. It was an astute choice of teams, since the Bad Boys—a nickname derived from the team's propensity for on-court violence—steam-rolled their way to the title. Stauth's focal point is Piston general manager Jack McCloskey, a career basketball man who carefully built the team from league doormat into contenders. Stauth also emphasizes the leadership of veterans Isiah Thomas and Bill Laimbeer. This is a special book that brings fans as deep inside the NBA as they're likely to get without actually suiting up. —*Wes Lukowsky*

Switzer, Barry and Shrake, Bud.
Bootlegger's Boy.
Morrow, $19.95. 401p.

When Switzer resigned last year as head football coach at Oklahoma, he was among the winningest coaches in history and the architect of three national championship teams. Though revered by Oklahomans and admired by many others, Switzer has had his share of detractors, among them the NCAA, which kept a close eye on the Oklahoma program. The anti-Switzer camp would have one believe he played fast and loose with the rules, specialized in recruiting an unsavory type of athlete, and was less a coaching genius than a Pied Piper recruiter. This volume, not exactly an autobiography, offers a pugnacious "Oh, yeah?" reply to the critics. While the ultimate question of Switzer's integrity will be determined by a less subjective study, if at all, what emerges here is the gale force of his personality. From humble origins—his father really was a bootlegger—Switzer used his intelligence, his wit, and his cunning to rise to the top of his chosen field. It was a hard road and a rough climb, as he makes clear, and he apologizes for nothing. —*Wes Lukowsky*

Tapply, William G.
Opening Day and Other Neuroses.
Lyons & Burford, $16.95. 240p.

There may be more skillful anglers than William Tapply (indeed, his deficiencies are a mournful refrain thorughout this varied collection of essays and reminiscences), but few are more passionately, even obsessively, devoted to their sport. Few also are so adept at communicating its profound allure. In Tapply's treatment, dunking worms for horned pout in a local New England pond becomes as pleasant a pastime as one could desire. Fly-casting for trout in the famed rivers of the West—the Bighorn, the Henry's Fork, the Frying Pan—or questing for tarpon in the coastal waters of Belize becomes high adventure. Despite his disclaimers, Tapply—author of the Brady Coyne mystery series —is an expert fisherman, and he passes along a wealth of angling lore. More than that, though, he imparts an appreciation for the experience of fishing. Readers run the risk of getting hooked. —*Dennis Dodge*

Thompson, Charles and Sonnenschein, Allan.
Down and Dirty: The Life and Crimes of Oklahoma Football.
Carroll & Graf, $18.95. 284p.

Thompson, a star quarterback at Oklahoma under former head coach Barry Switzer, is presently in prison for conspiracy to distribute cocaine. The latest in a long series of books intent on bashing collegiate sports (most of it justified), this is the first from a player. Though Thompson professes remorse, he gleefully chronicles the debauchery of his stay in Norman, when he was either drunk, stoned, gambling, or fornicating. Most of his transgressions were, he says, made with the knowledge or at least unstated approval of Switzer. As a matter of fact, Thompson claims that he used to get his booze at Switzer's house, where the coach would help fill the trunk of Thompson's car, which was supplied by an avid Sooner booster. Thompson's own words reveal a self-indulgent, self-serving, manipulative oaf. Then and now. But he was tolerated because he could win games for the old alma mater. A very depressing account that will, sad to say, no doubt make its author a pile of money. —*Wes Lukowsky*

✓ Thorn, John and others, eds.
The Whole Baseball Catalogue.
Simon & Schuster/Fireside, $17.95. 369p.

Committed baseball fans will clasp this tome to their hearts, purr contentedly, and disappear for a few days of delicious indulgence. Editor John Thorn, the ringleader of this cooperative venture, is well known to fans as the editor of *Total Baseball* and coauthor of *The Hidden Game of Baseball*. Assisted by a capable corps of contributors, Thorn critically assesses everything from baseball songs (i.e., "Johnny Podres Has a Halo 'round His Head") to stadium architects to fantasy camps to baseball newsletters. Other chapters cover baseball tours, collectibles, equipment, games, computer software, and literature. Whenever possible, addresses and phone numbers are included. An extraordinary volume with which to start the new baseball decade. Indispensable. —*Wes Lukowsky*

Visions of Sport.
Viking, $29.95. 158p.

The international sports picture agency Allsport has assembled a few pictures from its apparently vast archives and produced a light, playful, and happy book of photographs reproduced in vivid colors. An intense Seve Ballesteros peers out from a jungle of trees; a young Chris Evert stares contemplatively out of a window; Katarina Witt, bedecked like Papagena, swoops across the ice; the ever-sweet Walter Payton strides across a sea of bodies. So many are here, and they make the body seem strong, full of character, fluid, all-accomplishing. But there are bikes and motorbikes, too; and crowds and cricketers (the gentleman's sport) with broken noses and arms, and Mary Decker crying after her accident with Zola Budd. Sport is about play and expresses our faith in the world's plasticity, with we the children in it; but it is also about dignity, regality, pride in what we are. Yet, to tell the truth, this isn't a book to inspire philosophy. Even the "essays" that decorate the pictures like doilies are as bodiless as clouds. What we admire here is the spirit of worship. —*Stuart Whitwell*

Wartman, William.
Playing Through: Behind the Scenes on the PGA Tour.
Morrow, $18.95. 288p.

Professional golf is a subject of great interest to most golfers and an absolute bore to everyone else. This revealing if a bit dyspeptic look at the PGA Tour shows why the increasingly popular game has never really made it as a mass-market spectator sport. The reason, of course, is image. Professional golf is sponsored by corporations, makes most of its profits from TV commercials sold to corporations, and appeals directly to the corporate mentality. As Wartman makes abundantly clear in following the tour through the 1988 season, golf is the "Disneyland of sports: a carefully controlled arena in which corporations rather than families can invest their money and have a life-affirming experience." It's the corporate image that turns off bleacher bums, but beneath the white-bread package there is a terrific game that needs no apologies. Wartman examines the on-the-course action—"theater in the oblong"—in depth, profiling the players (he likes regular guy Curtis Strange but can't hide his antipathy toward press-conscious Greg Norman), describing the action at key tournaments, and providing insightful analysis of why some win and others lose. Like the pro tour, golfers will love this book, others will ignore it. —*Bill Ott*

✓ **Will, George F.**
Men at Work: The Craft of Baseball.
Macmillan, $19.95. 320p.

Political opinion maker George Will is, as his many champions know, a rabid baseball fan (with a particular allegiance to the Chicago Cubs). Here, Will accomplishes what he no doubt has wanted to do for a long time: write a baseball book with style and authority. He definitely succeeds, though his literary influences will be obvious to readers of such baseball writers as Roger Angell or Thomas Boswell. Melding a Boswellian fascination for the players and managers with an Angell-like respect for the sport's history, poetry, and irony, Will focuses on four major figures in the game—the Oakland Athletics' Tony LaRussa, the Los Angeles Dodgers' Orel Hershiser, the San Diego Padres' Tony Gwynn, and the Baltimore Orioles' Cal Ripken—offering freewheeling discussion of their special talents. Will's basic emphasis on individual skills (LaRussa's strategizing, Hershiser's pitching, Gwynn's hitting, and Ripken's fielding) provides multiple opportunities for digression on the exploits of many past and present stars of the game and for the interpolation of illustrative statistics. A rock-solid look at the game and its heroes. —*Martin Brady*

Williams, Dick and Plaschke, Bill.
No More Mr. Nice Guy.
HBJ, $19.95. 310p.

From 1967 to 1988, Dick Williams was arguably the best manager in major league baseball, winning pennants in Boston, Oakland, and San Diego, including leading the colorful A's to world championships in 1972 and 1973. Williams was also a constant source of controversy, since his undeniable success in bringing respectability to chronic losers was offset by his demanding on-the-field ethic, his sometimes gruff demeanor, and his refusal to tolerate the b.s. tossed his way by owners, general managers, and even superstar players. This volume, often frank beyond necessity, certainly captures the Williams persona, which isn't always a happy one. We learn first of Williams' humble St. Louis beginnings and his 13-year journeyman playing career. Then it's on to the Impossible Dream year of '67—when Williams led an unlikely bunch of Boston Red Sox to the World Series—and his other managerial stints for the A's, Angels, Expos, Padres, and Mariners. Williams and coauthor Bill Plaschke—who does nothing to reign in Williams' abrasive, often foul-mouthed style—tell some startling tales (of drugs in Montreal, for example), take potshots at the current brand of major leaguer, and name names all the way. Like Williams the ballplayer, this is hard-nosed stuff, sure to ruffle feathers among the baseball establishment and guaranteed to draw avid readers in the public library. —*Martin Brady*

Travel

Barth, Jack.
American Quest.
Simon & Schuster/Fireside, $8.95. 115p.

Move over, Charles Kuralt. Forget about Steinbeck's *Travels with Charley* —this is travels with Spunky and Barth, who is a contributor to *Spy* and *Premiere* and author of *Roadside America*. Gleefully trashing the "on the road" genre, Barth sets out across America on various quests. His itinerary emulates the style and tone of David Letterman's "Top Ten" lists, and he shares Letterman's peculiar brand of dumb-for-dumb's-sake irony. Barth's goofy quests include tracking down, meeting, and kissing "ten TV sirens of the 1960's," re-creating the journey of *Easy Rider*, and working in the world's largest McDonald's (Vinita, Oklahoma), for the Coca-Cola hotline, and at a multiplex movie theater. This is the "Stupid Human Tricks" version of the search for America: absurd and irreverent. Bound to attract Letterman and *Spy* fans and certainly worth the bargain price. —*Donna Seaman*

Sports & Recreation

✓ **Berger, Bruce.**
The Telling Distance: Conversations with the American Desert.
Breitenbush, $19.95. 243p.

Winner of the 1990 Western States Book Award for creative nonfiction, this volume belongs on the shelf with all great desert literature. Berger updates the traditional chronicle of the desert by admiring its vastness and mysteries while being acutely aware of its vulnerability. While Berger treads the same sliprock championed by Edward Abbey, he steps more gently, wary of destroying the fragile environment, reluctant to burn wood or encourage others to intrude on the rapidly shrinking wilderness. Berger tells us that, like having safe sex, we must have safe explorations—but without diminishing primal pleasure. He relates his experiences hiking, camping, rafting and birdwatching, all the while letting his mind travel into meditations on the deep psychic link between wilderness and dreams, music, literature, and the "joy of the mind." Berger's prose is as perfectly adapted to his thoughts as cacti are to the desert—readers will find quotables on every page. —*Donna Seaman*

Brook, Stephen.
Vanished Empire: Vienna, Budapest, Prague: The Three Capital Cities of the Hapsburg Empire As Seen Today.
Morrow, $21.95. 384p.

The former capitals of the Hapsburg empire are visited by Brook, who finds a completely different world from that of his previous travel book, *Honkytonk Gelato: Travels through Texas.* The author manages to preserve his hip and fresh attitude as a tourist, however, as he traces the remains of the Austro-Hungarian rulers, samples the local cuisine and alcohol, and visits one musty museum after another. And when tourist ennui begins to take hold, Brook turns to the locals for some aid and comfort—a ploy that yields some of the funniest and most charming moments of his book. These more entertaining passages are balanced by some serious topics—the exploration of the aftereffects of World War II and the presence of communist rule on some parts of the lost empire. Although some of Brook's observations have been outdistanced by the recent movement to freedom in Eastern Europe, his combination of historical reverie and present-day reality make for an exceptional voyage. —*John Brosnahan*

Conrad, Peter.
Where I Fell to Earth: A Life in Four Cities.
Poseidon, $18.95. 252p.

Australian-born teacher and critic Conrad is seemingly peripatetic as he travels the world, but when the writer does settle down, it is in one of four places: London, Oxford, Lisbon, or New York City. This group portrait of these cities functions as a map for Conrad's memoir, which evokes settings with particular distinction. The cultural disjunctions that Conrad experiences as he moves from one location to another—from domestic comfort with a Portuguese family to Greenwich Village squalor—may boggle the reader's

Travel

mind, but the writer calmly accepts his lot in each place as though it's his due. Combining magnanimity and open-mindedness under all these varied conditions can't be easy, but Conrad's intriguing traversal of his familiar stopping places makes for a number of marvelous and disturbing images of the human condition. —*John Brosnahan*

Critchfield, Richard.
An American Looks at Britain.
Doubleday, $21.95. 512p.

Journalist Critchfield examines the interrelated history and cultures of Great Britain and the U.S., two countries united by more than shared language and social traditions. On the way to forming his American's view of Great Britain as a once powerful and now distant mother country, Critchfield interviews a wide range of British subjects and residents, from Paul Theroux to Jeremy Irons, to get their opinions of Margaret Thatcher, the intelligence industry, social progress, economic recovery, and the still present and powerful class system. Digesting all this material, he assesses the present condition of British culture and peers into the future, offering several provocative suggestions of what might repair the shaky foundations of British society. A fascinating look at the other side of the pond. —*John Brosnahan*

Dickey, Christopher.
Expats: Travels in Arabia, from Tripoli to Teheran.
Atlantic Monthly Press, $18.95. 240p.

The author of *With the Contras* travels into another politically charged region with this description of his trips throughout the Arab world. Traveling from North Africa to the Middle East, Dickey meets up with Americans and Europeans who have lived and worked in these Arab countries for many years and documents the disjunction between Western and Islamic societies. The expatriate experience, with all of its advantages and drawbacks, is sympathetically portrayed, perhaps more so than many current developments, which the author describes with less kindliness but with an equally vivid tone. The collision between these cultures receives a dramatic representation here, even if Dickey's treatment is sometimes less than politically incisive. —*John Brosnahan*

✓ Dunbar, Tony.
Delta Time: A Journey through Mississippi.
Pantheon, $19.95. 260p.

Dunbar first traveled to the Mississippi Delta in 1968 at age 19. Since then he has been enamored of this strip of fertile America running east of the Mississippi River from Memphis to Vicksburg. His book is a portrait of Delta life—native personalities and local politics in a place where "plantation society" is immediate history and of immense cultural influence, a community aware of its problems with flooding, poverty, education, population desertion, and Wal-Marts invading small towns. But it is also a region whose people are devoted to a way of life that boasts Delta blues, black elected officials, and the "miracle of peace between races." Dunbar affectionately records the insights of social workers, politicians, and old friends like Tiny Man Brown ("You used to call the Ku Klux Klan's name twenty-five years ago and it would make my heart skip a beat. Now it seems like you would say, 'We're gonna chew some bubble gum.'"). A stirring account of the American South, painstakingly documented by a man who believes that its citizens could teach the world some lessons. —*Kathryn LaBarbera*

✓ **Greenwald, Jeff.**
Shopping for Buddhas.
Harper, $8. 160p.

Journalist Greenwald, hoping to finally write a novel and having discovered that Nepal inspires him, seeks enlightenment through the acquisition of a "flawless little statue of Buddha." His quest sparks musings on Brahmanism and Buddhism, the differences between Western and Eastern art, and the corrupt and poverty-stricken state of Nepal. He recounts his sojourns, especially his time in Kathmandu, with startlingly inventive descriptions. The landscape is teeming with deities and sacred cows, the shops crammed with cheap, imitative art. Greenwald's narrative runs on two parallel paths—observations of his surroundings and his inner struggles. He maintains a Woody Allenesque amusement about himself while witnessing the revolutionary changes shaking "the World's Only Hindu Kingdom." In conclusion, in true Zen fashion, he discovers that he cannot have his Buddha until he is willing to lose it. Cogent and funny. —*Donna Seaman*

Hartmann, William K.
Desert Heart: Chronicles of the Sonoran Desert.
Fisher Books, $35. 216p.

Astronomer Hartmann doesn't offer a strictly scientific account of the Sonoran Desert but instead combines the history of its exploration with an account of its unique geologic features. The author sifts through early descriptions made by Indians and Spanish explorers and updates these with more recent tales of how astronauts trained there for exercises in moon research methods. As for the numerous craters and other evidence of volcanic activity, Hartmann relates the results of his analysis in an easy, informal style that depicts both beauty and desolation while recognizing the environmental changes human encroachment has created in this ecosystem. Illustrated with an excellent series of color and black-and-white photographs. —*John Brosnahan*

Hitchens, Christopher.
Blood, Class, and Nostalgia: Anglo-American Ironies.
Farrar, $19.95. 321p.

Hitchens offers an appealingly ironic view of how the British Empire influenced U.S. response to world events in the twentieth century. England, he

THE BOOK BUYER'S ADVISOR

Travel

suggests, stage-managed America's debut as a world-class player only to find
the apprentice supplanting the mentor in a classic *All about Eve* scenario.
Hitchens covers a number of historical events—the two world wars and the
cold war in Europe—that illustrate this transatlantic transfer of power and
influence as Great Britain prompted U.S. involvement and later witnessed a
not-quite-hostile takeover of its original domination and prestige. Hitchens
supplies a sturdy historical setting for his views, which predict both a poor
future for Anglo-American political supremacy and a good chance for recipro-
cal philosophical benefits. Read this in conjunction with Critchfield's *An
American Looks at Great Britain. —John Brosnahan*

Mayle, Peter.
A Year in Provence.
Knopf, $19.95. 240p.

As the title states, this is a recounting of Englishman Mayle's year's worth of
experience as a resident in the French province of Provence. He and his wife
set up housekeeping in a farmhouse and got busy with the business of gaining
firsthand knowledge of the lay of the land. In chronological arrangement,
January to December, Mayle relates with iridescent detail his observations
and impressions of, among other things, the charm of the domicile that he
and his wife occupied during their sojourn, the soon-digested but easily
remembered meals they consumed, the seasonal fluctuations in weather and
flora and fauna, and, most engagingly, the personalities of the characters they
encountered. With a graceful, direct, and humorous style, Mayle is a first-rate
travel writer. —*Brad Hooper*

✓ **McIntyre, Loren.**
Exploring South America.
Clarkson N. Potter, $40. 207p.

South America suffers from a PR problem in terms of its image in North
American eyes. One vast jungle with little or no differentiation from one
country to another is the commonly held opinion. To the contrary, insists
veteran travel and nature photographer McIntyre; and if one book can
disabuse the *norteamericano* of the idea that South America offers little in
the way of visual splendor and cultural diversity, his photographic journey
around all four corners of this provocative continent fills the bill. From Brazil's
rain forests, where the Indians' eons-old pristine existence is being threatened
by encroachments of "civilization," to the café-lined streets of Argentina's
sophisticated capital, Buenos Aires, not unlike those of Paris and Rome, to
Ecuador's majestic live volcanoes, and to the vast grasslands of the south-cen-
ter of the continent, where cattle roam Texas style, the reader is ushered
through South America's multiformity by way of a series of spectacular—but
sensitive and never garish—photographs, which often fill double-page
spreads. And—not incidentally—appearing at the beginning of chapters are
essays giving background information on geographical, biological, and his-

torical features and also highlighting McIntyre's own involvement in South America over the several decades of his explorations. —*Brad Hooper*

McPhee, John.
Looking for a Ship.
Farrar, $17.95. 242p.

Travel writer McPhee moves from land to sea with this firsthand look at the life of merchant marine Andy Chase and his fellow sailors aboard a freight ship bound for South America. McPhee's potent tales of piracy, smuggling, storms, and even the mundane days at sea that he experienced aboard the *Stella Lykes* are rife with adventure, yet offer testimony to the creaking, atrophic status of America as a civilian naval power. "From No.1 in the world in total ships, the United States Merchant Marine has dropped to No.13, while Panama and Russia are ascendant." McPhee's case for regenerating U.S. shipping is heartfelt but unobtrusive for readers who simply wish to read about the adventures of modern seamanship and revel, as did McPhee, in the lure of the sea. —*Denise Perry Donavin*

Michener, James A.
Pilgrimage: A Memoir of Poland and Rome.
Rodale, $14.95. 75p.

In 1988, Michener was invited to Poland, ostensibly by the Union of Polish Writers; the government had actually issued the invitation in order to award this formerly banned author with the nation's highest medal of honor. From Poland, Michener flew to Rome to visit another Pole, Pope John Paul II. It was actually their sixth meeting; Michener and Karol Wojtyla were old acquaintances from the author's wanderings and research in Poland. Just as the reader grows convinced that there is little exciting about Michener's "story of my winter vacation," the author imparts a few tidbits, picked up at an ambassador's dinner party, about the Oliver North conspiracy. Fans of *Poland* will certainly want to read about the fall-out from that best-seller and will be pleased to know that the royalties from this book will go to the Young Polish Writers Fund. —*Denise Perry Donavin*

✓ **Millman, Lawrence.**
Last Places: A Journey in the North.
Houghton, $18.95. 242p.

First reaction: what a good idea for a book, to follow the trail of the Vikings from Norway to Newfoundland. Second reaction: this man writes so well he'd make going from Walmart to Waldenbooks spellbinding. Travel is Millman's subject because "bodies in motion tend to drop their guard and immediately get on with their stories," and it's the stories that really interest him, whether they involve the sexual adventures of an Icelandic trawling captain, the boasts of a drunken murderer, or the geologic musings of a scientist standing at the volcano mouth of Hell. Not that he slights the art of description: we see the windswept North Atlantic Isle of Folta, "Eden minus all the damned

Travel

Travel

creeper vines"; an Icelandic tundra where the glacial discards are "battered busts of Roman emperors arranged in a semicircle"; a rural slum in Canada that "looked like Appalachia crossbred with a gypsy encampment and then struck by an earthquake." —*Pat Monaghan*

Seff, Philip and Seff, Nancy R.
Our Fascinating Earth.
Contemporary, $12.95. 304p.

The husband-and-wife authors of a syndicated column on scientific curiosities cull from it to produce this potpourri bearing its name. Chapter by chapter, the diversity of material is impressive but, unfortunately, sometimes distracting, since related subjects are not organized together. All the major scientific disciplines are represented, as are most of the historically significant accomplishments—the pyramids, ceremonial wild animal hunts in Asia Minor, the Phoenician discovery of glass, etc. The Seffs also explain many myths and mythological beasts like the unicorn and the white whale (Moby Dick) in empirical terms. A delightful book for casual science readers. —*George Hampton*

Shukman, Henry.
Sons of the Moon.
Scribner, $17.95. 192p.

On the high Andean plateau called the Altiplano, between Bolivia and Peru, dirt tracks lead from one small Aymara village to another. These Aymara, descendants of a pre-Columbian people conquered by the Incas, live in limbo between their old ways and the ways of the twentieth century. Pickups roar across salt lakes almost evaporated from the equatorial sun; fiestas celebrate the energy of food goddess Pacha Mama; entrepreneurs try to find minerals to mine and services to sell. Shukman brings us a vivid picture of a beautiful but forbidding land and of indigenous people caught between an imperial but vanished past and an uncertain future. —*Pat Monaghan*

✓ **Smith, Anthony.**
Explorers of the Amazon.
Viking, $19.95. 252p.

Five centuries of exploration and adventures are represented in Smith's profiles of the men and women who traveled up the Amazon River in search of gold, power, and scientific knowledge. From the Spanish explorers of the sixteenth century down to the early environmentalists and medical researchers of the nineteenth and twentieth centuries, Smith chronicles the great expeditions that traversed the river's immense length. Even today, the author says, changes in the river's path make it in some ways a relatively unexplored phenomenon. Among the people who challenged the river were Portuguese sailor Pedro Cabral, the European discoverer of Brazil; Baron von Humboldt, the German naturalist; and American explorer and engineer Walter Hardenburg, who helped expose the terrible conditions for rubber plantation workers. Smith invests each of their stories with appropriate drama and detail, making this remarkable sequence of events a galvanizing experience. —*John Brosnahan*

Theroux, Peter.
Sandstorms: Days and Nights in Arabia.
Norton, $18.95. 261p.

Drawn to Arabia by the allure of mystery, magic, and other sexy fantasies, Theroux began his career in Cairo teaching English and then turned journalist, albeit a reluctant one. His fluency in Arabic landed him a job as bureau chief for an English-language newspaper in Riyadh, the insular capital where his mail was censored and his phones tapped. His real interests were not in his official field of business news, but rather in the many facets of Arabian society where religion governs every aspect of life and petrowealth has distorted old systems. Theroux has a good ear for conversation and a flair for colorful language and humor. Sensitive to the inadequacies of generalizations, he concentrates on particulars. The result is a tangy blend of good-natured cynicism and curiosity. This memoir is brimming with vivid sketches of life in a volatile, often contradictory, ever-intriguing culture. —*Donna Seaman*

Thomas, G. Scott.
The Rating Guide to Life in America's Small Cities.
Prometheus, $34.95. 535p.

Statistics aren't always entertaining, but these come close. The figures on 219 cities and surrounding areas defined as "micropolitan" (smaller, but not part of metropolitan areas) are a treasure trove of useful and tantalizing information. Ten criteria are used: climate/environment, diversions, economics, education, sophistication, health care, housing, public safety, transportation, and urban proximity. Each is broken down into more specific areas, played off against metropolitan problems. "Public Safety," for example, asks how many crimes occur and how many are violent, and how good are police and fire services. Ratings relate to the national average—the U.S. average monthly pay for public school teachers is $1,789, which puts Fairbanks, Alaska, with $3,015, in first place and Hinesville, Georgia, in last with $989. The numbers, placed in a national context with introductions to each section, come from sources like the U.S. Census and professional associations, collected between 1980 and 1988. This unavoidably wide range for national data combines with good organization and pertinent commentary to give a solid sense of place for these cities. —*Virginia Dwyer*

Thomsen, Moritz.
The Saddest Pleasure: A Journey on Two Rivers.
Graywolf, $9.95. 304p.

Thomsen, though American, has spent much of his adult life in Ecuador, first as a Peace Corps volunteer—his experiences chronicled in *Living Poor* (1971)—and later as a farmer, from which perspective he wrote his second book, *The Farm on the River of Emeralds* (1978). In this, his third work,

Thomsen turns curmudgeonly; not since Paul Theroux (who, incidentally, provides an introduction) in his iconoclastic *Kingdom by the Sea: A Journey around the Coast of Britain* has a travel writer been so cranky. Though many critics and readers felt Theroux had no reason to be so negative toward his adopted homeland in *Kingdom*, it is perfectly understandable why Thomsen is grousing. He relates how he was ejected from the farm in Ecuador he had worked so hard to make productive; leaving Ecuador, he went to Brazil, to wander and ponder. Sixty-three years old at the time, Thomsen, while gathering luscious impressions as he toured Brazilian cities and countryside, simultaneously reflects on the frailty of the flesh and the propensity of humans toward selfishness. Superior travel writing. —*Brad Hooper*

Visalli, Santi.
San Francisco.
Rizzoli, $49.95. 224p.

In his third oversized city-as-siren album (after *Chicago* and *Boston*), Visalli finally gets around to what everybody assumes is America's most voluptuously lovely burg—the town you would have thought he'd do first—good ol' Baghdad by the Bay. To it he applies the same eye for bold geometries (built or natural) and lustfully luscious palette he employed to portray the Second City and Beantown. Here, more than in the earlier books, the saturated and brilliant colors he prefers (the book's introducer, Kevin Starr, rightly compares Visalli's vision to that of Maxfield "Dayglo" Parrish) are appropriate. San Francisco can seem incredibly colorful while you're there, and after you've left, it gets even more colorful. Visalli's version of it corresponds to your most romantic, got-to-go-back-there memories. Buy it and watch your patrons disappear, all bound for the bay. You go, too. —*Ray Olson*

True Crime

Deakin, James.
A Grave for Bobby.
Morrow, $19.95. 352p.

Confirmed losers Carl Hall and Bonnie Heady were executed for the 1953 kidnapping and murder of Bobby Greenlease, the young son of a prominent Missouri businessman. The pair received $600,000 in ransom, but only half of it was ever recovered. *St. Louis Post-Dispatch* reporter Deakin wants to know what happened to the missing loot. After beginning the story with the sad inevitability of Bobby's death (the kidnappers killed the boy even before they had the ransom in hand), Deakin follows the missing cash through FBI and police investigations, through money laundering in Michigan's Upper Peninsula and a brief stay in an allegedly Mob-owned bank on the South Side of Chicago, to secret interviews conducted during Robert Kennedy's historic tussle with Teamster boss Jimmy Hoffa. The money is still missing, but

Deakin gives a good idea where it's been and why. Although this account is sometimes a bit littered with distracting asides from the author, it offers a fascinating glimpse into how the Mob's long arm snaked its way into a sordid crime by two small-timers who were in over their heads. —*Peter Robertson*

Denton, Sally.
The Bluegrass Conspiracy: An Inside Story of Power, Greed, Drugs, and Murder.
Doubleday, $19.95. 336p.

Lexington bluebloods Drew Thornton and Bradley Bryant were not, it seems, what they appeared to be. The respected Kentuckians headed an organization called "the Company" that ran guns to South America, smuggled drugs into the U.S., corrupted cops, and ultimately engaged in murder and assassination over a period of 20 years. The author, an investigative reporter for a Lexington television station when the Company began to unravel in the early 1980s, meticulously re-creates the activities of Thornton and Bryant, and also of Kentucky State Police officer Ralph Ross, the man most responsible for their downfall. Denton is less convincing when she tries to implicate better-known figures from the realms of politics and sports in the Company's illegal activities, using the flimsiest kind of guilt-by-association in an apparent attempt to hype the controversy level of her material. This is not only distasteful, it is unnecessary. The core story, which is admirably substantiated, is engrossing enough. —*Dennis Dodge*

Englade, Ken.
Beyond Reason: The True Story of a Shocking Double Murder, a Brilliant and Beautiful Virginia Socialite, and a Deadly Psychotic Obsession.
St. Martin's, $19.95. 353p.

The breakthrough to solving the gruesome double murder of Virginians Derek and Nancy Haysom came in a suburban London department store when a detective noticed two shoppers committing fraud. Suddenly, the apparently motiveless killing with ritualistic undertones had suspects—the Haysoms' youngest daughter, Elizabeth, and her German boyfriend, Jens. Englade works hard at exposing the psychotic underpinnings that explain this truly weird young couple: both are sexually disturbed, self-absorbed individuals with impressive intellects and trauma-filled backgrounds. Elizabeth, in particular, was the victim of molestation by her mother, brutal beatings she endured during a trip to Europe, and various troubles at the exclusive English boarding school where her parents sent her. Like so many true-crime epics, Englade's account offers pleasure on two levels: following the carefully orchestrated investigation and marveling at the seemingly insurmountable problems of being a rich kid. —*Peter Robertson*

True Crime

✓ **Graysmith, Robert.**
The Sleeping Lady: The Trailside Killings above the Golden Gate.
Dutton, $19.95. 419p.

The hills surrounding the Bay Area are a mountain paradise for hikers and nature lovers. Murdering and raping to satisfy an uncontrollable sexual urge, David Carpenter, a nearsighted, middle-aged man with a bad stutter, dominating parents, and a history of sex offenses, stalked these hills and nearby areas from 1979 until 1981. Robert Graysmith, a political cartoonist for the *San Francisco Chronicle*, tracks Carpenter's mayhem in a detailed, relentlessly researched true-crime odyssey. Combining interviews with many near-victims, witnesses, and Carpenter himself, who emerges as an elusive yet articulate creature, Graysmith produces a work that is notable both for the author's reluctance to dwell on the gore and the emphasis on his own visual/naturalist slant. The murder scenes are brought into sharp focus, and the reader is made aware that a beautiful environment is being poisoned even as a vicious crime is taking place. *The Sleeping Lady* represents the more honorable aspects of a genre often found lacking in good taste. —*Peter Robertson*

✓ **Johnson, Joyce.**
What Lisa Knew: The Truths and Lies of the Steinberg Case.
Putnam, $19.95. 304p.

In the novel *In the Night Café* and the memoir *Minor Characters*, Johnson has written of a woman's search for sexual and emotional satisfaction. In this book, she examines one woman's realization of such a quest. That woman, however, is Hedda Nussbaum, lover of Joel Steinberg, the New York attorney convicted of first-degree manslaughter in the death of the couple's illegally obtained "daughter," Lisa. Johnson thinks Nussbaum was also Steinberg's criminal accomplice. She is indignant that the prosecutorial and media depiction of Nussbaum as a battered victim excused her from trial or even scrutiny. As Johnson sees it, "the Lisa Steinberg case turned into the Hedda Nussbaum cause," reflecting "the fact that as a society we care far less about the interests of children" than of "even blameworthy [adults]." Johnson's eloquent book is, perhaps, necessary reading in order to rebuke the ideologues of adult female victimization and to restore a sense of proportion to a nation in which there is "far more activism . . . on behalf of the unborn than there is on behalf of living children." —*Ray Olson*

Kaplan, Joel and others.
Murder of Innocence: The Tragic Life and Final Rampage of Laurie Dann.
Warner, $19.95. 352p.

Laurie Dann lived in affluent Chicago suburbs with parents she thought cold and distant. She never finished college, her marriage crumbled, she let herself decompose. Close to 30, directionless, on various forms of medication, a child-woman with a handgun license and several weapons, Laurie Dann lashed out at a hostile world: boys who had jilted her, families that no longer required her as a baby-sitter—they received packages of poisoned food. She tried to set fire to one school. At another she opened fire. One boy was killed. Later, holed up in a nearby house, she took her own life. Three *Chicago Tribune* reporters have produced this detailed and dry account of the Dann story in which they steer clear of quasi-fictional analysis. Instead, much of the text is based on the biased testimony of Laurie's former husband, Russell Dann. The reader is left with a series of disquieting questions and a profound sadness. How could a disturbed woman, known to police in several townships, come to be running free, armed, and occasionally employed as a baby-sitter? This baffling fact, never fully explained, may require the fruits of other journalistic accounts in order to be put in its proper perspective. True-crime fans, especially those who followed the well-publicized case, will be interested. —*Peter Robertson*

Kessler, Ronald.
The Spy in the Russian Club: How Glenn Souther Stole America's Nuclear War Plans and Escaped to Moscow.
Scribner, $19.95. 320p.

In several striking ways, spy Glenn Souther's story bears similarities to the John Walker case. Both men were naval officers, both had access to secrets (Souther was assigned to a naval intelligence center in Norfolk, Virginia), and both spied for the Soviets. Souther, unlike Walker, was never caught, and his motives appear ideological and psychological rather than financial. He defected in 1986, committed suicide later in Moscow, and was given a hero's burial. As he was never caught, the impact of his spying is impossible to calculate, although his security clearance gave him the run of the Norfolk center, where he had unlimited access to lists of American nuclear targets and details of military surveillance operations. On a psychological level, Souther and Walker were also similar; both were chronic womanizers, both liked to drink, both had personalities that tended toward immaturity. Curiously, both men were turned in by their abandoned wives, and, in both cases, the navy and the FBI were slow to investigate. Kessler, former correspondent for the *Washington Post*, turns the Souther story into a marvelous exposé of a twisted life, showing how Souther's hate for his father grew into hate for his country, and how, despite achieving success at almost everything he tried, Souther harbored deep feelings of insecurity. In addition to supplying all the known facts about the case, Kessler constructs a fascinating character study of the modern traitor. —*Peter Robertson*

Schechter, Harold.
Deranged.
Pocket, $4.50. 306p.

When Schechter asked Robert Bloch why so many continue to be fascinated by Ed Gein (prototype of Bloch's *Psycho*, Norman Bates), the novelist replied it's because they don't know about Albert Fish. A murderer of children whom he tortured before dispatching and, he confessed, eating, Fish was sexually aroused by his excesses, which he was instructed to do by "divine" voices. He

True Crime

liked self-torture, too. Caught in 1934, Fish seemed—as he had for years—a harmless, decrepit old man who had, paradoxically, been the responsible parent of six children. Nevertheless, with considerable ingenuity, he had kidnapped and killed perhaps 15 children and molested hundreds more before he started slaughtering his victims. Schechter relates Fish's crimes, apprehension, and sensational trial with the flair and popular tone that made his book about Gein, *Deviant*, so unputdownable. His second criminal bio, of a figure who must be reckoned the ultimate real-life boogeyman, is even more compelling, even more grippingly fascinating-repulsive. —*Ray Olson*

Wick, Steve.
Bad Company: Drugs, Hollywood, and the Cotton Club Murder.
HBJ, $19.95. 271p.

In the early 1980s, Karen ("Laney") Jacobs arrived in Miami, where she saw young Cubans entering the drug market. She watched and learned. Then, when she had her bankroll, she split for L.A. and the movie world, where she met Roy Radin, who wanted to be a producer. They both met Robert Evans, maker of *Chinatown*, who was desperate for a new hit. The three pinned their hopes on *The Cotton Club*. But Radin got greedy and was trying to cut Laney out of the deal when the pair met for dinner to discuss their differences. That was the last time Radin was ever seen alive. The question of whether Laney engineered Radin's murder is never resolved—no one has been formally accused of the crime—but the open-endedness only serves to remind us this is not a movie scenario. *Bad Company* starts out like a top-notch true-crime story; Laney in Miami has a palpable breathlessness—she's greedy, clever, exploitive, and charismatic. Unfortunately, when the story gets to L.A. and Radin shares center stage, the energy dissipates. But Wick, a Pulitzer Prize–winning reporter, avoids both psychobabble and the true-crime writer's tendency to rely on fictional reconstruction. A grim but involving tale. —*Peter Robertson*

FICTION

General Fiction

✓ **Abbey, Edward.**
Hayduke Lives!
Little, Brown, $18.95. 318p.

George Washington Hayduke, ecowarrier and absolute wildman, is back in the late Edward Abbey's last book. Rumored dead at the end of *The Monkey Wrench Gang*, Hayduke and cronies (Doc Sarvis, Bonnie Abbzug, and Seldom Seen Smith) return to the battlefield—the desert and canyon country of southern Utah, for another round of "ecotage." Hayduke is a macho Vietnam vet and master escape artist; Sarvis is a successful surgeon who burns down billboards in his spare time; Bonnie is his gal and one tough lady; and Smith is a river guide and a jack Mormon with three wives. They all love the glorious Colorado River country and come to its defense by destroying bulldozers, oil rigs, and mining operations. This sequel finds Doc, Bonnie, and Smith older and more cautious after their arrests for the monkey business they committed earlier. But Hayduke, quite alive and just as mad, stirs them back into action. Their target is the Super Giant Earth Mover, Goliath, a huge dragline excavator. They tangle once again with their archenemy, Bishop Dudley Love, but now they have some allies from real life, the Earth First people. *The Monkey Wrench Gang* inspired the Earth First movement, and now it's the author's turn to pay tribute to the group. But Abbey can't help but be irreverent, mocking conservationists as much as mining companies. While this novel doesn't sparkle as brightly as its predecessor, it is full of laughs, high adventure, and some potent commentary on our times. Abbey is as ornery, opinionated, outspoken, outrageous, and original as ever. His fine prose caresses every inch of desert, canyon, river, slickrock, and juniper tree, while his machismo is deliciously obnoxious. Hayduke, constantly pissing outdoors due to his nonstop beer guzzling, admires his output and thinks, "Thank God I'm a man." Thank God for Edward Abbey—an artist with purpose, humor, and true grit. Abbey lives! —*Donna Seaman*

Adler, John Morel.
The Hunt out of the Thicket.
Algonquin, $14.95. 208p.

In old-fashioned, exacting prose, Adler presents 10 short stories set in the woods, thickets, and swamps of the rural South. Although the physical action of hunting, farming, and fishing is always presented straightforwardly and in authentic detail, the narratives usually harbor deeper themes, such as racial discrimination and fear of loss. In "Two Moons," Adler enters "thirtysomething" territory and transforms it with a hard-hitting portrayal of a young man coming to grips with his fear of commitment. In the disturbing title story, a lovesick hunter compares the thrill of stalking and killing a deer to his broken love affair, concluding "the dead animal is his in a way she never could have been." For all the simplicity and directness of Adler's prose, it fairly seethes with big emotions, and the effect is both startling and impressive. —*Joanne Wilkinson*

Agosin, Marjorie, ed.
Landscapes of a New Land: Short Stories by Latin American Women Writers.
White Pine, $19. 194p.

Editor Agosin turns attention to female voices in the Latin American literary tradition with this anthology of short fictional pieces from the 1970s onward. Although earlier twentieth-century figures such as Maria Luisa Bombal and such well-known writers as Luisa Valenzuela are included, the book's emphasis is on introducing younger, less well known authors. The stories reflect a variety of styles, subjects, and settings; several pieces are collected under sections reflecting shared concerns and themes. The two final sections supply examples of magic realism and of children's literature. Although only one part of the book deals with overtly political topics, the history of the region and the authors' awareness of their countries' social and cultural development form an undercurrent that runs throughout. —*John Brosnahan*

Akins, Ellen.
Little Woman.
Harper, $18.95. 230p.

A somewhat humorous tale of criminal women in Wisconsin turns scary and serious with death and betrayal. Beauty, a successful and strikingly large young woman, finds sudden marriage and motherhood (of twins) so startling she comes a bit undone and flees. Nearly ending up on skid row, Beauty hatches a scheme to build a retreat for troubled women in the wilds of Wisconsin with funding from an eccentric benefactor, known as Clara Bow Cole. After assembling their crew of sometimes sad, sometimes amusing misfits, the women stake their northern claim and begin to get on with it. Just as Beauty's notion of taking over the place for herself when the rest drop out seems to be coming true, she discovers she wants to make the communal dream work. And Clara Bow, who has progressed from swindled eccentric to beloved friend, reveals an even more surprising truth. Part mystery, part human tragicomedy, this strange work fascinates both in plot and characterization. A most original and almost unclassifiable novel. —*Deb Robertson*

✔ **Alther, Lisa.**
Bedrock.
Knopf, $19.95. 326p.

Small-town New England life hasn't been so torridly portrayed since *Peyton Place*—or erotic agonies so hilariously overwrought, either. Alther, author of *Kinflicks*, settles her readers down in the midst of the tranquil, snow-draped beauty of Roches Ridge, Vermont, and waits for the spring thaw to uncover the winter's accumulation of junk that lies below the wind-blown drifts. Unfortunately, all the dirt isn't on the ground, but Alther isn't afraid to dish it all out in spirited fashion, as she exposes all sorts of dangerous liaisons, unrequited passions, and just plain weird behavior. On a single visit to this snake pit of desires, a New York photographer becomes so enchanted with the picturesque village—at least with the winter version of rural serenity— that she leaves Gotham, her husband, her children, and her friends to set up an idyllic new life. But her urban sophistication and previous globe-trotting existence certainly don't prepare her for what she uncovers in Roches Ridge or, indeed, in her own life. While there are plenty of targets in this comedy, Alther's humor is never savage or mean-spirited. She documents the wonder of sexual attraction—between men and women, between women and women, and between men and men—in all of its power, frustration, and ultimate acceptance. A novel that is as funny as it is moving in its portrait of the complexities of life and love. —*John Brosnahan*

Amis, Martin.
London Fields.
Crown/Harmony, $19.95. 480p.

A cunning suspense tale of physical and psychic mayhem. For a variety of reasons a beautiful young woman has decided to become a murder victim and sets out in a methodical manner to choose her own killer. This bizarre scheme is hindered by the narrator, who becomes a key player in the resolution of complex emotions and motives. Having set up a meeting in a pub with two likely suspects—a sexually avaricious bounder and a disappointed husband— the woman manipulates their desires to her own unsavory ends. This scheme develops into a darkly comic *liebestod* that climaxes at a surreal dart championship, with the winner, the loser, and the victim all determined within the novel's final pages. Another caustic portrayal of human desires from the author of *Success*, this time heightened by a more deeply sinister and squalid atmosphere. —*John Brosnahan*

Anderson, Lauri.
Hunting Hemingway's Trout.
Atheneum, $17.95. 176p.

This quirky pastiche of short sketches, all related to Ernest Hemingway either through theme or character, is sandwiched between factual snippets on Hemingway's life. Several of the lead characters are obsessed with Hemingway's work; in "A Short Unhappy Life," for example, a frustrated college professor persuades his dim-witted girlfriend to simulate the final death scene from "The Short Happy Life of Francis Macomber," complete with a rampaging if ancient buffalo and a Mannlicher rifle. Other selections take a more lighthearted approach, as in the title story in which two cousins set out to fish the Big Two-Hearted River but end up dining on road kill. Although the exact tone of the collection is hard to pinpoint, it seems to waver between two extremes. Anderson is either saying that the modern world is too banal a setting for Papa's outsize appetites or that his fictional heroes were, in fact, the same brand of immature, unhappy adults she draws with such devastating accuracy. —*Joanne Wilkinson*

Appel, Allen.
Till the End of Time.
Doubleday, $19.95. 412p.

Alex Balfour, the time-traveling hero of the immensely popular *Time after Time* and *Twice upon a Time*, returns in these pages to continue his involuntary excursions along the space/time continuum. In this outing, Alex travels back to World War II in the Pacific, where he becomes directly involved in the attack on Pearl Harbor, a PT boat mission in the South Pacific, the plight of Allied prisoners of war, and the development of the atomic bomb. As Alex ping-pongs back and forth through time, he also meets up with a host of luminaries that includes Albert Einstein, Franklin Roosevelt, John F. Kennedy, and Betty Grable. Appel is neither subtle nor profound in his writing; however, his love of history combines with a terrific premise and a decent story line to carry the day in a novel his growing audience is sure to enjoy. —*Steve Weingartner*

Appelfeld, Aharon.
The Healer.
Grove Weidenfeld, $16.95. 128p.

Widely recognized as one of the most powerful writers of the Holocaust, Appelfeld escaped from a concentration camp when he was eight and survived by hiding in the forests of the Ukraine for three years. Now living in Israel, Appelfeld has written eight novels that have been published in English. His latest is written in the same spare and ironic style as the previous ones. The healer of the title is a rabbi who fails to cure a Viennese businessman's emotionally ill daughter but turns her and her mother to religion. This family of assimilated Jews is thus divided, as the father remains rooted in the secular world. *The Healer* is set on the eve of World War II and the Holocaust and uncomfortably hints at the horrors to come. Like his other novels, a small but invaluable jewel. —*George Cohen*

Auchincloss, Louis.
The Lady of Situations.
Houghton, $20.95. 275p.

Auchincloss' modern morality tale features Natica Chauncey, a young woman from an old New York family whose fortune was lost during the Depression.

Natica is determined to improve her status, but when she marries minister Tommy Barnes and they settle in at the Averhill school for boys, it seems that social climbing is out. The appearance of an Averhill alumnus with looks, money, and charm presents Natica with new opportunities. She is soon divorced and remarried despite the social disapprobation of the 1930s. The story, told from Natica's view, is perfectly reasonable—she is a bright, talented young woman, who eventually becomes a lawyer (Auchincloss' highest kudo) plagued by bad luck. On the other hand, Natica's Aunt Ruth, who shares the novel's narration, sees her as a scheming, unladylike figure. This sense of the duality of Natica's nature adds even more interest to the well-told tale. —*Denise Perry Donavin*

Auster, Paul.
The Music of Chance.
Viking, $18.95. 217p.

Auster loves extremes, capturing them within the structure of his architectural prose. Author of the acclaimed New York Trilogy and *Moon Palace*, Auster delves again into his love for odd, compulsive journeys and labors. Former firefighter Jim Nashe finds himself addicted to cross-country drives, covering thousands of miles for no defined reason. Almost out of money, he picks up Pozzi, who plays poker for a living. Nashe ends up staking him in a game with two big-time lottery winners living on an isolated estate in Pennsylvania. The enigmatic millionaires use their wealth to indulge in peculiar hobbies, including the acquisition of 10,000 large stones that once made up an Irish castle. When Pozzi loses every cent and then some, he and Nashe agree to work off their debt by building a wall out of the castle stones. This Kafkaesque tale of psychotic adaptation, or "warped voodoo logic," with its fine gallows humor, is highly recommended. —*Donna Seaman*

Baker, Sharlene.
Finding Signs.
Knopf, $18.95. 243p.

Sharlene Baker's debut novel—about a mid-seventies hitchhiker committed to "adventure"—has the kind of heroine who really grows on you. Criscrossing the country several times over many months, Brenda wends her way to Al in Spokane, who wants to marry her. Brenda's ambivalence about the proposed marriage lengthens the trip considerably, though, and it's no surprise to find, when she finally arrives, that he's married someone else. The journey to Al is only the framework for a remarkably well-assembled first novel. Our hero finds many literal and spiritual signs in her distinctly humble quest, and her creator's self-restraint is tangible. Vagabond Brenda's hippie friends and on-the-road escapades always manage to swerve to safety before they become laughable, and every authentic scene adds a piece to the story. —*Deb Robertson*

General Fiction

Banville, John.
The Book of Evidence.
Scribner, $17.95. 224p.

In an insidious voice, cultured killer Freddie Montgomery details the sordid events leading up to his brutal, seemingly motiveless murder of a scullery maid. Freddie is a failed scientist who, though married and a father, leads an aimless life island-hopping in the Caribbean. Spending most of his time drinking in low-life resort bars, he incurs a large gambling debt with a local mobster and is forced to leave his wife and child as ransom while he returns to his native Ireland. Moving in an alcoholic stupor, bitterly wrangling with his widowed mother, Freddie feebly attempts to extract money from his relatives. In a last pathetic effort to cover his debt, he steals a valuable painting and viciously beats an innocent bystander. An unreliable narrator (How much of this "confession" is really true?) who is filled with self-loathing, Freddie is a disturbing, haunting figure. Author Banville's formidable writing skills are everywhere evident in this revealing portrait of a killer's dark heart. —*Joanne Wilkinson*

Barthelme, Frederick.
Natural Selection.
Viking, $18.95. 208p.

Barthelme's latest novel involves characters that would fit comfortably into the landscape of his stories collected in *Moon Deluxe* —divorced and remarried men and women who fit the "thirtysomething" mold but who resist easy categorization and who quickly discover that talking about their problems and needs neither solves nor fulfills them. The prime example here is Peter, who is very concerned about the decline of family values, as well he should be: his roles as husband and father suffer from aimlessness and numbing self-recrimination that do nothing to help resolve his indecisiveness as a mate and parent. Barthelme's deadpan rendering of his character's complaints about life in general and his situation in particular are as off-the-wall and riveting as ever, even if the novel's conclusion promises an even darker, more tragic world to come. —*John Brosnahan*

Bausch, Richard.
The Fireman's Wife and Other Stories.
Simon & Schuster/Linden, $17.95. 205p.

When Bausch writes about marriage and family relationships, he shows a cranky, cracked surface, while at the same time offering a peek at the expansiveness of what's brewing underneath—where connections are really made and broken. Throughout these short stories there is the palpable sensation that life has been poured into something that can't possibly contain it, and what you see—what leaks out of the cracks—are the repetitive details of everyday existence, the irritations of sharing so much. Bausch is a remarkable writer and a confident one. He assumes that the reader will recognize this world and intuit its meaning. Although his prose is lean and exact, his stories are fluid and not at all tightly controlled. One precise, fleeting detail

General Fiction

can lead us far into a character that we may feel quite on our own. In "The Brace," a stable, married daughter, Marilyn, gives a hug to her oft-absent, pompous, famous playwright father: "I put my lips to his cheek, and he pats my arm, turning a little, as if already looking for a way out." The little turn is so perfect a gesture for the man we know at this point, but then Marilyn goes on to say that he "is essentially a timid man," and the turn takes on a deeper meaning—he becomes whole, and we see more than we necessarily even want to see. Bausch is the least showy of writers, yet he is able to show so much. —*Frances Woods*

Baxter, Charles.
A Relative Stranger.
Norton, $17.95. 223p.

A well-established and admired composer of short stories, Baxter is also a published poet (*Imagined Paintings*), and the precision and economy of poetry shape each of the tales in this volume, his third collection of stories. Baxter's timing and descriptive vocabulary are perfect and his emotional pitch subtle and sure. In "Fenstad's Mother," he depicts the finely honed power of mind within the age-weakened body of an elderly woman, while in "Westland," he writes about a man depressed by the degradation of nature. People cope with the unfamiliar in the title story, which is about adoption, and in "The Disappeared," where a Swede on business in Detroit has a strange encounter. Love between men and women at different stages of life is the theme of a triad of short, sharp stories titled "Three Parabolic Tales." Issues of communication are at the heart of each tale—an aspect of love and life well understood by this word artist. —*Donna Seaman*

Bell, Madison Smartt.
Barking Man and Other Stories.
Ticknor & Fields, $19.95. 256p.

This is Madison Smartt Bell's second short story collection. The first, *Zero db and other Stories*, was excellent; *The Barking Man* is even better. These memorable tales take place in Bell's native South; on the streets of New York, London, and the French Riviera; and even inside a mouse's cage. Each setting is fully realized, perfectly expressing the space and pace of each environment. His characters are striking creations: misfits and loners, visionaries and atypical heroes, their lives pulsing with menace. Bell confronts life's essentials, whether in "Holding Together," told from the perespective of a philosopher mouse whose wisdom helps him survive captivity, or in the southern stories, all with the same precision and melancholy patience that distinguished Bell's last novel, *Soldier's Joy*, or in the New York stories, which portray homelessness, child abuse, and the relentlessly lonely and grim routine of the streets. His characters are sometimes noble, sometimes weak, but always solitary, living on the edge. Bell is the prose poet of aloneness, offering us an unflinching and compassionate interpretation of a hostile world. —*Donna Seaman*

Berger, Thomas.
Orrie's Story.
Little, Brown, $18.95. 282p.

Prolific novelist Berger's newest is based on an old, enduring tale—the Greek Oresteia tragedy. Set in small-town America at the end of World War II, Orrie is Orestes, Augie Mencken is Agamemnon, Esther is Clytemnestra, E. G. is Aegisthus, Ellie is Electra, Gena is Iphigenia, and a college acquaintance of Orrie's named Paul fits the role of Pylades. Berger has a great time setting the story in motion, embellishing it with twentieth-century twists and appropriately flawed characters. Augie fakes going to war to get away from his evil wife and her lover, cousin E. G. He sends postcards bragging about his combat exploits while working down South at a defense plant and romancing a virginal clairvoyant. He returns to get a divorce . . . you know the rest. Entertaining and snappy, Berger makes good use of the classic framework. —*Donna Seaman*

Bernard, April.
Pirate Jenny.
Norton, $18.95. 240p.

Connie Frances LaPlante drugs her loneliness with shoplifting and the dark, wild music of Kurt Weill and Lotte Lenya. Stuck in a dead-end New England town with a neglectful mother and an absent, manipulative father, she takes up her dad's flimflam values and lies and cheats her way to New York City. Shedding her past and her persona, Connie transforms herself into Jenny, a "German" immigrant, and climbs the social heights with one con after another. Like a tightrope walker, Jenny mesmerizes the reader with her skill and daring and the dangers of her enterprise, which go beyond discovery to the death of her authentic self. In simple but vivid and engrossing language, Bernard has written a coming-of-age novel about a failure to come of age. Jenny's exploits are fun, but as she lurches from one lie to the next, she leaves Connie ever further behind and draws ever nearer to the heartlessness and violence of her much-admired prewar Berlin. —*Leone McDermott*

Bloch, Robert.
Psycho House.
St. Martin's, $16.95. 224p.

Someone in Fairvale couldn't leave well enough alone. They had to rebuild the burnt-down Bates house and motel, hoping to snare tourists intrigued by the butcher-knife murders ol' Norman did 30 years back. And no sooner is the place ready to open than an 11-year-old girl gets hacked down while snooping around. That brings true-crime writer Amy Haines to town to do her own kind of snooping. Fairvalers are not amused nor very helpful, although they are increasingly interested in her presence as more citizens are hacked up. Bloch's second *Psycho* sequel is more a whodunit than a horror-screamer, but it's a good one that keeps you guessing all the way. Meanwhile, there is Bloch's marvelous bargain-basement prose, full of well-turned clichés and wry cracks, such as the characterization of the local country club: "like thousands of others—a recreational center for wealthy businessmen who have not yet been indicted." Reliable entertainment from a practiced hand. —*Ray Olson*

Bodett, Tom.
The Big Garage on Clearshot: Growing Up, Growing Old, and Going Fishing at the End of the Road.
Morrow, $18.95. 288p.

More of the little stories that the homey-voiced Motel 6 spokesman delivers first, and with yokelly panache, on the radio. The characters—Argus Winslow, the town grouch with the heart of gold; conscientiously bemused town manager Emmitt Frank; benighted ne'er-do-well Doug McDoogan; feminist-environmentalist harridan Tamara Dupree; earnestly pubescent eighth-grader Norman Tuttle; and the rest—all reprise their acts from *The End of the Road.* And they're all mellowing, which is the one thing you can be sure will happen to everybody in Bodett's Alaskan answer to Lake Wobegon. Despite such genuine tragedies as Ed Flannigan losing his right arm, End of the Road is the most comforting small town in any form of American fiction since Andy Griffith's Mayberry, and fans of that classic sitcom really ought to be told about it if they don't already know. —*Ray Olson*

Bottoms, David.
Easter Weekend.
Houghton, $17.95. 198p.

It's almost Easter, and the Holtzclaw brothers of Macon, Georgia, have plans—Carl owes money to the Mob, and he's enlisted the help of his brother, Connie, a former boxer, in a kidnapping-extortion scam. But the plans go horribly awry when Connie befriends an old bum, oversleeps at his girlfriend Rita's house, and returns to the hideout in the morning, forsaking the cover of night and risking the success of the entire venture. From the book's title onward, Bottoms (an award-winning poet, anthologist, and novelist) creates a study in juxtapositions, a subtle clash of light and dark, hopes and realities, and goodness and evil. And from the first sentence on, the reader is drawn into a world where terror and courage go hand in hand. Most compelling, however, is the incongruousness of Bottoms' poetic voice describing the brutal actions, creating a heart-stopping, thickly nightmarish mix of sweetness and death. This novel proves that hearts of gold are one-half fool's gold (as the bum says, regarding humanity, "It's a mix. I seen a bunch of 'em and it's a real mix . . . and that's the problem, ain't it?"). A problem, indeed, and who will rise to live again after this *Easter Weekend* is anyone's guess. —*Eloise Kinney*

✓ **Bourjaily, Vance.**
Old Soldier.
Donald I. Fine, $18.95. 172p.

En route to salmon fishing in Maine, retired top sergeant Joe McKay stops in New York to see his brother, Tommy, hard-driving fiddler-leader of a

General Fiction

successful bluegrass band and a competition-level Scots piper. Tommy plans to go to a Highland Games in Nova Scotia and drop in on Joe afterwards. Both brothers operate in milieus that reek of machismo, but Tommy goes Joe one better as a man's man—he's gay, as Joe's long known and accepted. Unfortunately, he does not escape the fate of so many hard-living gay men: he has AIDS. This discovery and its disclosure to Joe precipitate the violent climactic events of Bourjaily's incident-packed short novel. Writing with Hemingwayesque economy, Bourjaily's tough enough to please Norman Mailer but also as tender as the late James Jones could be with similar characters. Despite a few errors on the subject of piping and an overabundance of sensational happenings, his is the most unusual AIDS novel to date and a terrifically appealing portrait of true brotherly love. —*Ray Olson*

Bowering, Marilyn.
To All Appearances a Lady.
Viking, $18.95. 336p.

A novel about time passing and time passed. It is also about a curious, middle-aged man who hardly considers himself sentimental, yet has an unforgiving need to find out about parents he never knew. Robert Lam, half-British, half-Chinese, leaves Vancouver Island shortly after his stepmother's funeral to sail from Victoria to the Charlotte Islands. His stepmother's ghost "accompanies" him on the journey, whereby he unravels the circumstances of his birth. Fogs, ghosts, chilling stories, unpleasant memories, damp sea air, and the loneliness of the voyage add immeasurably to this introspective and brooding saga. At its melancholy end, Lam sets fire to his boat, stranding himself on D'Arcy Island, a leper colony at the turn of the century and the place where he was born. —*Cynthia Ogorek*

✓ **Bracewell, Michael.**
Divine Concepts of Physical Beauty.
Knopf, $18.95. 261p.

Since his earlier *Crypto-Amnesia Club*, a rather grand attempt to rewrite Ellis' *Less than Zero* in the style of Evelyn Waugh (though sadly aping *Brideshead* rather than the droller and slicker *Scoop*), Bracewell has acquired a major American publisher and a grander, more ambitious storytelling mode. He still insists on trying to find meaning behind every shallow utterance and artfully struck pose his upper-class British characters (Sloanies) can summon, but, despite that, his rich tale of tormented love is remarkably, even breathlessly, readable. Bravely reworking the low-fiction device of multiple coincidences, Bracewell crosscuts among a series of troubled, truly bizarre relationships, chief among them being the doomed love of performance artist Kelly for Miles Harrier. (Hanging stock still from the ceiling and covered in body paint—she's the centerpiece in a living art exhibit—Kelly watches as Harrier cuddles with another woman; Kelly releases her safety harness, and both women are killed.) While his characters are largely self-centered—either the charmed elite or reckless bohemians—

Bracewell manages to penetrate their shells for some chilling and astute observations. This most ambitious novel essays a stark portrayal of youthful individuality run amok and destined to be persecuted and abhorred—twin tactics the class-fixated British know only too well. Just ask Evelyn Waugh. —*Peter Robertson*

✓ **Braverman, Kate.**
Squandering the Blue: Stories.
Ballantine/Fawcett Columbine, $17.95. 241p.

Twelve linked stories by poet and author of the critically acclaimed novel *Palm Latitudes*. The central figure in each of these unsettling tales is a woman on the verge of 40 who writes and teaches poetry and has a daughter, often hostile. The women are also alcoholic, obsessed with poetry, and dangerously porous to the malignancy of the world. The title story, told from the daughter's point of view, is an indictment of the mother's bohemianism. "Falling in October" is a startling vision of our times as a continuation of the Dark Ages. Other stories find the poet struggling with the incapacitating demons of alcoholism. Often in a trance of helplessness, she lets men boss her around and abuse her. Braverman creates the monotone of confession and the disorienting crackling of intermittent sanity. Her image-saturated and piercing prose is a mosaic of mirror shards reflecting a cruel, fragmented world in which her heroine is finally redeemed. Cathartic and written with a poet's precision. —*Donna Seaman*

Breton, Marcela, ed.
Hot and Cool: Jazz Short Stories.
NAL/Plume, $9.95. 336p.

This is a brave collection, in that fiction about jazz has usually been savaged by jazz critics who also write about books, i.e., a majority of the profession. Fortunately, from the music's beginnings, fiction writers have liked it and set stories in its milieu. The 19 selections here span from the 1920s Harlem renaissance of both literature and music in Rudolph Fisher's "Common Meter" through the revolutionary 1960s in LeRoi Jones' "Screamers" to somewhat later in Toni Cade Bambara's perfectly pitched domestic monologue, "Medley." These and contributions by the likes of J. F. Powers, Langston Hughes, Ann Petry, Terry Southern, James Baldwin, Maya Angelou, and Richard Yates ensure high quality in the fiction. From Peter De Vries and Al Young come sketches that aren't necessarily fictional, and pungent stories by Josef Skvorecky and Julio Cortázar add international flavor. In all, a strong collection that well may bring short story connoisseurs to jazz (and jazz fans to short stories). —*Ray Olson*

General Fiction

General Fiction

Brookner, Anita.
Lewis Percy.
Pantheon, $17.95. 261p.

Lewis Percy is a young doctoral student in Paris researching his thesis on the hero in nineteenth-century French literature. Shortly after he returns home to England, his mother dies and he marries Tissy Harper. (Given to romantic fancies, Lewis has cast himself in the heroic role, as emancipator of Tissy from the "thraldom" of her mother's home.) Unfortunately, he soon finds himself enslaved to a demure but agoraphobic spouse, who, once her spirit is freed through Lewis' efforts, leaves him and joins a women's liberation group. Lewis' jousting with the mundane realities of life and his determined efforts to achieve a semblance of heroism make for a serpentine emotional journey, but one that Brookner's loyal audience will want to follow. —*Denise Perry Donavin*

Brown, Larry.
Big Bad Love.
Algonquin, $16.95. 228p.

Brown is a writer who knows about life and about rejection, two concepts that are often synonymous for writers. Many of the stories in his collection pertain to "the writing life," while others celebrate, or diminish, life in general. Although Brown's stories range in scope from the excruciatingly imaginative to the tawdry and sad, they are all remarkably readable, permeated with sex, lust, anger, bitterness, and particularly good writing. He reveals relationships between men and women, men and men, fathers and children, writers and editors, most of whom are rural characters who do a lot of drinking and driving around. In one story, "The Apprentice," the husband of an author remarks, "I don't know where this writing thing came from or what caused it, but it's a part of her now, like her arms or her face." For Brown, the art of storytelling is as intrinsic as that, as a careful reading of these stories will demonstrate. —*Ivy Burrowes*

Buckley, John.
Statute of Limitations.
Simon & Schuster, $19.95. 385p.

Thomas O'Malley is on top of the world as a speechwriter for the newly inaugurated president, but his lofty position becomes precarious as old college roommate Dave Nicole threatens to expose O'Malley's youthful misdeeds. Nicole has yet to mend his dope-dealing ways and has, in fact, become an out-and-out criminal, a career that impels him to coerce the hero into a scheme to smuggle cocaine aboard *Air Force 1*, of all conveyances. Exposure is the predictable result as the wordsmith gets canned and the media feeding frenzy begins. Sure this plot is microwaveable, but all the ingredients for preparing a Beltway brouhaha are here—the contending ambitions, the cocktail gossips, the news leaks, and so on. A good effort from a professional politico with a feel for the power game and its frequent trivialities. —*Gilbert Taylor*

Buechner, Frederick.
The Wizard's Tide.
Harper, $13.95. 128p.

Teddy Schroeder is 11 and his sister and playmate Bean is 7½ when the family fortunes hit bottom. Their father, ineffectual son of an ineffectual man who wed wealth, thinks he sees a way up in a friend's scheme to make glass less brittle. To finance it, he wheedles money from his scornful mother and sells his wife's stock without her consent, after which they fight and she contrives to humiliate him in front of Teddy. The venture fails, leading to tragedy. Teddy, singularly innocent for his age, sees all but experiences it from the distance of childhood and its preoccupations with amusement and horrid imaginings, the loss of parents chief among them. Buechner's intent here is to relate childhood memories in an unanalytic, childlike style. This forces him to fill the story with the physical details and sensual recollections that bring it to life. Readers who treasure such lookings backward as Hamner's *Homecoming* (source of "The Waltons") and Maxwell's *So Long, See You Tomorrow* will most enjoy this quiet novella. —*Ray Olson*

Burdekin, Katharine.
The End of This Day's Business.
Feminist Press, $24.95. 190p.

The premier edition of an extraordinary book written just before World War II: a remarkably well thought out feminist utopia set 4,000 years hence in a steady-state world order in which women and men are strictly segregated after puberty except for sexual encounters. Women run things and constitute the entire educated class. Men are reared to submissively labor and play sports, without knowing their fathers or anything of the male-run societies of long ago, all extinguished in a great mid-twentieth-century war. It is a peaceful existence but one without sexual equality or love. An artist named Grania intrudes on this tranquillity. Feeling that loving, egalitarian relationships between women and men are possible, desirable, and historically inevitable, she teaches her son history—an offense punishable by death for both. Burdekin was influenced by Marxism, and her account of a Communist golden age after the great war and her trust in dialectical materialism are now embarrassments. But her logical working out of the political consequences of psychosexual differences is fascinating and enthralling. —*Ray Olson*

Buzbee, Lewis.
Fliegelman's Desire.
Ballantine, $7.95. 208p.

For Fliegelman—recently divorced and young at heart, bored with business in an office tower—desire is all consuming. Whereas others seem to know what they desire, "he could not decide which of these forms was the one he yearned for most." So he quits business to work in a bookstore/coffeehouse that seems filled to brimming with other people's wants. One day he is attracted to a customer named Mimi. Has Fliegelman finally found what he

General Fiction

desires, or are the days conspiring against him? Buzbee's use of simple, voluptuous language about everyday objects in an urban environment—the humorous personification of night and day, the witty conversations in the bookstore, and the self-conscious postmodernist dialogue ("He told her that he knew, and he knew that she knew that he really knew")—forces us to journey with Fliegelman in his search. Set against smooth-talking, sue-for-damages 1980s San Francisco, this is the first in a projected trilogy. Readers will eagerly await the next installment from this language lover. —*Danny Rochman*

Byatt, A. S.
Possession: A Romance.
Random, $22.95. 546p.

No one is going to give this book a bad review. Who would want to say anything nasty about this formidably intelligent woman who, in an act of extraordinary bravado, has attempted to refashion the novel in the form of a romance—overlaid, in the manner of a pastiche, with long passages of philosophical verse, symbolist storytelling, and a narrative of detection—about two inhibited academics. In a way, the double narrative (a relationship between nineteenth-century poets foreshadows that between the academics trying to uncover its secret) creates a postmodern novel bent on introspection; its contortions are fascinating. Nonetheless, virtue is not the same as art, and this novel ends up where most English novels come to rest: in the realm of the hollow good. The problem is perhaps that the English no longer have a relationship with their language: they either distrust or revere it. There are exceptions (one thinks, for example of Graham Swift). But contrast just five pages of Byatt's prose with that of Salman Rushdie or Patrick White (Indian and Australian), and you will see how clearly her work resembles a handsome but empty seashell. Admirers of John Fowles and Iris Murdoch, on the other hand, will regard this criticism as fallacious; they will focus on the novel's undeniable strengths. —*Stuart Whitwell*

Champagne, John.
When the Parrot Boy Sings.
Lyle Stuart, $8.95. 205p.

The author of *The Blue Lady's Hands* again has a young gay New Yorker tell his story. Just out of college in the early 1980s, Will's a collage artist eking out a meager living by cleaning the apartments of better-off men and looking for a love commensurate with his idealism. That would be a "polygamous monogamy," sexually safe (as he and his fellows start worrying about AIDS) but providing some variety. He thinks he finds something like his goal when he falls for Dennis and Scott, although they caution him not to impose on them (they're content with their promiscuous "open" relationship). Will ignores what they say and eventually must face what Dennis compassionately tells him: "People . . . want different things, they learn different things from life." Very similar thematically to Reidinger's *Best Man*, Champagne's book is not quite as good because of Will's irksome, long-winded fantasies about the titular symbol. Still, Will is convincing, particular, and vital, and so is his story. This sexy second outing consolidates Champagne's place as one of the best new gay novelists. —*Ray Olson*

Cheuse, Alan.
The Light Possessed.
Gibbs Smith/Peregrine Smith, $19.95. 325p.

Cheuse is on a roll. His last book, *Tennessee Waltz and Other Stories*, was well received, as was his previous novel, *The Grandmother's Club*. His newest is a bold undertaking; he's written a novel based on the life of Georgia O'Keeffe. In an amalgam of polyphonic narration, time shifts, letters, and journal entries, Cheuse first invents a mythic beginning for his character, artist Ava Boldin, and than closely follows the trail of his real-life subject to Chicago, South Carolina, Texas, New York, and finally, New Mexico. At first the pace is awkward, more like a slide show than a film, but once Ava hits New York, Cheuse's prose comes alive. His descriptions of O'Keeffe's paintings show a genuine affinity and seasoned familiarity with her uncompromising autobiography, which accompanies the magnificent 1976 Viking/Studio book of her work. He has tapped into her consuming vision, eroticism, and dedication but has also made her an otherwordly creature, leaving humanity to the other characters, including his intriguing version of Alfred Stieglitz. O'Keeffe has recently become a sort of icon, and many believers will seek out and enjoy this valiant effort at telling her story. And then, hopefully, they'll return to the source: her own expressions of light, life, and earth. —*Donna Seaman*

✓ Clewlow, Carol.
Keeping the Faith.
Poseidon, $16.95. 119p.

The stultifying effect religion can exert upon a life is searingly conveyed in Clewlow's somewhat impressionistic novel. As a young girl, the narrator, Maud, was totally enveloped in the fundamentalist Christian beliefs and practices of her family's church. Now, from the plateau of adulthood, Maud relates, with increasing cynicism and remorse, the scenes of adolescence that resulted in her alienation from her parents. Clewlow limns the prayer scenes, especially the one involving the baptism, so realistically that the reader is immersed in Maud's experience and comprehends totally her innocence and desire for eternal security—not to mention her emerging doubts and rebellion. —*Denise Perry Donavin*

Clifford, Sigerson.
The Red-Haired Woman and Other Stories.
Dufour Editions/Mercier Press, $9.95. 94p.

There are 17 stories in this slight volume, some of them, singly, richer than the complete output of many a fashionable minimalist. They're all Irish country stories, set in the author's native Kerry. They're about such matters as how illiterate Old Tim gets his will written only to tear it up, how crazy Red Ellie makes a greater fool of improvident James Moylan, how John Dan's

General Fiction

daughter in America sends him a bullfighter's jacket, how diminutive Jureen Madden finds a new home after 65 years with his behemothian brother Dan, and whether social-climbing Aeneas MacCarthy is the true descendant of the legendary king of Munster. The voice that speaks them is that of a wise, gentle public-house raconteur with, of course, a twinkle in his eye, and their language is sweetly full of the witty metaphors, Gaelicisms, and lilting inversions of fine Irish speech. One might object that they are sentimental and commonplace—the reply to which is that the common people and events Clifford so effortlessly brings to life (because he *knows* them) are worthy of sentiment of the noblest kind. —*Ray Olson*

Collins, Jackie.
Lady Boss.
Simon & Schuster, $21.95. 608p.

Lucky's back. Last seen in *Lucky*, Collins' story of life among the rich and overstimulated, our heroine is up to her old tricks, trying to wield power, maintain an active sex life, and dodge hitmen. As always, Collins knows how to hold readers' attention; even if those attention spans are short, some of her chapters are only a page long—a good fit. Using her knowledge of Hollywood—the glamour, the tawdriness, the hilifers and the scum, Collins massages sex scandals into power-mongering and comes up with—What else? A potential miniseries. Here the story hinges on Lucky's efforts to take over a Hollywood studio—her actor husband doesn't like the higher-ups. Unlike most spouses who can only listen sympathetically to work-related complaints, Lucky can actually do something about Lennie's problems, but she runs afoul of some nasty men along the way and temporarily alienates Lennie, too. Boy, you can't win for losing. Fortunately, despite people trying to kill her, Lucky is still lucky. Which makes another sequel likely. Does that make *us* lucky, or what? —*Ilene Cooper*

Colwin, Laurie.
Goodbye without Leaving.
Poseidon, $18.95. 249p.

Geraldine Coleshares frets: "My life was a cloud of gnats." A rock 'n' roll fanatic, she opted out of graduate school to go on the road as the "white Shakette," a backup singer with a black R & B group. She acquires an admirer, Johnny, who manages to lead a double life—an ardent rock and roller as well as a successful New York lawyer. When the Shakette gig is up, Geraldine tries to avoid marriage because it's what her snobbish mother wants, but she loves Johnny and gives in. She suffers anxiety about adult life. (How do people know what to do?) She loves being a mother and can't understand why she has to "be" anything else; she finds joy in pure experience: singing, dancing, holding her infant son. Geraldine is funny, independent, self-deprecating, and genuine, squirming with discomfort at smug dinner parties and engaging in witty repartee with her ever-patient husband. Colwin is known for wry, entertaining fiction, but this is a cut above her earlier works. The tone here is disarmingly light, the humor intimate, and the plot inventive. A cheerfully irreverent look at an identity crisis and its unexpected resolution. —*Donna Seaman*

Compo, Susan.
Life after Death and Other Stories.
Faber and Faber, $18.95. 228p.

A slick collection of tales about post-punk scenesters set in L.A. and London. The title piece is a novella about Zelda Zonk, a Marilyn Monroe freak, Vex, a David Bowie disciple, and Cruella, a vamp with a penchant for puns. Zelda communes with Marilyn and discovers that her long-lost diary was buried with her. Zelda and her cohorts break into the vault, take the diary, and flee to London where they get involved with a prince and the press. The short stories share characters and an aura of grubby manipulation and aggressive pointlessness. Compo, ever deadpan and hip, dissects the phenomena of dead celebrity worship and its relationship to the concept of an afterlife. The predoomed search for meaning in life leads her garishly attired characters to emulate Sid Vicious one day and convert to Catholicism the next. Smart, sassy, and tough, Compo is a facade-buster. —*Donna Seaman*

Conley, Robert J.
Go-Ahead Rider.
Evans, $15.95. 159p.

George Tanner is a mixed-blood Cherokee. His parents were killed during the Civil War, and he was raised in an orphanage. A kindly minister has provided him with a Harvard education, but since teaching holds little appeal, George returns to the Cherokee nation where he hesitantly takes a job as deputy to Go-Ahead Rider. In the midst of a vehement debate over the railroad coming into the nation, a reclusive drunk is blamed for a murder. Go-Ahead and George investigate, only to find a connection to the rail controversy. Veteran novelist Conley works on three levels: murder mystery, frontier political potboiler, and the search for personal identity. Intelligent and entertaining, this novel contains all the standard western plot elements plus a great deal more depth. —*Wes Lukowsky*

Cornwell, Patricia D.
Body of Evidence
Scribner, $17.95. 387p.

For all the wrong reasons, Cornwell's debut novel, *Postmortem*, generated a storm of publicity. Her coroner/sleuth Kay Scarpella pleased the critics and drew the obligatory comparisons with Paretsky's Warshawski and Grafton's Millhone. But it was the welter of forensic details that created the hoopla; the more delicate mystery readers apparently like murder fine but don't have the stomach for postmortems. That's a pity, because Cornwell deserves credit for being a crafty prose stylist whose characters possess a dignified strength pleasingly devoid of hard-boiled overload. In *Evidence*, Cornwell cuts back on

General Fiction

the grisly deluge and squeezes a few extra nuances out of her plot, which revolves around the death of an author, Beryl Madison, who seemingly opened her door to the person she knew wanted to kill her. More deaths follow, leaving Scarpella to sort out the answers from the available forensic evidence, including a multitude of unusual fibers found on Beryl's body. Cornwell's minor characters need some flesh tones, and, like Warshawski, Kay could stand to lighten up some. Still, *Evidence* is an accomplished novel; with the autopsy gore wisely downplayed, other, quieter narrative strengths are allowed to emerge. It's difficult to say if Cornwell will attain the popularity of the Paretskys and Graftons, but she certainly wouldn't be out of place in their company. —*Peter Robertson*

Cornwell, Bernard.
Sharpe's Waterloo: Richard Sharpe and the Waterloo Campaign, 15 June to 18 June 1815.
Viking, $17.95. 378p.

Here, at last, is the ultimate battle of the Napoleonic Wars as fought by Cornwell's perennial hero, Richard Sharpe. At Waterloo, Lieutenant-Colonel Sharpe serves as military adviser to the Dutch prince of Orange—a hapless military strategist who sends legions to their deaths before Sharpe takes matters into his own hands. Harper, the huge Irishman who has guarded, quarreled with, and fought beside Sharpe through 11 earlier novels, is again present—here as a civilian, since he mustered out following the last battle. Along the way, Sharpe settles an old score with Lord John Rossendale, who previously cuckolded him and helped deprive him of his hard-earned fortune. Cornwell graphically depicts the grime and horror of the battlefield, including cavalry charges, cannon bombardments, and infantry attacks. A sublime work of historical fiction. —*Denise Perry Donavin*

Coulter, Hope Norman.
Dry Bones.
August House, $17.95. 280p.

When a large bone segment is discovered in a remote town in Arkansas, nearly everyone has their own interpretation of its origin and significance. Some believe it is an Indian relic; others hope it may be a dinosaur; another group is certain that it can be used to prove the tenets of the creationists. Throughout all the flurry caused by this discovery, Coulter never loses touch with the feelings of the boy who discovered the bone—a 10-year-old dismissed by his older brother, dismayed by his father's affair with the preacher's daughter, and cheered only by the ugly, loyal puppy he has found at the discovery site. Coulter packs her novel with genuine people and their equally real hopes, deceits, and ordinary pursuits. The controversial issue (evolution versus creationism) remains an underlying theme not a trumpeted message. Beautifully wrought fiction from the author of *The Errand of the Eye* (August House, 1989). —*Denise Perry Donavin*

Courter, Gay.
Flowers in the Blood.
Dutton, $19.95. 585p.

Courter's latest lavishly detailed historical novel, set in Calcutta, concerns a late Victorian Jewish family's dealings in opium ("the flower trade"). The action begins with a tragedy that sets the tone for the rest of the story: six-year-old Dinah Sassoon, the narrator and chief protagonist, awakens one morning to find her mother bloodied in bed, presumably killed by a jealous lover known to Dinah as friendly Uncle Nissim. Dinah's father, Benu, rushes home to Calcutta from a business trip in China, where he spends most of his time, just as the trial winds down and the unsavory Nissim is set free. Angrily, Benu whisks Dinah away from her only known family and into a new life filled with risks and adventures and focused for the rest of Dinah's days on exacting revenge. Courter creates a mesmerizing family saga, subtly etched with historical detail. Certain to please the *Shogun* and *Thorn Birds* crowd.
—*Mary Banas*

Covington, Vicki.
Bird of Paradise.
Simon & Schuster, $18.95. 192p.

For Honey Shugart, 30 years of widowhood have proved unexpectedly enriching. Her tormented marriage to an alcoholic was filled with passionate suffering, but since her husband's death she has reined in her emotions, thrown herself into community work, and fashioned a more structured life, buttressed by the support of her many and lifelong friends. When she inherits a good deal of money and the family home, her small, ordered world starts to unravel as her niece pressures her to rezone the land and sell it at a handsome profit to a black-owned business, much to her neighbors' consternation. At the same time, she is being courted by a sweet, handsome lawyer who slowly wears away her emotional armor. This warm novel, filled with the rituals of life—burying husbands, tending to wills, baking cakes, singing in the choir—offers a dignified, comforting vision of old age. Confident enough to speak her mind and wise enough to change it when she's wrong, self-sufficient but not too proud to admit love when she finds it, Honey is a captivating character.
—*Joanne Wilkinson*

Coyle, Beverly.
The Kneeling Bus.
Ticknor & Fields, $18.95. 224p.

The milieu of this coming-of-age novel is unusual —small-town Florida in the 1950s. Carrie, the daughter of a Methodist minister, is a feisty and wondering child with a sense of holiness and an awareness of the power of thought. She is a marvelous witness to all sorts of events: some funny, like the strange romance between the direct-dialing man and her Aunt Dove; some tragic, like the death of the orchid growers' young daughter; and some just weird, like the mad boy who keeps leeches for a hobby. Coyle brilliantly captures self-consciousness and the struggle between weakness and strength that typify the child's mind. Inevitably, though, Carrie grows up and becomes a hazy, middle-aged character, and her eccentric, larger-than-life parents are reduced to frail, otherworldly creatures. But Coyle's concluding image, that of Carrie's mother on a kneeling bus—a bus that lowers itself to the sidewalk to help disabled and elderly passengers board—is full of hope and humor. A fine first novel, imbued with the sadness of the past and full of memorable scenes and personalities. —*Donna Seaman*

Crews, Harry.
Body.
Poseidon, $18.95. 223p.

A visceral new novel from southern humorist Crews. His last book, *The Knockout Artist*, was about a boxer; here he brings us into the fanatic world of bodybuilding, particularly female bodybuilding. The contest for Ms. Cosmos is being held in Miami, and the two top contenders are Marvella Washington, a black-skinned monument to female power, and Shereel Dupont, perfection sculpted from the body of Dorothy Turnipseed, poor white trash from Waycross, Georgia. Shereel's farcically rowdy, fat, hairy, and barbarous family has shown up for the big event. The scariest of the bunch is Shereel's "feeandsay" Nail, a knife-caressing dude sporting a perforated outline of a heart on his chest with the instructions "Cut Here, If You Can." There's enough tension generated between the mutant, competitive bodybuilders and the Turnipseed contingent to light up the South. There's also plenty of sexual antics among the "walking collection of minor miracles" and some good old suspense. Crews' dialogue is hilarious and his descriptions of the harsh techniques of bodybuilding fascinating. A blustering, pumped-up chunk of fiction. —*Donna Seaman*

Crichton, Michael.
Jurassic Park.
Knopf, $19.95. 413p.

Crichton's been spinning best-selling science-spiced adventure tales since *The Andromeda Strain* and has reached a peak with his latest. The Jurassic Park of the title is an amusement park on a fog-shrouded island off the coast of Costa Rica with a startling main attraction: real, live dinosaurs. The people of InGen, a genetic engineering firm, have succeeded in cloning 15 species of the prehistoric creatures and believe that their designer dinosaurs cannot reproduce or survive in the wild. But they're wrong. After some "accidents," the head man brings in some "consultants" to assess the situation: two paleontologists, a disgruntled programmer, and a mathematician who specializes in chaos theory. He also flies in his two grandchildren to prove that everything's A-OK. Soon his consultants and grandkids are running for their lives, pursued by tyrannosaurus rex, intelligent and vicious velociraptors, and cearadactyls. With near misses (and plenty of direct hits) on every page, Crichton whips up the suspense while dispensing a mindstretching condemnation of the perils of ungoverned genetic engineering. An irresistible mix of action and thought. —*Donna Seaman*

Cussler, Clive.
Dragon.
Simon & Schuster, $19.95. 416p.

In his tenth novel Cussler brings back Dirk Pitt, special projects director of the National Underwater and Marine Agency (NUMA), who has a "razor hardness about him that even a stranger could sense," a man who spends "almost as much time on and under water as he does on land." The plot involves a crashed B-29 bomber that was carrying a third atomic bomb to Japan in 1945—the nuclear cargo having been buried in the Pacific Ocean for 45 years—and a group of Japanese extremists who seek to blackmail the U.S. with nuclear weapons strategically planted in several large U.S. cities. In addition to compelling action, there's lots of authentic talk about microelectronic computers, buoyancy compensators, and regulators here; Cussler fans will lap up every detail. —*George Cohen*

Dahl, Roald.
Ah, Sweet Mystery of Life.
Knopf, $18.95. 132p.

These seven stories date from the late 1940s when Dahl was living in England's Buckinghamshire countryside and just beginning his career. The remembered people and settings of this rural region come to life vividly, Dahl converting them into a series of tales that explore a surprisingly deep and engagingly humorous vision of humanity (especially for an author as young as Dahl was at the time). His characters are refreshingly ordinary and full of life: a poacher who is able to outsmart the gamekeeper but not his prey; a gambler who targets a ringer at an illegal greyhound race; and an antique dealer whose impeccable eye and less-than-dainty morals are no match for rustic intrigues. Although most of these stories have appeared in other of the author's collections, here, in a single sequence, they form a graceful introduction to Dahl's world and writing. —*John Brosnahan*

Davenport, Guy.
The Drummer of the Eleventh North Devonshire Fusiliers.
North Point, $19.95. 144p.

The completion of a trilogy that includes *Apples and Pears* and *The Jules Verne Steam Balloon* finds adolescent hormones rampant again at a Danish boys' school. Male bonding of a particularly intimate and emphatic nature again takes center stage—in Freudian terms most of these characters have stalled at the oral, homoerotic stage of sexual development, although the foreplay is innocent and gleeful rather than perverse. The four stories and a longer novella make up the volume, but the distinctions between the individual pieces are fairly meaningless. Instead of structure, Davenport's virtuoso style carries the day, mingling classic and contemporary references along with lyrical descriptions of nature and human nature just as the ripening bud of sexuality has reached its bursting point—and before guilt and torment have polluted these freewheeling young psyches. —*John Brosnahan*

General Fiction

Davis, Christopher.
Dog Horse Rat.
Viking, $17.95. 231p.

It is the mid-1970s and the Vietnam War is still a recent and troublesome memory to dishonorably discharged army veteran Van West. This seems to explain why Van commits murder when he and his younger brother Royal are caught in the act of burglarizing the summer house of a wealthy Connecticut family. But as the story unfolds, we come to see Van as a natural-born loser, much like his father and virtually every other male in his town. Royal, being more self-aware than most, is disturbed by what Van has done, but somehow cannot avoid committing further acts of violence—almost as if he were fated to do so. It is not clear from all this what Davis wants to tell us about Vietnam, or rural culture, or men in general. What is clear is this: he has written a powerful, and powerfully sad, novel. —*Steve Weingartner*

De Carlo, Andrea.
Yucatan.
HBJ, $21.95. 216p.

This is the tale of an odd spiritual quest in which the principals—a famous international filmmaker, his young assistant, and his rich producer—become soul searchers more out of ego and ennui than from any particular energy. The director, Dru Resnik—an appropriately self-absorbed artist—wants to film a novel about a New York musicologist who makes a spiritual journey to Mexico. In Hollywood to meet with the enigmatic author, Resnik begins receiving obscure messages that seem to suggest the existence of a profound mystery. Throughout the novel, Resnik, the assistant, and the producer slavishly obey the increasingly explicit (but also mundane and ridiculous) instructions—go to Mexico, wear green clothes, go swimming. These three are remarkably unimaginative and literal—but plucky, too. They don't know what they're doing, but they feel like philosopher detectives anyway, bumbling along, trying to be spiritual guys in the face of what appears to be a meaningless game. De Carlo has written a thoughtful novel full of sneaky wit and charm. —*Frances Woods*

Dee, Jonathan.
The Lover of History.
Ticknor & Fields, $19.95. 256p.

Dee, an editor for the *Paris Review*, has set his debut novel in the Manhattan of the young, white, and alienated. Warner teaches history at a fancy private school and resents his good-looking, privileged, insular, and smug students. For economic reasons, he shares an apartment with Kendall, a beautiful, unfriendly woman who works night shifts at an all-news radio station. The big story is the terrorist murder of the secretary of state and the protests against the government's retaliation. Private fears and sadnesses mesh with the dread aroused by the threat of war. Dee depicts the guarded, unhappy milieu of *Slaves of New York* or *When Harry Met Sally*, but without being as hiply clichéd or as funny. A shrewd mood-setter, he examines the repercussions of history, both social and personal, and the elaborate defense mechanisms adopted by lonely people. Thoughtful and well crafted. —*Donna Seaman*

De Ferrari, Gabriella.
A Cloud on Sand.
Knopf, $19.95. 416p.

With her quirky, compelling characters and sun-drenched locales, first-novelist De Ferrari has hit the ground running. Through a combination of letters, shifting points of view, and great cinematic chunks of descriptive prose, the narrative lurches forward, giving off a choppy but distinctive sense of time and place. Set partly in Italy during the 1920s and partly in Latin America, the novel revolves around a group of vibrant characters: the imperious Donna Dora, who flaunts her great wealth and many love affairs but remains emotionally hollow; the elegant Count Mora, a wise, kind man who becomes a second father to Donna Dora's neglected children and who can see both her selfishness and her brilliance; the daughter Antonia, who struggles to free herself from her mother's domination; and the world-weary Arturo, who rescues Antonia by marrying her and finds himself rescued in return. De Ferrari suffuses her material with an original artistic vision, so it's not surprising that maverick moviemaker Martin Scorsese has bought film rights to the book. For once, a novel that lives up to the PR hype preceding it. —*Joanne Wilkinson*

Delibes, Miguel.
The Stuff of Heroes.
Pantheon, $19.95. 295p.

Like Hugo Claus' *Sorrow of Belgium*, which depicted a young boy growing up in fascist Belgium on the brink of World War II, Spanish writer Delibes' coming-of-age novel is set during the equally politically charged and tempestuous time of the Spanish civil war. Gervasio has had premonitions of hero status since he was a mere child: his neck hairs stood on end when he heard military marches, and he has been susceptible to sudden mystical swoons as well. Eventually, as a naval recruit, Gervasio will get the chance to become a real hero, but by this time his indoctrination will cancel all the expected glory and pride, and death will seem a more likely reward for the truly heroic deed. But even before this moral flash point, Gervasio's family and their position in conservative Spanish society also become problems for Gervasio, as sides in the forthcoming battle are chosen and his relatives divide in their patriotic allegiance. English readers may not catch all of the historical resonance of Delibes' story, but the depiction of Gervasio's family life resounds with laughter and anguish. —*John Brosnahan*

General Fiction

✓ **Devine, Eleanore.**
You're Standing in My Light and Other Stories.
Beacon, $17.95. 126p.

The fact that this is a 74-year-old author's first book will probably grab some attention, but these 13 stories are remarkable because they're tart, taut, touching, economical, elliptical, sharp, sensuous, and sexy—i.e., just about everything we want in short stories. A former news reporter, Devine favors short words and sentences and intelligent, responsible, middle-class suburbanites, most of them middle-aged and older. In the title piece, an MIA widow finally decides it's time to move on, even though that means putting mother in a retirement home. In "Goodbye, Charlie," a 39-year-old daughter intends to tell her parents about her female lover but defers it to minister to her embitteredly retired father. In "Pietà," a teenager tells of her much-older brother's return home to die. In "A Certain Difficulty in Being," Bea Harrison, widowed less than a year, lets herself be wooed by a longtime admirer, a widower himself now, and likes it, but . . . Such homely situations, keenly and sympathetically observed, constitute a richly rewarding body of short fiction.
—*Ray Olson*

Doane, Michael.
Six Miles to Roadside Business.
Knopf, $18.95. 240p.

When Vance Ravel (rhymes with *travel*) was only seven years old, his daddy walked into a blaze of bright light and disappeared from the world. No corpse, no coffin, no *proof* of death. Searching the mythologies of all religions and cultures, Ravel tries for many years to understand his father's last act. As an adult, Ravel discusses this great myth of his childhood with a stranger, who interprets the story his own way and deifies Ravel, now the unwilling focus of a religious cult. Ravel's mystical, searching story unfolds between chapters concerning his father's pathetic, tired life. Stationed in the deserts of the western U.S., where nuclear bomb testing is an ordinary occurrence, Ravel, Sr., awaits the elusive promotion to sergeant, watching his military friends die of radiation exposure. Realizing that he, too, is poisoned, Ravel, Sr., walks resolutely toward ground zero during detonation, secure in the knowledge that "a death in combat" will leave his family in financial security. In exploring the nature of myth and reality, Doane reveals how a father's journey and a son's journey take them down divergent roads but lead to similar conclusions.
—*Kathryn LaBarbera*

Dodge, Jim.
Stone Junction: An Alchemical Potboiler.
Atlantic Monthly Press, $19.95. 372p.

The epic quest, like the best detective novel, has always proven to be internal as well as external; the hero, in his exploration, learns as much about himself as he does about the object of his pursuit. In *Stone Junction*, Daniel, the precocious young protagonist, is seeking not only his mother's killer, but also a powerful diamond with supernatural powers and, ultimately, some pretty potent knowledge. But knowledge comes in all shapes and forms, and with a price, as Daniel learns through a series of tutors, including Wild Bill (who teaches him the powers of meditation); Willie Clinton (who shows him how to pick locks); Jean Bluer, the master of disguise; and Volta (who instructs Daniel in the fine art of literally vanishing), the leader of a mysterious secret society called AMO (Alchemists, Magicians, Outlaws). The plot can be rather confusing; nevertheless, outlandish and freaky characters, witty and occasionally profound dialogue, and a tripped-out and often-inspired zaniness make this cross-country romp of sure appeal to fans of Tom Robbins and his kind. —*Benjamin Segedin*

Doig, Ivan.
Ride with Me, Mariah Montana.
Atheneum, $18.95. 384p.

To conclude his Montana trilogy (see also *English Creek* and *Dancing at the Rascal Fair*), Ivan Doig moves forward in time—and then looks back. What narrator Jick McCaskill calls "memory storms," unprovoked assaults from the past, drive the action in this ruminative look at growing up and growing old, western style. A teenager at the time of the events in *English Creek*, McCaskill is 65 in 1989, a recent widower, and struggling to hold on to his beloved ranch in the face of massive societal change ("Maybe what I have known how to do all my life, which is ranching, simply does not register any more"). Reluctantly, he agrees to accompany his daughter, Mariah, a photographer, and her ex-husband, Riley, a reporter, as they tour Montana in a Winnebago, on assignment for a newspaper, gathering human-interest stories relating to the state's centennial celebration. Personal history mixes with Montana history as the trio dodge buffaloes, visit the site of Chief Joseph's surrender, and deal with unresolved familial and marital discord. Doig continues to excel at creating a sense of place, and, as before, the grandeur of the West is effectively set against the ineffable sadness of human lives—the misconstrued motives, the coming together and the breaking apart, the private sorrows and the unrealized hopes. —*Bill Ott*

Dorfman, Ariel.
My House Is on Fire.
Viking, $17.95. 167p.

This collection of stories by the author of *Mascara* illustrates the Chilean writer's political passion and faith: most of the selections seem to be set in the recent Pinochet dictatorship of his country. A young soldier confronts his pacifist father when he is ordered to guard political prisoners; an inquisitor is distracted from his torture when he asks medical advice from the doctor he is interrogating; and a censor struggles with both his high reputation and the hard issues he faces in reading his manuscripts. While the literary style— most often first-person with interior musings, or third-person with a lot of dialogue—doesn't consistently capture the emotional and physical horrors of these situations, at his best Dorfman has created stunning and soulful portraits of people on the edge of endurance. —*John Brosnahan*

General Fiction

Dunne, Dominick.
An Inconvenient Woman.
Crown, $19.95. 416p.

Dunne's new glitz and sleaze epic (following *People Like Us*) concerns billionaire financier and presidential adviser Jules Mendelson; his high-society wife, Pauline, and fractious stepson, Kippie; a bunch of other gangsters and Hollywoodites who are either business associates, friends, or antagonists; and Flo March, Jules' curvacious, decidedly nonblueblood mistress, who comes to know too much about everyone else's less-than-licit dealings for her own good. Screams, curses, threats, snubs, murder, skulduggery, and anything but legitimate, everyday activity (including sex, the paucity of which seems downright daring in this kind of novel) hog the pages. Nearly everybody dies before the end, and the wrong culprits are punished. This beach-blanket accessory will never be mistaken for realistic fiction, but Dunne's devotees aren't likely to care one whit. —*Ray Olson*

Ellison, Emily.
The Picture Makers.
Morrow, $18.95. 280p.

Ellison reveals seven characters through their own narratives in this slightly sad, warm, witty tale of a southern family moving from the 1950s into the 1980s. There is Henry, the preoccupied patriarch with a heart his daughter Eleanor compares to a "'56 Plymouth station wagon," and his wife, CoraRuth, who teaches Powder Puff Mechanics and has to remind Henry to change the oil in his truck. Eleanor, a painter, bears the eldest child's responsibility for worrying about both of them. And there are her husband, the over-achiever Will; his sister, Marilyn; Fitz, environmentalist, activist, Eleanor's ex-mother-in-law and best friend; and Ben Bolt, who moves through the story like a shadow. All are picture makers, whether with mind, memory, photography, or oils, sustaining their dreams as they change over time. Ellison succeeds in depicting the feeling of family and the distinct flavor of the South with delightful descriptions and flair for incredibly lucid storytelling. —*Ivy Burrowes*

Emecheta, Buchi.
The Family.
Braziller, $17.95. 240p.

When her parents immigrate to England, Gwendolyn remains in her small Jamaican village with her grandmother. It's a hard life; they constantly worry about money, yet they are rich in friends and have an active social life revolving around their church. When Gwendolyn is molested at the age of nine by a family friend, her small, loving world is shattered, and she eagerly anticipates the move to England, where she rejoins her parents. And though her life there is better in many ways (just as her village friends predicted), the coldness of the climate and the people is hard to get used to. Then her life takes a familiar, sickening turn when her own father forces her to have sex. She soon becomes pregnant, but, ironically, in her darkest hour she begins to find the inner strength and purpose to forge a better, more independent life. Emecheta's touching portrait of a resilient teenager is shot through with telling social commentary, and her formal, cerebral prose style is softened by the silky patois of native Jamaicans. —*Joanne Wilkinson*

Endo, Shusaku.
Foreign Studies.
Simon & Schuster, $18.95. 232p.

Japanese author Endo's pessimism about the West's ability to understand the East (and vice versa) is the obvious theme that binds these three stories. Although Endo says in his introduction that he is more sanguine these days than he was when he first conceived these works, it is the doubt that comes through. The result is something that reads very much like Graham Greene (one of Endo's champions in the West): slow, moral fiction that turns on a point of ambiguity and the failure to sort that ambiguity out. In "A Summer in Rouen," for example, one of the first Japanese students to study in the West after the war is confused and dismayed by the expectations placed on him as well as the unconscious Western arrogance of his kindly, perhaps neurotic hosts. This story has no real mood, no drama, no real philosophical profundity, and, as always with Endo, no sparkling prose, but in its subtle, understated way it gets under your skin. Just how autobiographical these three stories are is confusing. Endo's attempts to distance himself from them in his introduction invite one to think they are more autobiographical than one would have at first guessed. —*Stuart Whitwell*

Falco, Edward.
Plato at Scratch Daniel's and Other Stories.
Univ. of Arkansas, $18.95. 165p.

This disarming collection of short stories is so compassionate at heart that one might be tempted to dismiss its artistry. Whether detailing an inner city kid's initiation into hustling or a college dropout's confrontation with his draft board in the 1960s, Falco presents his characters with a great deal of empathy. In "Gifts," a father's almost unbearable sadness over his son's death is eased when he spends a week in the cabin willed to him as part of his son's estate. In "Prodigies," a young genius who was taught to play chess by his father enters a series of competitions after his father dies as a way of keeping the legacy alive. Presenting people at their most vulnerable—indeed, every other character seems to have a bad case of the shakes—Falco also skillfully presents them at their most compelling. —*Joanne Wilkinson*

Farris, John.
Fiends.
Tor, $4.95. 438p.

The fiends in question are the *Huldufólk*, some of Eve's children who, according to legend, were cursed in Eden by the wrathful Old Testament God. Strictly nocturnal (like that other horrific race oft associated with Transylvania), they live forever and fly with wings made of human skin flayed from

General Fiction

living victims. They also "turn" or recruit humans to their ranks. In Grand Guignol maestro Farris' newest, these monsters turn up in the east Tennessee town of Dante's Mill in 1906, are successfully put down, only to rise again in 1970, when they bedevil a set of mostly teenaged protagonists, whom Farris brings vividly, particularly to life. With his characteristic inventiveness and gift for small-town local color as well as his flair for characterization, Farris forges another expertly entertaining horror thriller. What's more—and very welcome given the current fad for mixing sex and horror—he portrays sex, long a leitmotiv in his work, as a positive, healthy force that is part of what makes humans good and of which the evil *Huldufólk* are incapable. —*Ray Olson*

✓ **Fogle, James.**
Drugstore Cowboy.
Dell/Delta, $9.95. 224p.

Usually, book precedes movie—unless it's a so-called novelization—but not in this case. Apparently, the film starring Matt Dillon had to be a hit before anybody'd back the novel. It's easy to see why publishers balked. Fogle, a convict for 35 of his 53 years, has a prose style that's half oral history, half 1950s pulp paperback—so rife with clichés, obvious metaphors, junkie slang, and bull-simplicity that no professional author would even try to get away with it. (The only one who's close is William Burroughs when he writes inside the junk experience, but he's never—he doesn't intend to be—this direct, raw, and real.) The story of what turns out to be the last days of Bob Hughes, addicted since he was 13 and the boss of a four-person crew that specializes in knocking over drugstores and hospital pharmacies, is absolutely convincing as Fogle tells it. Riveting, too, with just the right blend of outlaw romance, outsider humor, and grim naturalism. Maybe it's a classic. Rough as hell, but a classic. —*Ray Olson*

✓ **Fox, Paula.**
The God of Nightmares.
North Point, $18.95. 224p.

Using simple words, Fox writes with a kind of radiant intelligence that knows the brutal and the good and "an ordinary desolation." Helen Bynum has a late coming-of-age at 23 when she finally leaves her cheery mother's run-down resort near Poughkeepsie, New York, for exotic New Orleans. It's 1941, and war is raging in Europe; the talk—from Proust and Wright to politics and painting—is heady and unrestrained; Helen's Jewish lover is about to be drafted; her alcoholic aunt, Lulu, domineering and helpless, is dying. A lot happens (including murder, passionate encounters, and betrayal), but the drama explodes in the loneliest moments, as when Helen confronts her long blindness to the terror beneath her mother's smiles. As Aunt Lulu says, "The more I know about myself, the less confidence I have in life." Helen discovers that true sympathy includes that dark knowledge, even while she finds renewal in remembering the good of things past. Fox has won the highest awards for her uncompromising books for young people. In this, her seventh adult novel (the last was *A Servant's Tale*), she forces you to remember those intimate moments when you were startled into new, disturbing awareness. —*Hazel Rochman*

Frayn, Michael.
The Trick of It.
Viking, $17.95. 172p.

Oh, to have a pen pal such as Richard Dunnett—he always writes back. And back and back—long, literate, witty monologues to a fellow scholar in Australia, which try to pound out for posterity the timeless literary trick: what makes a writer write. Kingsley Amis' Lucky Jim never had it so hard. Skeptical and academically knowing as his fictional predecessor, Professor Dunnett is a more dedicated and thorough scholar, who unwittingly embarks on a striking method of literary study—he meets, courts, and marries the subject of his literature course synopsis: a female novelist. Scoring the literary coup of his career, he begins to lovingly dissect the Grand Muse in proximity, to unveil the creative leaps she performs in her celebrated novels. In this subtle and sublimely ironic epistolary novel, monologues of intelligently considered literary life fly across the oceans and time zones as Dunnett struggles to pin down, before they become evanescent, his marriage to a creator and his own orbital existence as interpreter of the mystic writing process. Graceful metaphors are the iron frame of this book, giving substance and humor to the doubts and struggles of those subscribing to a creative life. Its words leave few answers as to how, but a faint glow of hope for the why. —*Deanna Larson-Whiterod*

Freeman, Cynthia.
Always and Forever.
Putnam, $19.95. 384p.

Published after Freeman's death, this last novel by the author of *Seasons of the Heart* is a touching, elegantly drawn tale. Set in post-war America and Europe, the story traces the love affair of David Kohn and Kathy Ross. This pair of U.S. college graduates meet when they volunteer to aid concentration camp victims in Germany. Their romance is stifled by David's overwhelming grief at the loss of his immediate family (who remained in Germany while David was sent to study in America). David's opportunistic cousin, Phil, moves in and woos Kathy. Shortly after her marriage to Phil, Kathy realizes that she has made a mistake and pours her energy into forging a career in the women's fashion industry. Freeman excels when it comes to filling in the fashion details and has created a timely subplot involving the animal rights issue (Phil is heir to a multi-million dollar furrier business). And because she pays as much attention to politics as she does fashion, the background of the novel is rich in detail. —*Denise Perry Donavin*

General Fiction

Frucht, Abby.
Licorice.
Graywolf, $18.95. 256p.

Frucht's description of summer also describes her novel: "Still the summer goes on, in its strange, slow, spellbound way." *Licorice* is moody, mysterious, and sensual, saturated with dread and longing. It tells the tale of a summer in an unnamed midwestern town that is silently and steadily losing its population. People just disappear, especially women. Liz, the narrator, is frightened and fascinated by this creepy exodus. She delivers mail, takes long walks, and is a sort of witness to things, including her own puzzling desires. People are occupied with curious activities: making lingerie out of old wedding dresses, re-creating the execrable soup remembered from a concentration camp, spying. Liz seems to be slipping off into never-never land, but is rescued by her loving, life-giving husband. A haunting and exotic work about love and loss, "the wedding of fragility and strength." —*Donna Seaman*

Fuentes, Carlos.
Constancia and Other Stories for Virgins.
Farrar, $18.95. 204p.

Mexican Fuentes is a member, with Mario Vargas Llosa of Peru and Gabriel García Márquez of Colombia, of the great triumvirate of living Latin American fiction writers. He is a practitioner of the hallmark of that region's fiction, magical realism, a wondrous mixture of fantasy and verisimilitude. While Fuentes has published one collection of short stories previously, *Burnt Water* (1980), his high international reputation rests more on his novels than on his production in the shorter form. But the five stories appearing in his latest collection show his talent to be no less radiant in confined focus. Take, for instance, "Viva Mi Fama," which is an exemplary demonstration of Fuentes' gifts—and challenges. Rubén Oliva is approaching middle age, living unhappily with his wife and children in a four-room apartment in Madrid. But Rubén is no ordinary Madrileño; he is a has-been bullfighter. He dreams of reentering the ring for a finale that will secure his fame into perpetuity. In the process of such dreaming, his consciousness is melded with that of Pedro Romero, a matador of long ago, made immortal in a Goya painting. This story's difficult narrative structure is matched in impact by its luscious language and winged imagination. —*Brad Hooper*

Gale, Patrick.
Little Bits of Baby.
Dutton, $18.95. 288p.

This comedy of manners suspensefully reveals unexpected connections among its colorful cast of Londoners. Peter and Andrea Maitland run a nursery school at their home. Andrea's closest friend is Faber, a black painter whose adopted daughter Iras is a prodigy born without eyes. The Maitlands' only child, son Robin, disappeared at age 21 under vague circumstances. He has lived in a monastery on a remote island, and has now, eight years later, returned at the request of his closest childhood friend, Candida, a popular early morning TV host. Candida married their mutual friend, Jake. Their marriage is linked in some shadowy way to Robin's strange, incommunicado exile. Robin is the catalyst behind a taut series of events that unfolds with the rhythm and control of a good mystery. Every character and setting pulses with charged detail and dramatizes the various kinds of love and guilt that grow between parents and children, men and women, and men and men. The isolation of blindness and madness, as well as the concealment of same-sex love, are explored with sensitivity and humor. A praiseworthy work by a young writer who already has four earlier novels to his credit. *—Donna Seaman*

Ganesan, Indira.
The Journey.
Knopf, $18.95. 192p.

Sensitive Renu, her younger, Americanized sister, Manx, and their widowed mother leave their home on Long Island to return to their native island off the coast of India for the funeral of Renu's beloved cousin, Rajesh, who has died in a train accident. On the fictitious island of Pi—a place of overwhelming beauty, gods, and ghosts—the sisters find themselves swept back in time, to a place rife with mysticism and the secrets and eccentricities of an extended family. Many journeys are taken in this inventive, captivating, gently humorous tale—journeys instigated by wanderlust and curiosity, journeys that are escapes and quests. Ganesan masterfully contrasts cultures and explores repercussions of the past. A lyrical and spell-casting debut. *—Donna Seaman*

✓ **García Márquez, Gabriel.**
The General in His Labyrinth.
Knopf, $19.95. 304p.

Colombian García Márquez's magnificent and universally adored novel *One Hundred Years of Solitude* has become a monolith, casting its shadow over all of Latin American fiction. Upon publication of every novel from Mexico and Central and South America for the past 20 years, the first question on readers' and critics' minds is always the same: Is it as good as *Solitude*? But García Márquez himself never seems intimidated by his adoring public's expectation that he meet the standard he set for himself. Obviously, it is his intention that each post-*Solitude* novel explore its own sociocultural territory. Here we find García Márquez adhering closer to historical fact than ever before, achieving a shimmering, heartbreaking portrait of the great Simón Bolívar, the George Washington of South America. The author sets as the perimeters of his novel Bolívar's last days, when the general was broken in health and reputation. The Bolívar that emerges here is a man old before his time, angry and appalled that the good work he had wrought—the liberation of most of a continent and its unification into one strong state—was falling into ruin, his dreams destroyed by others less able than he. As good as *Solitude*? Different—but astonishingly beautiful by any standard. *—Brad Hooper*

General Fiction

García Márquez, Gabriel.
Collected Novellas.
Harper, $22.95. 256p.

These three novellas, published originally at various points in the distinguished Colombian writer's career, serve as excellent supplementary reading for those who have been intoxicated by García Márquez's novels, which include of course the wondrous and fabulously popular *One Hundred Years of Solitude* (1970) and the most recent, *The General in His Labyrinth*, a fictionalized portrait of General Simón Bolívar. All three novellas gathered here, *Leaf Storm* (originally published in 1955), *No One Writes to the Colonel* (1961), and *Chronicle of a Death Foretold* (1983), are prime examples of this Nobel laureate's characteristic setting aside of traditional narrative forms and his adroitness in handling fantasy and hyperbole. —*Brad Hooper*

Garrett, George.
Entered from the Sun.
Doubleday, $19.95. 368p.

The third in a series of historical novels including *Death of the Fox* and *The Succession*. Once again, Garrett submerges his readers in the contentious atmosphere of Elizabethan England. A young player, Hunnyman, is hired, by force, to investigate the murder of poet Christopher Marlowe, stabbed to death at a tavern under suspicious circumstances. Rumor has it that Marlowe, who was a bad drunk, an atheist, and liked boys, was also a spy. Hunnyman sleuths between happy hours with his lover—the young, beautiful, and wealthy widow, Alysoun—who runs a print shop and has visionary dreams. Marlowe's murder is also being reexamined by an old, scarred, and famously ugly soldier, Barfoot. A secret Papist, Barfoot cavorts with two hefty Dutch whores when he isn't tracking down the truth about Marlowe or musing on his pain-filled past. Told at a leisurely pace, the story allows for digressions into the concerns of the times: the Plague, religious intolerance, political intrigue, even commentary on the issue of extravagant attire. Garrett's strong and well-informed imagination brings a colorful, complex past to life via multifaceted characters and clever narration. Sure to delight historical novel enthusiasts. —*Donna Seaman*

Geha, Joseph.
Through and Through: Toledo Stories.
Graywolf, $8.95. 144p.

Short stories about a Toledo, Ohio, community of Arabian immigrants. Even though Geha immigrated from Lebanon decades ago, he has vividly recreated the many awkward incidents associated with adjusting to life in a foreign country. His characters struggle with English, the uselessness of old customs in an alien setting, superstition, fear, and the generation gap between immigrant parents and their American-born children. In the first story, "Monkey Business," a young widower plans to remarry so that his six-year-old son has a mother, but it is the ill-at-ease, timid father that needs mothering, not the boy. The title of the story "Everything, Everything" pointedly mirrors a daughter's frustrated response to her old-fashioned mother's inquiries: "Nothing, nothing." And in "News From Phoenix," an Arab family befriends a Jewish family. A worthy addition to the literature of immigration. —*Donna Seaman*

Gerber, Merrill Joan.
King of the World.
Pushcart/Norton, $18.95. 279p.

Winner of the Eighth Annual Editors' Book Award for overlooked manuscripts, this somber novel was nominated by Cynthia Ozick. It is a powerful, sad, and haunting tale of love and madness. Ginny is a shy young woman afflicted with a severe spinal deformity. Her self-image is warped by this physical flaw, making her humble and weak. Enter Michael, handsome, strong, extravagantly emotional and sexual. They fall in love and marry; Ginny worships her husband. A tremendous sense of foreboding builds relentlessly as Michael's behavior becomes more and more irrational and violent. Gerber's perfectly balanced prose brings the reader inside both Ginny's and Michael's psyches. Her depictions of Ginny's fierce loyalty and Michael's complex madness are gripping. She effectively captures both the baffling fascination of insanity and the devouring aspect of love. This novel may have been "overlooked" by commercial publishers due to its deep sadness and complete lack of sensationalism. —*Donna Seaman*

✓ **Gifford, Barry.**
Wild at Heart: The Story of Sailor and Lula.
Grove, $17.95. 176p.

Sailor Ripley and Lula Pace, the doomed lovers in Barry Gifford's stunning *roman noir*, are the Romeo and Juliet of the South. Sailor's on parole after doing two years in a North Carolina prison camp for killing a man in self-defense (or, as Lula puts it, "Because Sailor was a shade more sudden than that creep Bob Ray Lemon he gets punished for it. The world is really wild at heart and weird on top"). The first two-thirds of this deliciously sensual book show us the "wild at heart" part, as Sailor and Lula, on the run from a private detective hired by Lula's mother, drive through the South—talking, smoking, eating, and making love at various ports of call along the way. There is a definite desperation in their frenzied flight that gives the story its edge, but there is also a marvelous tenderness and a wondrously life-affirming sexuality that make Sailor and Lula far more than just another randy couple used to evoke the steamy nihilism of Jim Thompson or David Goodis. This is no modern imitation of the pulp novels Gifford reprints when wearing his other hat as publisher of Black Lizard Books; neither is it anything like David Lynch's film adaptation of the story; no, the saga of Sailor and Lula is a purebred original. When the world finally takes its toll on these courageous lovers—the "weird on top" part asserting itself in the end—we grieve both for

General Fiction

them and for missed opportunities everywhere. Wild hearts often grow cold, but Sailor and Lula make us remember what it is to burn. —*Bill Ott*

✔ **Gilchrist, Ellen.**
I Cannot Get You Close Enough.
Little, Brown, $19.95. 418p.

Over the course of several novels and short story collections, Gilchrist has been successfully apprenticing herself to greatness. In her latest book, three interrelated novellas, she proves her nearness to the eminent Eudora Welty in not only understanding the peculiar southern temperament but also the mythical dimensions of storytelling. In excruciatingly honest prose, a deep sensuality beguilingly standing behind her straightforward style, Gilchrist lends clear appreciation of the domestic dilemmas besetting the Hand family of Charlotte, North Carolina. In the first novella, "Winter," famous writer Anna Hand involves herself in the custody fight between her brother and the woman who has been a thorn in the family's side for years; "De Havilland Hand" features another child of Anna's brother, who had been long-lost but turns up in North Carolina wanting to live with her kin; and "A Summer in Maine" finds both of these children taking a New England trip with friends and relations and coming to terms with burgeoning adulthood. Gilchrist demonstrates impeccable sensitivity to not only details of her characters' environment but also the ecumenicity of their plights and triumphs. —*Brad Hooper*

✔ **Gordimer, Nadine.**
My Son's Story.
Farrar, $19.95. 277p.

Gordimer's previous novels, *Burger's Daughter*, *July's People*, and *A Sport of Nature*, tell stories of lives warped by apartheid. Here, in her most accomplished and finely tuned work, she again examines the psychology of the struggle for freedom in South Africa (see also the accompanying Gordimer interview). The tale is narrated by a young man who is witness to the gradual politicization of his family. Will's father, Sonny, was a teacher dedicated to serving his community. He and his wife, Alia, believed in "living useful lives" within the limits proscribed for blacks. But Sonny quickly finds himself embroiled in the liberation movement and is arrested. While in prison, he meets Hannah, a white activist. Upon his release, they fall in love—a love charged with the passion and eroticism of secrecy. Sonny lives a double life, forced to conceal his risky resistance work while at the same time using it as a shield for his relationship with Hannah. His son (unwillingly privy to his affair), daughter, and self-possessed wife must cope with his absences and their own political consciences. Within this pentagon of souls, Gordimer examines the nuances of commitment, conflict, guilt, love, and need, and illuminates each facet of the clandestine—the lies and silences, the play-acting both at home and in public. Gordimer has reached new levels of precision and emotional timbre in this stunning work. —*Donna Seaman*

Gordon, Jaimy
She Drove without Stopping.
Algonquin, $17.95, 372p.

Gordon writes like a woman with a gun to her head. She crowds her paragraphs with startling, outsize metaphors that perfectly encapsulate the wild coming-of-age of 21-year-old Jane, an aspiring adventurer. Because her wealthy father is so stingy, Jane is perpetually low on cash and eager to earn his disapproval. At college in Ohio, she moves out of her dorm room and into an abandoned house on the outskirts of town, where she lives with her artist-boyfriend Jimmy who seems to have moved straight from boy wonder to derelict. When a local yokel misconstrues Jane's footloose life-style and sexually attacks her, Jane heads west in a 1951 money-green Buick and ends up in L.A. A serious run-in with the police and assorted misadventures with a beguiling group of misfits finally convice Jane that enraging her father is not a suitable raison d'etre. This feminist updating of the road novel works on a number of levels—the vigorousness of its writing style, the way complex themes snake through one chapter after another, the sheer virtue of the lowlife heroes who pop up throughout—all of which will convince readers to hitch a ride with Jane. It's well worth the trip. *—Joanne Wilkinson*

Hale, Robert D.
The Elm at the Edge of the Earth.
Norton, $19.95. 352p.

A beguiling novel about an unusual childhood in rural America between the two world wars. David is sent to live with his aunt and uncle during his mother's prolonged and serious illness. His stern but loving aunt is head cook at the County Home, a cozy sanitarium ensconced on a thousand-acre farm complete with woods, pond, garden, and an abandoned house—paradise for an eight-year-old. David, the only child, readily befriends the residents, especially Adeline, who hates to wear clothes and teaches him "fertility dances," and Rose, his confidante, interned for murdering her abusive husband. David gets quite an education. Hilarious escapades drive the plot, but the true story is David's capacity for empathy and love. Hale has re-created the glow and freshness of a time before TV when people spun their dreams around trees. Pure joy. *—Donna Seaman*

Halligan, Marion.
The Hanged Man in the Garden.
Penguin, $7.95. 183p.

From a top Australian fiction writer, a collection of 20 attractive short stories. Halligan deals with "up-shorts"—those moments when circumstances catch persons in vulnerable situations in which they consequently make decisions that are life-changing. For instance, in "Blue Fornications," a woman falls into a momentary sexual dalliance—the time and setting and man having proven too alluring to resist. "Use More Hooks" is a brief but pungent narrative about a couple on holiday at the beach, the sun steering the woman's thoughts to a seduction (one that does not involve her husband). And in

"Paternity Suit," Gerry is glad his friend Sybil's unborn child is not his—she then can't force him to pay child support—but, ironically, once he knows he is off the hook, he shocks himself by asking her to marry him. Halligan's style is not so much minimalist as poetic, the economy of her prose richly intense rather than flatly connotative.
—*Brad Hooper*

Handke, Peter.
Absence.
Farrar, $17.95. 117p.

An enigmatic parable about post–World War II Europe? Or merely an enigmatic parable? With Handke, one can never be sure about the time or setting of his narratives. In the Austrian writer's latest novel, four people meet on a train and embark on a journey across borders and across the four seasons, which rapidly and inexplicably follow one another, if not in the usual order. Geography and history seem to determine the route that takes these people from a large city to a rural wasteland, which holds the evidence of battles and desolation. The final monologue works as a contemplation on the disappearance of one of the four travelers; this has political reverberations that could apply as well to leaders who may or may not be discredited. Handke's style weaves its customary spell as the book manages to suggest multiple layers of meaning without revealing much of the author's intentions.
—*John Brosnahan*

Hansen, Brooks and Davis, Nick.
Boone.
Summit, $19.95. 416p.

Cast in the form of an oral biography, this inventive novel displays a startlingly subtle understanding of recent pop culture. The subject is Eton Arthur Boone, a tragic, enigmatic figure who dominated the arts scene of the late 1960s and early 1970s with his stunning club performances. As a sort of hybrid comedian-actor, he did haunting impersonations of celebrities that were dubbed "exposures" because of their devastating accuracy. However, when he began to practice his art form on audience members, many an ugly scene resulted and he ended up leaving the country at the height of his notoriety. He went to work writing scripts for a television comedy series in England, next made an avant-garde film, and then wrote a memoir of his mother—all of his work considered a revolutionary reworking of the form. His death in a motorcycle accident at the age of 26 virtually sealed his cult status. Like *Edie*, *Boone* is told through a series of distinctive voices that draw a rich picture of a compelling character. Authors Hansen and Davis have really pulled off a mini-coup here: borrowing a page from New Journalism, they've taken a pop cultural framework and given it a fictional twist, breathing new life into the form. —*Joanne Wilkinson*

Harrison, Sue.
Mother Earth Father Sky.
Doubleday, $19.95. 356p.

In the tradition of Jean Auel's *Clan of the Cave Bear*, Harrison tells the story of an Aleutian woman living around 7000 B.C. When her village is destroyed by a hostile tribe, Chagak flees to her grandfather in the Whale Hunter tribe. Along the way, she finds safety with old Shuganan, but her trials do not end there. She endures brutalization and childbirth—but finally finds safety. Ten years in the planning and execution, Harrison's fine first novel is based on thorough research into the life-style and beliefs of ancient Aleutians; exquisite detail imparts great viability to her characters. Although occasionally lapsing into noble-savage clichés, this book should gain Harrison as many readers as Auel's classic did for her. *—Jill Sidoti*

Hegi, Ursula.
Floating in My Mother's Palm.
Poseidon, $17.95. 158p.

"The name Adolph Hitler was never mentioned in our history classes. Our teachers dealt in detail with the old Greeks and Romans; we'd slowly wind our way up to Attila the Hun, to Louis the Eighth who had six wives, to Kaiser Barbarossa, to the First World War; from there we'd slide right back to the old Greeks and Romans." For Hanna Malter, growing up in postwar Germany, life was circumspect in more ways than history class. Because the past—either in national or in personal terms—was not a topic open for discussion, information had to be gleaned through shrewd observation, careful listening, and bits of gossip picked up from the dwarf librarian, whose aborted "romantic episode," like her stunted growth, stands as a metaphor for a generation caught in the vice of history. These carefully crafted, interconnected vignettes place the same demands on the reader that Hanna's world exacted from her; as we read of "The Woman Who Would Not Speak," or of an illegitimate son's desperate attempt to learn something of his G.I. father, we are forced to interpret silence, to find passion in the way a housekeeper caresses a new potato. It is a triumph of both literary technique and human resilience that such passion is there to be found. *—Bill Ott*

Herr, Michael.
Walter Winchell.
Knopf, $18.95. 176p.

Before there were Oprah and Geraldo, there was Walter Winchell. One of his editors once said that the rambunctious and provocative journalist was "a terrible price to pay for freedom of the press." But it was indeed Winchell's defiant irreverence and rousing muckraking that were the keys to his enormous success. An entire generation was familar with his flamboyant style and could recognize his distinctive voice—"Good evening, Mr. and Mrs. America and all the ships at sea. . . . Let's go to press. Flash!" Herr, known for raising a few hackles himself with his groundbreaking journalistic account of Vietnam, *Dispatches*, here chooses fiction to relate the story of the demagogic commentator's tumultuous rise and fall. Herr takes liberties with Winchell's life and with the presentation of his career, concocting a literary hybrid of sorts that utilizes cinematic devices (flashbacks, pans, montage sequences) to produce a Howard Hawkes–style newsroom biopic. With locations like the infamous Stork Club and cameos by such Winchell contemporaries as Damon Runyon, Ed Sullivan, Ernest Hemingway, Josephine Baker, Roy Cohn, and a smattering of well-known gangsters, Herr effectively (and lovingly) evokes a much romanticized era. Fast paced with ample witty dialogue, this account of the little man who became as big as his mouth portrays Winchell as a megalomaniacal star-maker, a sharp pundit of his times, and, ultimately, a man who couldn't change with the times. —*Benjamin Segedin*

Hiller, Catherine.
17 Morton Street.
St. Martin's, $16.95. 240p.

What happens when the female au pair you've been expecting turns out to be a young, handsome, virile Italian instead? Do you show him how to care for the baby or how to baby you? Acquaint him with the house or lure him into the boudoir? These tantalizing options are all open to Sara Lenox Jennings when, unexpectedly pregnant with her third child, she hires 28-year-old NYU grad student Carlo Rinaldi to help out. But the adventure is just beginning, for Carlo also has options—namely, the two Jennings sisters, Perri (a gorgeous model-turned-filmmaker) and Lucy (a young academic type), who have flats in the Lenoxes' brownstone. Hiller weaves a thoroughly charming yarn whose memorable, full-bodied characters are the pièce de résistance of this otherwise fluffy concoction. —*Mary Banas*

✓ Hillmore, Susan.
The Greenhouse.
New Amsterdam Books, $16.95. 125p.

In this chilling modern allegory of attachments and detachments and how nature affects them both, a greenhouse is personified within a dynamic world of good and bad, growth and decay, observing the evil that drapes over the seasonal ebb and flow with an uneasy serenity, a glassy, vacant stare. Reluctantly attached to a country house and its handicapped mistress, yet accepting of its bonds, the greenhouse nourishes and propagates her life and plants within glass walls and is willing to protect the lives it supports to the death. The story weaves spells, with the rhythms of language and events and inexorable sudden turns of the seasons. Fantastic, almost surreal descriptions of the moon's ashen light and of overripe autumnal grapes with splitting skins pervade the battle of the greenhouse for the roots, and souls, of the lives it has nurtured in its consistent moisture and warmth; the descriptions provide images with harsh outlines, without the benefit of soft shadow or lesser truth. In a Jamesian ghost story of immense intensity, Hillmore's preternaturally still prose captures, with the emphasis of a silent film, the movements of humans in tandem and at odds with a natural and moral world, orchestrated throughout in the eerie slow motion of truths revealed. —*Deanna Larson-Whiterod*

✔ **Hoffman, Alice.**
Seventh Heaven.
Putnam, $18.95. 256p.

Can magical realism be successfully transplanted to a Long Island subdivision? Hoffman's latest novel suggests that it can be done, and in the process of treating both everyday and fantastic events as equally valid experiences, it transforms the dreary existences of people caught in the middle-class dream trap of late 1950s–early 1960s America. The story encompasses one year in the life of the people who live on Hemlock Street, just as the decade is turning from the complacency of the Eisenhower era to the promise of the Kennedy decade. But the residents of post–World War II suburbia are almost totally unaware of these larger switches; they are involved instead with the minutiae of their lives—cutting the grass, raising the kids, earning a living. At first they don't sense all the possibilities that are now theirs to seize, but a divorced woman with two young children is the catalyst for raised consciousness and enlarged perspectives. Nora is a lady who doesn't fit the mold of her neighbors; she dresses flashily, she loves her kids but doesn't fuss about their not-too-clean clothes, she's no Betty Crocker in the kitchen, and most importantly, she has no husband. In short, Nora's presence hits the neighborhood like a home-lending institution's redline. In the course of a year people's lives are turned inside out, both by the normal course of fortune and by Nora's influence. Hoffman employs just enough weirdness and magic—the hint of witchcraft, the possibility of ghostly apparitions—to push her characters over the border of normal behavior into a psychological depth and vividness that mere realism couldn't accomplish. The wonderful trick is that this makes these people not odder or stranger, but more vivid and engaging while they struggle out of their mundane ways into a brave new world. —*John Brosnahan*

Holland, Cecelia.
The Bear Flag.
Houghton, $19.95. 423p.

Holland seamlessly interweaves fact and fiction in order to vivify California's reluctant incorporation into the United States. Widowed during an arduous trek across the Sierra Nevada, Cat Reilly is compelled to carve out a unique niche for herself on the western edge of the continent. When she joins forces with a motley band of homesteaders and misfits at Sutter's Fort, her fate becomes inextricably entangled with that of her adopted frontier homeland. Though she is drawn to a mysterious Russian count employed as a spy by the Mexican Army, the conflict between their visions of California's destiny forges a seemingly insurmountable barrier to their love. During the inevitable clash between the settlers and the powerful dons, Union military forces seize the opportunity to conquer California. Detailed historical fiction populated by a

General Fiction

distinguished gallery of supporting characters including Kit Carson and John Charles Frémont. —*Margaret Flanagan*

Holt, Victoria.
Snare of Serpents.
Doubleday, $19.95. 384p.

Set in nineteenth-century Edinburgh, Holt's new novel follows the transformation of Davina Glentyre from sheltered young Scot to South African schoolteacher. When a cherished governess is fired for thievery and the replacement, Zillah Grey, cites her last place of employment as the lead singer for the Three Redheads, 16-year-old Davina senses that her life is in trouble. She watches as her righteous banker-father succumbs to the influence of a flamboyant, titian-haired female. His sudden death, due to arsenic poisoning, arouses suspicions; but it is Davina, not Zillah, who winds up in the dock. The verdict, "not proven," hangs like a specter over the young woman's life. She migrates to South Africa where she hopes—futilely, it turns out—to escape the scandal. Holt's romantic suspense has little of the latter—the ending is fairly obvious—but the story has a fitting store of intriguing moments, sprightly characters, and chaste love affairs. —*Denise Perry Donavin*

Homes, A. M.
The Safety of Objects.
Norton, $17.95. 173p.

This collection of short stories is for adults who like fiction with a jolt. The mundane is a facade for the bizarre in these unsettling tales of suburban life. Homes homes in on the peculiar things people do in private—like a lawyer who urinates in office plants after hours, kids who molest a Barbie doll, or a couple who fall apart when their children are away. Her plots also include insanity at a mall, a boy rejected by his kidnapper, and a mercy killing. Garish as this sounds, Homes coaxes a sort of queasy poetry out of these unravelings, an empathy for the emptiness people feel within their roles of child, husband, mother. David Lynch comes to mind as does John Cheever, cranked up a notch or two. Strong stuff from a writer bound to attract attention. —*Donna Seaman*

Houston, James.
Running West.
Crown, $19.95. 320p.

In his widely praised novel *The White Dawn*, Houston probed the sense of wonder, the excitement, and the tragedy that so often unfolds when an aggressive Western culture confronts the static, passive culture of some native American tribes. He returns to a similar theme in his current novel. Based on historical characters and events, the novel relates the story of William Stewart, a Highland Scot who is forced into exile, and Thanadelthur, a young Indian woman of the Dene nation. Set against the stark vastness of the Canadian north in the early eighteenth century, the chronicle of these tragically doomed lovers is both exciting and moving. The author shows a rare ability to tell an epic tale without dwarfing the personal aspects of a romantic

248

relationship. Houston, who lived in the Canadian Arctic for 12 years, again displays superb technical knowledge of the terrain and of the traditional cultures that once flourished there. —*Jay Freeman*

Howard, Elizabeth Jane.
The Light Years.
Pocket, $18.95. 434p.

A rich domestic drama arises from the pages of Howard's captivating novel, set in England in 1937 and 1938. The Cazalets are an upper-crust London family comprising the three grown sons of William and Rachel Cazalet and the sons' wives and children. As the novel opens, the extended family is undertaking its summer relocation to the country house in Sussex. During the course of this summer and the next, readers—especially those who love the familial depictions of Virginia Woolf and Rebecca West—become witness to the public and private selves of the individual family members. Beguilingly, those selves are often at odds. Adding to the novel's allure is the fact that even with the luxuriousness of detail, the pace is swift. Howard is a highly esteemed writer in her native Britain, and her latest will undoubtedly draw high praise from the reading public on this side of the Atlantic as well. —*Brad Hooper*

Howatch, Susan.
Scandalous Risks.
Knopf, $21.95. 387p.

Scandalous Risks is the fourth in a projected six-novel series about the Church of England in the twentieth century, preceded by *Glittering Images*, *Glamorous Powers*, and *Ultimate Prizes*. Howatch has taken as her general theme in this sequence of books the conflict between adherence to spiritual values and the day-to-day temptation of earthly delights, namely those of a sexual nature. This latest in the series finds young Venetia Flaxton, daughter of a peer of the realm, falling in love with her father's closest friend, Neville Aysgarth, who is not only a married man but also dean of Starbridge Cathedral. In the form of a remembrance of times past, in this case the year 1963, Venetia recalls all the exquisite, painful details of their affair. "I never recovered from him," she confides. With sculptor's hands fashioning rich, lustrous three-dimensional characters, Howatch brilliantly shows how and why the situation between Venetia and her "Mr. Dean" arose, flourished, then died away. —*Brad Hooper*

Israel, Phillip.
Me and Brenda.
Norton, $17.95. 214p.

The "me" in this charmer is Russ, driver for a car service in Queens and frequent customer at a bar under the el. Here he meets Dave Winger, who quit college to work with his hands and meet "real people." Russ, who barely earns enough for wife Brenda and kids, is wary of Dave's choice to live poor for some "theory." He assumes he's one of the "real people" Winger's talking

General Fiction

about and wonders, "Is it a compliment or an insult or what?" Winger's idealism vanishes as he falls hard for the scams of con man Al Croppe. Croppe is a terrific creation, the archetypal fast talker hustling Winger into an Atlantic City scheme with high stakes. Russ gets lured into the game too but is protected by his innate realism and Brenda's love. Israel is a modern Damon Runyon—his book is funny, insightful, and satisfying. —*Donna Seaman*

Jaffe, Rona.
An American Love Story.
Delacorte, $19.95. 432p.

Jaffe, best known for *The Best of Everything*, has another winner on her hands, this one starring a cad and the four women who almost wreck their lives because of him. The book's weakest character is its centerpiece, Clay Bowen, influential television mogul—at least for a while. Clay marries ballet dancer Laura Hays because he loves her, but she also looks mighty good on his arm. Clay claims to adore their daughter, Nina, too, but when the television business moves to Los Angeles, Clay moves along with it, leaving Laura to become anorexic and Nina to grow up craving her father's love. Susan Josephs, a fledgling screenwriter, falls hard for Clay, who reciprocates for 10 years or so, until a blandly developed mid-life crisis moves him into the arms of avaricious Bambi Green, the discomfort of his decidedly unsuccessful old age. Though Bowen's magnetism is more talked about than shown, Jaffe writes her women well, especially Susan, who plays her role as the other woman with sympathy and style. In a situation of her own making, she is willing to take the consequences. Setting is a strength here, too: Jaffe's Hollywood scenes, exploiting the farce and foibles of La-La Land, are particularly sharp. A book begging to be read while sitting around the pool. —*Ilene Cooper*

James, M. R.
A Warning to the Curious.
Godine, $10.95. 257p.

Briton James (1862–1936) was a scholar and antiquary. His splendid supernatural tales, consequently, are imbued with his knowledge of college life and ancient times. At once sinister and elegant, these 13 ghost stories sport perfectly crafted—perfectly creepy—atmospheres. James' apparitions—unlike those created by the other famous ghost-story writer surnamed James (Henry, that is)—are certain and definite, i.e., there is no ambiguity in terms of whether the ghostly presences actually exist or are simply hallucinations. An engaging introduction is contributed by esteemed British mystery and psychological-thriller writer Ruth Rendell. —*Brad Hooper*

Jenkins, Victoria.
Relative Distances.
Gibbs Smith/Peregrine Smith, $15.95. 144p.

An elemental drama. Myra Wells, 36, independent and tough, returns to her home turf where her long-abandoned son, Tom, is working for Arlen Dyer, a man Myra's been in love with since she gave herself to him at the crazy age of 13. Arlen's an ambitious rancher, mean and miserable, still unhappily married. He hires Myra, who works alongside Tom and Arlen's son, Neal, sharing the hard labor of running a ranch. Arlen is still unattainable; it's Neal who wants Myra. Everyone is gruff and wary. The energy of unspoken tensions is mirrored in animals—an insatiable bull, heifers and cats who won't mother their young, a horse trapped in a wire fence. Dreams are crushed by reality, and the distances between people are as vast as the landscape. A deliberately constructed and resonant first novel, lonely as a memory-haunted, destinationless, predawn drive across the plains. —*Donna Seaman*

Johnson, Charles.
Middle Passage.
Atheneum, $17.95. 288p.

In 1830 former slave Rutherford ("Illinois") Calhoun becomes a stowaway on the *Republic* rather than escape his debts by a forced marriage. What he doesn't know is that the ship's captain is the sadistic dwarf Falcon, famous for his intellect and his various escapades, and that the ship is headed to Africa for a cargo of mysterious slaves, the Allmuseri. The captain has brought one additional thing on board—whatever it might be, it is kept in a massive crate, feared by all, and drives the cabin boy insane when he is sent to feed it. Using the colorful language and colloquialisms of the time to vividly describe the voyage, characters, and actions of the crew, Johnson creates an odd and stirring adventure, filled with stench and rot and the terror not just of ancient sea travel, but also of what humans can and have done to one another. Illinois, whose journal forms the tale, is a thief and a scoundrel whose spiritual awakening is told with verve, wit, and compassion. —*Eloise Kinney*

Johnson, Wayne.
The Snake Game.
Knopf, $18.95. 224p.

In spare, mesmerizing prose, first-novelist Johnson details the downward spiral of a group of Ojibway and Chippewa Indians. A dozen main characters are featured in a group of connected stories set from the 1950s to the 1980s, playing bit parts in some and major parts in others. This telescopic shifting of viewpoint is extremely effective, for it serves to underline the unraveling of a culture as it portrays each character coming to grips with heartbreak and failure. In "What Happened to Red Deer," a talented Indian pitcher uses the racial jeers of the crowd to feed his hatred, which in turn feeds his skill on the mound, only to lose control of his emotions and seriously injure the batter. In "Bear, Dancing," a local priest asks a young Indian boy, Bear, to play Santa at the annual Christmas party, but Bear finds himself paralyzed by embarrassment and fear until he saves himself by performing a tribal dance around the tree. A powerful, impressive debut. —*Joanne Wilkinson*

General Fiction

Jones, Stephen and Sutton, David, eds.
The Best Horror from Fantasy Tales.
Carroll & Graf, $17.95. 264p.

In an effort to revive the spine-tingling tradition of the pulps of the 1930s and 1940s, the British *Fantasy Tales* is heir apparent to *Weird Tales*, which was perhaps the most influential newsstand pulp in the horror genre (it spawned the careers of such popular authors as Robert Bloch, Robert E. Howard, and Fritz Leiber). In this collection, editors Jones and Sutton have selected a sample of the best stories to have appeared in *Fantasy Tales*, including an author list that reads like a veritable who's who in the world of modern, macabre fiction (Clive Barker, Ramsey Campbell, Charles L. Grant, etc.). The stories range in quality from effective hack work to the truly terrifying. Francis Wellman's "Don't Open That Door" is the sort of classic scary tale that one would tell on a dark and stormy night. In "A Place of No Return," Hugh B. Cave spins a voodoo yarn worthy of an E.C. comic. In a potent piece of urban fright, "The Forbidden," Barker transforms a run-down housing estate into a den of unspeakable evil. The tales are embellished by the art of contemporary illustrators. —*Benjamin Segedin*

Jönsson, Reidar.
My Life as a Dog.
Farrar, $17.95. 220p.

A picaresque series of adventures awaits Swedish teenager Ingemar Johansson—not the boxer, but an unfamous young man who hilariously confronts all the obstacles that life throws in his path. Growing up in the 1950s with a celebrated but unrelated namesake is only part of the hero's problems: his father is absent, and his perpetually sick mother is an infrequent visitor. Young Ingemar is shifted into the homes of relatives according to their convenience; even Ingemar's poor dog is put up for adoption. What saves Ingemar is his indomitable spirit and a taste for imaginative exploration that is mirrored in his love of reading. This novel served as the basis for the film of the same title, and this connection may help attract readers to Jönsson's little gem of a book. —*John Brosnahan*

Joyce, William.
The Recorder of Births & Deaths.
Watermark Press, $9.75. 190p.

Seven powerfully inventive short stories by the author of the controversial novel *First Born of an Ass* (Watermark, 1989). Joyce's style is perhaps best characterized as quirky; his subjects inhabit the very fringes of society. But the starkly naked truth Joyce exposes cuts to the nerve of human conscience. Although the author's bluntness may shock many readers, his intent is less scatological than satirical, pointing with wry humor to our universal foibles and failings. From the title story, in which an arrogant philosophy graduate student scorns his mortician-dating mother for, ironically, living life while he only dreams about it, to "My Grandfather's Bones," about a steel-mill crane operator who dies in an industrial accident, this collection focuses on working-class laborers and their families, whose seemingly ordinary lives are shown in full harsh detail to be chillingly surrealistic and sadly incomplete. An astounding work of contemporary absurdist literature. —*Mary Banas*

✓ **Just, Ward.**
Twenty-One: Selected Stories.
Houghton, $22.95. 389p.

Just celebrates 21 years of published fiction with as many finely crafted stories. Introductorily, he mentions the Americans in whose story-writing company he presumably wants to stand: "Fitzgerald, Faulkner, Hemingway, O'Hara." Of those, the touchstone for Just's achievement is O'Hara. More than that underread master of the form (readers still seem to prefer his mostly clumsier novels), Just writes about people of consequence—politicians, journalists, bureaucrats, and other professionals who believe in what they do and try to do it well. Like O'Hara, Just crystallizes crises in the lives of his personae that are all the more momentous and powerfully affecting for their quietness, their lack of noisy confrontation. In the great tradition of realistic fiction, Just strives to conjure place, time, and circumstance through physical and psychological detail. When he succeeds (constantly in this collection), he produces the likes of "Honor, Power, Riches, Fame, and the Love of Women"— along with O'Hara's "The Doctor's Son," one of the great stories at any length about the predicament of the drunken Noah, of the heroic father stripped bare before his son. —*Ray Olson*

Kabakov, Alexander.
No Return.
Morrow, $14.95. 100p.

Publication of this potent novella by a Moscow journalist has caused quite a stir in the Soviet Union, where readers are not accustomed to unrestricted literature. *No Return* is dystopian, the opposite of utopian. The narrator is a prognosticator, a scientist who can travel through time. Two officials instruct him to write about the events taking place in the near future. The time frame then shifts, plunging the reader into a brutal scene on the nighttime streets of Moscow, which is in the grip of violent chaos, as various ethnic groups, armies, and terrorists are on the rampage. Here, in the time of "Great Leveling," people who wanted reforms are rounded up and exterminated. What Kabakov seems to be saying through his bleak vision is that perestroika must be given the support needed to make it work because there are no alternatives. A dark and thought-provoking work that has already captured international attention. —*Donna Seaman*

Kaschnitz, Marie Luise.
Circe's Mountain.
Milkweed Editions, $9.95. 128p.

Kaschnitz, while unknown to many Americans, was one of Germany's most acclaimed and prolific post–World War II writers and the recipient of that country's major literary awards. Even today (she died in 1974), her stories

General Fiction

sparkle with timeless insight into the human condition. The 12 stories collected here show the range of Kaschnitz' considerable talent to full advantage. They are set in both Germany and Italy, the author's main residences, during the 1960s and 1970s, and are in style and substance not unlike Hemingway's fiction in their crisp exploration of emotion, subtle use of autobiographical elements, and fatalistic bent. From the opening story, which hauntingly evokes a happily married couple's fated, unkept appointment to buy the house of their dreams (much to their good fortune), to the closing title story, about a grieving widow's struggle to overcome guilt and rage and let life continue to unfold, these gracefully sculpted tales reflect the author's delight in life in the face of sobering experience. Highly recommended. —*Mary Banas*

✓ **Kees, Weldon.**
Fall Quarter.
Story Line Press, $18.95. 288p.

Best known as a poet of the depressed ilk of Jarrell and Berryman, Kees—who disappeared near the Golden Gate Bridge in 1955—also aspired to be a novelist. Of four attempts, only this book remains. It's so good that its publication more than 40 years after Kees abandoned all hopes for it is one of the events of the year in American fiction. It's about William Clay's first college teaching job after a very successful student career. He arrives at a university in a typical heartlands town full of an enthusiasm that is blasted by the indifference of his tenured superiors, the vapidity of faculty interaction, and the stupidity of his students. In self-defense, he falls to boozing with the only intellectual peer among his colleagues, to partying with the town's fast set, and into love with an alluring but erratic young lounge singer who makes him forget about his fiancée back home. The closest relative to *Fall Quarter* is undoubtedly Jarrell's *Pictures from an Institution*, but Kees' book is far more sardonic, even hopeless about the academic life. It is, however, no less funny, but its laughter is bitter with the kind of aftertaste left by some noir pulp-novelist—Jim Thompson, say, or David Goodis, who, if he could write about professors in situ, might have come up with just such a book. —*Ray Olson*

Kilworth, Garry.
The Foxes of Firstdark.
Doubleday, $18.95. 304p.

In a book reminiscent of *Watership Down* (though darker and lonelier in tone), Kilworth imaginatively explores the joys and terrors of the fox clan. His tale follows the fortunes of country vixen O-ha and her family as they struggle to survive in woodland and town. To the natural history of the fox, Kilworth has added a fascinating lore of fox language, mythology, and mores. O-ha's youthful happiness with her first mate and cubs is traumatically curtailed by a foxhunt, at the end of which her mate is dug out of their burrow and killed before her eyes. After a period of mourning, O-ha accepts the affections of Camio, a zoo escapee, and the two settle into an auto dump to rear their three cubs. The trials and dangers endured by the little family are presented in vivid and moving detail—the winter starvation, the bloodcurdling threats of fox-hating dogs, the motiveless cruelty and occasional, baffling kindness of human beings. Through it all, O-ha is sustained by her faith in the fox-spirits of the Firstdark, the time before the coming of Man. A haunting and dramatic work of wide appeal. —*Leone McDermott*

✓ **Kincaid, Jamaica.**
Lucy.
Farrar, $18.95. 163p.

Lucy Josephine Potter, 19, has left her home on Antigua for life as an au pair in a northern American city, determined never to return. She is angry and unforgiving, slow to warm to her genuinely friendly and generous employer and the cold, alien environment. Lucy is critical and clinical, observing the failings of people and trying to "invent" herself. She explores sexuality, discovers the alchemy of photography, and watches the disintegration of her employer's marriage. Gradually, the source of her bitterness emerges—her intense relationship with her mother and her resentment at never having her intelligence recognized and encouraged, never being seen as an equal to her brothers. And it goes beyond that: Lucy is angry about racism, colonialism, about having to come to America as a servant. She is stunningly frank and indomitable, firmly following her path to wisdom. Kincaid continues to hone the poetic style of her acclaimed novel *Annie John*. Her prose is sensual, surprising, vibrant, and candid. Her characters are deep wells of emotions that we can draw from again and again. —*Donna Seaman*

King, Stephen.
The Stand: The Complete and Uncut Edition.
Doubleday, $24.95. 153p.

This edition restores most of what was cut from the first publication of King's already plethoric sixth book. As he says in a preface, plot and personae are all the same, only the characters do more stuff. The plot is still about how a supervirus escapes from a biological warfare lab, killing more than 99 percent of the world's people, and how the U.S. survivors divide into forces of good and evil, the former animated by a quasi-charismatic quasi-Christianity, the latter by a supernatural personification variously known as the Walkin' Dude, the dark man, and by several names all having the initials R. F. The book's structure is still a cinematic cross-cutting of characters' stories, and virtually every chapter contains splendidly vital writing and slabs of King's trademark gore. Unfortunately, it all adds up to less than the sum of the parts, an epic without sufficient intellectual or religious or fablistic strength to support its great length. But the fans have demanded all of it (King says he still withheld some 100 pages he thinks should stay out), and they won't want to skip a word. —*Ray Olson*

General Fiction

King, Benjamin.
A Bullet for Stonewall.
Pelican, $17.95. 240p.

In recent years, proponents of assassination conspiracy theories have ranked just below gossip columnists on the scale of literary contempt. It is refreshing to come across an exciting and well-crafted novel that restores one's faith in the genre of conspiracy thrillers. The author begins with the premise that Stonewall Jackson, second only to Robert E. Lee in prestige among Confederate commanders, fell victim to a Union-organized conspiracy; the consensus has always been that Jackson was accidentally shot by his troops. Jackson's nemesis is a shadowy loner whose intelligence, competence, and icy relentlessness recall similar qualities in Frederick Forsyth's memorable Jackal. The assassin is opposed by a young and occasionally befuddled Confederate major who is determined to expose the plot, despite the inertia and disbelief among Confederate bureaucrats. This is a gripping and often convincing first novel that keeps us interested, guessing, and always entertained right up to the dramatic conclusion. —*Jay Freeman*

King, Thomas.
Medicine River.
Viking, $18.95. 261p.

Will, a native American now 40, returns after his mother's death to his Canadian hometown, Medicine River, to open a photography shop and sift through his past. Clearly etched characters, led by Harlan Bigbear, the town's basketball coach, matchmaker, and unofficial historian, amble through these sketches of small-town life. Scattered within these stories are Will's childhood memories of his father, a rodeo rider who abandoned him and his brother, James, when they were young, and his mother, who managed to raise the children on her own. There's humor, gentleness, and insight without sentimentality in Will's search for roots and identity among a people anchored in tradition. Warm and satisfying. —*Candace Smith*

Kingsolver, Barbara.
Animal Dreams.
Harper, $19.95. 288p.

In this skillfully told novel by the author of *The Bean Trees*, a young woman returns to her hometown to care for her father and, without knowing it, herself. As usual, Codi is seeking to avoid life, but instead she finds plenty of it. She begins a complicated romance with a former boyfriend, corresponds with her sister, Hallie, who is kidnapped and then murdered in Nicaragua, tries to convince her father that his declining mental abilities are interfering with his work as a physician, and attempts to save the town from the evil Black Mountain Mining Company, which is poisoning the river and threatening the region's future. In alternating chapters, Kingsolver gives us Codi and her father, Homer, adroitly melding two viewpoints of one history. The book's southwestern setting proves particularly evocative: lush hot springs, dramatic vistas, and ancient pueblos are ideal envelopes for characters in deep introspection or loving embrace. The mixed Anglo and native American culture is equally colorful and unusually well developed. It's hard to find fault with this book—it manages to push all our emotional buttons without sacrificing fine craftsmanship. —*Deb Robertson*

Kinsolving, William.
Bred to Win.
Doubleday, $19.95. 624p.

Kinsolving artfully interweaves melodrama, romance, and racing, effectively transforming an otherwise conventional horsey saga into an epic triumph. Alternately neglected and abused by her alcoholic father and brutal brothers, 15-year-old Annie Grebauer determines to escape the poverty and cruelty of her wretched childhood. Seizing an unexpected opportunity to flee to New York, she is befriended by a two-bit gambler who procures her employment at Belmont Park race track. Embarking upon a clandestine affair with Samuel Cumberland III, the sophisticated heir to a great fortune and a superlative stable of horses, Annie becomes addicted to the exhilarating world of thoroughbred racing. A disastrous marriage to Sam's best friend enables her to begin her own breeding operation, competing against her lifelong lover in a frenzied quest to produce a potential Derby winner. Unfortunately, unsavory connections from her past surface and threaten to destroy her security and success. The briskly paced action culminates in an explosively violent climax that will not disappoint expectant readers. Superb entertainment heightened by the author's extensive knowledge of the glamorous thoroughbred business. —*Margaret Flanagan*

✓ **Kis, Danilo.**
Hourglass.
Farrar, $19.95. 272p.

It is remarkable that a writer as brilliant as Kis (Yugoslavian by birth) is almost unknown in this country—though, on reflection, hardly surprising. (An ordinary writer like Boll wins the Nobel, while Grass is overlooked. Kundera grabs the fame, while writers like Kis have trouble getting translated.) Never mind, this is now the fourth of his works to make it into English, and even if this is all a little late for the author (he died last year), these are not the sort of novels that wear thin with time. It is true that some of his techniques are derived. The opening pages of *Hourglass* are pure Robbe-Grillet, and there are passages that read like the catechism chapter of *Ulysses*. But the techniques are perfectly true to the novel's tortured subject: the last months of a minor Hungarian functionary's life prior to being sent to a Nazi concentration camp. This is the world of Broch and Kafka seen in a new and riveting way. Obscure, nightmarish, anguished, and pathetic, the tale never blossoms into something one would call a story. It is an image, a metaphor, of humanity's cruelest, basest moment. —*Stuart Whitwell*

General Fiction

Konwicki, Tadeusz.
Bohin Manor.
Farrar, $18.95. 230p.

Konwicki, Poland's preeminent author, fused memories of his Lithuanian childhood with musings on politics in his last book, *Moonrise, Moonset*. Here, in this mythic romance, Konwicki delves further into his and his country's past. His narrator (himself?) imagines a pivotal event in the life of his grandmother, the beautiful Helena Konwicka. Helena lives on a wooded estate in Lithuanian Poland in the late nineteenth century, after the failed Polish uprising against Russian rule. Motherless and bound to her fanatically grieving father who has not spoken a word since the uprising, Helena is being pressured into marrying a man she cares nothing for. Suddenly, an enigmatic stranger appears, a young redheaded Jew, Elias. The magnetism between Helena and Elias is undeniable and cataclysmic. On one level, this is a classic love story, on another, it's a brooding contemplation of legacy and fate. An exquisite and insightful fable. —*Donna Seaman*

Kraft, Eric.
Reservations Recommended.
Crown, $18.95. 288p.

Kraft's last novel, *Herb 'n' Lora*, garnered rave reviews, and his latest should fare just as well, although it's a darker work. Matthew Barber is an executive in a toy company by day and a restaurant reviewer by night. Writing for the trendy set in Boston under the pseudonym B. W. Beath, he smugly assesses the dining scene, briefly escaping the problems of the real-life Matthew. Each chapter centers on a restaurant meal at which Matthew struggles with his self-consciousness while making mental notes for his review and eavesdropping on the other tables. These dining scenes are hilarious, perceived through Matthew's inner skirmish between his insecurity and B. W.'s sophistication. Matthew, we observe, is hurt by his wife's departure after 14 years of marriage and is trying to remake himself, with little success. His reviews become more and more personal; they're about what happens between him and his guests rather than about the restaurant. The war between his two personalities intensifies until Matthew loses control and finally gives way to his repressed anger. A shrewd, adroit, and spirited novel. —*Donna Seaman*

Krantz, Judith.
Dazzle.
Crown, $21. 502p.

Once again, Krantz has supplied her readers with another entertaining, stay-up-all-night-to-finish novel. Jazz is the hottest celebrity photographer in town. Together with her two partners and their rep, she runs Dazzle, the most successful photography studio in Hollywood. Jazz is the daughter of Mike Kilkullen, owner of 100 square miles of prime, undeveloped land along the Southern California coast. As we've come to expect, however, trouble awaits our heroine. Jazz's almost-husband, who left her the day of their wedding, returns, now wanting studio space at Dazzle. Jazz, meanwhile, is caught between two other men, megastar Sam Butler and distant cousin Casey Nelson, trying to decide which one she loves more. Her half-sisters, who have hated her since her birth, are scheming with a group of superwealthy New York businessmen and Mike's ex-wife to get control of the ranch and turn it into a playground for the wealthy. Worst of all, Jazz is cheated out of a chance to photograph her beloved L.A. Lakers by her scheming rep, Phoebe. Krantz is at the height of her frothy, escapist form here. This is a hot book, bubbling with sex, intrigue, and—most of all—money. Her fans won't want to miss it; others will see its very existense as proof of the decline of the novel. —*Jill Sidoti*

Kureishi, Hanif.
The Buddha of Suburbia.
Viking, $18.95. 283p.

The author of the screenplay for *My Beautiful Laundrette* brings to this first novel some of the same quirky virtues that made that movie such a surprising hit. As in the film, the conditions of Asian immigrants living in London, the racism of the British class system, and the sexual ambiguity of his characters are the themes that preoccupy Kureishi. Karim faces a full load of adolescent conflict in his young life: he's attracted to both boys and girls, his Moslem father has suddenly turned into a Buddhist guru and left Karim's mother, his school career seems to be bogged down in indifference if not outright hostility, his relatives seem caught unawares between East and West, and Karim himself observes all kinds of success for everyone but himself. In Kureishi's tragicomic view of the world, however, Karim's vulnerability and persistence eventually pay off. Meanwhile, Karim suffers through a string of experiences that are by turns hilarious, poignant, and threatening before fortune begins to smile, change is accepted, and murmured promises are fulfilled. —*John Brosnahan*

Latiolais, Michelle.
Even Now.
Farrar, $18.95. 185p.

Even now, almost grown up, Lisa feels responsible for her parents' happiness. But their divorce and custody battle have left bitterness and misunderstanding, making Lisa's self-imposed job all the harder. She feels she should live with her father for longer periods—to make him happy—but fears the unhappiness she would cause her mother. Life with each is a series of stressful situations, as Lisa vacillates between innocently enjoying herself and struggling to say and do the right things. Most convincing here is the way the author uses the child's belief that she controls the universe and is, therefore, the carrier of blame. The knot in Lisa's stomach, her fears and tension, can almost be felt. Latiolais also skillfully portrays the vivid fantasy life that consumes the adolescent, as well as the inability to be either fully child or fully adult. This distinctive first novel probes a common theme with new depth and without dreariness. —*Deb Robertson*

General Fiction

Lawrence, Karen.
Springs of Living Water.
Random/Villard, $17.95. 288p.

Photographer Min McCabe sets out in her van on a months-long journey doing research for her planned book on hot springs. As she drives from site to site, she is inundated by painful memories from her childhood—the slow death of her cancer-stricken mother, the endless demands of her needy younger sister, the desultory conversations with her grieving father. Little wonder, then, that Min left her provincial hometown in Canada just as soon as she could and settled in Southern California, which gave her the freedom to remake herself. Just prior to her cross-continental trip, however, her live-in lover has begun to press her for a more serious commitment, and her old images of family—of being cornered, hounded, deeply unhappy—come flooding back. A visit with her ailing father and a side trip to Europe with her younger sister force Min to rethink her attitudes toward marriage. This slow-moving, lyrical novel contains some wicked commentary on the California life-style as well as much insightful analysis of the often oppressive nature of hearth and home. —*Joanne Wilkinson*

Leffland, Ella.
The Knight, Death and the Devil.
Morrow, $22.95. 720p.

A biographical novel about Hitler's number-two man, Herman Göring? Not a seemingly tantalyzing subject, given the fact that Göring was the mastermind behind the dreaded gestapo and performer of other notorious deeds during the ignominious Third Reich. But—*but*—in Leffland's intelligent and artistic hands, this work develops into an infinitely absorbing portrait of one man's seduction by power, one who, without the moral grit to resist it, falls victim to the lure of corruption open to those in power. Leffland traces Göring's life holding tightly to fact, but, while ringing with authenticity, the novel also achieves all the fluidity and drama necessary to good fiction. There is a big distinction between sympathy and understanding; it is the novelist's charge, in such a project as this, to capture the latter, and Leffland does so splendidly. Certainly one of the most stylish historical novels to appear in a long while. —*Brad Hooper*

Levi, Primo.
The Sixth Day and Other Tales.
Summit, $18.95. 222p.

The late Primo Levi's two vocations—as a scientist and as a writer—are brought together in this volume of short stories examining the way technology has made a better tomorrow yet ignored the implications of scientific advances for today. Levi's technological huckster, Simpson, makes multiple appearances, luring his clients with the many possibilities for his amazing new machines and sending their owners' imaginations off always in the wrong, if completely logical, direction. A duplicating machine performs in three dimensions; a *kalometer* is intended to measure beauty objectively, but the setting can be adjusted to the operator's weird purposes; and cryogenic engineering takes an unfortunate erotic turn. Consequences can be sorted later, while science strides ahead, says Levi in these witty and mordant little fables that document the ongoing battle between the promise of the future and the sad reality of the human mind. —*John Brosnahan*

Littlepage, Layne.
Wonkers.
Dutton, $18.95. 288p.

At 37, disgruntled feminist Barbara Jane McGrath is *so* disenchanted (especially with men) that she can hardly abide even her New Age women's group. On top of that, the snack she grabbed while racing to the weekly group meeting is disagreeing with her in a big way. She races to the bathroom, upchucks, but still feels strange—bigger somehow, and then there's that twisted, lumpy feeling down there. My goddess! She's a man! What's more, she's a handsome, strong, thoroughly heterosexual man—now called B. J.—who immediately finds himself and Mr. B. J. (i.e., his, uh . . . wonker) newly interested in his erstwhile sisters. But he's just as uninterested in feminist claptrap, especially the misanthropic variety Barbara Jane edited for a living. Writing a romp worthy of a latter-day Thorne (*Topper*) Smith, Littlepage twits feminism's worst exaggerations as he argues that there is such a creature as a good, regular guy. Of course, B. J.'s that way because he retains Barbara Jane's basic decency and pragmatism while losing her angry disappointment. His odyssey from shock to love is a sprightly, hilarious, romantic, and wise comic fantasy. —*Ray Olson*

Lovecraft, H. P. and others.
Tales of the Cthulhu Mythos.
Arkham House, $23.95. 529p.

This is not the first time out for this set of stories about the giant, malevolent extraterrestrials created by pulp horror writer par excellence H. P. Lovecraft. To make up for that fact, Jeffrey K. Potter's illustrations *are* new and the volume conforms with the four books of re-edited Lovecraft that Arkham House has recently put out (*The Horror in the Museum and Other Revisions* is the latest). Only two of Lovecraft's many Cthulhu tales—"The Call of Cthulhu" and "The Haunter of the Dark"—appear. The other 20 entries are by horror hands from Lovecraft's heyday and on—Robert E. Howard, Robert Bloch, Colin Wilson, Stephen King, etc. —*Ray Olson*

✔ **Mahfouz, Naguib.**
Palace Walk.
Doubleday, $22.95. 512p.

Doubleday, which recently published three volumes of the Nobel Prize winner's fiction, now offers the first installment of the Egyptian writer's masterly trilogy dealing with three generations of a Cairo family in the first half of the twentieth century. The emotional and physical struggles of these middle-class people are depicted with a great deal of sympathy and honesty, from the torments of adolescent love through the banked passions of an established marriage. The first volume begins with a series of domestic scenes featuring the five children of a merchant and his wife; later, the setting shifts to Cairo nightclubs, coffee shops, and stores as Mahfouz re-creates the everyday existence of his characters in almost Dickensian detail. Meanwhile, on a larger scale, the proclamation of the British protectorate redefines these people's lives in unexpected ways. Later volumes in the series will explore the political and economic ramifications of Egyptian history as the country evolved during the reign of King Farouk and after the military revolution masterminded by Gamel Abdel Nasser. Mahfouz makes the whole texture of Egyptian society come alive, with glimpses of the various classes and their relationships to one another woven into a vivid portrait of a people and a place. —*John Brosnahan*

Matthews, Greg.
One True Thing.
Grove Press, $18.95. 352p.

If this novel were a movie shown on television, *TV Guide* would say: "Violence; sexual situations; strong language." But it isn't tube fare, it's a complex, grim, and fascinating family saga set in a small Kansas town. World War II vet Lowell Kootz has a vision that he translates into reality: The Thunderbird Motel. A circle of 20 cement tepees with a larger tepee in the center for home and office, the cabin complex is a great success in its early years, but Lowell dies in a car crash, leaving his only son, Ray, with his bitter, loveless mother. All Ray wants is to run the Thunderbird and succeed at raising a happy family. Instead, he must deal with an unfaithful wife, a rebellious stepson, and a son who accidentally murders his mother. The twisting plot carries the reader into psyches bubbling with anger, confusion, guilt, fear, and love. Matthews, author of the well-received historical novel *Heart of the Country*, excels at revealing the survival instinct that propels people through tragedy. His visual imagery expresses mental states perfectly, and he tells a solid story. —*Donna Seaman*

Matthiessen, Peter.
Killing Mister Watson.
Random, $21.95. 416p.

The author of *In the Spirit of Crazy Horse* and *Far Tortuga*, among others, uses his skills as a nonfiction writer and novelist to create docudrama out of the life, adventures, and misdeeds of E. J. Watson, the reputed killer of outlaw queen Belle Star (and one mean outlaw himself). Matthiessen uses a *Rashomon*-like montage of accounts, narratives, and testimonies to portray the career of Watson, particularly the period at the end of his life when he lived and worked in the Florida Everglades around the turn of the century. Watson was accused of a series of murders and gunned down by his neighbors in 1910 in a violent instance of vigilante justice. Matthiessen begins with this notorious incident and moves backward through a series of flashbacks to reconstruct and review Watson's reputation and responsibility for a string of unsolved killings. Unfortunately, the book doesn't hold together, as episodic impressions and contradictory evidence build up to confusion rather than resolution. Matthiessen's characteristic interests—the region's landscape and wildlife, the minority condition of native Americans and blacks, the true-crime aspects of the incident—are all present here, but the novel reaches it startling climax more through exhausted relief than powerful conclusion. —*John Brosnahan*

Mayerson, Evelyn Wilde.
Well and Truly.
NAL, $18.95. 400p.

A fetching tale, written with exacting ease, that serves up a rich slice of small-town Vermont life. Maggie Hatch, age 40 and newly widowed, somehow must make sense of her life, which in the past had been neatly arranged by her physician husband. But her attempts at self-direction run amok: her best friend accuses Maggie of flirting with her husband; her adored but cantankerous daughter, Kristen, drops out of college and back into Maggie's household; and her self-absorbed, oft-married mother, Sybil, returns, adding to Maggie's parenting chores. Worse yet, Maggie is called to jury duty on a case involving a daughter accused of murdering her own mother, forcing Maggie to reexamine the forces shaping her own life. Bright flashes of humor and delightfully fresh characterizations enliven this touching saga of self-discovery. Film rights have been optioned by the producer of *Sophie's Choice* and *On Golden Pond*, which should add to this novel's popularity. —*Mary Banas*

McCall, Dan.
Triphammer.
Atlantic Monthly Press, $18.95. 320p.

Despite the thriller-style title, this touching character study isn't really anything of the sort. The hero happens to be an Ithaca, New York, cop named Triphammer, but the story is not about solving murders. While Triphammer occasionally comes on macho and heroic, mostly he's just getting by, searching for small victories in an uneventful life. McCall is a restrained prose stylist, more intent on capturing his characters in tightly written scenes of verbal and emotional interplay than on expanding his plot beyond a few light narrative brush strokes. His protagonist has a job that tends to depress him, a growing fondness for the bottle, and a teenage son with all the requisite problems. Countless scenes are tender gems of understated emotion: the father liquored-up and ashamed when the son brings a girl home; the son calling dad to ask for a ride home after a long night of partying; the father at work, confronting and comforting the parents of a boy found dead, an apparent suicide victim. A heartfelt novel, infinitely sad but not without moments of hope. —*Peter Robertson*

McCorkle, Jill.
Ferris Beach.
Algonquin, $18.95. 380p.

McCorkle keeps getting better. *Ferris Beach*, the story of a girl's growing up, is her most focused work yet: gone is the overwriting that crept into her previous three novels. The central metaphor is the place that gives the book its name—a place associated with ideas of sex, freedom, and broken dreams, as well as Katie's mysterious older cousin, Angela, and her best friend's eccentric, fun-loving mother. Ferris Beach brings Katie a powerful dose of reality, complete with the requisite suffering, but it is all rendered so wistfully and obliquely that we never lose that sense of a child's wonder and terror. At the same time, though, McCorkle skillfully builds tension with the judicious placement of multiple forewarnings of the tragedies that await her young heroine. Still only 30 years old, McCorkle, already with four fine novels to her credit, seems poised to join the ranks of this country's premier fiction writers. —*Deb Robertson*

McCullough, Colleen.
The First Man in Rome.
Morrow, $22.95. 915p.

The best-selling author of *The Thorn Birds* offers an infinitely more demanding and rewarding piece of historical fiction. The first installment in a projected series outlining the demise of the Roman republic and tracing the origins of the Roman Empire, this volume commences in 110 B.C.E. and revolves around the smoldering political ambitions of two seemingly unsuitable statesmen. Lacking the requisite patrician pedigree, stolid and wealthy Gaius Marius, a brilliant general, acquires respectability by marrying into the irreproachable Julian dynasty. Deprived of his noble birthright by a dissolute and profligate father, the impoverished and curiously amoral Lucius Cornelius Sulla resorts to murder in order to claim an inheritance and purchase his way into the senate. Branded as outsiders, Marius and Sulla forge a formidable alliance, culminating in a succession of unparalleled military and political triumphs. An abundance of authentic information detailing the customs and mores of ancient culture is artfully interwoven into the fascinating narrative. McCullough's massive work will mesmerize motivated readers. —*Margaret Flanagan*

McEwan, Ian.
The Innocent.
Doubleday, $18.95. 288p.

In 1950s Berlin, a British telephone technician finds his military mission is not to help the Americans crack Russian communication lines as he initially supposes but to help spy on American intelligence operations. McEwan, however, uses the framework of the spooks-and-spies genre—based on an actual case, by the way—to create a psychologically oppressive comedy of errors that seems as much an homage to Alfred Hitchcock as to John le Carré.

Adding his own poignant twist to the espionage-happy atmosphere of Berlin, McEwan involves his technician antihero with a beautiful German woman who has her own problems, including an alcoholic ex-husband who contributes most of the plot's complications and grisly humor. Collaboration on all sorts of levels ensues, and the novelist exerts a chilling mood of deceit and seduction as he traces his characters' experiences in their descent into the sinister depths of the human condition. *—John Brosnahan*

McEwen, Todd.
McX: A Romance of the Dour.
Grove Weidenfeld, $17.95. 192p.

Novels intent on massacring the mythical "Masterpiece Theatre" image of Old Blighty have been legion of late; Martin Amis' *London Fields* and Hanif Kureishi's *The Buddha of Suburbia* are but two examples. So far Scotland has escaped. It's still the land of mist and heather, romantically dangerous in the works of R. L. Stevenson, comically quirky in the films of Bill (*Local Hero*) Forsyth. With *McX*, American author McEwen launches the first anti-tartan salvo in prose that at times hits Joycean levels of beauty and undisguised bile. Twin Scotlands exist side by side in the novel, with old-world romance governing the life of the fair Siobhan and contemporary dourness coloring the existence of her unlikely suitor McX, a weights-and-measures man whose job entails ensuring that public houses selling drams not short-change the thirsty punters. McX does his own imbibing at the Auld Licht, with legions of solitary Scottish drinkers, faceless souls crippled by Calvinism and harsh weather, pale faces sunk in pint glasses, lusting after the girl on a lager can or the one hidden behind the displays of salted peanuts. When content to play the role of caustic observer, McEwen hits the mark unfailingly. He has sardonic opinions on crisps, on ads on buses, on the gruff brutality of the language, and even on how to curtail smoking (limit the supply of matches). Once the author heads into the murky waters of his lovers' dreams, though, he gets a bit lost in seas of creative fancy. We're never quite sure what McEwen is saying or just how he feels about the real Scotland. Is it somewhere between Robbie Burns and Saturday night in an inner-city public bar at closing time? But which does he prefer? Both, perhaps. Or neither. In the tension between the two lies a remarkable, if partially unrealized, novel. *—Peter Robertson*

McFarland, Dennis.
The Music Room.
Houghton, $18.95. 26p.

After just a few pages of this debut novel, you know you're in good hands. Marty Lambert's younger brother has committed suicide. Marty, recently separated from his wife, travels from California to New York City to find out what led up to his brother's unexpected death. What follows are Marty's memories of his peculiar childhood and his attempt to come to terms with his past and present. His wealthy father is an alcoholic who has nothing in common with his Vegas showgirl wife except the comfort of drink, and she

General Fiction

keeps him from the one activity that brings him pleasure—playing the piano. McFarland perfectly captures the rhythm of drunken banter and the alienating effect it has on Marty and Perry who, unlike their father, are able to nurture their musical abilities but are left scarred by their careless upbringing. Without his brother, Marty is adrift in the arbitrariness of life, faced with the aching why of a suicide. But he does put together some of the pieces of Perry's death and is able to heal himself. The book's resolution, while a bit melodramatic, is a bid for a more generous life. In spite of the somberness of the story, this is a lyrical and often funny novel full of surprise and pleasing nuance. —*Donna Seaman*

McGahern, John.
Amongst Women.
Viking, $17.95. 184p.

McGahern is one of the most highly regarded contemporary Irish fiction writers, and anyone who picks up his latest novel will immediately understand why. It's an uncompromising yet ironically endearing tale of a curmudgeon—Michael Moran by name. "Daddy is old now," say his daughters to each other, and he is a frustrated, angry oldster. Back in his prime he fought the British in Ireland's war for independence; in his dotage he now fights with his wife and daughters, who, despite the abuse he heaps on them, continue to feel it is their job to give the old guy positive stimulation. Oddly enough, regardless of Michael's inability to reconcile past and present, to let himself show and be shown love, he remains the core of his wife's and daughters' existences—a fact that most poignantly comes home to them upon his death. This is not a novel of plot, but one of character, of psychology. And McGahern, in a style at once tough and lustrous, beguilingly insinuates a comprehension of Michael's fears and will. —*Brad Hooper*

McKnight, Reginald.
I Get on the Bus.
Little, Brown, $17.95. 296p.

Adrift in Senegal, a dropout from the Peace Corps, Evan Morris feels as alienated from the West African community where he can barely speak the language as he feels from his black upper-middle-class Denver home and the perfect woman he left behind. Is it malaria? A jinni-demon that someone has put on him? Madness? "What's wrong with me? I mean, I hallucinate, I black out, I get headaches . . . I stand. I smoke. I pick up the telephone . . . Did I kill?" The book's too long; there's only so many times we can read about his headache. But the style, both jerky and hypnotic, is like a powerful drumbeat, the relentless *I* is like a pursuer. The hallucinations are a torment, but they also promise release from the imprisonment of that individual consciousness. The surreal is rooted in a strong sense of the place, and the characters, Senegalese and American, are funny, touching, and mysterious. McKnight's first novel depicts the search for identity of Evan (Everyman) with a candor that challenges easy clichés about roots. —*Hazel Rochman*

McLeay, Alison.
Passage Home.
Simon & Schuster, $19.95. 590p.

McLeay's monumental first novel features an indefatigable nineteenth-century heroine engaged in an arduous transatlantic struggle to control her own destiny. Abandoned by her nomadic husband on the outskirts of the American frontier, decorous Rachel Gaunt adopts the guise of a notorious French singer in order to earn her return passage to Liverpool. Back in England, she conceals the more questionable elements of her past and marries the pompous director of a prosperous shipping firm. Unfortunately, the mysterious Adam Gaunt resurfaces to reclaim her heart, and two formidable enemies attempt to destroy her social and economic well-being. Torn between love and duty, a mature Rachel confronts her shortcomings and achieves a sense of independence, which enables her to marshal her emotions and chart her own course for the future. A gloriously romantic adventure underscored by vivid characterizations and authentic historical detailing. —*Margaret Flanagan*

McMurtry, Larry.
Buffalo Girls.
Simon & Schuster, $19.95. 328p.

Following closely on the heels of *Some Can Whistle* —a tale of family love and reconciliation set on a ranch in present-day north Texas—McMurtry returns to his specialty: the Old West. His main character is none other than Calamity Jane, though the Jane he resurrects here is an aging drunk. Interspersed with letters Jane composes to her daughter but never mails, the narrative is brimming with typical McMurtry color: authentic detail about rustic lifestyles, with particular emphasis on lively plains and mountains characters so well drawn their unhygienic smells fairly waft off the page. History and storytelling mix well met here. —*Brad Hooper*

Merle, Robert.
Vittoria.
HBJ, $19.95. 394p.

Set against the background of sixteenth-century Italy, this engaging novel recounts the story of Vittoria Peretti. Blessed with beauty, charm, and intelligence, Vittoria evokes passion, devotion, and even violence from those closest to her. Ultimately, the very attributes that inspire such reactions lead her to a tragic fate. Vittoria's story is narrated by a series of "witnesses," including a mute priest, a Moorish concubine, Vittoria's neurotic and misogynistic twin brother, and a cardinal who schemes and manipulates with a ruthlessness and cynicism that Machiavelli would admire. Through their eyes we encounter a civilization both brilliant and corrupt, in which a drawn dagger often lurks behind the sweetest smile. It is a society that outwardly cherishes females; yet it takes brutal, merciless revenge upon those women who deviate from male-imposed norms. Merle displays a good understanding of the culture and institutions of the late Renaissance, and his story is rich in detail and replete with finely drawn characterizations. —*Jay Freeman*

Metz, Don.
King of the Mountain.
Harper, $18.95. 304p.

In this fine sequel to Catamount Bridge (Harper, 1988), ex-hippie Walker Owen returns to rural Vermont and discovers that what he remembers best from boyhood is almost gone. What begins as a journey to visit mad, dying Frouncy Audette (more of a mother to him than his own ever was) and part native American but now Yankeefied Claire (his former lover) becomes a struggle to save the woods from condo developers. Frouncy's son, Junior, an angry, paraplegic Vietnam vet, has sold his inheritance, betraying his family's long tradition of stewardship of the land. The Abenaki tribe has also been lured by the chance of prosperity: Claire's great-grandfather, Eale-In-the-Wind, was the Abenakis' last great shaman, but her father, Horton, is "best powder monkey in northern New England," a dynamiter working for the condo developers. As legal means fail to stop the developers from tearing up the land, Walker joins rascal farmer Snoot Audette in acts of sabotage. Are they too late? Can anyone save the land? In a surprisingly dramatic climax, Metz draws to a close this compassionate tale of compromise and chances lost. His flawed characters find the courage to make peace and accept their guilt.
—*Danny Rochman*

Michaels, Leonard.
Shuffle.
Farrar, $17.95. 162p.

The author of *The Men's Club* returns with more tales of the incompatibility of modern men and women in his latest collection of autobiographical confessions. "Journal" and "Sylvia" are the latest battlefield reports on the psychosexual hostilities, but the other stories in this collection find Michaels in a mellower, more nostalgic mood, recalling his father's life or one of his teachers who first stirred his ambition to be a writer. Still, it's love and sex—and their absence—that compulsively drive Michaels' characters to distraction, a condition of horny angst that the author limns to near perfection. —*John Brosnahan*

Micou, Paul.
The Music Programme.
Birch Lane Press, $16.95. 240p.

The U.S.–funded Music Programme in Timbali, Africa—mostly inebriated, eccentric, middle-aged musicians with little time for music but plenty of time for sunbathing, chasing the opposite sex, and watching the tranquilized monkeys dropping out of trees—is in trouble. A U.S. congressman has sent his envoy, Charles ("Crack") McCray, to ferret out the financial truth, bad notes and all, and ensure, perhaps, a grand finale to the program. First-novelist Micou's whimsical farce, published last year in England, centers around Crack's efforts to maintain neutrality after meeting the earnest conductor, Dr. Lord; sharing an apartment (and clothes) with bogus Irish speechwriter Dan O'Connor; and falling in love with the elegant wife of the composer in residence, Kastosis, whose tape recorder, accidentally left on, promises to provide a opus not soon to be forgotten. A comic satire on the tangled strains of bureaucracy, with catchy catch-22's and an ending that can almost be met with applause. —*Eloise Kinney*

Miller, Sue.
Family Pictures.
Harper, $19.95. 352p.

If the expression *multigenerational saga* implies a work of fiction lacking in depth, then the latest novel by the author of the widely applauded *Good Mother* will disabuse the reader of such a notion. Miller extends her tale over a 40-year period, following the full effect a special son has on the lives of not only his parents but also his siblings. David Eberhardt is a psychiatrist living with wife, Lainey, in the Hyde Park section of Chicago; their third child is autistic, and in rapid succession David and Lainey have three more children as a sort of compensation for little Randall's impairments. In a steady buildup of sonorous detail—with good narrative tension but without an ounce of sentimentality—Miller explores the ramifications of such an adjustment in all of those (mother, father, sisters, and brother) having to deal with the boy until the day he dies. —*Brad Hooper*

✔ **Monette, Paul.**
Afterlife.
Crown, $18.95. 288p.

The author of the fine AIDS memoir *Borrowed Time* now gives us a fine AIDS novel. In it, three men whose lovers all died in the same hospital during the same week decide how to live as they await their own illnesses. Steven, well-off proprietor of a travel agency, reencounters a man he used to despise but who, chastened by his own "seropositivity," now seems vulnerable, approachable, finally lovable. Dell, an immigrant Mexican gardener consumed by anger over his loss and public homophobia, pursues a vendetta against a TV evangelist who preaches that AIDS is God's *blessing* to gay men. Sonny, a gay Adonis, plunges back into the promiscuous sexuality he's indulged in since puberty but also searches for New Age deliverance from his compulsion. Monette interweaves their stories with melodramatic flair, keen gallows humor, and sweeping romanticism. His novel is old-fashioned in its vivid scene-setting, rich characterization, psychological penetration, and its ambitiousness to speak for an entire segment of society. That ambition is largely realized, nowhere more strikingly than in sex scenes (too often just a routine feature of gay-male fiction) that are as meaningful and relevant as they are graphic. A major achievement. —*Ray Olson*

General Fiction

Moore, Brian.
Lies of Silence.
Doubleday, $18.95. 208p.

In Northern Ireland, an act of political violence triggers a personal crisis for a hotel manager, his wife, and his lover. Michael Dillon was about ready to call an end to his marriage and leave for London for a new life with a younger woman, but an IRA bombing at his hotel complicates his plan when circumstances and a vengeful wife turn him into a reluctant hero. Moore injects his usual perplexing moral questions into this novel, as Dillon agrees to identify one of the terrorists and thus puts his own life on the line again. But Dillon begins to equivocate once he has escaped his native country: Isn't it best to leave all these modern troubles behind him, to remove himself from the ethical quagmire that is sinking his country? Moore ends his fable with an incident that eliminates all thought of the possibility of scrupulous action in a single blunt moment of revelation that banishes even the chance of fragile hope. —*John Brosnahan*

Morgan, Seth.
Homeboy.
Random, $19.95. 416p.

Seth Morgan has lived life the hard way. Son of Frederick Morgan, poet, founder and editor of the *Hudson Review*, he could have followed a more tranquil path, but alcohol, drugs, and crime proved too magnetic. Fortunately, all the heroin and booze didn't drown the poetry in his blood: this autobiographical first novel—the story of street and prison life in and around San Francisco—pulses with the power of a natural writer. Joe Speaker is a junkie-pimp with a conscience and a kind heart. He and his lover, stripper-whore Kitty Litter, try to keep their hustles small-time and harmless, but they get dragged into a series of mishaps—mostly involving a rare and cursed diamond—that make for classic thriller action: murder, theft, blackmail, pornography, tragedy, and comedy. Morgan paints the prison scene in flinchless detail: AIDS, scams, gangs, sex, brutality, and the criminality of the guards. Of course, life on the outside isn't too pretty, either; various junkies and whores suffer torture and star in snuff films. Morgan can describe anything from a sunrise to a decapitated corpse, and he uses more terms for sex than any slang dictionary. He reels off pages of slow, creeping suspense relieved by jolting violence, and he mixes street talk with a book-lover's vocabulary. And there's a happy ending: he plays the failings of the justice system against the gruff, sustaining love between outcasts, and the outcasts survive and thrive. Homeboy is a bit too long, as though Morgan couldn't bear to end it. Let's hope this means we'll be seeing more of his work. —*Donna Seaman*

Morris, Phillip Quinn.
Thirsty City.
Random, $17.95. 256p.

If the heart of the South is Alabama, and the heart of Alabama is Sumpter County, then the heart of the county is the Reynolds family—good looking, wealthy, intelligent, and boisterous. Though poor as a child, now-rich boot-legger Doddy Bennie J. has always given his children, Winn and Wright, everything, and in the summer before Wright goes off to college, he tries to give them up, even though he would like to keep them forever in his mansion, Big House. Wright, however, is intent on simply having the best time he can, sleeping with his beautiful, death-obsessed cousin, Hanna, drinking beer and driving fast cars, and only occasionally thinking about his past or his future. Morris paints an evocative, vernacular portrait of the late-1960s South, where coon-dog funerals are de rigueur, new money is merely more eccentric than old, and despite what encyclopedias and textbooks say, "Dixie" is the state song. As the maid points out, "Thangs has to end. New thangs has to start." Morris does a fine job with both. —*Eloise Kinney*

Mortimer, John.
Titmuss Regained.
Viking, $19.95. 281 p.

Never one to let altruistic politics stand in the way of selfish personal revenge, British Conservative minister Leslie Titmuss seemingly switches philosophy when he is caught in the middle of an ecological muddle. Titmuss' constituency is located in one of those green and pleasant English valleys, not an absolute beauty but, so far, relatively undisturbed. Then a real-estate developer starts buying up farmland cheap and designs a new town that will cater to the nouveau riche and Margaret Thatcher's privatization schemes. Titmuss would seem to welcome such progress, but, unfortunately, it comes just as he purchases a grand old country house that will soon be surrounded by the new development. Since the house is to be the magnet with which Titmuss catches a new wife and, moreover, plays a key role in his attempt to retaliate for old social snubs, Titmuss is at a loss to know what to do. The complications come fast and furious on both sides of the conservation issue, with Mortimer catching all the quirks and pecadilloes of his characters as they exhibit their basest concerns for their own welfare. A sequel to the author's *Paradise Postponed*, this sardonic look at English village life in the modern era is certain to please the "Masterpiece Theatre" crowd. —*John Brosnahan*

✓ **Murray, Sabina.**
Slow Burn.
Ballantine, $7.95. 160p.

Spoiled and bored, the children of Manila's wealthy families have nothing to do but make trouble for each other, playing out their dramas at nightclubs, parties, even a wedding, ignoring the squalor and social unrest that simmer outside their gates. Isobel de la Fortuna, the young, beautiful, and miserable narrator of this bewitching debut novel, appears to be invincible. She chain-smokes and tosses drinks at men, but at heart she's confused, sad, and hopeless. She gets involved with an arrogant and manipulative man who marries another and expects her to be happy as his mistress. And why not? Everyone has affairs, including her stepfather. But Isobel can no longer play

General Fiction

the game; her long-smoldering anger drives her to seek the aid of a fortune-teller with portentous consequences. Murray's tightly wound, efficient, pungent prose and milieu of tragic decadence is reminiscent of Hemingway, especially *The Sun Also Rises*, but with a feminine spin. This is the genuine article—an incandescent piece of work. —*Donna Seaman*

Nagy, Gloria.
A House in the Hamptons.
Delacorte, $18.95. 374p.

A surprisingly satisfying soaper bubbling with plots and personalities. It's summer and all the wealthy New Yorkers leave town for the beach, softball, and predictable parties. But this summer is different. A blast from the past, in the form of a luscious blonde named Fritzi, unsettles the lives of two couples. Other households are also having their troubles with, what else, drug abuse and adultery. The locals are not immune; they get dragged into the chaos of the summer people by love and employment. The plot gets too hectic, but the characters are colorful, thoroughly likable, and include Match, a six-foot, redheaded masseuse; Louie, an Ethiopian orphan; and China, whose girlish journal entries offer a second perspective. Fast-paced and funny, Nagy mocks the artifice of the Hampton life-style and celebrates good old-fashioned love and loyalty. —*Donna Seaman*

Narayan, R. K.
The World of Nagaraj.
Viking, $18.95. 185p.

A return to the fictional Indian village of Malgudi, the setting of some of Narayan's most memorable novels and tales. This time the focus of attention is on Nagaraj, a middle-aged man whose quiet existence in the village is disrupted when his nephew and the outside world intrude on his familiar if aimless routine. A family squabble over an inheritance forces the nephew and his new wife into Nagaraj's home, distracting him from his life's work: a scholarly study on a Hindu sage that has remained in the incubating stage of wishfulness for years and years. All the unsettling turmoil that ensues is treated with Narayan's humorous yet fond concern for his characters' welfare. Although this short novel stretches the writer's narrative skill—Narayan is more masterly in his briefer works—it is yet another loving depiction of a world he has defined so exceptionally in the past. —*John Brosnahan*

✓ O'Brien, Edna.
Lantern Slides.
Farrar, $18.95. 256p.

J. P. Donleavy's portrait of Irishmen—and women—in *A Singular Country* only scratches the surface of the physical and emotional vicissitudes endured by that country's inhabitants. O'Brien's short stories expand on the anguish and brutality endemic to modern Irish lives, and her characters have more than their own secret problems to brood and moon about. Through a process

272

of communal festering spurred by rumor and gossip, whole rural villages cluck and keen over other people's misfortunes, raising their torment by an exponential ratio. A middle-aged woman who lives with her brother is unhinged when he becomes engaged, not so much for the domestic changes the new wife will introduce, but for the threat the marriage will pose to an incestuous relationship. A very merry widow's second marriage revives tales of what—and who—may have caused the first husband's death. And long-term passions are disrupted by the ties of marriage and the temptations of short-term dalliance. Even leaving Ireland can't quell the hold of this moralism; on holiday in Europe or living in London, the magnetic presence of the homeland draws these characters into morose contemplations of failed relationships between the sexes. O'Brien mines her home territory to splendid effect with her glinting looks at what the Irish have made of their struggle and what Ireland has made of their unhappy lives. —*John Brosnahan*

✓ **O'Brien, Tim.**
The Things They Carried.
Houghton, $19.95. 273p.

"In the end . . . a true war story is never about war. It's about sunlight. It's about the special way that dawn spreads out on a river when you know you must cross the river and march into the mountains and do things you are afraid to do. It's about love and memory. It's about sorrow. It's about sisters who never write back and people who never listen." In Tim O'Brien's world, of course, a war story is all that—and more. The author of the National Book Award–winning *Going after Cacciato* offers us fiction in a unique form: a kind of "faction" presented as a collection of related stories that have the cumulative effect of a unified novel. The "things they carry"—literally—are prosaic things: amphetamines, M-16s, grenades, good-luck charms, Sterno cans, toilet paper, photographs, C-rations. But the men in O'Brien's platoon—Curt Lemon, Rat Kiley, Henry Dobbins, Kiowa, and the rest—also carry less tangible but more palpable things such as disease, confusion, hatred, love, regret, fear, what passes for courage; in short, the prototypical psychological profile of the youthful Vietnam vet. There are 22 pieces here in all, some of which were previously published in such diverse literary arenas as *Playboy*, *Granta*, and *GQ*. The prose ranges from staccato soldierly thoughts to raw depictions of violent death to intense personal ruminations by the author that don't appear to be fictional at all. ("On the Rainy River," O'Brien's account of the time he almost fled to Canada after receiving his draft notice, is particularly moving.) Just when you thought there was nothing left to say about the Vietnam experience . . . there's plenty. —*Martin Brady*

Odier, Daniel.
Cannibal Kiss.
Random, $16.95. 176p.

Frenchman Daniel Odier is best known in the U.S. for four hip mysteries—including *Diva*—published under the pseudonym "Delacorta." This is the first of his Odier novels to appear here. A phantasmagorical journey across

General Fiction

America and into the realm of imagination and creativity, it is the story of a young, enigmatic, sensual woman named Bird, who is linked to saxophonist Charlie Parker in more ways than her name. A seductress, vagabond, and artist, she is involved with one character called the Writer and another called the Chameleon. She wanders into people's lives: a fat prostitute in L.A., an old man living along the Mississippi, and a family of cannibals, placing herself in bizarre and dangerous situations. Meanwhile, the Chameleon watches and the Writer waits. But who is writing the book? Yes, this is one of those novels about writing novels—but with the mind-stretching fluidity and meaningful obscurity of the best modern jazz. To read it is to travel in a dream world made real through Odier's spare, witty, elegant, and intrepid prose. *—Donna Seaman*

Olmstead, Robert.
A Trail of Heart's Blood Wherever We Go.
Random, $19.95. 416p.

Eddie Ryan is a young mortician trying to survive a profession that requires his wife and children to live in the house where he prepares the deceased for burial. Their surprisingly happy home is set against the backdrop of a town inhabited by intriguing Northeasterners. The novel chronicles a growing friendship between Eddie and Cody, a logger whose partner's gory death opens the story. Chapters flow from Eddie's casework to stories of bouts with alcohol, sexual frustration, male-female misunderstanding, and mechanical accidents. This trail of heart's blood swerves around some inspired moments, especially the Christmas Eve dream sequence involving Eddie and his family. Olmstead's strong writing paints both gruesome pictures of the awfulness of life and beautiful scenes of life's richness. Unexpected biblical references almost seem out of place against the technical language of bulldozers and heating systems but provide some of the book's most original and effective passages. A provocative view of what life must be like for a youthful mortician who lives with the people he'll one day bury. *—Kathryn LaBarbera*

Parini, Jay.
The Last Station.
Holt, $21.95. 290p.

Tolstoy died in 1910 in the Astapovo stationmaster's house after finally leaving his wife of nearly 50 years, Sofya, and the comfortable life he felt so uncomfortable with. Parini, drawing upon biographies and the many published diaries of Tolstoy's family members and friends, has written a beautiful, deeply moving historical novel about Tolstoy's last days. He surrounds the reader, lovingly and intelligently, with Tolstoy: the man, the varying influences on his life, his belief in "love unsullied by false interpretation," often quoting from Tolstoy's diaries, letters, and novels. In chapters with alternating viewpoints—of Tolstoy; Sofya; the leader of the Tolstoyan movement, Chertkov; the secretary, Bulgakov; the doctor, Makovitsky; and Tolstoy's daughter, Sasha (and including his own poetry)—Parini depicts the final clashes between Chertkov and Sofya regarding the copyrights to Tolstoy's work. What emerges are sympathetic, poetic portraits of those who were only human, dealing with one they deemed a saint. Parini so skillfully portrays the growing madness of Sofya that her appearance at the window of the stationmaster's house, against Tolstoy's wishes, is nearly terrifying; it is ironic, and tragic, that her definition of love would run so far afield of his. —*Eloise Kinney*

General Fiction

Parris, P. B.
Waltzing in the Attic.
Doubleday, $18.95. 240p.

In her first novel, a chilling gothic, Parris piles cruelty upon cruelty for a young woman growing up on a Nebraska farm. As a child, Hannah Meier is allowed no pleasure by her father, a man who uses his disturbed interpretation of religion to repress and imprison her. As she grows up, every avenue of escape closes off. Her mother dies, her sister is crippled in an accident, and her brother rapes and impregnates her. A single night of affection with a man from town 25 years later provides Hannah's second sexual experience and second child. A good-natured child at first, Paulie quickly becomes as twisted as the other two men. Paralyzed by duty, fear, isolation, and her "religious" upbringing, Hannah survives on naive girlish hopes and belief in God until the disastrous climactic scene set off by the telling of family secrets. *Waltzing in the Attic* could be accused of carrying forth an underlying "men bad, women good" viewpoint, but the author can be forgiven since she tells her story with such enthusiasm and, at the same time, with uncharacteristic restraint in the most unexpected places. This excruciating horror story deserves notice. —*Deb Robertson*

Pazzi, Roberto.
The Princess and the Dragon.
Knopf, $18.95. 160p.

In the dreamy, sad, lonely world of Pazzi's novel, the young, consumptive brother of Tsar Nicholas II sits among the mountains of Georgia, Russia, and suffers the anguish of powerlessness and illness and waits for his death. At times the Grand Duke George seems like a Russian Huysmans; the prose itself sometimes reads like a cross between the *Four Quartets* and the mystical essays of Maurice Maeterlinck. In other words, it's an odd mixture, often obscure, often teasingly beautiful, often difficult to distinguish from nonsense. By the time the rather wooden realism of the opening chapter has given way to a 75-year coach ride across time, the reader is likely to have become disenchanted with all this business about several selves in the same self, all these mirrors, all this languid chatter about fate and destiny and the circularity of life. These days one hardly expects general readers to attack mystical or pseudomystical thinking with much vigor, but for those few iconocalsts in search of something exotic and rare, Roberto Pazzi will be a find. —*Stuart Whitwell*

General Fiction

Penner, Jonathan.
Natural Order.
Poseidon, $16.95. 136p.

For Connecticut beekeeper Jerry Hook, life seemed to make sense; it followed a natural rhythm and order—that is, until a serious competitor sent his business into a tailspin, his feelings for his first wife led him astray from his second, and his college-age son, Eli, was lured into a malevolent cult of reincarnationists. Now Jerry is a man divided, and the chasm is growing especially wide between himself and his son, threatening, quite literally, to swallow up Eli. With skillful craftsmanship and a deliberately askew narrative, this inventive novel exquisitely captures the meaning of "a house divided." Hook is a man who never quite belongs—to his family, his social clan (he's a poor South Ender who made good and now lives in the town's respectable North End), and to himself. And life's darker forces, metaphorically embodied in Jerry's droning bees, seem to have descended. A fascinating character study wrapped up in a jarring parable for modern times. —*Mary Banas*

Perec, Georges.
Things and A Man Asleep.
Godine, $19.95. 221p.

French author Perec used aspects of his life as markers for exploring the murky waters of alienation and uncertainty about how to live in his somber and ironic novels. *Things: A Story of the Sixties* (1965) brought Perec instant fame in France. It concerns a young couple who freelance haphazardly as market researchers while longing for all the material goods they're not willing to work hard enough to afford. An omniscient narrator reports on the pair with clinical detachment, an obsession with settings, and no dialogue. First published in the U.S. in 1968 as *Les Choses*, it was neglected, receiving only one review—in BOOKLIST, July 1, 1968. This is the first U.S. edition of *A Man Asleep*, a masterful and probing tale about a student who loses the will to live. He becomes a zombie, following a routine of sleep, long walks, solitude, and silence until he attains neutrality, a perfect vacuum, only to discover the futility of indifference. Perec should be read by everyone interested in the international novel. —*Donna Seaman*

Perry, Elaine.
Another Present Era.
Farrar, $18.95. 244p.

An exceptional first novel set in a possible present (or the just-barely future). The earth is poisoned. New York City is assaulted with violent storms, floods, and brown-outs. Elegant and mulatto, Wanda is a young, dedicated, and inspired architect, estranged from her white father, and uneasy about her fair looks. Her boyfriend is also a light-skinned mulatto and is losing his mind. Wanda falls in love with an artist, former Bauhaus teacher Sterling Cronheim, who is mysteriously "too old to still be alive." Concealing his identity, he collects art and grieves for his lost loves. His memories of prewar Berlin, occupied Paris, and postwar America mingle with the drama of the present. In both eras, decadence mixes with artistic energy as people face the unfaceable. Perry fluidly handles racial, sexual, and societal conflicts and aesthetics with resonant insight. Intelligent, sentient, and striking fiction. —*Donna Seaman*

Perutz, Leo.
By Night under the Stone Bridge.
Arcade, $17.95. 208p.

Late-sixteenth-century Prague is a cash-poor city ruled by a madman—the Holy Roman Emperor Rudolph II. Rudolph's loves are his wild animals, art, and Esther—a beautiful Jewish woman married to the wealthiest man in Prague. Their liaison, real or dreamed, is at the heart of this collection of interrelated stories. Perutz takes us through the labyrinthine city where the Great Rabbi communicates with angels; where the neglected visionary Johannes Kepler lives in abject poverty; and where many strange occurrences take place, all fraught with cosmic irony. Dogs speak; icons appear; spirits call the names of the living who will soon die. Legend and superstition, paradox and fate, intermingle freely. While Perutz's other recently translated and reissued novels, *The Marquis of Bolibar* and *Leonardo's Judas*, focus on one group of people and one central event, this book contains a splendid variety of personalities and situations. Each chapter is a fable within itself. Perutz is a master storyteller, adept at juggling humor, pathos, suspense, and mystery, and at bringing the distant past to life. —*Donna Seaman*

Petrakis, Harry Mark.
Ghost of the Sun.
St. Martin's, $18.95. 288p.

This sequel to *A Dream of Kings* (1966) has the physically battered, emotionally contrary, spiritually resilient Leonidas Matsoukas returning to Chicago after the death of his son and five long years of torture and imprisonment in his native country. Things change: his daughters have grown up, his former wife has married a rich man, and his Halsted Street neighborhood is almost unrecognizable. Matsoukas' emotional adjustment to coming home proves equally jarring. He encounters his prison torturer and is torn between vengeance and forgiveness; his love for his lost son is transferred to a young unmarried woman with a baby boy; and he struggles to adjust to his still-alluring ex-wife and her new husband, who inexplicably reveres him. Attempting to give Matsoukas' story the grandeur of an epic, Petrakis mixes allegory, irony, and coincidence with abandon, teetering at times on the edge of melodrama but always managing to veer away at the last moment. A florid, stylized writer, Petrakis is a passionate observer of the interplay between emotions and dreams. —*Peter Robertson*

Petrovics-Ofner, László.
Broken Places.
Atlantic Monthly Press, $19.95. 252p.

Childhood and adolescence in the Hungary of the 1940s and 1950s is the setting for this quasi-autobiographical reminiscence. Taking us through those troubled times of war, Holocaust, and communism, narrator Pisti manages to retain a comforting amount of innocence. One relative's explanation of artillery shelling, for instance, conjures in the boy's mind an image of mollusks contending in a lake. The novel proceeds by multiplying such encounters between the cares of the adult world with those of the child's, interspersing them with much symbolic imagery. The apparent goal is to present psychological allusions about the development of personality, and young Pisti eventually matures by the time of the 1956 anti-Russian revolt, when he is wizened enough to know which side to fire his gun at. Despite the terrifying drama of the period, the novel moves at a very languid pace. Perhaps this mood would appeal to readers who, like the author, had to grow up all too quickly in Eastern Europe. —*Gilbert Taylor*

Phillips, Caryl.
The Final Passage.
Penguin, $7.95. 205p.

Phillips' *Higher Ground* appeared in 1989, and now an earlier work has been released for the first time in the U.S. It is the tragic tale of Leila, a young West Indian woman who marries the cold, enigmatic Michael (though he continues to stay with his lover, Beverly, and their son). Leila's mother, seriously ill, goes to England for treatment, and Leila, Michael, and their infant son follow. Where their Caribbean island was poor and oppressive, at least it was beautiful and warm—home. Phillips' London is a cold, ugly hell where blacks are despised. The mother dies, and Michael abandons Leila. Phillips knows the psyche of prisoners—people trapped by prejudice, poverty, and inertia. This novel is a chant of steady sorrow. In simple, weighted prose, Phillips creates vivid, substantial characters who speak sparingly; their homes are bare; their lives circumscribed by oppression. The only light is the love the women have for their children. An evocative, gracefully powerful novel. —*Donna Seaman*

✔ **Pickering, Paul.**
The Blue Gate of Babylon.
Random, $17.95. 304p.

There's just no pigeonholing this one. Pickering's novel recalls Richard Condon's *Manchurian Candidate*, but it's also a meditation on the lies that become our history. Reluctant British spy Toby Jubb is a well-meaning, amiably bent classicist-turned-diplomat whose tryst with a French politician's wife gets him sent to cold-war Berlin. Assigned to run a brothel to trap a former Nazi who is now an East German soldier, Toby indulges his passion for "that old liar" Herodotus and models his brothel on ancient

Babylon and the Temple of Ishtar. The brothel prospers; the operation founders. By turns, this book is frighteningly real and surreal. It's comedy—as high, weird, and low as British comedy can be. It's also cynical and tragic. Pickering's Berlin, circa 1960, rings true—and the characters are memorably quirky. A terrific novel by a terrific writer. —*Thomas Gaughan*

Pilcher, Rosamunde.
September.
St. Martin's, $22.95. 544p.

Pilcher's fame grew considerably with *The Shell Seekers*, which was transformed into a made-for-television movie. In her new, enrapturing intergenerational saga, which features a minor figure from that earlier novel, Scotland is more than a backdrop. The scenery is raved about (even by locals), Scottish customs are played up, and the characters are primarily lairds and ladies from distinguished, hard-working Highland families. Pilcher writes safely—crises are introduced then quickly disposed of before one even gets a chance to fret over the outcome; potential acts of murder, adultery, and other illicit deeds are nipped in the bud. However, she does have the ability to pull readers straight into her created world and make them glad when such family, romantic, and financial difficulties are smootdy out. Even though it lacks the depth of *The Shell Seekers*, *September* is wonderful romantic fiction. —*Denise Perry Donavin*

Popham, Melinda Worth.
Skywater.
Graywolf, $17.95. 208p.

Albert and Hallie Dunham have lived in the desert near Yuma, Arizona, for 40 years, eventually naming the desert creatures, their "neighbors," after the trash they pick up. Thus does the reader become acquainted with the coyotes Kraft, Kodak, Salem, Chieko (named after a Japanese candy-bar wrapper), Boyardee, Dinty Moore, and the aloof, enigmatic leader, Brand X, all of whom are forced to leave the area after the Dunham's well is poisoned. Popham's utterly charming tale of the creatures' journey to find water, led only by their spirits and the determination of Brand X to find Skywater, the ancestral drinking place of the "moon callers," is underpinned with the horrors of humankind's tainting of the earth—the tailings from copper mines that have ruined the water, the testing of bombs, the dumping of waste. All this is seen from the animals' point of view, with occasional human asides (letters from Hallie, the inane car conversations of highway travelers) and interventions (the drunken trapper who catches Chieko). Popham doesn't sentimentalize nor anthropomorphize but instead draws upon the coyote's role in native American lore, its long existence as a predator, and mainly, the desire and right of all living things to "live a completed path." This unfalteringly eloquent and often sorrowful book, which paints the desert landscapes as lovingly as it does the animals who populate it, becomes a poignant and telling indict-

General Fiction

ment of those who are murdering not just the land, but its inhabitants. —*Eloise Kinney*

✓ **Price, Reynolds.**
The Tongues of Angels.
Atheneum, $18.95. 176p.

A middle-aged artist—a painter—remembers the summer of 1954 when he was a counselor at a boys' camp in the Great Smoky Mountains. At a time in his life when he was determined to gain immortality by way of his art, he encountered 14-year-old camper Raphael Noren. The mystique borne by this uncommon adolescent influenced the narrator's painting for years to come; but more to point is the fact that the narrator himself was too much an influence on his charge. This obsession with patterning himself on the artist leads in the end to Raphael's death. What the narrator learned from this experience was that to inspire anyone else to attain levels of artistic grace was *none* of his business. This is perhaps Price's most beautiful novel, written with sublime humor and poetry. (Referring to the campers' propensity for pulling stunts, Price has the narrator assert early on that "I rightly suspected I'd hardly begun to experience their virtuosity in ways to smuggle farts like anarchist bombs into the highest and most sacred scenes of camp life.") Without sentimentality, Price honestly tugs at the heartstrings. —*Brad Hooper*

Pringle, Terry.
Tycoon.
Algonquin, $17.95. 300p.

Pringle's latest tale of love and ambition is set against the boom and bust economies of Texas in recent years, and like his earlier *A Fine Time to Leave Me*, it showcases the author's talent for strong setting and characters. Over the novel's span from the sixties through the eighties, two families, the old established Brewsters and the upstart Gaineses, are featured. Billy Brewster—William the Third—comes complete with colorful granddad and unambitious, rich-boy ways. Go-getter Stan Gaines becomes Billy's father's favorite "son" and an oil and real-estate tycoon. Stan also gets Billy's best friend, Sally Ann, for a wife, to Billy's utter amazement and chagrin. But Billy and Sally Ann continue their sexual fireworks through the years despite their separate spouses and children. In this refreshing retake on the one-note "Dallas" routine, Pringle wisely packs plenty of years into his scenario, rounding out his characters and preventing their descent into the usual tired caricatures. He also allows a little ambiguity to seep into his narrative, which fosters a more realistic air. We're never completely sure what ultimately motivates his characters, and for once, that isn't a fault; it makes them seem human. —*Deb Robertson*

Proffitt, Nicholas.
Edge of Eden.
Bantam, $18.95. 384p.

Proffitt serves up the old Argonauts gambit and salts it with amateur anthropology in this updated (set in 1978) tour of the territory Robert Ruark trod so best-sellingly in *Something of Value* and *Uhuru*. Just as Jason gathered the guys to go for the gold in Colchis, Nairobi police inspector Peter Odongo gets up a group to track some highly successful ivory poachers who believe in gruesomely killing the competition as well as the animals. Now Odongo's black, but his cohero is the youngest of the great white hunters, whom Odongo recruits because blacks, forbidden by old colonial law to use firearms, don't shoot well. As the rest of the crew evidences, however, blacks can still hunt up a storm, each according to the ways of his ethnicity, which Proffitt pedantically spells out. If this all smacks of some old jungle movie (hey, it even drags a *girl*, a hiply foul-mouthed reporter, along for the ride), be assured that, thanks to Odongo's role in it, it's also a bit of a *roman policier* and that if you read it fast enough, it's plenty entertaining in both respects.
—*Ray Olson*

✓ Pynchon, Thomas.
Vineland.
Little, Brown, $19.95. 385p.

"Whole problem 'th you folks's generation," says a member of Billy Barf and the Vomitones, "is you believed in your Revolution, put your lives out there for it—but you sure didn't understand much about the Tube. Minute the Tube got hold of you folks that was it, that whole alternative America, el deado meato, just like th' Indians, sold it all to your real enemies, and even in 1970 dollars—it was way too cheap." In Thomas Pynchon's long-awaited fourth novel (his first in 17 years), it's 1984, though it's clear that the author's heart, soul, and mind are somewhere in the 1960s, when the Cause was worth marching for—even if it did share a lot of screen time with "The Brady Bunch" and "Gilligan's Island." Our tale begins in Vineland, an old logging community north of the City where still-hippified Zoyd Wheeler, performer of stupid human tricks, lives with his daughter Prairie. Enter Hector Zuniga, henchman for evil federal prosecutor Brock Vond, who's interested in tracking down Prairie's mom, Frenisi Gates, once Vond's lover and a former FBI undercover agent and member of a group of documentary filmmakers who captured the Revolution in all its impotent glory. While the feds hassle Zoyd, Prairie goes on the road with the Vomitones, but is soon swept away by her mother's old countercultural colleague Darryl Louise Chastain (aka DL) to L.A., where they spend the day reliving, via film, Frenisi's (apparently traitorous to the Cause) life and activities. With Reagan budget cuts forcing hippies-turned-informants out from their lives on the underground dole, the power-mad Vond freaks, then exercises his obsessive commitment to keep Frenisi from reuniting with her daughter. Not that it matters much, the counterculture wins its first battle in decades in this evocative, maddeningly insistent satire of anyone ever afflicted with Me Generation–itis. Pynchon's

General Fiction

virtuosic display of literary fireworks comes complete with wacko song lyrics, a keen feel for modern-era slang, lickety-split dialogue, and an innovative, frenetic approach to shifting points of view—sort of like Neal Cassady commandeering a wireless remote. —*Martin Brady*

Quarrington, Paul.
Whale Music.
Doubleday, $17.95. 224p.

Powered by the talent of composer, performer, and all-around musical genius Desmond Howell, a rock group called the Howl Brothers achieves great success in the 1960s, with only the Beatles offering serious competition. By the 1980s, though, Howell has become a recluse, having undergone a Brian Wilson–style crash-and-burn cycle. Insulated from the day-to-day world by millions in royalties, his drug-honed imagination, and an endless supply of stale jelly doughnuts, he devotes himself to mastering the ominous Yamaha 666 synthesizer and producing his magnum opus—an electronic symphony intended for an audience of whales. Among the eccentric characters—derived from actual personalities in the entertainment world as well as from author Quarrington's ample imagination—is a diminutive runaway mental patient named Claire. Scraping the bottom of the groupie barrel by shacking up with Desmond, she evolves from a source of distraction to the elusive inspiration needed in his music and his life. Witty, irreverent, and moving, this is one of the more enjoyable pop-culture satires to come along since William Kotzwinkle's *The Fan Man* (Avon, 1974). —*Elliott Swanson*

Raymo, Chet.
In the Falcon's Claw: A Novel of the Year 1000.
Viking, $17.95. 222p.

In tumultuous tenth-century Europe, where many expect the Second Coming, abbot Aileran feels his life has always been shaped by others. From his Viking and Irish heritage to his priestly vows, from friendship and passion to betrayal, he appears to be "a sparrow caught in the falcon's claw." He is torn between heaven and earth, between his love of God and his love and sexual passion for his beautiful pupil Melisande. The story is told through flashbacks to Aileran's youthful friendship with the licentious adventurer Gerbert (who later becomes pope) and to his love affair with Melisande; through letters between the friends and lovers; and through the church inquisitors' interrogation of Aileran. Raymo's lyrical prose style incorporates biblical and classical tales to illuminate eternal ethical questions: Can love remain constant in a world of flux? Is every action equally capable of expressing good and evil? A challenging historical novel. —*Danny Rochman*

Richler, Mordecai.
Solomon Gursky Was Here.
Knopf, $19.95. 413p.

As Moses Berger finds out in Richler's newest novel, Solomon Gursky is a near-legendary figure who was not only here, but here, there, and everywhere, taking part in this century's seminal events—even, apparently, after his reported death. Early in the novel we find out that Solomon, the most dynamic of the three Gursky brothers (heirs to a Canadian distillery dynasty) was killed in an airplane crash. Yet, Moses—who has devoted his life to writing a biography of the family—uncovers odd hints of an afterlife on Earth (around the world, in fact, and in many different guises) for the vigorous, mysterious Solomon. Moses is determined to untangle truth from fiction and family history from braggadocio. The Gurskys brag that their Canadian roots reach back to the sole survivor of the doomed Franklin Arctic expedition of 1846, who went on to preach his own randy version of Judeo-Christianity to the Innuits while fathering three legitimate sons and countless illegitimate descendants. But can the truth be recognized when it's seen? The ethnicity and eccentricity of Richler's characters open the door for plenty of jokes, one-liners, and subtle ironies. A richly humorous novel from the author of *The Apprenticeship of Duddy Kravitz* (1959). —*Denise Perry Donavin*

Rigby, Kate.
Fall of the Flamingo Circus.
Random/Villard, $16.95. 224p.

To open Lauren Schnazer's diary is to enter the tough London scene of the fertile lower class ("my mums have popped out the little pills pink and blue pretty reguler") and the underworld of the punk movement. With an awkward start, presumably the voice of a seven-year-old, the sporadic entries grow in eloquence as the adolescent Lauren matures. Her consistent disregard for property, work, and school are understandable in light of her abusive father, whose violence follows Lauren and even intrudes upon the lives of her friends. Blunt, matter-of-fact statements of this brutality will shock the reader into understanding why Lauren is the way she is—an anti-establishment lost soul who rebels against anyone who "doesn't like people . . . doesn't want their blood or sweat or sex or tongue or intelligence." In her first novel, Kate Rigby introduces a provocative, questioning heroine who is "scared of meeting me" but rises to the occasion. —*Kathryn LaBarbera*

Robbins, Tom.
Skinny Legs and All.
Bantam, $19.95. 422p.

The release of a new Tom Robbins novel is no small thing to all those who find grave import in the near-hallucinogenic, self-referential ramblings of this aging icon to a former counterculture. Robbins returns to familiar territory, contriving an elaborate tale in which Ellen Cherry Charles, another one of the author's "small-town girls with big-time dreams," moves to Manhattan to be an artist but ends up working as a waitress at a restaurant owned by an Arab and a Jew—located across the street from the UN—where a belly dancer named Salome is far more popular than the *baba ghanoug*. Ellen Cherry's husband, Boomer, a redneck welder, inadvertently gains a reputation as an artist and moves to Israel, where he makes political sculpture. Meanwhile,

General Fiction

her Uncle Buddy, an evangelical preacher in search of a TV ministry, dreams about the Second Coming and Armageddon and plots the destruction of the Dome on the Rock and the construction of the Third Temple. Also in the cast are an odd assortment of anthropomorphized objects—Painted Stick, Conch Shell, Can o' Beans, Silver Spoon, and Dirty Sock—who are also on a quest to the Promised Land. The text is divided into chapters, each representing a stage of Salome's Dance of the Seven Veils; in her climactic dance, as each veil falls, some sort of revelation is disclosed as illusions are peeled away one by one. Robbins takes on the Arab-Israeli conflict and the meaning of art as he combines revisionist biblical scholarship with spiritual and artistic exploration, illuminating the common origins of warring peoples and concluding that the earliest deity was female. A whimsical novel laced with "significance." —*Benjamin Segedin*

Robinson, Buffy Shutt.
Creative Differences.
Soho, $18.95. 275p.

A captivating autobiographical novel about one woman's rise to the top of the Hollywood film industry. Robinson knows whereof she speaks, or writes, for she herself rose from secretary to president of marketing at Columbia Pictures. The author effectively employs a novel of "interiors," with the main character talking as if to herself, to capture the dislocation experienced by the nameless narrator as she rapidly rises through the corporate ranks and loses a bit of herself along the way. It's an imaginative novel, invested with subtle humor and just the right dose of realism to keep the pages turning. And in the end, the working-girl heroine learns an important lesson or two about having it all. Unfailingly good entertainment. —*Mary Banas*

Robinson, Sue.
The Amendment.
Birch Lane Press, $17.95. 237p.

An exciting novel pitting pro-lifers against a pro-choice group in the year 1998. The country has finally ratified a pro-life amendment to the Constitution. During the celebration in New Orleans, a local abortion clinic is raided and in the action the doctor and his patient are killed. In the aftermath, the patient's mother, Frances Foster, joins her daughter's best friend and the clinic's nurse to abduct the first lady, who is also president of the Rights for the Unborn League. Foster, it turns out, knows that the first lady herself once had an abortion. She reckons that a $100 million ransom would in some way make up for her daughter's death by funding a safe and legal clinic in Sweden plus international transportation costs for American women in need. Tightly written, this is a white knuckler to the last page. —*Cynthia Ogorek*

Rossner, Judith.
His Little Women.
Summit, $19.95. 366p.

"The fiction writer always seems to be breaking a contract with reality that her friends and relations were sure she signed." In this choice novel of love and libel, readers may wonder how many of her own contracts Rossner has broken. Certainly her characters, for all their quirkiness, resonate with an honesty that makes them seem based in truth. The story is told by Nell Pearlstein, daughter of movie mogul Sam Pearlstein, who has four daughters by three different wives. Nell, who was abandoned by Sam when he began his new family, is surprised to learn he's done the same thing to an older daughter, Louisa. Despite Sam's shocking lapse in fatherly responsibility, both girls are deeply enamored with their charismatic dad and must learn to understand the profound impact he has on their lives. Intertwined is the story of Louisa's libel case: she has been sued by a man acquitted for murder who feels she has stolen his story for her best-selling novel. Rossner gets it just right—the Hollywood ambience, the sibling rivalry, and the effect the burgeoning feminist movement has on both sisters. Details of the libel trial, often revealed through court transcripts, also show veracity. Though most intense at the beginning, when details of everyone's lives are tantalizingly dispensed, the book will continue to hold readers until the end. Rossner, best known for *Looking for Mr. Goodbar*, has another winner here in a story both entertaining and insightful. —*Ilene Cooper*

Roth, Henry H.
Boundaries of Love and Other Stories.
British American Publishing, $17.95. 224p.

In this 19-piece story collection, Roth spins prose of great power and attractiveness. Essentially, these stories deal with the clash and clank of discordant relationships. For instance, "Dealing" is a short monologue between two old college chums, with the discomfort between them—due to the difference in their financial situations—made obvious. And in "When Flynn was Drinking," the reader is told in no uncertain terms how, when the narrator's friend Flynn was imbibing, life was benevolent to everyone around him. But when reasons of health demanded Flynn give up the bottle, he was no longer considered fun, and the world then saw him as a lout. All the stories resemble prose poems in imagery and rhythm, are wrought from honest sentiment rather than easy sentimentality, and demonstrate a gentle authorial hand guiding them toward resolution. —*Brad Hooper*

Roth, Philip.
Deception.
Simon & Schuster, $18.95. 208p.

Roth replays themes from his recent work in his latest novel. In fact, the text is presented as excerpts from a writer's notebook, with a final twist added at the very end. Each incident involves a famous writer and his latest mistress, and unlike Portnoy, this character has few complaints. In these lovers' chats,

General Fiction

the topics ramble from scene-setting foreplay to postcoital recriminations on the adultery that has just taken place. Complications arise, however, when the current mistress senses the writer may have yet another candidate in the wings or, worse yet, may have scheduled a few unannounced matinees with an alternate cast. All of this conversation makes for galvanizing eavesdropping, but Roth's performance may be a bit of a letdown from *The Counterlife*; still, *Deception* is a necessary entry in Roth's canon, even if it will send the reader back to his earlier versions of the basic story, some of which are readily identifiable by clues dropped into the dialogue. —*John Brosnahan*

Rothschild, Michael.
Wondermonger.
Viking, $17.95. 228p.

The blurb on this collection of stories will tell you that Rothschild is another García Márquez, another Faulkner, another Hawthorne, and no doubt there is something in this claim. But Ted Hughes, Dylan Thomas, and Gerard Manley Hopkins, though all old world writers, might have been better choices. They're also all poets, and the title story reads very much like poetry. Of course, when people start throwing around names like this they're either trying to cover up some inadequacy or desperately trying to put their finger on something distinctive. The latter is definitely the case here. "Wondermonger" is actually a novella, and it stands out from the other pieces like the work of an adult stands out from the work of a child. It is dense, breathless, at moments brilliant, earthy, mythic, difficult, sometimes pretentious. Frankly, it's difficult to assess how good Rothschild really is. He is such an original that only time and rereading will really tell. If he can build on what he learned writing "Wondermonger" he might be the first major writer to appear in this country for a very long time. —*Stuart Whitwell*

Rushdie, Salman.
Haroun and the Sea of Stories.
Viking, $18.95. 210p.

No verses here, satanic or otherwise, just a few lines of doggerel in Rushdie's latest story, which was written during the last year while the author was in hiding after an Iranian death threat was placed on his life for blasphemy. Composed in the form of a magical folk story, the book is addressed and dedicated to Rushdie's young son and comes complete with all the trappings of a classic fairy tale, from a kidnapped princess to a magic potion to a happy ending. Typically, Rushdie is not content to rest with a witty surface narrative; comments on his life and his art pop up throughout the story, the author pondering his own situation in the midst of plotting his characters' ordeals. There's even some hilarious if poignant self-mockery in the portrait of a storyteller who loses his voice and his wife in a single moment. But the story does go on for just a bit too long, both the joke and the underlying reality of Rushdie's situation reaching an impasse that even an often brilliant style can't overcome. —*John Brosnahan*

Sanchez, Javier Garcia.
Lady of the South Wind.
North Point, $19.95. 240p.

This 1985 novel was a great success in the author's native Spain. While the author is Spanish, all his characters are German. The style is old-fashioned and reminiscent of Thomas Mann. Most of the book consists of a monologue: Hans Kruger is telling Andreas Dorpfeld about his overwhelming fascination with Olga Dittersdorf. His dutiful, exhaustively thorough, even clinical, account lends a certain atmosphere of detachment, even of eavesdropping, to the story. The three of them work at an explosives manufacturer—a well-chosen occupation as the patient reader will discover. Kruger's life is reduced to his preoccupation with Olga. He studies her eyes, lips, nail-bitten hands with hopeless passion. She tolerates his worship, spending hours with him at bars and then returning to her athlete lover. She is, allegedly, the lady of the south wind—a hot, dry wind that hastens the ripening of fruit and stirs the desires of women—but Olga remains in control of hers, and Hans ends up in an asylum. A demanding but intriguing novel that tinkers with the notion of subjective realities wherein anything is possible. —*Donna Seaman*

Sanders, Dori.
Clover.
Algonquin, $15.95. 196p.

Ten-year-old Clover Hill is devastated when her beloved Daddy is killed on his wedding day. Her own grief overshadowed by that of her relatives and seemingly strange stepmother, Clover tries to behave normally and stay out of the way. Told from a simple, decidedly childlike point of view, this first novel gently examines the unsettling ideas a child can experience after a parent's death. Clover's sadness and insecurity are convincing as she grapples with her sense of loss and her uncertainty about where she now fits in. Her kind and loving stepmother and aunt and uncle reassure her as the family members join together to repair the chain broken by Gaten Hill's death. The fact that Clover is black and her stepmother white provides Sanders with further opportunity to dwell on the cultural differences that fuel the insecurities of these two people with nothing in common but their loss. The author clearly knows and loves her characters, who are imbued with individual strengths and forgivable faults. —*Deb Robertson*

Schott, Max.
Ben.
North Point, $17.95. 165p.

Schott, author of the well-received *Murphy's Romance*, offers a second novel that doesn't disappoint. *Ben* is a well-knit drama about love and loyalty. Max, the young, watchful narrator, has been befriended by Ben, a horse trainer and rancher. Max's mother, victim of a brain tumor, requires constant care from her patient, kind, but distracted husband, Myron. Ben's gruff affection and his world of horses, fields, and rodeos provide a refuge for Max, while Max's uncritical trust and admiration is a balm for Ben, whose young wife

General Fiction

has left him. Paced to the rhythm of the swing of a shovel or the gait of a burro, Schott's prose conveys the depth of repressed feelings his gentle, reticent characters contain out of respect and love. —*Donna Seaman*

Schraft, Constance.
Instead of You.
Ticknor & Fields, $19.95. 256p.

Charlotte and Louise are sisters. Charlotte is dynamic and decisive. She is the one people notice, fall in love with, set their lives to. Louise is not. But this is her story, and it is set to her tentative rhythms. It is the story of a woman whose life has been looked at in terms of someone else's, and whose positive attributes are discussed in negative terms—she doesn't make waves, she doesn't cry. Although Louise is the novel's narrator, we don't really feel as if we get inside her—hers is not a noisy inner life. But when Charlotte, still in her thirties, dies in a car accident, Louise steps right into her place. She takes a leave of absence from her job in New York, moves back to her home town, and in with Charlotte's husband and two daughters. What seems like certain emotional suicide becomes a real opportunity to test her ability to become herself. Schraft tells this story with an appropriate economy of words. It is no small accomplishment that Louise does emerge—without a dramatic inner struggle and without an obvious effort, but fully intact and fully herself. —*Frances Woods*

Seidler, Tor.
Take a Good Look.
Farrar, $18.95. 261p.

Despite the fact that this coming-of-age-in-the-big-city story is streaked with elements of perversity, its tone is never anything less than bucolic. Nice guy Paul Motley moves to the Big Apple with the intention of writing a screenplay and making contacts in the film industry. His aspirations are sidetracked when he becomes obsessed with the beautiful woman who lives in the brownstone across the street. He follows her one day, discovers that her name is Stevie Farr and that she works in an upscale restaurant, and lands himself a job as a waiter so that he can be near her, though she's not exactly encouraging. The wait staff consists almost entirely of aspiring actors and includes two strikingly handsome twin brothers. Their stormy, possibly incestuous relationship is about the strangest, most fascinating thing Paul has seen and considerably alters his touching if naive view of the world. Paul ultimately discovers a new, more attainable dream girl and a wiser outlook in this upbeat, colorfully drawn portrait. Seidler is the author of several well-received books for young people, including *The Tar Pit.* —*Joanne Wilkinson*

Shields, Carol.
The Orange Fish.
Viking, $17.95. 199p.

Shields is the kind of writer who can make anything seem interesting—especially the kind of thing that is usually interesting only to the person to whom it is happening. Universalizing the mini-epiphanies we all have and making them shimmer with mysterious possibilities, she brings to the fore a "lesser world," a world that usually seems passive, matter-of-fact, nearly mute. She gets inside that world and reveals "its covered pleasures, its submerged pattern of communication." In the title story, a nearly middle-aged couple not happy with each other and terrified of aging (but whose boldest expression of that fear is an occasional flash of pain in the upper colon), purchase a lithograph of an orange fish. They hang it, with its "wide, ungreedy eye," over the breakfast table, where it speaks to them of agelessness and of a place where it is enough just to be. They emerge from their unhappy selves, suddenly capable of great feats of sympathetic imagination. Shields understands the poetry of change, and she reports the transformation it brings about with a wry, matter-of-fact tone that is absolutely right.
—*Frances Woods*

Shiner, Lewis.
Slam.
Doubleday, $18.95. 240p.

Poor Dave. He's 39, has just been paroled from the slammer, and all he needs is a breather to think through his future. Perhaps a low-stress job as caretaker of a Texas coast beach house would suit him just fine. Unfortunately, the house won't let Dave relax; it exerts a strange gravitational attraction: among its visitors are a UFO worshiper, drug dealers, two treasure hunters, women half his age or women of "a certain" age, and more than a few cats. These folk, guided by a few boisterous plot complications, foil Dave's best efforts to maintain his sanity and freedom from the parole officer. The hilarious catharsis arrives when our good-natured protagonist, exasperated at all his uninvited guests, gets rid of the problem by torching the beach house. A zany, imaginative novel. —*Gilbert Taylor*

Shriver, Lionel.
The Bleeding Heart.
Farrar, $19.95. 415p.

Over the past 10 years, 32-year-old expatriate Estrin Lancaster has made plastic boots in Galilee and ashtrays in Amsterdam; she's picked grapes in Champagne and lemons in Greece. When she lands in Belfast, she's tired of traveling but wary of settling down. Especially after she meets Farrell O'Phelan, former free-lance bomb disposal expert turned politico. Their skittish romantic relationship embodies their almost pathological fear of contentment. Meeting in a hotel room at odd hours of the day and night, they regularly fight, make love, and talk about leaving for new countries. As they struggle to deny their increasing love for each other, their personal relation-

General Fiction

General Fiction

ship becomes the focal point of a fringe terrorist group. Shriver's expansive, full-tilt prose mixes personal and political themes with abandon as she skillfully dissects the ills of a pair of modern lovers and a country in conflict. —*Joanne Wilkinson*

Siddons, Anne Rivers.
King's Oak.
Harper, $19.95. 576p.

Maybe it would be wrong to say Diana Andropoulis was born on the wrong side of the tracks in Atlanta, but she certainly was not brought up in the kind of neighborhood her future husband came from. Marriage into the high and mighty Calhoun family, therefore, is not a success for Diana; and, eventually, she and her little girl flee Atlanta for a small town—namely, Pemberton, near the Big Silver Swamp. "I had wanted banality in Pemberton," Diana says, but she gets the very opposite. She meets a man who exists on a less earth-bound level than she, and her affair gets her embroiled in a controversy surrounding a nuclear plant's spoilage of the Big Silver. A nice big robust soap opera with a suitably responsible message. —*Brad Hooper*

Silman, Roberta.
Beginning the World Again.
Viking, $19.95. 410p.

Mixing historical figures with fictional characters, Silman tells a compelling if somewhat claustrophobic story of the "women of Los Alamos," the wives of the scientists who created the atomic bomb in the early 1940s. Filtering the narrative through the character of bright, vivacious Lily Fialka and her brilliant young husband, the author deftly interweaves the domestic details of family life with the larger issues spurred by the scientists' deadly work on the "gadget." Enforced isolation in the barren New Mexico desert prompts Lily to forge fast friendships with History Lerner, an outspoken woman disowned by her family for marrying a Jew; with Jacob Wunderlich, a complex man with a passion for science, who is trapped in a disastrous marriage; and with Erik Traugott, a world-renowned scientist who becomes convinced that the atomic bomb will unleash a new kind of madness upon the world and does his best to convince Churchill and Roosevelt that they must put a stop to the research. For all of its weighty moral and historical themes, this novel is also an interesting and insightful group portrait of highly intelligent, motivated people focused on a common goal. —*Joanne Wilkinson*

Simon, Rachel.
Little Nightmares, Little Dreams.
Houghton, $18.95. 212p.

A brilliant tapestry of short stories—16 in all—that memorably displays the slender threads that tenuously connect people. Virtually no manner of relationship escapes this prizewinning writer's astute eye and tender wit: the bonds between mother and daughter, husband and wife, friends, and extended family all are explored, but from a female's point of view. The title story—the collection's best—uses symbolic dream imagery to poignantly portray a wife's growing awareness of her husband's impending death and the bittersweet quality of her need to spiritually let go after some 40 years of being part of a couple. "Breath of This Night" turns a rock 'n' roll hero into an intimate symbol of mother-love and loss as a mother tenderly reflects on her three daughters' growing up and away from her. "The Greatest Discovery of Them All" turns motherhood inside out in its darkly comic portrait of a bored Jewish housewife turned drug runner, whose daughter, whom she inadvertently murdered, watches disapprovingly from Heaven, waiting for her mom's return "home." Simon is an expert at weaving popular culture into short, personal narratives studded with analogy and laced with meaning. —*Mary Banas*

Sinclair, Clive.
Cosmetic Effects.
Viking, $18.95. 247p.

Film professor Jonah Isaacson is spinning out of control, caught in the metaphorical equivalent of clear-air turbulence, which he encounters on a flight to Israel. Things run amok after Jonah cheats on his wife with the robust Stella, who drugs him, breaks his arm, and sets it with high explosive packed into the cast. Jonah becomes an "animated time bomb" in a bizarre tale that mixes a bit of espionage (terrorists, Palestinians, Israelis), questions of identity in an ambiguous world, and a veritable barrage of film lore (Jonah hates Meryl Streep, mostly because she kept her breasts hidden in *Sophie's Choice*). Our sense of reality keeps shifting as Jonah's mind wanders through various points of view, including that of the broken arm, which assumes a voice of its own. Sinclair's dark and often quite dirty humor features plenty of Monty Python–like juxtapositions—loftily artistic utterances spot-welded to more earthy concerns—along with sound advice on such practical matters as orifice etiquette during immersion in a tidal wave. Sinclair isn't always perfectly focused, but the depth of his vision and his spiraling inventiveness lure the reader into a world of chaotic fancies, submerged truths, and even some somber reflection on the Israeli-Palestinian conflict ("two people in a single land"). —*Peter Robertson*

Smith, Charlie.
The Lives of the Dead.
Linden Press, $19.95. 366p.

Buddy Drake makes gory, hyperkinetic films and is desperate for funding for his next production. He travels to western Florida to ask his ex, Bess, for money. Bess farms and takes care of her mad brother, R. B. Buddy and R. B. get along great; they both live within the haze of madness. Buddy is possessed by the script he's writing, especially the murderous exploits of his character D'Nel Boyd. He talks about Boyd so much that one wonders if Boyd and his crimes are real. Buddy replies: "It's true, it was told to me; and I made it up." Oh. But what about Buddy's saturated, cinematic memories of violence and ferocious sex? Real or imagined? Smith erects great arcs of burning imagery and metaphor that support hellish and nihilistic visions. This paean to menace and lust—which captures you in the way a deer is mesmerized by the headlights of a car—is Smith's third and most powerful novel. —*Donna Seaman*

Smith, Mitchell.
Stone City.
Simon & Schuster, $19.95. 576p.

Bauman, a middle-aged college professor, finds himself in the slammer for taking someone's life while driving under the influence. The world of prison, he finds, is divided between those who want to stay out of trouble and those who want to cause it. Bauman must walk a fine line between the two when he, under duress by authorities, carries out an under-wraps, in-house investigation into a series of prison killings. Forcefully written, Smith's novel creates for the reader every detail of an environment where life has less meaning than a pack of cigarettes, sexual tension hangs in the air like water vapor, and alliances are more necessary for survival than they are in international diplomacy. To its jolting climax, this novel exudes a delicious sordidness. —*Brad Hooper*

Smith, Pauline.
The Little Karoo.
St. Martin's, $15.95. 172p.

Smith's collection of short stories (first published in 1925) is set in the still, hot, parched Karoo, an area of near empty veld inhabited by isolated Afrikaner farmers close to the Old Testament and far from town and change. Whereas Olive Schreiner's *Story of an African Farm* (1883) is anti-pastoral, focused on a liberated girl who rebelled against the constraints, stasis, and cruelty of the isolated farm, Smith's elemental stories are about the poor white Afrikaners on those farms, struggling innocents for whom the Bible is law and family and work the only bonds in the huge desolation. When a stranger asks for shelter, it's the will of God—even when he brings betrayal. Two stories, "The Pain" and "The Schoolmaster," are masterpieces, heartbreaking in their simple humanity. Novelist Caroline Slaughter says in her introduction that these sad, wise stories reveal the psychology and strength of the old Boers, and she asks "if these qualities could only be extended beyond clan and color, what could not be achieved in the country that produced them?" —*Hazel Rochman*

Soister, Helena.
Prophecies.
Bantam, $18.95. 352p.

Soister's remarkable first novel is set in Antwerp during the mid-1500s. The narration by English merchant Sara Lathbury, a widow who has taken over her husband's trading business, draws the reader straight into the congested streets of the Flemish port and straight into the most threatening elements of the Reformation. Ruled by Philip II of Spain, Flanders is as dangerous a locale for Protestant mutterings as Sara's native England under the rule of Philip's bride, Queen Mary. Sara has come to Antwerp to find a new business representative and happens upon one who is not only engaged in smuggling heretical pamphlets but is also haunted by the ghost of his father's partner. To complicate matters further, Sara is traveling with her widowed niece, who falls in love with the new representative and is determined to rescue him from his haunted state. Political and religious intrigue are drawn with heart-stopping tension; the scenic and period details are just as engrossing. —*Denise Perry Donavin*

Stead, C. K.
Sister Hollywood.
St. Martin's, $15.95. 224p.

In remote but effective prose, New Zealand author Stead details the life story of Edie Harper, who runs away from her hometown and never looks back. Because her Australian boyfriend, Rocky, is an aspiring actor, the duo settles in Hollywood where Rocky hopes to break into the film industry. Before long, Edie takes a job as secretary at a major studio, and Rocky is entrenched in the crash-and-burn cycle of hope and despair (augmented by excessive amounts of alcohol) that is the lot of many young actors. Because she is quick and level-headed, Edie is promoted at work, acts as a consultant on story projects, eventually becomes a screenwriter, and is soon attending parties with the likes of Bogart and Bacall. She falls into a passionate but doomed relationship with the head of the studio, and Rocky sinks further and further into an alcohol-induced torpor. Stead's absorbing story line bogs down every once in a while when the point of view switches to that of Edie's young brother, but for the most part, this bittersweet view of the old Hollywood is a poignant, compelling read. —*Joanne Wilkinson*

Steel, Danielle.
Message from Nam.
Delacorte, $21.95. 416p.

Certainly this latest novel is a notch above Steel's usual effort. Her story centers around Paxton Andrews, a UCLA college student, originally from Savannah, Georgia, who decides to go to Vietnam after her fiancé dies there. As the Saigon-based reporter for the *San Francisco Morning*, writing a column headlined "Message from Nam," Paxton journeys to a war in a land far from home where she falls in love again, this time with an officer who investigates the tunneling systems of the Vietcong. Colleagues die, Paxton's lover is captured, she's caught in an attack and finally ordered home to California. Steel tells us a lot about the war, its escalations, and the tragedies it wrought; but often the significant events read like news bulletins interrupting the regularly scheduled program. Steel has earnestly tried to make sense of the feelings of people who fought in Vietnam, and her effort will tug at many hearts. The usually slick Steel style is muted with an appropriate respect; however, to anyone who has pored over the potent fiction on Vietnam that has emerged in the past few years, this novel will appear only glib. For Steel's

General Fiction

many fans, though, the romantic wartime adventures of Paxton Andrews may at least bring the war into starker relief. —*Denise Perry Donavin*

✔ **Stegner, Wallace.**
Collected Stories of Wallace Stegner.
Random, $21.95. 544p.

A well-honored American fiction writer—winner of prizes, fellowships, and critical applause—Stegner is better known for his novels, which include *The Big Rock Candy Mountain* and *The Spectator Bird,* than his short stories. This retrospective of Stegner's short fiction, pulling together 31 stories covering his long and distinguished career, loudly broadcasts his high level of accomplishment in the shorter form. A master of the effortlessly beautiful metaphor, Stegner writes in a lush but never mannered style. His stories are brief yet do not hint of abbreviation or truncation; there is a sense of spaciousness and expansiveness in each story's few pages, arising from the author's ability to create with well-chosen phrases quick but complete portraits and concise but fully engrossing narratives. Stegner's abiding interest in the American West permeates his work, as does his consciousness of the influence of the past on people's present lives. "The Berry Patch" is quintessential Stegner, presenting a farmer couple going berry picking and capturing the subtle but important communication that transpires between them during those few hours. This collection represents a milestone not only in Stegner's impressive career, but also in recent American publishing. —*Brad Hooper*

Sterchi, Beat.
Cow.
Pantheon, $19.95. 353p.

Here's a novel that comes with a publisher's warning that makes it out to be a bovine equivalent of *The Satanic Verses.* Certainly, *Cow* is not for the squeamish, but if the reader can stomach one of the more vivid episodes of "All Creatures Great and Small," there should be no problem with Sterchi's very realistic story of a milk cow's life, from pasture to slaughterhouse. The human element in this tale is a Spanish immigrant who comes to the Swiss Tirol as a guest worker and who, despite many linguistic and cultural obstacles, finds himself at home with the animals, if not with the local populace. Sterchi's novel also raises some hard food-chain issues: where does our daily sustenance ultimately come from, how safely and humanely is it produced, and will the reader gag on the next Big Mac that is ordered up? Certainly the relationship between human and animals has never been portrayed with such intimacy and power as in the pages of this novel, nor have the implications of this animal-human dependency been illustrated on such an elemental level. —*John Brosnahan*

Straczynski, J. Michael.
Othersyde.
Dutton, $18.95. 288p.

Teenagers are the prime movers in Straczynski's latest venture into frightdom, which draws its impetus from an individual's yearning to belong. New-kid-in-town Chris wants to make a good impression on his classmates, but they don't give him a chance. The only person he connects with is another outsider, "Horseface" Roger Obst, a smart and cynical classmate who turns out to be a punching bag for his alcoholic father and the target of countless school bullies, none of whom think twice about adding Chris to their hit lists. Then the pair encounters a bum, who passes to them an evil gift that feeds on Roger's desire to get back at the people who have hurt him so badly. Straczynski evokes a nightmarish scenario filled with tiny creatures of the dark that suck, bite, and choke and kill at Roger's whim. For those willing to suspend disbelief, the genre conventions are here and the pacing is good. So what if there's a loophole or two? What's more, Straczynski has made certain that the promise of evil extends well beyond the boundaries of the last page. —*Stephanie Zvirin*

Stratton, Richard.
Smack Goddess.
Birch Lane Press, $18.95. 516p.

Despite the lurid title and probably because of its author's criminal past (he wrote the book while in prison for importing marijuana and hash), this novel contains some surprisingly good characterizations of major players in the drug world. Sonia ("the Smack Goddess") Byrne-Downes is a highly intelligent drug dealer to the stars, busted and tried amid a flurry of tabloid headlines. After their star informant is murdered, the prosecution arrests Sonia's punk-rock pal, Rickie Rude, as a way of putting pressure on her to give up her drug connections. Rickie turns the court proceedings into a veritable showcase for his mystical-radical brand of politics, and Sonia refuses to reveal her sources. Sentenced to life imprisonment, she masterminds a daring escape to Jamaica. For its convincing depiction of a circle of hard-core, high-living drug dealers with their contingent of lawyers, and for its fast-moving plot, readers will "just say yes" to *Smack Goddess*. —*Joanne Wilkinson*

Swift, Edward.
Mother of Pearl.
British American Publishing, $18.95. 240p.

You know you're onto a good book when right from the start—the very first sentence, in fact—the narrative reaches out and yanks you headlong into a rollicking, whimsical tale that never loses its momentum nor its hold on your imagination. Such is the case here. Pearl and Wanda Gay McAlister are bickering old biddies who take sibling rivalry to hilarious extremes. Perhaps as they sit and reminisce on the porch, the sweltering heat of southern Texas has gone to their heads. More likely, the sisters' eccentricity is a family

General Fiction

heirloom—brazenly displayed with outlandish pride to shocked neighbors. Swift brings a rapier wit and good-natured fun to his depiction of this fictional family of lovable eccentrics, which includes a brother who sought arrest so he could use his jail cell as a "think tank." One of those rare novels that brims with life—and whose underlying dark humor tugs at the heart with its piercing insights. —*Mary Banas*

Thomas, D. M.
Lying Together.
Viking, $17.95. 238p.

What was originally referred to as a trilogy has now become the Russian Nights Quintet, and with this final chapter, Thomas concludes his ambitious, elegant, and difficult experiment in literary improvisation. To his cast of Russian writers and poets, now in England for a literary conference, Thomas has added himself as a character, the interpreter of dreams. At night, over alcohol, the stories begin: a sexually tormented servant girl confides in a famous psychiatrist, two lovers lie motionless, coupling, minds freed and spinning like film frames through a projector. Thomas also talks of real people—Isabella Rossellini, her mother, famous writers either worshiped or despised, even Freud, long a nonspeaking presence in Thomas' world, now briefly assuming center stage. As in Philip Roth's recent *Deception*, Thomas narrows the gap between fact and fiction, continues to expand his use of sexual imagery, and narrowly escapes descending into a parody of his own considerable talents. The publisher's claims notwithstanding, *Lying Together* will prove formidable indeed for anyone unfamiliar with the preceding novels. For the faithful, though, this last movement in a five-part symphony of desire once again extends the gray boundaries of dream and daylight, of love and lust. —*Peter Robertson*

Thomas, Rosie.
A Woman of Our Times.
Bantam, $18.95. 512p.

The woman in question is Harriet Peacock, a young British entrepreneur who loves the fray of business and the exhilaration of winning. Her life is set on a faster course when she discovers her photographer-husband cameraless with a model. Their breakup inspires a quest: Harriet returns to her mother's hometown to search for her unknown father. Instead she finds Simon Archer, a man who befriended her then-teenaged mother. Archer is a former British army officer who was imprisoned by the Japanese in World War II. He survived his ordeal by inventing "a game of skill and calculation" painstakingly constructed from matchsticks and other scraps. Harriet's visit surprises and disarms him, and he gives her his game, never imagining that she would mass-produce it as "Meizu" (Japanese for maze or labyrinth) and build a multimillion-pound corporation. Harriet is the ultimate workalcoholic. Her zeal to succeed distorts her judgment and strains her relationships with friends, family, and a pair of egomaniac lovers—a drunk movie star and a rich and evil businessman. Thomas has packed a lot into the money-power-sex framework, creating a "meizu" of plots and characters, and elevating the usually trite formula by contrasting Harriet's life with that of two women friends, thus dramatizing the meaning of work, power, and freedom. —*Donna Seaman*

General Fiction

Thompson, David.
Silver Light.
Knopf, $19.95. 328p.

In 1950, western photographer Susan Garth is 80 years old. She knows and despises John Ford, barely tolerates John Wayne, and is the daughter of legendary cattle driver Matthew Garth (the character played by Montgomery Clift in *Red River*). Her lifelong friend is western writer Bark Blaylock, who may be the bastard son of Wyatt Earp, or of Ethan Edwards (John Wayne in *The Searchers*), and who thinks, at a tender age, that folks are referring to him when they talk about the Kid. Susan, Bark, and the other real and movie-born characters who populate this sweeping saga of the old and new West have a great comic mythic quality. But Thompson's wonderfully wry, earthy details keep the proceedings well grounded. As in his earlier *Suspects*, which did with film noir what he does here with westerns, there are astonishing moments when you suddenly get inside some movie myth you've seen a hundred times. After the child Bark crosses the Pecos River on horseback—certainly a familiar sight—his companion cries, "Great God, Bark . . . don't ever forget you crossed this river. When you're an old man it may be the best thing you have." Thomson shows it to us in a way that makes this sentiment utterly believable. —*Frances Woods*

Thurm, Marian.
Henry in Love.
Bantam, $8.95. 272p.

When Henry and Kate marry, he is 69 and she is 28. Despite the age difference, they are convincingly in love. One year later, as happy as any couple on the coast of Maine, they have a baby girl, Darlan. Within the framework of this potentially quaint setup, Henry and Kate emerge as strong, unique individuals whose relationship is not defined by their diverse years. Thurm uses the situation, though, to force us to rethink how we see people. Henry, in particular, emerges as strongly as he does because of the context in which we see him. When he has a brief, passionate reunion with his sixtyish ex-wife, plays with his tiny daughter, or makes love with Kate, we keep having to remind ourselves that he's in his seventies. And then, remarkably, when he is stricken with an illness that leaves him unable to do even the simplest task for himself, we find ourselves amazed again—we keep having to remind ourselves that his body no longer works. It is a constant shock. This is a wonderfully poignant but never sentimental or condescending look at love and aging. —*Frances Woods*

Tilghman, Christopher.
In a Father's Place.
Farrar, $18.95. 214p.

Weighted down as they are by the heartache and the pleasure of family bonds, Tilghman's characters seem altogether unfit for literary typecasting. They're quite unlike the urban, success-oriented characters that populate much of contemporary fiction. In the story "Hole in the Day," for example, 29-year-old Lonnie abandons her husband and four children because she's pregnant with another. Running from her isolated homestead to the lights of the city, "she cannot believe she has come so far for this—a baked island of neon." Whether she likes it or not, her family means everything to her. And that's pretty much the way it is for most of the characters in this collection— for the young man who struggles to accept his mother's marriage to a former ranch hand; for the frightened boy who witnesses his father murder a waterman on Chesapeake Bay; for the infertile woman whose husband casts her off so that he might remarry and father a child. The sharp tangle of family life is the essence of this graceful, stirring group of stories by a writer whose voice and vision are all his own. —*Joanne Wilkinson*

Trevor, William.
Family Sins & Other Stories.
Viking, $18.95. 251p.

Irish writer Trevor mines his home territory to spectacular effect in his latest collection of short pieces. In these investigations of the human condition, love and death blend, although in the Irish sensibility there's definitely an excess of death and a paucity of desire with which to contend. An unhappily married man meets with his wife's latest lover, hoping against hope that this time he will be rescued by divorce from the marital trap; no such luck. The emotional aftereffects of a horrible mass murder in a small village are multiplied by the sensational reporting of a tabloid newspaper. And a boyhood friendship ends on the rocks with devastating consequences. There are one or two clinkers in Trevor's latest lot, but they are only brief departures from the writer's unusually high standards. —*John Brosnahan*

Truscott, Lucian K.
Rules of the Road.
Carroll & Graf, $18.95. 336p.

For his third thriller-with-soldier (after *Dress Gray* and *Army Blue*), Truscott trots out the kind of plot and extra characters that Elmore Leonard would burn down the house with. But Truscott's no Elmore. The tale of how, when reassigned near his southern Illinois home after a decade abroad, Major Sam Butterfield gets involved in a big bribery-and-murder political scandal just flickers along like a fairly good TV movie. Perhaps the main problem is that instead of pitching the plot from the viewpoint of a quirky crook or working stiff—despite the fact that Sam's accomplice is a young petty hood who could easily walk away with the book—Truscott uses "Good Sojer" Sam. And Sam is only a little less obnoxiously macho-virtuous than his tinny superior officer, a stooge left over from some John Wayne epic. But there's worse entertainment fiction out there, and Truscott at his worst is still a competent writer. —*Ray Olson*

Tryon, Thomas.
The Wings of the Morning.
Knopf, $22.95. 592p.

Tryon's latest novel is an elaborate, even overwrought, soap opera. Based on the Romeo and Juliet, star-crossed-lovers concept, *Wings* features as its Montagues and Capulets the two New England clans of Talcott and Grimes. Naturally, a Talcott girl and a Grimes boy fall in love; and the contrivances their families undertake to keep them apart take the reader on a sleigh ride through a plethora of details about various corners of the early-nineteenth-century globe. Characters rarely extend themselves beyond the two-dimensional; and Tryon's writing style is stodgy. But romance is the leavening factor: hearts beating wildly beneath period costumes will carry readers of historical pageants through to the last page. —*Brad Hooper*

✓ **Updike, John.**
Rabbit at Rest.
Knopf, $21.95. 544p.

As Updike ages, so, too, does Rabbit Angstrom. Through *Rabbit, Run* (1960), *Rabbit Redux* (1971), *Rabbit Is Rich* (1981), and now in the fourth and last in the lauded series, Updike's vulnerable hero has seasoned from young manhood to mid–middle age. As time has passed, as the Rabbit books have appeared at decade intervals, Updike seems to understand Rabbit more, to more easily sympathize with the compulsions that have not only plagued but determined the form of his life. *Rabbit at Rest* finds our hero at age 55, he and wife Janice in the habit now of spending half the year in Florida; the time is the winter, spring, and summer of 1989. "Everything falling apart," Rabbit discerns as he looks out over the landscape not only of his own life but also of the country at large, "airplanes, bridges, eight years under Reagan of nobody minding the stores, making money out of nothing, running up debt, trusting in God." Rabbit's heart is bad, his son Nelson remains a disappointment, and even infidelity has too high a price tag these days. Rabbit is face-to-face with immortality and is finding it difficult not to blink. Comedy and pathos have been the warp and woof of the Rabbit cycle; now, with more compassion than usual woven into its fabric, the conclusion is less Rabbit's shroud than his banner. —*Brad Hooper*

Urquhart, Jane.
The Whirlpool.
Godine, $17.95. 238p.

The year is 1889. The location is the Canadian town of Niagara Falls—except for the prologue and epilogue, which concern the death of Robert Browning. Why is this Canadian story bracketed by an English poet's death? Because this is a novel of poets and poetic sensibilities. Maud, recently widowed, takes

General Fiction

on her husband's business—running a funeral home. For years, her son doesn't speak. When he does, his startling vocabulary and manner of communicating make it apparent that he has been listening intently. Meanwhile, Patrick, a young poet given to long walks in the woods, happens upon a whirlpool in the river and observes a woman reading nearby. They share a fascination with the whirlpool, and soon he falls in love with her—or at least with the fantasy of her. The circular pull of the whirlpool is echoed in the novel's plot and the characters' interactions. Urquhart has created a lyrical and magical realm. Her exploration of the meaning of patience and loneliness and the influence of place on people's emotions is subtle and penetrating—prose with the depth of poetry. An accomplished debut. —*Donna Seaman*

✓ **Vargas Llosa, Mario.**
In Praise of the Stepmother.
Farrar, $18.95. 149p.

The Peruvian novelist offers an extended story that charts the erotic attraction between a young boy and his stepmother and how their ultimately requited sexual passion leads to O. Henry–like consequences. Actually, this case of April-November incest is hardly the most fascinating aspect of the brief tale. Instead, a series of elaborate sexual fantasies based on literature and art that serve to inspire the father and stepmother's marital union is much more prominently featured, often subduing much of the more obvious *Lolita* comparisons of sexual role reversals. And then there are the illustrations that accompany these passages, reinforcing the classic sources of the couples' desires. This sexy little ode to sensuality was created by Vargas Llosa just before he became a presidential candidate in the 1990 Peruvian election. —*John Brosnahan*

✓ **Vaughn, Stephanie.**
Sweet Talk.
Random, $16.95. 164p.

Welcome a new name to the ranks of fine short story writers: Stephanie Vaughn. Most of the 10 stories in her superb first collection are interconnected, narrated by a young woman named Gemma whose father is an exacting military man, not easy to live with. Gemma and her brother learn the art of restraint while coping with their parents' troubled marriage and the loneliness of living on army bases and moving frequently. Every landscape reflects the emotions of the characters. While Vaughn excels at capturing the aura of youth, she is equally sensitive in portraying the adult world. With gentleness, humor, and grace, the women in these stories face duplicity, accidents, and illness. They respect people, including themselves, and they can handle adversity. Vaughn's irony is warm and perceptive, and her imagery sparkles with beauty: a figure walking across a frozen river; a woman making a snow angel late at night; the dreamy reflections in glass beads. Thinking about these stories, with their perfectly modulated prose, is like holding an egg—they are smooth and edgeless, cool and elegant, filled with life. —*Donna Seaman*

Vonnegut, Kurt.
Hocus Pocus.
Putnam, $19.95. 304p.

Old soldiers never die, they just babble one hip truism after another—or so it goes in Vonnegut's latest novel. Eugene Debs Hartke is as unlikely a West Point graduate as one is likely to come across, but he manages to make it through his military tour of duty to become a Vietnam vet, college instructor, prison administrator, and, when the inmates revolt, an army commander again. Vonnegut lards Hartke's life and experiences with a full load of concerns, quips, and rambling opinions on war, politics, society, drugs, and the counterculture, all caught in a time warp of 1960s mentality. Since the narrative is set in the early twenty-first century, however, Vonnegut is also able to progress beyond such historical events as the Holocaust and the bombing of Hiroshima to more contemporary dilemmas like the Japanese takeover of U.S. business and the progressive materialization of American civilization. All of this is set within a structure that jumps from one point to another, held together by a stylistically thin and philosophically bland mortar that produces the easy-to-swallow irony that Vonnegut's readers expect. —*John Brosnahan*

Walser, Robert.
"Masquerade" and Other Stories.
Johns Hopkins, $35. 202p.

A new collection of Swiss writer Walser's short fiction rounds out the impression left by his *Selected Stories* . The selections encompass every phase of Walser's career, from journalistic fillers to pieces that were composed just before and during the author's descent into insanity and creative silence. The result is a fine representation of Walser's scope and development as a writer, as well a sampling of the contradictions and complexities of his seemingly naive style. Novelist William Gass pens the appreciatory foreword, while translator Susan Bernofsky briefly surveys Walser's career and literary reputation. —*John Brosnahan*

Weesner, Theodore.
Winning the City.
Summit, $17.95. 202p.

Dale Wheeler, 15, had always worked hard and played by the rules. Basketball was more than a game to Dale. It was his ticket out of a life limited by poverty and his loving but unpredictable alcoholic father. Winning the city tournament was his dream, his only chance to change his life. When Dale is kept off of his dream team by the sponsor who wants to play his own son in Dale's position, Dale learns the painful fact that sometimes life just isn't fair. Weesner captures the emotional ups and downs of the teen years in this touching coming-of-age story about a boy who learns, in his disillusionment, to fight back. —*Candace Smith*

Weill, Gus.
Flesh.
St. Martin's, $15.95. 224p.

Meet the Caesers, who prove that the rich are different. More than money sets them apart, however, as protagonist Marion Anderson discovers during his extended stay at their isolated island mansion off the coast of Maine. He visits at the behest of Justin Caeser, with whom he is writing a musical. One quirk he immediately notices is the family's ravenous passion for devouring meat at dinnertime, matched only by their appetite for the nocturnal enjoyment of each other's assets afterwards. It becomes even weirder when Marion slowly connects the mysterious disappearance of another house guest with the nightly repast. Once he realizes that he is to be the main course at the next meal, he becomes involved in a race with his hosts to see who beats the Grim Reaper. A ghoulish tale, perfect for stormy nights. —*Gilbert Taylor*

Weldon, Fay.
The Cloning of Joanna May.
Viking, $18.95. 265p.

Weldon, unrelenting in her growth as a tantalizing novelist, deals mostly in her fiction with personal relationships, with particular attention paid to women as mothers. Her latest novel is no exception to the rule; additionally, it possesses another Weldon quality: making the weird seem perfectly real. The novel rests on the premise that when Joanna and Carl May, now in late middle age, were considerably younger, Carl (quite unbeknownst to his wife) had a doctor remove an egg from her womb, which was then subsequently divided into four eggs and placed in other women, who gave birth to Joanna clones. Now, in the present time, there exist four women who haven't a clue about their genetic and birthing history. In the meantime, Carl has divorced Joanna for infidelity; but the time comes when Joanna learns of the existence of her four daughters/sisters, and, proving the old adage that apples do not fall far from the tree, the stories of their lives and loves bear the unmistakable imprint of the woman from whom they were cloned. Typically Weldon—in other words, a bizarre delight. —*Brad Hooper*

Wesley, Mary.
A Sensible Life.
Viking, $18.95. 364p.

The author of *Not That Sort of Girl* presents another novel brimming with capricious characters. Wesley's story opens in pre–World War II Brittany, where 10-year-old Flora Trevelyan, the footloose daughter of self-centered English parents, meets up with two upper-class, randy teens—Cosmo Leigh and his friend, Blanco Wyndeatt-Whyte. The boys are infatuated with Flora; her independence is especially appealing to them because their every move is dictated by their families. (Flora's parents prefer to spend afternoons in bed, leaving Flora free to explore the coastal town and subsequently become wise beyond her years.) The influences of Ford Madox Ford and Virginia Woolf are evident here, but Wesley finds a voice all her own in relaying the tale of Flora's maturation. Wesley does not write pat romantic fare; her realistic characters undergo clashes and suffer untidy resolutions. —*Denise Perry Donavin*

West, Morris.
Lazarus.
St. Martin's, $19.95. 293p.

The noted author of *The Shoes of the Fisherman* (1963) and *The Clowns of God* (1981) looks once more into the closed world of the Vatican, offering a story rife with drama, political intrigue, and foreboding. Pope Leo XIV is a stern ruler who undergoes heart bypass surgery and receives a change of heart as well as physical restoration. The pope's plans to add heart (compassion) to the Catholic Church involve decentralizing authority and smoothing out certain procedures. Under fire is the Congregation for the Doctrine of the Faith, which has been responsible for condemning individuals without giving them an opportunity to argue their case or state their views. Throughout his recuperation, the pope and the people around him are threatened by an Islamic terrorist group and protected by ruthless members of Mossad, the Israeli intelligence agency (which the Italian government cavalierly permits to operate on this most sacred turf). Marketed as the culmination of a trilogy, West's newest novel carries few references to the earlier books. Although West often allows suspense to lag when it could easily be tightened, the story reads smoothly and demonstrates that he has not lost his touch for portraying backstairs life at the Vatican. —*Denise Perry Donavin*

Westlake, Donald E.
Drowned Hopes.
Mysterious, $18.95. 422p.

How many ex-cons does it take to retrieve a coffin filled with $700,000 from under 50 feet of water? There is no one punch line here, but several; and the third time's not the charm, but the straw that breaks the backs of an odd lot of salvagers in Westlake's newest comic caper. When Tom Jimson robbed an armored car and buried the money, he never expected a dam to be built directly on top of it. And being a 70-some-year-old new parolee, he asks his former cell mate, John Dortmunder, to help (who asks his friend, telephone-obsessed software-thief Andy Kelp, who asks his friend, fat, moist, computer-nerd Wally Knurr, and so forth). Amid harebrained escapades and snappy dialogue (including a convincing conversation about Yuppies being aliens— Why else would they hide their feet in sneakers, live only in lofts, and eat tofu?), the group learns that money is not all, that no one should be trusted, and that love can smooth the rough edges off any disappointment. As obese Wally points out, "The trouble with real life is, there's no reset button." Fast-paced and funny. —*Eloise Kinney*

Wharton, Edith.
The Stories of Edith Wharton.
Carroll & Graf, $18.95. 310p.

American novelist and short-story writer Wharton (1862–1937) was a close friend of literary god Henry James. Wharton, like James, wrote razor-edged analyses of the manners of the late nineteenth- and early twentieth-century well-to-do. But Wharton should not be "feared" by contemporary readers; while certainly a refreshing change from the contemporary fascination with minimalism, her fiction is not stylistically creaky, and thematically her work is timeless. This collection of 14 short stories was selected from the author's considerable output by award-winning British novelist Brookner. It features stories falling into two general categories: social satires of the society of "Old" New York, and ghost stories. Some of the tales—"Autre Temps . . . ," "After Holbein," and "Pomegranate Seeds," for instance—are famous; others, such as the delectable "Atrophy," in which the respectable Nora Frenway pays an unsettling visit to her ill lover, will be new even to readers familiar with Wharton. —*Brad Hooper*

White, Michael C. and Davis, Alan, eds.
American Fiction: The Best Unpublished Short Stories by Emerging Writers.
Birch Lane Press, $12.95. 358p.

This volume, comprising 24 short stories, pared down from the approximately 550 entered in a national contest, is a must-read collection for all short-fiction enthusiasts. From the first-prize winner, "The Color of Scars," by Florri McMillan, in which a young woman describes her own brain surgery, to the other stories, all close contenders for the coveted top honor, the anthology is a wealth of imagination and talent. While some of the tales are quite disturbing—one detailing a gentle stepfather's losing battle with cancer; another, a young girl's struggle to give up the child she conceived with her own grandfather—all are wonderfully crafted and gripping. As guest judge Anne Tyler states in the introduction, "Judging these twenty-four finalists was no easy task, but reading them was a pleasure." Tyler has accomplished the unenviable task of choosing the top three prizewinners, leaving nothing to the reader but enjoyment. —*Ivy Burrowes*

✔ **Wideman, John Edgar.**
Philadelphia Fire.
Holt, $18.95. 240p.

In his much-acclaimed *Brothers and Keepers*, Wideman wrote a staggering memoir about his life as a writer and his brother's as a prison inmate. In his most recent collection of short stories, *Fever*, he further demonstrated the sobering eloquence of his voice in picturing various elements in the constant friction between black and white societies in America. His latest novel is, as the title reflects, centered on the 1985 destruction of the Philadelphia headquarters of an organization called MOVE. The narrator is a black American who has removed himself from his homeland and taken refuge from the cares of life on an easygoing island in the Aegean. Nevertheless, when news of the MOVE incident reaches him, he becomes obsessed with its meaning—to him personally, to black Americans in general. In a perambulatory narrative, the protagonist wanders back through his past, searches the terrain of his present, and peers with bated breath into an uncertain future, all within a post-Philadelphia-fire consciousness. As richly upholstered as it is sturdily framed, Wideman's painful novel is, like the fiction of the great James Baldwin, both loud and beautiful. —*Brad Hooper*

Wideman, John Edgar.
Fever: Twelve Stories.
Holt, $16.95. 161p.

Wideman's newest collection of short fiction finds the writer both expanding into new stylistic areas and delving back into familiar territory. The best items are those that relay further episodes from Pittsburgh's Hometown ghetto— the setting for several of the writer's novels—and the title story, a powerful meditation on history and race set during a yellow fever epidemic in Philadelphia but filtered through a very contemporary attitude. Several stories recall black music and musicians as Wideman witnesses the richness of black popular culture, while more disturbing episodes explore the gulf between black and white society and black and white lives. A few of the more experimental works don't succeed completely, but this is nonetheless an estimable addition to Wideman's work. —*John Brosnahan*

Williams, Jana.
Scuttlebutt.
Firebrand Books, $18.95. 198p.

Buddy novels about sailors are commonplace, but in Williams' book, the sailors are women—naval recruits at boot camp in the early 1970s. Weston, from southern Arizona, who can't get warm in Maryland; Taylor, a smarter-than-streetwise black from New York City; Yont, whose sleepwalking could get her discharged; Harper and Jones, an interracial couple who enlisted under the "buddy system"; and Bates, who sleeps with her duffel bag and misses her man—all come to life as they learn about themselves, each other, and survival in a system that dictates everything from the lipstick you must wear to whom you may love. The interaction between the characters, their instructors, the navy—and by extension, society at large—during basic training percolates questions about authority, race, and friendship. We care about the women's progress from "baby boots" to graduation and assignment to their first duty stations. The story is *yar* (nauticalese for easy to handle), and the scuttlebutt is that we should be hearing more about Williams after this fine first novel. —*Marie Kuda*

General Fiction

Williams, Joy.
Escapes.
Atlantic Monthly Press, $18.95. 180p.

The characters in Williams' short stories share various commonplaces of the writer's fictional world: a child who died young, a parent who died in midlife, or old couples who seem to have outlasted emotional attachment to their partners. Williams offers minimalist contemplations of the human condition, isolating a moment in each instance and, with a few convincing details, sets out a whole fateful scheme that overflows with the inevitability of a passage on to yet another stage of life. Ranging from grim comedy to resigned despair, the mood of these pieces isn't all that varied, but the brooding emotions are telegraphed sharply and clearly. These stories first appeared in *Esquire*, *Granta*, and other magazines; four were selected for inclusion in *Best American Short Stories* volumes between 1978 and 1987. —*John Brosnahan*

Wilson, A. N.
A Bottle in the Smoke.
Viking, $18.95. 290p.

Readers of Wilson's masterful *Incline Our Hearts* will be thrilled to discover that the story of Julian Ramsay's coming-of-age in postwar Britain is continued in this equally distinguished sequel. The bemused narrative voice that supplied the rich, melancholic edge to Ramsay's recollections of his youth in an English village is again present as the tale shifts to London in the 1950s, where Ramsay is struggling to establish himself as a writer and actor. Characters from the first book are still in evidence, but the narrator's world has enlarged dramatically to encompass a group of tipsy bohemians who gather in a seedy Soho pub where Ramsay tends bar. Set against the comic pronouncements of these gin-inspired philosophers is the unraveling of Ramsay's marriage to Anne, an event that brings home the very unromantic way that lovers "inflict so much hurt on one another." Though the story of a naive, would-be literati who learns about pain is anything but fresh, Wilson reverses our expectations by making us see that the aging narrator, embittered and suffering from "atrophy of the heart," is really the foolish one. We "return gratefully to obvious truths, like Keats' 'I am certain of nothing but the heart's affections.'" —*Bill Ott*

Wilson, Wayne.
Loose Jam.
Delacorte, $17.95. 263p.

When Henry Brown sees Miles Duckworth hobbling toward his Southern California house, he knows he hasn't been able to escape his past after all. Serving in Vietnam with Miles, performing with him after the war in a rock band that, briefly, seemed on the verge of hitting it big, watching the band and Miles disintegrate in a haze of drugs and craziness—that was all part of what Henry was hoping to forget by rejoining the conventional world. Soon, though, he is farther from the safety of that world than ever. Miles is on the run from Monroe, a Vietnam rival turned psycho, and Henry, protesting all the while, finds himself helping his onetime friend escape. At times, this uneven book has all the visceral power of the best Vietnam coming-home novels (say, Robert Stone's *Dog Soldiers*), but at other times it sinks under the weight of too many 1970s tunes being played the same way too many times. Give Wilson a chance, though; he possesses enough talent to bear watching. —*Bill Ott*

Winterson, Jeanette.
Sexing the Cherry.
Atlantic Monthly Press, $19.95. 180p.

We're told that "time is one," and indeed time is fluid in this inventive tale by an award-winning young British author. Dog Woman is a shape-changer living in London in the 1600s. She has strange powers and tremendous strength. Finding an abandoned baby by the Thames, she names him Jordan and raises him along with her hounds. Eventually Jordan takes to the sea, and his wanderings bring him to many fantastic lands—places where people don't use floors, and words are scrubbed from the sky to clear the air. Suddenly it's 1990, and Jordan is seemingly reincarnated as a young seaman who lives with a woman whose life is dedicated to fighting water pollution. Then we're back in seventeenth-century London, by the "stinking Thames." Winterson has spun us around, making us accept the inexplicable and visualize the improbable, and while we're spinning, she douses us with a bracing shower of feminism and ecological warning. Well received in England, this phantasmagorical novel is certain to please anyone who is willing to take chances with the contemporary novel. —*Donna Seaman*

Wolf, Joan.
The Edge of Light.
NAL, $18.95. 384p.

Ninth-century England was a murky, fragmented, and violent world of petty and often competing Saxon kingdoms. Only the chronic threat posed by pagan Danish invaders provided impetus for military cooperation. The figure of Alfred, king of Wessex and the only English monarch to bear the title "Great," stands above this dreary jumble as a man of genuinely heroic dimensions. In the final installment of her trilogy on England's Dark Ages, Wolf brings to vivid life both the man and his era. Alfred is revealed as a brilliant political and military leader who held the Danes at bay while setting the stage for the eventual unification of the Saxon kingdoms. While often a gentle and loving husband and father, Alfred is quite capable of decisive, even ruthless action in defense of his interests. The Danes are seen as tough, brutal, yet intensely human foes who are determined to carve a place for themselves on this green, temperate island. This is an interesting, exciting, and occasionally inspiring saga in which the personal story of Alfred is expertly interwoven with broader historical themes. —*Jay Freeman*

Wolfe, William J.
Benedict Arnold.
Paideia Publishers, $26. 413p.

As both patriot and traitor, Benedict Arnold remains one of the most elusive, enigmatic figures in U.S. history. In Wolfe's meticulously researched novel, Arnold is portrayed as a man riddled with contradictions. While devoted to the Revolution, he despised the "mob" and was far from egalitarian in attitude and behavior. He seemed possessed of great physical courage and natural leadership qualities; yet he often allowed petty slights to enrage him and to seriously cloud his judgment. Wolfe, who died shortly before his novel was published, tells Arnold's story in a slow and occasionally ponderous manner. At times, the sheer weight of detail can overwhelm the reader. Nevertheless, this is a fine work of historical fiction: the characters, both real and fictitious, are compelling; the dialogue, although invented, is succinct and plausible; and Wolfe beautifully describes the majesty and squalor of the Revolutionary War. —*Jay Freeman*

Wright, T. M.
The School.
Tor, $17.95. 288p.

Frank and Allison Hitchcock lost their only child, Joey, in a freak accident more than 10 years ago, but he still lives, very painfully, in their memories when they move into an abandoned school in rural New York. It was theirs for a song, but their friends and new neighbors think they got a bad bargain. When they start seeing elusive people in the building, smelling strong but fleeting odors in it, and finding flaws in the walls and ceilings that become catastrophic overnight, they start to agree, but they can't leave because being there seems somehow to be bringing them closer to Joey. They're right, of course. The school is haunted, not just by the children and teachers who died in it, but also by the past selves of many others, eventually including the Hitchcocks themselves. Wright plays down gore and violence while, by coolly, skillfully managing the narrative, he maintains a deliciously creepy aura from first page to last. It's quite a performance, and those who like their horror subtle and insinuating as a trickle of icewater down the spine should adore it. —*Ray Olson*

Yamashita, Karen Tei.
Through the Arc of the Rain Forest.
Coffee House, $9.95. 214p.

Yamashita, award-winning playwright and short story writer, offers a sly, rambunctious, and wise first novel of global dimension. Cleverly exploiting the converging dramas and extreme characters of a soap opera, Yamashita spins interconnected tales of devotion and corruption that ridicule the heedless drive for wealth and power. The tale is set in early twenty-first-century Brazil, when a mysterious *matacao* ("vast plastic mantle") is found as sections of the rain forest are cut down. The matacao becomes a mecca for entrepreneurs of many ilks including a three-armed man running a corporation, an Indian who's use of feathers as a calming device catapults him to dubious celebrity, and a Japanese man with his own personal satellite—a small ball that spins in front of his face. The changes that sudden fame and riches bring to people's lives parallel the effects industrialization and materialism have had on the environment—they unbalance and sicken. Incisive and funny, this book yanks our chains and makes us see the absurdity that rules our world. —*Donna Seaman*

Zahava, Irene, ed.
My Father's Daughter: Stories by Women.
Crossing Press, $20.95. 291 p.

This anthology of women's short stories about fathers and daughters covers a surprisingly dark spectrum of conflict, illness, and death. In Edna O'Brien's story, the father is in a nursing home. Joyce Carol Oates' contribution is titled "Stroke," and the father has just died in Alice Walker's contribution. Many stories are studies of paternal relations shattered by divorce, including Marianne Rogoff's "Meeting My Father Halfway," a crushing denial of love. "Letter to My Father" by Carolyn Gage is a fierce indictment from a daughter who was sexually abused by her father. A few stories have a more affectionate tone, such as Irini Spanidou's tale of a stern father who pushes his daughter to test her strengths. Laura Davis' "Waiting for the Beep" is a funny tale of role reversal in which a 70-year-old dad with a heart condition drops acid. A sensitive mix of well-known and less-familiar writers from diverse cultural backgrounds. —*Donna Seaman*

Zielinski, David.
A Genuine Monster.
Atlantic Monthly Press, $17.95. 252p.

Nick Ames is certifiable but not certified. A hulking ex–Vietnam vet and ex–minor league ballplayer, he lives in San Diego, where the vestige of his normality is alternately fueled and skewed by the only people who can even remotely be called his friends. There's Argo, the author of pseudonymously published cheap thrillers starring one Elvis Elvesizer. And then there's La-Wanda, a well-endowed tart of a waitress who wouldn't think of giving Nick a tumble yet remains the object of his erotic daydreams. In manic first-person oratory filled with references to grade-B horror flicks and reminiscences of his Vietnamese girlfriend, Nick struggles to make contact with Argo, LaWanda, his UFO-obsessed landlady, a piggish liquor clerk—anybody who can step into his living nightmare and make things right again. Alas, Argo gets behind the wheel of a car drunk, and, with Nick in the shotgun seat, the two embark on a deadly joyride. This is weird stuff, indeed, but it is oddly compelling. Zielinski's narrative drive can't be ignored, especially as expressed via his protagonist's synapses-gapped thought processes. —*Martin Brady*

Mystery & Espionage

Ashford, Jeffrey.
A Conflict of Interests.
St. Martin's, $15.95. 192p.

An anti-blood-sport group's acts of destruction are coming close to being outright terrorism. Sanderson, the man with information about the group's next strike, which may threaten members of the royal family, is protected by a new identity. Should Bowles, a former bobby in charge of the criminal informant program, blow Sanderson's cover by revealing his identity to King, the pushy copper in charge of the investigation? Matters are complicated by the fact that Sanderson isn't terribly happy with his new life, his new wife, and the sudden painful intrusions of his former life. Ashford, author of the previous *A Question of Principle*, writes cerebral tales of stretched loyalties and allegiances. From Bowles on down, actions are questioned, moral positions constantly redefined, and twisted hearts and minds gradually revealed beneath stuffy British exteriors. —*Peter Robertson*

Asimov, Isaac.
Puzzles of the Black Widowers.
Doubleday, $19.95. 253p.

Once a month the Black Widowers meet—to pontificate, to argue, and ultimately to solve a puzzle, or rather, to let the club's urbane butler, Henry (who also happens to be a member), solve the puzzle. Asimov, who makes no secret of the debt he owes to P. G. Wodehouse and his much-loved Jeeves, has been writing these Widower short stories for years; most of them first saw the light of day in *Ellery Queen's Mystery Magazine*, although two new tales are included in this fifth collection. Whenever the Widowers gather for food, brandy, and cigars, a guest is invited—not just any guest, but someone who has a delicate problem requiring brains and cunning to solve. Naturally the feisty diners consider themselves equal to the task. And, equally naturally, they come up far short. From dealing with a mean-spirited academic to guessing the meaning of a dying man's last word, Henry saves the day. Anyone who relishes wordplay, sharp wit, cruel jokes, and all-around bitchiness should find themselves very much at home with the Widowers. —*Peter Robertson*

Barnard, Robert.
Death of a Salesperson and Other Untimely Exits.
Scribner, $16.95. 288p.

A roundly applauded British mystery writer follows 18 novels with his first collection of short stories. Sixteen in number, his stories reveal an appreciation of the form's great ability to deliver effect. Murder and mayhem are at large in his stories, of course, and Barnard deftly, given the few pages allotted a short story, handles the problem of untimely death—evoking, in each and every story, a delightfully twisted atmosphere populated by scintillatingly idiosyncratic characters. The perfect book to have at hand when time does not permit reading a full-length mystery. —*Brad Hooper*

Barnes, Linda.
Coyote.
Delacorte, $17.95. 256p.

Before the sated public calls for a halt to the slew of tough-talking female detectives following in the considerable wake of Sara Paretsky and Sue Grafton's redoubtable sleuths, space should be left in the ranks of the front-runners for Linda Barnes' creation, Boston's own Carlotta Carlyle. Sure, she carries just a few too many mean credentials testifying to her toughness: ex-cop, part-time cabbie, master of a blues-guitar lick, close to six-feet tall, part Italian, possessor of a mean spike (as in volleyball). Offsetting the outsize hard-boiled résumé, though, is Carlotta's wonderful, skewering wit, which is all her own and which she wields with gutsy abandon as she plows through Beantown's meaner streets. What she finds this time are two Hispanic women, both dead and both with the same name. One has a green card, which just might be real. Two INS guys are investigating. One's a dweeb, but the other's a hunk. Carlotta falls hard and fast. Meanwhile, there are more murders and revelations of kickbacks involving illegal work and illegal workers. A full plate for Carlotta, to be sure, who must also find time to humble a vicious opponent on the volleyball court, appease a Little Sister, and drive her cab to pay the bills. Life's hard, even for six-footers. —*Peter Robertson*

Blain, W. Edward.
Passion Play.
Putnam, $19.95. 320p.

Passion with its power for destruction is Blain's theme in his gripping first novel. A young male prostitute is found dead of a broken neck in a New York porno house, and soon afterwards the corpses start piling up at a genteel Virginia boarding school. Virtually everyone at the Montpelier School for Boys suffers passion of some common type—including the English teacher's obsession with his ill and beautiful wife, the student Lothario's drive for sexual conquest, and the drama director's uncontrollable rages—but which of these covers a passion for murder? Blain keeps the reader guessing as he deftly shifts point of view and suspicion from one character to the next. Pacing is quick, and boarding-school life is drawn in convincing and often humorous detail. In sum, an exciting and thought-provoking debut. —*Leone McDermott*

Block, Lawrence.
A Ticket to the Boneyard.
Morrow, $18.95. 288p.

This time, former cop, recovering alcoholic, and dick-without-a-license Matthew Scudder is his own case. Twelve years past, in order to protect himself and a hooker friend, Scudder framed a man, James Leo Motley, who had it coming. Motley's out of prison now, and guess what? He hasn't mellowed.

Block is working with some of crime fiction's most clichéd situations: we know the killer, and we know that the path back to Scudder will be littered with stiffs. Somehow, though, it doesn't matter; we still get our nerves stretched like catgut as the inevitable plays itself out. *Boneyard* stands as further evidence of Block's rightful place in the major leagues of mystery writers. The dialogue never wastes a second, and though Scudder is a sentimental shamus, Block manages to make such stock scenes as the AA meetings, the confabs in dreary drinking dives, and the hero's Irish hoodlum buddies all seem like the genuine goods. Maybe the call girl is a little cloying for earthy crime palates, but the killer is a psychotic to savor—monk-style haircut, hands that seek out points of intense pain, mind darker than the bars Scudder once soused himself in. —*Peter Robertson*

Boyer, Rick.
Gone to Earth.
Fawcett/Columbine, $16.95. 256p.

Doc Adams, the crime-solving oral surgeon, can't seem to stay out of trouble. The proud owner of a new getaway in the Berkshires, Doc is just settling into the country-gentleman role when his handyman discovers four Harley Davidson motorcycles hidden in the barn. Soon the bikes' owners turn up—in shallow graves. Thanks to a little publicity in the local paper, the killer—a nearly seven-foot sociopath named Buddy Franz—gets it into his warped head that Doc Adams is the cause of all his troubles. As Buddy goes on a killing spree—mere warm-ups for his date with Doc—it becomes clear that the Adams' idyll in the country has become *Straw Dogs*, Massachusetts style. This isn't one of the best in the series—too much reliance on a stock thriller premise, too little interplay between characters—but, that said, Boyer deserves credit for generating plenty of tension. We may know we're being manipulated, but the idea of a madman coming to get us in our home—"He's cut the phone line!"—always strikes a responsive chord. —*Bill Ott*

Brandon, Jay.
Fade the Heat.
Pocket, $18.95. 342p.

After the quirky characterization and fascinating micro-detail of *Predator's Waltz*, which followed several critically acclaimed paperback originals, Brandon seems set to scale the walls of bestsellerdom. This legal thriller, which features enough courtroom lore to invite comparison to Scott Turow's *Presumed Innocent*, has already been optioned by Steven Spielberg and is to be published with all the fanfare that a hefty advertising budget can supply. The novel focuses on San Antonio DA Mark Blackwell, whose son, David, is accused, tried, and convicted of rape. The case against David is strong, his alibi truly lame, and the emotionally charged testimony of the victim compelling. In addition to his deftly handled courtroom scenes, Brandon is an accomplished stylist and excels at creating complex minor characters. For example, the odious hoodlum from whom Mark extracts information possesses an almost charming honesty, especially when contrasted to the legions of legal eagles scrambling over financial and human carrion. A publisher-proclaimed "breakthrough novel" that actually lives up to its hype. —*Peter Robertson*

Braun, Lilian Jackson.
The Cat Who Lived High.
Putnam, $15.95. 240p.

After living for three years up north in Pickax City, Jim Qwilleran, retired journalist and conditional heir to the Klingenschoen fortune, braves the perils of down below (noise, pollution, crime), ostensibly to escape the rigors of a Moose County winter, but actually to investigate the feasibility of saving a rundown apartment building from the wrecking ball and restoring it to its former elegance. "Qwill" has settled in at the Casablanca and met some of its more flamboyantly eccentric tenants when he discovers—thanks to his Siamese sleuth Koko, who sniffs out bloodstains beneath the carpet, a gold bracelet behind a sofa cushion, and a message on the wall—that his penthouse was the scene of an apparent murder-suicide. Neither the fate of the Casablanca nor the recent crime is as straightforward as it seems, however, and Qwilleran nearly loses his life before returning to the safety of Pickax. A little more complexly plotted than some of the earlier Qwilleran stories and offering the same brand of humor, this is a first-rate addition to the series, with the mustached newspaperman's pampered pets both in fine fettle—Yum Yum becomes addicted to water beds, and Koko learns to play Scrabble. —*Barbara Duree*

✔ **Burke, James Lee.**
A Morning for Flamingos.
Little, Brown, $18.95. 304p.

Most mystery writers establish a sense of place mainly to create ambience, with street names and landmarks strewn about in the manner an interior decorator arranges furniture and chooses wallpaper. Occasionally, though, setting becomes something more—the architect replacing the decorator—and a metaphor emerges that enhances meaning rather than just prettifying plot. James Lee Burke is an inspired architect; his interest in New Orleans extends well beyond the travelogue surface. Burke's Cajun detective, Dave Robicheaux, is once again battling personal demons—questions of fear and bravery, violence and compassion, pleasure and pain—and as he stalks an escaped killer and infiltrates the world of a Mafia drug lord, he finds reflections of his own torment wherever he looks. What it means to be Cajun is at the heart of Robicheaux's dilemma: he treasures the easy-living side of his heritage, but with the po' boy sandwiches and the pulsing beat of Zydeco music come the lure of violence and an obsession with bravery and personal honor that consistently puts himself and his loved ones at risk. Can you enjoy beignets at the Café du Monde, or hum a chorus of "Jolie Blonde," or sip a Dixie beer without at the same time wanting to bash the head of anyone who smiles at your girl? And when you do bash a head, are you really doing it to protect the things you love or because the simple act of bashing something gives you such a kick? Robicheaux's ongoing attempt to resolve these questions brings new levels of meaning to the way we see New Orleans in particular and the pursuit of pleasure in general. Is the Big Easy really all that easy? Can any of us ever get free enough from our own demons to really experience the pleasures that New Orleans—or life—offers? Keep James Lee Burke in mind the next time you're strolling down Bourbon Street. —*Bill Ott*

Butler, Gwendoline.
Coffin in Fashion.
St. Martin's, $14.95. 176p.

The world of high fashion is a cutthroat place—especially if the merchandise isn't the latest haute couture and the setting is the swinging London of the 1960s. Sergeant John Coffin isn't exactly a dedicated follower of the fashion industry, but events tied to the rag trade manage to disturb his attempts at a quiet existence. It all begins when Coffin's modest renovations on his new house uncover two buried bodies—one a long-missing child, the other a retired policeman. Another boy has recently disappeared from the local school, and evidence links the child's whereabouts to the disturbed son of Rose Hilaire, the owner of a cut-rate clothing factory. The buried man turns out to be Rose's uncle. Coffin now has to contend with a missing boy, two long-dead corpses, and the disturbing fact that he fancies Rose's ambitious young designer. The laconic, long-suffering bobby makes a fine hero, and Butler once again (see also *Coffin on the Water*) makes good use of period detail and a slyly underhanded approach to murder. —*Peter Robertson*

Butler, Gwendoline.
Coffin in the Museum of Crime.
St. Martin's, $15.95. 192p.

Butler, who also writes under the name Jennie Melville, is firing out coffin tales with speed and relish (see *Coffin in Fashion*). The secret to her freshness seems to be variety. She moves the pleasingly complex Coffin all over London, uprooting him from his old contacts and his old loyalties and creating a self-contained, slightly lonely, emotionally guarded, big-city bobby. Promotion has given Coffin command of a new district, the London docklands—a seething oasis of Yuppie aspiration clashing head-on with old-town crime and character. His new digs are a gutted church, which also houses a theater group. When a caretaker's head and hands show up, no one mourns a nasty soul's demise. But when his wife also dies and his backyard yields another buried corpse, there are questions about the relationship of all this to the unusual specialization of the local museum: heinous crime through the ages, both solved and unsolved. *Museum* really has too many dead bodies, and nowhere near enough strong characterizations. But Butler has the light touch of a master and a beguiling hero in the somberly monikered Coffin. —*Peter Robertson*

Chesbro, George C.
The Language of Cannibals.
Mysterious Press, $18.95. 208p.

Chesbro writes bizarre mysteries, some starring Robert ("Mongo") Frederickson, dwarf, Ph.D., private eye extraordinaire, and former circus aerialist. With brother Garth, who's unusual in his own right, Mongo butts heads in this novel with crazed ultraconservatives running a death squad in an artsy Hudson Valley town. Chesbro's villains, at least those Mongo confronts, are also bizarre—bigger-than-life, Bondish megalomaniacs. Often using real social and political concerns as motifs, Chesbro's stands on those issues are passionately held and stated. Here it's the danger of the far right-wing's effective manipulation of symbols and Orwellian double-speak and the suggestion that KGB sleeper agents are manipulating the manipulators. It's vintage Chesbro—and vintage Mongo: David versus Goliath, with David ultimately kicking right-wing butt, saving America from itself. And that's sure to delight Mongo's faithful fans. —*Thomas Gaughan*

Constantine, K. C.
Sunshine Enemies.
Mysterious, $18.95. 176p.

Actually, Rocksburg Police Chief Mario Balzic drunkenly gets it wrong: What he means to say is "sunshine enemas"—a barroom oxymoron suggesting that, even at its nastiest, life offers its share of pleasant surprises. The nasty part is visible right away, but the sunshine is a little harder to find, as Balzic must deal with a gruesome murder outside a porn shop—29 knife wounds in a man's body and a BMW parked nearby with a gun and a baggie full of white powder inside. Meanwhile, a local preacher badgers Balzic over the porn shop's merchandise. Unsurprisingly, the shop has mob connections; then the preacher turns out to be a fraud. This isn't really a tale of crime and detection, though. It's about family. While Balzic's breaks down, an abused woman comes to him, sure her son has committed a crime. Constantine lets his earlier clues fall where they may. The crime's solution is rendered secondary to the rugged yet tender protagonist's inner torments, barely visible through the tough-guy veneer. A slick, economical use of plot and patter from an expert craftsman. —*Peter Robertson*

Cook, Thomas H.
Night Secrets.
Putnam, $19.95. 320p.

New York private eye Frank Clemons has survived his daughter's suicide, his marriage breakup, and his latest girlfriend's departure. At the request of a rich, concerned husband, Frank, during the day, follows a blonde woman who travels to the Dakota and Trump Tower, pawns her possessions, and makes a drop in Central Park to a cop. Working nights for free, Frank and his portly partner, Farouk, visit a fortune teller who is murdered, and a sensual young woman—entranced by a gypsy belief in a pure blood line stretching back to

Mystery & Espionage

Jesus Christ—signs a false confession. Frank soon falls under her spell. Cook works his twin plots with admirable deftness; each would fuel a halfway decent mystery alone. He injects a fluid sense of shifting reality in the night work, and the day case has a clocklike precision. The twice Edgar-nominated Cook already has a legion of fans. Expect him to add a few more with this latest. —*Peter Robertson*

Cooper, Susan Rogers.
Houston in the Rearview Mirror.
St. Martin's, $14.95. 165p.

An apparent murder/suicide plan leaves Oklahoma cop Milton Kovak's sister in a coma (charged with the killing) and her husband dead. It also drags the beleaguered brother to a place he despises—Houston, the scene of the crime. Kovak never liked his sister's husband much, and he likes him even less when the dead man's amazing sexual conquests become public knowledge. He's certain his sister didn't do it. After meeting an attractive waitress at the watering hole where the murdered man did most of his scoring, Kovak is off exploring Arab oil connections and industrial fraud. The second novel in a new series (following *The Man in the Green Chevy*), this engaging tale confirms one's feelings from the first book: Kovak is a real treasure. No skirt-chasing dullard with a big gun, he is thoroughly likable, utterly without pretense, and something of a ladies' man, albeit a laid-back, charming one. Cooper has a definite winner on her hands. —*Peter Robertson*

Cork, Barry.
Unnatural Hazard.
Scribner, $16.95. 176p.

Scotland, golf, and castles provide the ambience in this clever variant on the familiar locked-room mystery—only here it's a locked links. When former touring pro Chas MacLiven turns his ancestral castle on a remote Scottish island into a hotel with adjacent golf course (accessible only by boat), it's time for the bodies to start dropping. And drop they do, in a tangled plot involving a celebrity golf tournament, Nazi loot, family secrets, and Highlands history. Fortunately, inspector Angus Straun—policeman, best-selling novelist, and low-handicap golfer—is on the scene to sort out why it doesn't seem possible to play nine holes without somebody dying. Golfers are certain to chuckle at the cruel fate of one of the victims, who pays the ultimate price for trying to cut the corner on a dogleg: while looking for his ball in the woods, he's pushed off a cliff. For those who like their mysteries delicately soft-boiled—long on local color and short on gritty reality—Cork's charming, lightweight diversion lands as sweetly as a Seve Ballesteros wedge shot. —*Bill Ott*

Cormany, Michael.
Rich or Dead.
Birch Lane, $15.95. 189p.

On a strict diet of Kools, cheap liquor, and Valium, private eye Dan Kruger has stumbled through two unusual, flawed, yet entertaining tales. The third has the Chitown sleuth still fueled on various intoxicants, still playing the blues late at night on a Gibson guitar, and still rooting for the White Sox even though he lives next door to Wrigley Field. The trouble starts with a stiff in a cheap hotel and a missing bag of money. The stiff is a Hispanic illegal whose stop-at-nothing sister claims the dough is hers. A local hood who deals in heroin and cut-price illegal workers claims it's his. Enter various lowlifes including a street gang called the Romeo Kings. As in the earlier Kruger novels, Cormany lets his plot wander unleashed for most of the tale, allowing the sleazoid atmosphere to take center stage. It all works fine as a hyper-kinetic rush through the ever-venial Windy City, but some variation on the theme may be called for the next time around. —*Peter Robertson*

Craig, Patricia, ed.
The Oxford Book of English Detective Stories.
Oxford, $10. 554p.

A trenchant introduction tracing the evolution of fashions in the detective short story precedes a splendid array—33 in toto—of prime examples of the genre. Ranging chronologically from the developers of the detective short story (Arthur Conan Doyle and Austin Freeman, among them) to current stellar practitioners (including Julian Symons and Michael Gilbert), the stories demonstrate one abiding characteristic: what is lost in investigative involvement because of the confines of the short story form (as opposed to the expansiveness of the detective novel) is more than made up for in the increase of intensity of effect. (And that's not a bargain to sneeze at!) —*Brad Hooper*

Crider, Bill.
Medicine Show.
Evans, $15.95. 184p.

Crider's Sheriff Dan Rhodes mysteries are understated gems of murder, detection, and human nature, and he brings the same style to his westerns. Ray Storey is traveling with Colonel Mahaffey's medicine show as advance man and sharpshooter. But it's not the money or the lure of frontier show business that motivates him—it's revenge. During a bank robbery a while back, Storey's mentally handicapped kid brother was killed by the Hawkins brothers, who eventually escaped. In a small east Texas town he finds them. A twist in the plot forces Storey to confront his own fortitude and realize that the fantasy of revenge is much different than the actuality. A wonderfully written western mystery. —*Wes Lukowsky*

Cross, Amanda.
The Players Come Again.
Random, $17.95. 240p.

The ever-popular Cross has written a mystery replete with feminist and literary ambience. Kate Fansler, English professor and amateur detective, is asked by a major publisher to take on a bit of literary sleuthing for a biography of one Gabrielle Foxx, whose fame is rooted in the fact that she was married to an author of Joycean stature. As Kate debates whether to take on this project, she meets the surviving family members, three women who entice her through a maze of family secrets, dropping hints that Gabrielle's contributions to her husband's work involved far more than playing the roles of muse and housewife. Devotees of Cross will be delighted; mystery fans weary of stories littered with dropping bodies will also relish this puzzling tale. —*Denise Perry Donavin*

Daniel, Mark.
Unbridled.
Ticknor & Fields, $18.95. 223p.

Georgie Blane is a man of many faults. The famed steeplechase jockey is a drunkard and a philanderer, and his professional ethics have been known to defer to the odd bribe. Blane has an Irishman's appreciation for a good horse, however, and Vantage, the hot favorite for the prestigious King George VI Stakes, is the best he has ridden. He draws the line at pulling Vantage despite inducements that would banish his persistent financial woes, but can he continue to refuse in the face of grisly threats to his family? Daniel gallops over terrain long dominated by Dick Francis, the master of the English turf thriller, and his straightforward story is sure to suffer from comparisons with the latter's ingenious plots. In deftly capturing the nuances of the racing scene, populating that scene with a teeming cast of warts-and-all characters, and bringing them together at the wire for a heartstopping finish, however, the newcomer more than keeps pace. This is a most promising debut. —*Dennis Dodge*

Dobyns, Stephen.
Saratoga Hexameter.
Viking, $16.95. 246p.

Three separate cases—a string of murders at a nursing home, a series of burglaries at a swank hotel, and the perverse harassment of a literary critic at an artists' refuge—conspire to befuddle Saratoga sleuth Charlie Bradshaw and to keep him away from his favorite track as the short racing season slips inexorably away. What's worse, all three cases involve poetry in one way or another, and Charlie, who would rather be scoping out the Daily Double, must pass himself off as a poet to catch one of the evildoers. (There's plenty of in-group irony here since Dobyns is himself a poet of considerable distinction.) Bradshaw and his pals, a skirt-chasing house dick and an alcoholic investigator with a delicate ego, are no Sherlock Holmes (nobody thinks to have the hotel guests keep their valuables in a safe), but they are as likable as a lone front runner on a speed-holding surface, and so is Dobyns' sixth Saratoga mystery. —*Dennis Dodge*

Easterman, Daniel.
Brotherhood of the Tomb.
Doubleday, $19.95. 336p.

Before the author completes his first, blood-spattered 100 pages, the secret crypt that housed Jesus, James, and Mary is discovered by an ambitious priest; Christian history is stood on its head; and, in the midst of a vaguely apocalyptic setting (complete with allusions to Revelation, the compulsory 666, and symbolic messages in Hebrew and Greek), a cult called the Brotherhood of the Tomb is born. Then Easterman makes a curious detour into Ludlum country. It seems that the Brotherhood is no small-time cult; with power to spare and agents all over the globe, the group is ready to organize a hit on the Pope. Also among the cult's intended victims is one Patrick Canavan, a reformed Brotherhooder himself and an ex-CIA agent to boot. But Canavan doesn't cooperate, and a dizzying round of escalating violence ensues. Despite both the excess blood and Easterman's annoying devotion to the Harlequin school of overlush romantic interludes, the novel manages to forge an effective combination of religious mysticism and straightforward spy-craft-hunt-and-kill. —*Peter Robertson*

✓ **Ellroy, James.**
L.A. Confidential.
Mysterious Press, $19.95. 496p.

They're all L.A. cops in the 1950s, but the similarities don't go much further: company man Ed, struggling to live up to an illustrious family legacy, goes strictly by the books; psychotic Bud, avenging his mother's killing by his father, slaughters other abusers of women; and celebrity wanna-be Jack, lusting after bright lights, sells lurid accounts of his celebrity drug busts to a lowlife mag. The grisly narrative jumps from prison beatings, to glimpses of the porn-mag industry, to a mass slaughter in a late night diner, to the brutal rape of a Hispanic woman. Ellroy, author of *The Black Dahlia*, merges raw-edged period detail with sleazy celluloid lore, pulling away occasionally for snippets of forensic reports, newspaper accounts, and showbiz gossip. The effect is dark and dazzling, the prose splattered with fifties idiom, the whole epic package easily justifying what would be a daunting length for most traditional crime tales. The three main characters interact, cross paths, fire off sparks, and finally—inevitably—explode. Categorizing mysteries is often a self-defeating exercise, but here the publisher's use of the term *noir procedural* seems perfectly apt. Ellroy has made the field his own. —*Peter Robertson*

Emerson, Earl W.
Help Wanted: Orphans Preferred.
Morrow, $17.95. 320p.

Emerson's Thomas Black mysteries, set in Seattle, have long been among the best in the genre. Now, with his second Mac Fontana novel, the fireman-author joins Robert Campbell, Neville Steed, and a handful of others who juggle their talents between two high-quality series. As in the last Fontana novel, *Black Hearts and Slow Dancing*, the techniques of fire fighting provide fascinating ballast for a novel that jumps from pastoral revery to bursts of grotesque violence. When a Staircase, Washington, fireman dies of arsenic poisoning, Fire Chief Fontana is forced to once again assume the additional title of acting sheriff. More killings follow, disturbing the sleepy tranquillity

Mystery & Espionage

of the quiet Northwest town. Emerson mixes Fontana's investigative efforts with plenty of amusing diversions, including some slightly sophomoric but undeniably funny scatological humor. (Famous for outrageous showdown scenes, Emerson outdoes himself here with a shootout in which one of the combatants hides in an outhouse by burying himself in . . . well, you get the idea.) Clever plotting, engaging good guys, pretty scenery, cheap laughs, and fire-fighting lore—it all adds up to solid, unpretentious entertainment. —*Bill Ott*

Epperson, S. K.
Brother Lowdown.
St. Martin's, $16.95. 272p.

The three protagonists of Epperson's riveting first novel are the walking wounded, abused—sexually or physically—as children and trying now to cope with their pasts. Terra Donlevy has retreated to a ranch outside Wichita, surrounded by her pets, firmly refusing to have anything to do with her family's cosmetic business, making herself look as plain as possible, and struggling with her desperate fear of men. Simon Brith, a Wichita homicide detective, is regarded by his colleagues as a misogynist, his scarred face a constant reminder of both his crazed mother's attack on him and his unease with women. And beautiful, Adonis-like Brother Lowdown, searching for his mother in order to take his revenge for the past, is always belatedly realizing that the pretty young blond women he slashes are not his mother. All in all, very strong stuff, but handled surely and swiftly in this tautly paced mystery. The interweaving of the lives of the three characters is skilful, convincing, and has an elegant resolution. A truly gripping story, not for the weakhearted, in which the violence is really evil. —*Stuart Miller*

Estleman, Loren D.
Sweet Women Lie.
Houghton, $18.95. 193p.

If anyone can be said to truly represent the traditionalist mode of private-eye storytelling, it would have to be Loren Estleman in his Amos Walker novels. Walker is a determinedly anachronistic, relentlessly hard-boiled Detroit sleuth, his patter dripping off the pages, his woeful self-pity raised to a fine art. Here he finds himself hired to protect his ex-wife's husband, a deadly CIA operative with secrets to trade. This isn't an especially elegant piece of crime plotting; strangely languid at first, the novel turns frenzied and confusing at the end as Estleman peppers the pages with false leads. It hardly matters, though, since Walker's fans are in it for nostalgia, not plot. To read an Amos Walker novel is to revisit every lovably hokey, oft-parodied trademark of the classic hard-boiled style: the perpetually smart-ass sleuth mumbling his hard-luck stories to good and bad women while drinking good and bad booze. —*Peter Robertson*

320

Estleman, Loren D.
Whiskey River.
Bantam, $17.95. 272p.

Book one in crime writer Estleman's projected Detroit trilogy. The narrative starts at the tail end of the thirties, with wise-guy reporter and mob-guy confidant Connie Minor hauled up before a grand jury to tell his side of the past ten years' illegal booze action across the Canadian Border. Connie lets rip, and there isn't a line that doesn't simmer with period authenticity. The author's prose has always had something retro about it, so perhaps this isn't surprising. The trouble is, by working backwards, Estleman gives away some of the best stuff early: there is no tension in the story of Jack Dance's rise and fall as he cavalierly takes on the might of major-league bootlegger Joey Machine (Estleman appears to have no shortage of evocative hoodlum names). So, too, everyone knows that Connie will stray a little too close to the crime figures he is supposedly getting the lowdown on. Nevertheless, certain scenes crackle (gunfire on the ice-bound river in the pitch blackness, as a secret tip-off has the bulls closing in), and while this is not prime Estleman, it's not half bad either. —*Peter Robertson*

✓ Fonseca, Rubem.
Bufo & Spallanzani.
Dutton, $18.95. 234p.

They like to call these "literary" mysteries—a slippery term that hints at something more enduring, difficult, and allusive than the usual—and invariably names like Umberto Eco are used to pin the concept down. But in this case, the comparison is fair. In the first seven pages, references are made to Tolstoy, Flaubert, Chagall, St. John Perse, Moravia, Baudelaire, and Occam; moreover, Fonseca is a better writer than Eco; he handles the style (Europeanized intellectual in conversation) quite brilliantly, and his mystery-within-a-mystery plot is skillfully executed. Actually there are three crimes— one banal, one beautiful, and one exotic and clever. Fonseca paces them eccentrically, keeping the reader off balance. But it is precisely his clever handling of plot that finally steals something from the novel's brilliance. For plot—no matter how clever—is inevitably banal; like a cadenza in a concerto, it draws attention from the music and to the performer. It is a curse of the mystery genre that this sort of thing has to happen at the end. The reader is sorely tempted to turn back to the middle. —*Stuart Whitwell*

✓ Francis, Dick.
Longshot.
Putnam, $19.95. 324p.

After the high-tech dabblings of *Straight*, Francis plunges headlong into the racing world again, delivering a edgy, spellbinding thriller with the usual racetrack lore and enough raw emotional angles to satisfy those addicted to the almost sensual lure of uneasy reading. John is close to starving as he waits for his first novel to hit the stores, and his second effort seems destined

Mystery & Espionage

to stay trapped within his worried head. So he takes a paying gig, living with a famous trainer, writing his life story, and eating regularly again. But the gig has a hidden price tag, and John, whose previous writings ran to survival guides, gets to put some of his old theories into practice. Fatal accidents start happening involving a stable girl, a rider, and sundry other backstretch types. And worse, John's survival tales seem to be providing the killer with many helpful hints. Francis remains one of the most incandescent talents in the mystery game. His plot positively shimmers, and his sleuth easily hurdles that always difficult jump from credible character to believable amateur detective. Perhaps best of all, Francis extracts a wealth of weird and wonderful shadings from his suspects, whipping up hidden admirations, suppressed angers, and raging jealousies. In short, all the good stuff. —*Peter Robertson*

Freeling, Nicolas.
Sand Castles.
Mysterious Press, $17.95. 224p.

Dutch policeman van der Valk has been delighting mystery fans for decades with his curmudgeonly mix of wisdom and world-weariness. Both qualities are in full bloom here, and van der Valk isn't even supposed to be working. He's on holiday with his no-nonsense wife, Arlette, but, naturally, he just can't keep his nose out of the nefarious. First there's a smut-peddling school principal to be dispatched, and then—somewhat more thorny—there's a neo-Nazi industrialist whose illusions of grandeur have turned lethal. All the bad guys get their various comeuppances, of course, but the pleasure in van der Valk is never plot. What makes the books live are all those little ordinary things that happen along the way: Arlette saying to her husband, "If you're going to undress me, do it without these loutish pleasantries," or van der Valk ordering his halibut with lemon juice because nobody in Holland can make hollandaise sauce. Everyday life in all its glorious particularity. —*Bill Ott*

Freemantle, Brian.
O'Farrell's Law.
Tor, $17.95. 320p.

CIA hitman Charles O'Farrell is pretty close to cracking up—what with struggling to limit himself to a couple of martinis a day, hiding the truth about his chosen profession from his trusting wife, and worrying about his son, his daughter, and especially his nine-year-old grandson, who is caught in a drug scandal at elementary school. Then there's an on-the-job problem. O'Farrell's first attempt at whacking a Cuban drug buyer ends in the car-bomb death of the man's innocent wife. O'Farrell's despondency increases, and he falls prey to the lure of the bottle all the more. Freemantle is the author of the excellent Charlie Muffin series—spy capers brightened by crusty and offbeat characterizations. This is an altogether more somber but no less fascinating work. Beset both by devils he knows and devils he doesn't know, O'Farrell manages to engage our sympathy despite his abhorrent career. Freemantle is to be credited for pulling off a rare literary feat—believable American characters created by a British author. *—Peter Robertson*

Gash, Jonathan.
The Very Last Gambado.
St. Martin's, $18.95. 288p.

After a mayhem-riddled sojourn to the Orient in *Jade Woman*, antiques expert Lovejoy returns to his home turf of East Anglia. He's up to his usual tricks: sniffing around for an antique bargain and showing no qualms about using dubious channels to close the deal. He also secures himself a lucrative gig as technical adviser to a movie mogul making a crime caper about a robbery at the British Museum. Trouble is, life is starting to imitate art. There's the murder of a reputed antique faker; there's the disappearance of an antique dealer who's involved with another dealer's wife; and there's the disconcerting fact that the police link Lovejoy to both events. Meanwhile, the harried hero falls into the arms of the movie mogul's delectable assistant. Lovejoy has always been cursed with a way with the ladies, an eye for a real treasure or a usable fake, and no luck whatsoever with the gendarmes. Gash fires off the usual salvo of cryptic dialogue, insider lore, and slick patter. Dedicated fans will chortle along contentedly. *—Peter Robertson*

Gerson, Jack.
Death Squad London.
St. Martin's, $17.95. 288p.

Berlin policeman Ernest Lohmann has fled Nazi Germany to settle in London, and while he no longer wields power or influence, he isn't forced to work for corrupt maniacs. A refugee adrift, Lohmann is slowly sinking into a self-pitying haze. His reputation, however, has preceded him. When a beautiful young journalist, on the trail of Oswald Mosley's Fascist Brownshirts, dies of an apparent suicide, Lohmann finds himself employed again, albeit in an unofficial capacity. Back in the saddle, he narrowly misses plunging headfirst from a high building, cripples two hired thugs with his Mauser and the back bumper of a Morris, receives unexpected help and a spot of physical solace from a wealthy socialite, and gets little encouragement from the boys in blue. The sequel to last year's *Death's Head Berlin*, this is another dark, driven, pulsating tale. Two winners so far in a series distinguished by its period authenticity and its resolute, resourceful sleuth. *—Peter Robertson*

✓ Gill, B. M.
Time and Time Again.
Scribner, $16.95. 192p.

After serving a brief prison sentence for throwing a brick during a demonstration, Maeve Barclay returns to her job as a stockbroker, but she is deeply scarred by the experience. Also scarred is the young policeman injured as a result of Maeve's action—and now a permanent fixture in Maeve's dreams.

Maeve becomes a social outcast, drifting away from her husband and increasingly drawn to Rene, her ex-con friend. That Maeve will slide inexorably into Rene's world of minor crime is soon apparent, but only gradually do we become aware of the horror beneath Rene's slightly seedy existence. Two-time Edgar nominee Gill delivers her taut tales of psychological suspense with all the verve and understated guile of Ruth Rendell. Here she breathes new life into the old British class-struggle gambit. Her character studies are minimalist masterpieces, and she reveals the story's dark deeds in an oblique, deliberately hesitant, and utterly captivating manner. —*Peter Robertson*

Gilman, Dorothy.
Mrs. Pollifax and the Whirling Dervish.
Doubleday, $17.95. 192p.

Mrs. Pollifax, the amazing CIA spy with an impeccable cover (she looks like, and is, a grandmother), meets up with the whirling dervish in Morocco, where he is part of a network of Polisarios, agents working to achieve the independence of the Western Saharans. Her mission begins as innocently as the previous eight have—with a phone call from her CIA contact, Carstairs, who suggests a minor job in an irresistible foreign locale. Mrs. Pollifax, who has just been fretting that perhaps she's getting too old for espionage work, readily agrees to fly immediately to Casablanca. As usual, the task proves perilous, while Mrs. Pollifax proves indomitable, whether she is swathed in veils and rendezvousing with an undercover agent, karate kicking an assailant, or fleeing across the desert. The countryside is depicted in great detail, and so are the native people. Gilman's eye for background matches her marvelous sense of adventure. —*Denise Perry Donavin*

Goldsborough, Robert.
Fade to Black.
Bantam, $17.95. 224p.

In the age of high fiber and power walking, it's a relief to spend time with Nero Wolfe: no leaving the beloved brownstone; beer pretty much round the clock; Archie to order around; orchids to dote over; meals that would lay a lesser man low. Of course, the odd case has to be taken on to pay for the meals, the beer, the orchids, and, since this is the 1990s, the computer that records the plants' germination records. In Goldsborough's last reconditioned Wolfe affair, date rape was prominent. Another modern disease appears here: industrial espionage. When two ads for rival soft drinks appear remarkably similar, the cranky beverage magnate from one of the companies isn't amused. And when a key player representing one of the ad agencies involved turns up dead, Wolfe takes the case. Goldsborough continues to drag the famous portly detective kicking and screaming into the present day, with new-fangled crimes elegantly applied to the trusty Rex Stout formula—set pieces full of furious wit leading to the classic confrontation in Wolfe's office, all delivered with verve and unerring respect for the form. In this case, the extremely rotund form. —*Peter Robertson*

Goulart, Ron.
The Tijuana Bible.
St. Martin's, $14.95. 192p.

When, early in this comic thriller about a cross-country scramble to find a bunch of very valuable old comic books, the characters use words like *deride* and *mayhap* in conversation, it seems that Goulart doesn't have the ear for the kind of (at least semi-) hard-boiled caper he's writing. Then about a third of the way into it, as the wisecracks, overly precise descriptive remarks, and sharply turned clichés mount up, it hits home. (By jingo! He's writing in comic-book style.) From there on out, the romp's sheer delight. The wife-left, desperate-for-a-gag, comic-strip ghostwriter hero and the curvaceous, blonde, alternately bright-and-dim-bulb heroine are more appealing, at least to grown-ups, than Batman and Robin ever were. The plot, with its heavies coming back like bad pennies, is the stuff of grade-B-movie dreams; the parties responsible for the old "Rockford Files" TV series ought to make a boob-tube flicker (modern equivalent of a quota quickie) out of it. Great cheap fun. —*Ray Olson*

Grafton, Sue.
"G" Is for Gumshoe.
Holt, $16.95. 261p.

Kinsey Millhone, America's favorite female private detective, returns in her seventh "alphabet" mystery, this one, like the previous *F Is for Fugitive*, showered with much media hoopla. (Everyone wants Kinsey: Literary Guild, Doubleday Book Club, Mystery Guild, six-figure paperback and foreign rights, audio cassettes. Can a movie be far behind?) Kinsey pursues a missing-person case that conceals a tangled web of violent family history; at the same time, she's trying to avoid a decidedly low-life type of hired killer. Kinsey's beloved VW is totaled in the course of events, and our heroine gets roughed up a bit herself. She also shares a brief but passionate dalliance with bodyguard Robert Dietz, one of the few male characters in a Grafton novel who is a genuine mental and physical match for Kinsey. (Might we see more of him?) Otherwise, this is standard (that is, pretty darn good) Grafton. (Kinsey's got to get off the antismoking soapbox, though. For heaven's sake, in that line of work? Let 'em smoke, Kinsey!) —*Martin Brady*

Granger, Bill.
League of Terror.
Warner, $19.95. 304p.

Despite glasnost and the crumbling of the Berlin Wall, the enigmatic Devereaux—the November Man—still functions, still chafes at the bureaucratic bit, still loves Rita, and still quietly emotes. This is the eleventh outing in a series that has come close to delivering some of the best in homegrown spy fiction: rough and ready prose, ambiguities aplenty, earthy talk at all the right moments, a sullen hero's facade masking inner torments. Here Devereaux's nemesis, Henry McGee, is converting terrorism into income. He recruits a ragtag crew of IRA zealots and, armed with nerve gas,

THE BOOK BUYER'S ADVISOR

Mystery & Espionage

proceeds to put the moves on the owner of an airline. The price is $4 million. Henry wants the dough. The IRA want arms and glory. But Henry also wants Devereaux. So he hits him where it hurts—he whacks Rita. Despite some agreeably gruesome twists near the end, and two of the genre's nastiest lady killers, Granger is spinning his narrative wheels here. The lover's talk has a tired, desperate feel, Rita is starting to resemble a doormat, and Devereaux, given a surfeit of unusually sappy lines, comes close to sinking in melodrama. These aren't developments that spy fans will relish, though the November Man audience should remain a loyal one through this weaker effort. —*Peter Robertson*

Haldeman, Joe.
The Hemingway Hoax: A Short Comic Novel of Existential Terror.
Morrow, $16.95. 224p.

Hemingway's lost novel, *Up in Michigan*, becomes the focal point for Haldeman's complex time-travel yarn. (The original manuscript and all carbon copies were apparently stolen from a train, circa 1921, and have never been recovered.) Agents from the Spacio-Temporal Adjustment Board attempt to stop John Baird, a university professor, from forging a flawless pastiche of the missing work. This seemingly insignificant event has the potential to change the course of history across a multitude of parallel universes. As the time cops repeatedly kill off incarnations of Baird in dimension after dimension, his persona begins to blur, gradually assuming the attributes of Papa Hemingway himself. This lively, cerebral novel is a fascinating addition to the Hemingway mythos. —*Elliott Swanson*

Hammond, Gerald.
Dog in the Dark.
St. Martin's, $14.95. 192p.

This new series from the author of the Keith Calder mysteries substitutes dog-training lore for gun-hobbyist trivia. Invalided out of the British army, John Cunningham sets up shop as a gun-dog trainer, specializing in spaniels, in the Fife region of Scotland. He soon inherits two loyal helpers, one a young local girl, the other a little older, married, given to bouts with the bottle and the occasional sexual advance (to which Cunningham succumbs). John also finds himself saddled with an odious collection of new neighbors—a mean-spirited farmer and two interfering old biddies. Soon one biddy is dead, and John is asked to account for his whereabouts by the local bobbies. These characters aren't half as jolly as the eccentrics who populate the Calder series, and Cunningham is a considerably more flawed hero than the unequivocally likable Calder. But that is as it should be in a tale considerably darker than any of the earlier books. All in all, Cunningham and his spaniels make a fine change of pace from Calder and his guns. —*Peter Robertson*

326

Hansen, Joseph.
The Boy Who Was Buried This Morning.
Viking, $16.95. 174p.

Fans of Hansen's gay sleuth Dave Brandstetter, breathe easy. He may have retired last time around (*Obedience*, but here he is, capering away once again and better than usual, thanks finally not to the plot (which is definitely okay, though) or the characters (who are okay, too) but to Hansen's considerable writing talents. Small-town, conservative-to-the-point-of-fascist Southern California—trying to make a killing in housing developments and new "sports" fads like combat games (as long as they don't have to sell to "those people," that is)—comes dryly, loathsomely to life through Hansen's lean, simile-phobic prose. Reading this book is like watching a topflight, downbeat TV or B-movie mystery; it's a gritty treat for the mind's eye. The plot? Oh, yeah, it's about how Dave discovers just who among a crowd of unsavory right-wingers killed a soldier-playing junior Nazi and his girl friend. —*Ray Olson*

Hardwick, Mollie.
Perish in July.
St. Martin's, $15.95. 208p.

The fifth Doran Fairweather mystery finds Doran and Rodney Chelmarsh still happily married. Helena, Rodney's crippled daughter from his first marriage, has just died, but their son Kit, now four years old, is thriving. Doran's antique business still flourishes, and Rodney is acting vicar at the small parish of St. Leonard's in the tiny village of Elvesham. The church is badly in need of repairs, and a fund-raising group hits on the idea of a local production of Gilbert and Sullivan's *The Yeoman of the Guard*. Enter the Chelmarsh's lovely neighbor, Paula French (or, as Doran calls her, "Perfect Paula"), whose warbling soprano gets her a lead part—until her decapitated body is found before a rehearsal, stuffed into one of the chests intended as a prop. Needless to say, Doran cannot help but get involved, with timely relief from maternal duties in the shape of her business partner's Welsh mother, a fascinating woman whose singsong voice and folk tales delight Kit. Hardwick is back in stride with this yarn, recapturing the lightheartedness of the earlier Doran stories, which was lacking in her recent *The Bandersnatch* (St. Martin's, 1989). —*Stuart Miller*

✓ Harvey, John.
Rough Treatment.
Holt, $17.95. 288p.

John Harvey received glowing press for his crime debut, *Lonely Hearts*, and here he is again, beating a barrage of startling effects and unfamiliar angles out of the police procedural. This rough slice of English life is cut from the cold, gray, industrial heart of the Midlands, the same spot frequented by Alan Sillitoe, and Harvey exposes it with Sillitoe's unflinchingly sardonic vision. And his caper detailing is near-flawless. Thieves break into a home and are surprised to find a kilo of coke; they offer it back—for an unusual price. The

Mystery & Espionage

husband, only storing the white powder, is desperate. Meanwhile, the wife is smitten with her new lover, and the cocaine's rightful owner is justly unhappy. Harvey's addition of a police-corruption subplot almost overloads the tale, but his rare gift for expanding the barriers of the genre without breaking the rules remains intact. Motivation and character are delivered in tense, rapid-fire, stripped-down narrative and souls are laid bare with unseemly ease. Definitely a series, and an author, to watch. —*Peter Robertson*

Hill, Reginald.
Bones and Silence.
Delacorte, $17.95. 312p.

In the gently sardonic hands of English author Reginald Hill, the formulaic odd-couple detective tale provides moments of inspired jocularity, sparkling cross-class conversation, and even a few savage emotional broadsides. This third mystery starring Superintendent Dalziel, the burly, blunt, endlessly cunning North Country copper, and his assistant, the thoroughly genteel Inspector Pascoe, lays out major and minor themes like train tracks, parallel for the most part, intersecting on occasion, and, once in a while, when the signals cross, colliding. The major theme has a wife committing suicide in the company of her lover, her husband, and, across the road, his eyes blurred by too many single malts, Superintendent Dalziel. Naturally, the three eyewitness accounts vary enormously. Dalziel also becomes involved with the curious doings of a local theater group and with another troubled woman close to suicide. Through it all, the rough-and-ready Dalziel is surrounded by the usual crew of effete, namby-pamby southern England types with no chins and plummy accents. Hill extracts a remarkable spectrum of nuance from his catalog of genre clichés and breathes new life into characters hired direct from the bad-British-sitcom wing of central casting. —*Peter Robertson*

Horansky, Ruby.
Dead Ahead: A Mystery Introducing Nikki Trakos.
Scribner, $17.95. 256p.

Readers with a preference for women characters and police procedurals should find Horansky's first mystery just the ticket. Nikki Trakos is a newly promoted detective whose supervisor is reluctant to give any serious assignments to a woman. So when the homicide of a small-time gambler occurs near Sheepshead Bay in Brooklyn, Nikki is grudgingly assigned the case and given only three days to show results. She also must deal with a partner who seems more concerned with another of his cases, one with a higher public profile. Matters become more complicated when the business card of a prominent Wall Street financier, recently deceased in a boating accident, is found in the victim's wallet. Are the deaths connected? Horansky has constructed a tight plot and keeps the reader guessing for a long time. The only possible weakness is the clichéd subplot—Nikki's alternating attraction/repulsion for her partner. But this is a minor quibble. While Horansky can hardly be said to have broken new ground in the popular procedural genre, she has written a solidly entertaining and engrossing mystery. —*Stuart Miller*

Huebner, Fredrick D.
Picture Postcard.
Fawcett/Columbine, $16.95. 288p.

Seattle lawyer and sometime sleuth Matt Riordan has an odd way of meeting women. In this, Riordan's fourth mystery, the barrister seizes his chance to cement a relationship with an attractive art dealer by agreeing to investigate the appearance of a postcard that seems to have been freshly painted by her famous grandfather, who has been presumed dead for 10 years. The ploy works, but it nearly gets Riordan killed as his search leads him too close to a forgery ring and a money-laundering drug lord, then back 50 years to a still-festering murder for which an innocent man was convicted. Riordan's obsessive nosiness is enough to alienate his love interest, but it does serve to propel Huebner's byzantine plot at breakneck speed. For that, for a sharply drawn cast of memorable characters, and for a wonderfully specific Pacific Northwest setting, Huebner's readers can again be grateful. —*Dennis Dodge*

✓ Izzi, Eugene.
Invasions.
Bantam, $17.95. 311p.

Eugene Izzi is churning out crime novels at a breakneck pace, each one a hard, sharp-edged gem of dark deeds in a dark city. Others have written about Chicago, but Izzi's city—a crime-sodden, Mafia hellhole littered with broken promises and shattered lives splattered over a finely drawn backdrop of inner-city sleaze—has all the visceral impact of Elmore Leonard's Detroit. Exposing crime, big time and everyday, from petty little betrayals to major heists, Izzi gives us characters who can never be pigeonholed, each one a potential bad guy. In *Invasions*, Frank Vale is a thief and an expert in home invasion. His brother, Jimmy, is back on the street after doing nine years in the slammer for protecting Frank. Jimmy is talked into whacking a big-name mobster for the bunch of militant racists who saved his hide in the joint. Against his better judgment, Frank helps. Izzi builds sympathy for the brothers, whose love for each other is stretched thin by too much hard time, but does it without any obvious keys to tell us these are good guys who do bad things. The gradual narrative buildup, culminating in a blood-drenched finale in a suburban mansion, is accomplished in slow, sinewy, relentlessly cunning prose. This may or may not be the book that lifts Izzi far beyond his competitors in the new-kids-on-the-mystery-block sweepstakes—say, Tom Kakonis (*Michigan Roll* and *Criss Cross*) and Andrew Vachss (*Strega* and *Hard Candy*)—but it hardly matters. *Invasions* is another virtuoso turn from a writer who just seems to keep getting better—and tougher. —*Peter Robertson*

Izzi, Eugene.
The Prime Roll.
Bantam, $3.95. 275p.

In the middle of the winning streak of his life, Chicagoan Lano Branka steals the girl, the dough, and the tenuous respect afforded near-moronic mobster

Mystery & Espionage

Tough Tony. Lano resurfaces in Atlantic City, his luck still intact and his winnings even more impressive. But he stakes it all on the essential goodness of a beautiful woman whose gambling debts threaten to turn her into a prostitute—a sucker bet if ever there was one. Izzi has already proved his narrative smarts in *The Take* and *King of the Hustlers*, both of which showcased a gang of dirt-encrusted, entertainingly amoral Chicago hoodlums. Now he seems determined to make his losers likable. He succeeds in spades, and if his dialogue still lacks the punch of George Higgins, he manages to avoid the stylization to which his more famous colleague sometimes succumbs. This novel explodes like firecrackers on a page-by-page basis, and the ending—big gambles, big losses, a small victory for the wiser Lano, and plenty of blood splattered all over the beach—is a set piece of accomplished crime writing. *—Peter Robertson*

Jackson, Jon A.
Grootka.
Countryman/Foul Play, $19.95. 336p.

Grootka's no longer a cop, but he is riding shotgun for a burnout in the abandoned car detail when they find a stiff in a trunk. A former pimp, hustler, and informant. Cut back to a thirty-year-old murder case that Grootka busted open and thought he resolved. He hadn't, and now he's in trouble. From the outset Jackson, author of the *The Diehard* and *The Blind Pig* (Macmillan, 1988) is playing a cunning narrative game, opening up his story like Russian dolls. The dead man's identity gets a little hazy, and Grootka's morals get a little tarnished. Meanwhile, the killer is thirty years older, an ugly, sweating man with a taste for vodka, building an endlessly complex computer program to track and rationalize his mounting evil. At times, Jackson is ambitious; maybe overly so. But his seamy Detroit evocation, as the city's sickos gear up for "Hell Night," and homeless winos hide from the cold winter "hawk," is a tight, relentless one. It's taken Jackson over 10 years to deliver this third Motor City urban-hell scenario, which is a damn shame. *—Peter Robertson*

✓ James, P. D.
Devices and Desires.
Knopf, $19.95. 352p.

What more can be said about P. D. James, the mystery writer with the soul of a poet? In *Devices and Desires*, James again serves up a superb tale of murder that provides an incisive look at the furtive, often twisted lives of accomplished people. James' stalwart protagonist, Commander Adam Dalgliesh, travels to the coastal Norfolk community of Larksoken to settle up the estate of his recently deceased aunt. Inevitably, Dalgliesh becomes embroiled in the affairs of the locals, many of them connected with the Larksoken nuclear power plant, which has brought a new economy to the area but has also stirred the juices of antinuclear protesters. Meanwhile, a mad killer called the Whistler is aprowl, savaging women with a bizarre modus operandi. Local inspector Terry Rickards, somewhat intimidated by Dalgliesh's presence, doggedly seeks the Whistler, then must shift gears when the power plant's aggressive administrator is murdered on the beach in Whistler-like fashion, but quite obviously by someone else. Egos, ambition, emotional repression, dark pasts, and thwarted love lie behind the stolid exteriors of the suspects. Dalgleish tries to stay out of Rickards' way but can't help offering his opinions on motives and methods. James at her best. —*Martin Brady*

Jeffries, Roderic.
Too Clever by Half.
St. Martin's, $15.95. 192p.

A new Inspector Enrique Alvarez novel is always cause for rejoicing, and Jeffries has not lost his touch in this ninth novel in the series. As usual, the setting is Mallorca, the victim and the suspects are English expatriates, and the inspector continues to love his brandy, his food, and his smokes. In this episode, the death of art expert Justin Burnett appears to be a suicide—until his sister, Phillipa, insists he was murdered. Alvarez, ever reluctant to exert himself too much—after all, exercise in the Mediterranean heat would never be wise—is forced to pay attention after evidence indicates both that the suicide note was not typed on Burnett's typewriter and that his fingerprints don't appear on the half-empty whiskey bottle found at his side, a liquor that his sister says he never drank. Jeffries has again produced a winner, combining intricate plotting and thoroughly agreeable characters. —*Stuart Miller*

Johnson, E. Richard.
Dead Flowers.
International Polygonics, $17.95. 204p.

It is always refreshing to find police procedurals set somewhere other than New York or California, and here's a particularly good one set in Minneapolis. When florist Raymond DeMeyere is found shot to death in the alley behind his shop, detectives Lonto and Runnion are disposed to believe that robbery was the motive, though the shop itself was not ransacked. (Curiously, that happens the next day.) Lonto also can't figure out why a florist would keep a set of scales in his office, but when a narcotics detective is shot, some tantalizing connections begin to appear between the two cases. Johnson never gets bogged down in the details of any aspect of police work; rather, he focuses on the process of examining leads, the theorizing based on available evidence, and the speculation on the "how-coulds" that, together, define detective work. This well-paced and soundly plotted mystery is bolstered by two extremely likable cops. A certain winner for all procedural fans. —*Stuart Miller*

✓ Kakonis, Tom.
Criss Cross.
St. Martin's, $17.95. 323p.

Kakonis' *Michigan Roll* was an explosive mystery debut. His second effort is even better: a brutally funny, hyperviolent, streetwise crime tale peppered in all the right places with the kind of seriocomic dialogue that fellow Michigander Elmore Leonard seems to whip up effortlessly. The scene of the

Mystery & Espionage

crime is a Grand Rapids department store, where the sensual Starla works the cash register and uses her charms to enlist security guard and confirmed loser Mitchell Morse in a heist scheme planned by her errant husband, Meat, and his twitching, skirt-obsessed sidekick, Ducky. The real brains behind the operation, though, is Dr. D. C. Kasperson, a longtime con man presently running a phony hair-growth operation. Kakonis is a truly fearless writer. His characters are blunt and unforgettable, and his dialogue, especially the scatological stuff between Meat and Ducky, is an unholy pastiche of vicious, ugly street truths that crack with authenticity. For the conclusion, he pulls out all the stops: in an orgy of blood and gunfire, everyone shafts everyone else; Starla gets to show a smidgen of goodness; Mitch shows a whole lot more; and the Doc uncharacteristically fails to account for the deep unhappiness of a nearly bald customer. Leonard better not relax; he now has a serious rival stalking his own psychological and geographic territory. —*Peter Robertson*

Kaminsky, Stuart M.
The Man Who Walked like a Bear.
Scribner, $16.95. 224p.

The last work to feature Soviet inspector Porfiry Rostnikov was *A Cold Red Sunrise*, which won the 1989 Edgar Award. Beset by the usual demons (including the plumbing in his apartment), visited by a few new ones, and still a thorn in the side of the Soviet bureaucracy, Rostnikov must deal with a host of problems in his sixth adventure: a plot to kill a Politburo member, shady deals in a Moscow shoe factory, and several demented nationalists who mastermind a scheme to destroy Lenin's tomb. Then there's the inspector's sick wife to visit in the hospital and the matter of getting his son out of the military, not to mention the equally vexing concerns of Rostnikov's partners, Karpo, who's fighting migraines, and Sasha, who would like to jettison his argumentative mother before moving to a larger apartment. All matters prove solvable, even the plumbing. Kaminsky continues to dazzle: the expertly interlocked plots and subplots and the superb procedural details would bring to mind Ed McBain even if Porfiry himself didn't go everywhere with a tattered 89th Precinct paperback in his coat pocket. —*Peter Robertson*

Kaminsky, Stuart M.
Poor Butterfly.
Mysterious, $17.95. 208p.

Whereas Kaminsky's somber chronicles of wayward Soviet sleuth Porfiry Rostnikov have won him critical acclaim (see the recent *Man Who Walked like a Bear*), his 1940s Hollywood mysteries, starring the effervescent Toby Peters and garnished with plenty of Tinseltown ambience, have allowed the film professor/author an opportunity to show his stuff. The Peters papers are definitely a lesser creation, although the madcap plotting, celebrity appearances, and hard-boiled wisecracks produce more than their share of good moments. Here the focus shifts from film to opera and from Southern to Northern California, as Leopold Stokowski's San Francisco performance of *Madame Butterfly* faces opposition from many sides. The local zealots are concerned with the pro-Japanese content of the opera (it's 1942), and more sinister trouble brews from the Phantom-like soul raising havoc from high above the stage. The maestro calls on Toby and his band of crack operatives— assorted dwarves, dentists, and an existentialist ex-wrestler—to sort things out. The mystery element is laughably light and the movie lore is missed, but the smart-ass one-liners and all-around daffiness keep things moving. —*Peter Robertson*

Kantner, Rob.
Made in Detroit.
Bantam, $3.95. 272p.

A rusted-out car explodes at a wedding party. The groom is a goner, and the former-building-super-turned-private-dick, Ben Perkins, is the cops' favorite suspect. The low-rent shamus sets out to clear himself and is soon swimming in deep waters. The trail leads from a mysterious blonde (a friend of the late groom's) to a dead drug dealer, a tortured woman in Detroit's notorious Cass Corridor, and to a gaggle of Motor City mobsters. This lean and wrenching novel, sparse yet evocative, has only one weakness: its period setting wobbles. Things appear to begin somewhere in the mid-seventies (the Allman Brothers, Pintos, and Gremlins) but soon we've inexplicably jumped to cellular phones, crack, Lee Iacocca, and Bon Jovi. Lamentable taste in music aside (although a liking for Fine Young Cannibals remedies things some-what), Perkins is a ruthless, sentimental, battle-scarred warrior—and a lot of fun as well. Kantner's vision is strictly street level, but his blurred, frantic action is executed with all the elan expected of a triple Shamus Award–win-ner. —*Peter Robertson*

Kellerman, Jonathan.
Time Bomb.
Bantam, $19.95. 432p.

Kellerman's independently wealthy, downright suave, humanely driven child psychologist, Dr. Alex Delaware, is prissy, self-righteous, and self-effacingly pompous enough to deserve a guest spot on "thirtysomething." But Kellerman's elegant forays into emotional child abuse form a fitting counter-balance to the more visceral methods of crime novelists Andrew Vachss and Eugene Izzi—who, in their works, wage no-holds-barred warfare with child abusers—and this, along with the mazelike intensity of his plotting, has given Kellerman the best-selling field all to himself. In *Time Bomb*, Delaware is first on the scene when a sniper opens fire in a schoolyard. The kids escape without physical wounds, but the shooter, a dull-witted local girl, is taken out by the bodyguard of a local political honcho visiting the school. Actually there are two honchos in attendance, representing both sides of the volatile busing issue, both hogging media space with their violently contrasting views. Delaware talks to the kids, helps them act out fantasies of hostility, and defuses their fears while their school is made to function as a test tube for experiments in racial and social integration. He also befriends the school's attractive young principal and gets to act out a few fantasies of his own.

Mystery & Espionage

Kellerman slots the parts together with his usual consummate skill. —*Peter Robertson*

Kennealy, Jerry.
Polo's Wild Card.
St. Martin's, $15.95. 224p.

Decked out in a rented tux, Nick Polo is playing poker with the in-crowd at a swank charity bash held in the outsize Pacific Heights mansion of a well-known San Francisco socialite. Nick's winning nicely, too, even at seven-card stud, which any poker player knows is a dope's game. Play becomes work when there's a burglary at the mansion, and Polo is hired by the socialite's father to retrieve stolen paintings. Kennealy is on number five in his Polo series; true to form, this latest entry offers a kinetic roller-coaster ride through San Francisco's highs and lows, from tony Nob Hill and Pacific Heights to the sleazy Tenderloin and low-rent Mission districts. Nick remains the urban hero surfing on a sea of sleaze, and, though Kennealy pretty much sticks to formula, there's usually a few surprises along the fast-paced way. Count on some low-budget laughs, some fresh angles on an overused crime locale, and damn few pauses for breath. —*Peter Robertson*

Knight, Kathryn Lasky.
Mortal Words.
Summit, $17.95. 316p.

Knight, a popular children's author (under the name Kathryn Lasky), has written a second mystery similar in style to her first, *Trace Elements*. Calista Jacobs, an acclaimed illustrator of children's books, reappears as the heroine, aided by her bright 13-year-old son, Charley. When a fellow author is gruesomely murdered and Calista receives threatening messages, Charley uses his computer skills to ferret out the villain. A sinister plot is exposed, involving creationists and psycho scientists out to prove their theory of a separate origin for the white race. Knight uses this novel to deliver kudos to librarians (one scene even takes place at an annual librarians' conference) and slam censors and anti-evolutionists. Fortunately, she is careful not to allow sermonizing to overwhelm the mystery and romance that make the book enjoyable. —*Denise Perry Donavin*

✓ **Leonard, Elmore.**
Get Shorty.
Delacorte, $18.95. 291p.

Nobody writes nice-bad-guys better than Elmore Leonard, and the nicest and best of the lot—at least since Ernest ("Stick") Stickley—just may be loan-shark-turned-movie-producer Chili Palmer. The Miami-based Chili is in Los Angeles looking for a dry cleaner who's behind on the "vig" when he encounters schlock moviemaker Harry Zimm. Soon Chili is pitching his own movie ideas—based mostly on his adventures in search of the dry cleaner—and helping Harry launch a "sure-thing blockbuster." But it's not all mineral water and soft pastels. There's a Mob guy on Chili's tale, and, worse yet, there's Bo Catlett (another hood gone Hollywood), who wants to produce Harry's blockbuster himself and sees Chili in the way. The delightful notion of street-smart, movie-loving criminals is what gives this offbeat comedy its zip. (On the other run from the Mob, Chili needs a place to hide and tries the Chateau Marmont, hoping to get Jean Harlow's room.) Leonard has put his own 20 years of movie-writing experience to good use here, producing not just another Hollywood insider's book, but instead an ingratiating mix of satire and celebration. As usual, the talk jumps off the page, and the characters are all stamped with an indelible individuality. This is Leonard's best book in several years, and he isn't even coming off a slump. —*Bill Ott*

Lescroat, John.
Dead Irish.
Donald I. Fine, $18.95. 293p.

Dismas Hardy is 38 years old, but it's been a hard 38. A Vietnam vet, former cop, former lawyer, and former husband, he now spends his time boozing and tending at in the Little Shamrock, an Irish pub on the corner of Ninth and Lincoln in San Francisco. The battered Hardy isn't pushing himself too hard anymore: a few games of darts, a few black and tans (a blend of ale and lager), a few more beers pounded at Candlestick Park on a cold afternoon. Things quickly change as a friend's apparent suicide (actually murder) throws Dismas back into action, hunting down the killer and exploring the deep tensions beneath seemingly tranquil generations of hard-living, gregarious Irish immigrants. Lescroat's portrayal of San Francisco isn't the usual one. He finds an oasis of tradition and an anachronistic family loyalty in the emerald sections of town, far removed from the surface sheen of tourists on the hunt for latter-day bohemia, cable cars, and goat-cheese pizza. An unusual and powerful mystery. —*Peter Robertson*

Lindsey, David.
Mercy.
Doubleday, $19.95. 528p.

Lindsey's previous thrillers have sold well and garnered critical acclaim (including a much-deserved Edgar nomination for the taut and absorbing *In the Lake of the Moon*), but they have yet to create the kind of feeding frenzy at bookstore and supermarket checkout counters achieved by numerous, less-deserving novels. Perhaps it's because his work is so unrelentingly dark. That doesn't change with *Mercy*, a compelling descent into sexual compulsion and emotional brutality. The cop is Carmen Palma; the serial-killer expert is FBI agent Grant; and the dead are middle-class Houston women—some married, some single, some young, some middle-aged. All they have in common is hidden lesbianism and a taste for sadomasochism. They each die in horrifying circumstances, which Lindsey explores in dispassionate, chillingly clinical prose. The one link between the women is a psychiatrist with his own dark secrets. His affairs with the women and his odd perversions make him the perfect suspect, but the battle-scarred Palma thinks it's all too easy. He's right. A relentless researcher, Lindsey never wallows in sexual psychobabble; his world is full of pitch-black souls, hidden societies, pasts full of pain, and stillborn futures. A spine-tingling novel that exerts a subversive pull on even the most wary reader. —*Peter Robertson*

Littell, Robert.
The Once and Future Spy.
Bantam, $18.95. 304p.

Let's not bury the spy novel quite yet. Gorbachev's glasnost and le Carré's *Russia House* delivered crushing blows to the once-thriving genre, to be sure, but here's Robert Littell hunkered over the victim administering CPR in the form of an ingenious new foray into the dark heart of espionage. On one level, this novel seems like a traditional anti-CIA thriller: working outside Company sanctions, a select subgroup is planning to explode an atomic bomb at a research center in Teheran, making it look like the Iranians did it by mistake. But somebody appears to be onto the plan, and the group's leader responds by hiring a retired admiral to "walk back the cat," or find the leak. What he finds is "the Weeder," an obscure Company computer expert who is obsessed with the Revolutionary War. It is a match between opposites: the admiral, for whom "there was only one truth and it was knowable" (and worth committing atrocities for), and the Weeder, for whom "spilled milk was the amniotic fluid of history" and any question of truth must always be prefaced by asking "Whose truth? Which truth?" Littell wants us to like the Weeder and fear the admiral, of course, but he makes us work for it; we never know if the Weeder is a modern hero or a crazy computer nerd who thinks he's Nathan Hale. What we do know is that with or without iron curtains, the words "Whose truth? Which truth?" will never lose their power, especially on a purely human scale. —*Bill Ott*

Lovell, Marc.
Comfort Me with Spies.
Doubleday, $14.95. 184p.

He's an unlikely spy: too tall (six seven), too distracted by the opposite sex, too easily given to bouts of schoolboy blushing. But after 13 assignments, Appleton ("Apple") Porter is finally on his first solo mission. His objective is to penetrate the world of Canadian wrestling and discredit "Bull Massive," a wrestler who supports terrorists. Along the way, he also encounters the alluring Agnes De Grace, whose alarming lack of modesty allows her to slip out of matching pantie-and-skirt combinations with what Apple considers frightening speed. Lovell has been cranking out these gossamer-like Apple yarns for years. Anything but realistic, the plots are set up with admirable offhandedness. But the affable Apple, a master linguist who is hopelessly inept at most of life's simple tasks, usually manages to blunder through with pleasing panache. Fans will especially enjoy his escapades in the wrestling ring as his gangly body and oddly misplaced bones somehow conspire to send a succession of more seasoned battlers to the canvas in ungainly heaps. —*Peter Robertson*

Lovesey, Peter.
Bertie and the Seven Bodies.
Mysterious Press, $16.95, 293p.

One of the major pastimes of the British upper class in the late Victorian and Edwardian eras was the shooting party: a week in the country, at a rambling mansion with sufficient bedrooms to accommodate any and all liaisons the guests might be involved in, with slaughter of game the order of the day and brilliant clothes and grand meals the order of the evening. No one was more keen on the country weekend than Queen Victoria's eldest son, the future Edward VII, called "Bertie" by family and friends. As veteran British mystery writer Lovesey would have it, Bertie Prince of Wales fancies himself an amateur sleuth. When he and the Princess of Wales are invited to Desborough Hall for a shooting party, the guests begin dropping like flies, and Bertrie assumes the search for the perpetrator of what at first seems to be a series of deaths either by accident or by suicide. Narrrated by Bertie himself, the voice here is perfectly accurate; Lovesey gives his main character just the right tone of sophistication, charm, anti-intellectualism, and savoir faire—mixed in with ennui. A wonderfully put together puzzle.—*Brad Hooper*

Ludlum, Robert.
The Bourne Ultimatum.
Random, $21.95. 640p.

While required reading for Ludlumites, this latest installment in the adventures of Jason Bourne (*The Bourne Identity*; *The Bourne Supremacy*) is a highly problematic piece of escapist fiction. First, much of the tension rests on readers remembering the bad guys from the earlier books. The tale begins with mild-mannered teacher David Webb attempting to expunge his violent alter-ego, the deadly assassin Bourne. It seems to be working fine until Bourne's archenemy, the dying but still formidable Carlos, turns up. There's also trouble brewing from that motley gang of Vietnam War cutthroats, the Medusa, now evolving into a sinister secret society of powermongers. Ludlum spends much time tying both plots together, using one enemy as a lure for the other, but the package tends to unravel at every opportunity. In addition, the author, normally no slouch at speed plotting, lets his narrative drag here and there. A Caribbean hit on Webb's family takes an eternity, even though few loyal readers can seriously expect the brave wife and kiddies to get viciously whacked. Carlos is now in his sixties and obviously ailing, and Bourne/Webb is a tired and bitter 50. At times, both seem about as deadly as Mr. Rogers. Always a somewhat mannered prose stylist, Ludlum tries for some unexpected zaniness in his minor characters, but it's a doomed and largely unnecessary gesture. This disappointing novel is certain to do well at the cash register, but most fans would be better off rereading the far superior

Icarus Agenda while they await their hero's next serving of transglobal death and intrigue. —*Peter Robertson*

MacLeod, Charlotte.
The Gladstone Bag.
Mysterious Press, $16.95. 192p.

In MacLeod's latest mystery, Emma Kelling is asked to oversee the summer home of an elderly friend and play hostess to a troupe of writers and artists who have been invited to stay in the guest cottages. Emma is not aware that the guests are gold diggers, in both the literal and figurative sense. Not only did the writers and artists plan to live off the gracious hospitality of a wealthy old woman, but they also have a scheme to locate a treasure supposedly cached by pirates long ago. A murder changes everyone's plans, and Emma calls for help from her niece, Sara, and Sara's husband, Max Bittersohn, both of whom have appeared in many of MacLeod's earlier mysteries (e.g., *The Recycled Citizen*). Another successful whodunit from the indefatigable MacLeod. —*Denise Perry Donavin*

Martin, Lee.
Deficit Ending.
St. Martin's, $15.95. 208p.

With a few days of maternity leave still left, Fort Worth policewoman Deb Ralston is standing in line at the bank with a fussy infant on her hands. Moments later a holdup occurs and a bank teller is abducted. Days later the teller's body is dumped in a public park late at night. The usually stalwart Ralston is somewhat frazzled here: newborn Cameron isn't taking to breast-feeding or to the concept of sleeping at night, and there are other mouths to feed—sundry pets and kids as well as an unhappy husband unable to continue flying helicopters due to a disability. The death of the 19-year-old teller hits Deb hard, and when the criminals strike again, she is more than ready. Martin, a former policewoman, has created another smart, believable procedural. In addition, her spirited, oft-put-upon detective is a revelation in the genre: compassionate yet driven; battling with motherhood, money, and murder; yet never resorting to stereotypical displays of hard-boiled angst. —*Peter Robertson*

Martins, Richard.
Sandman.
Atheneum, $18.95. 247p.

When open season is declared on Chicago's Iranian cab drivers, young and headstrong FBI agent Mary McCaskey and burned-out city cop Jack Corrigan approach Philip Hallet, a professor and expert in Middle East affairs. Little do the two law officers know that Hallet, between grim bouts with a gin bottle, is secretly engaged in running several undercover Arab agents within the U.S. While cabbies are dropping like flies at the hands

Mystery & Espionage

of a serial killer, Hallet's agents are being taken out in a series of contract hits. Martins, author of the critically acclaimed *The Cinch*, which also featured the plucky McCaskey, is adept at subdividing his plot: one fragment follows Usher, the plainly psychotic hitman, another charts the predictable yet believable romance between Mary, always looking for a lost sheep to mother, and Hallet, a prime candidate for mothering if ever there was one. Whether Hallet and his merry men are patriots or terrorists is, of course, the author's main surprise. He keeps the answer cleverly hidden inside a complicated grid map of intersecting alliances and loyalites, and he relates the action in prose that jumps from precise to powerful to passionate. —*Peter Robertson*

Matera, Lia.
The Good Fight.
Simon & Schuster, $17.95. 205p.

In this latest installment of wealthy San Francisco lawyer Laura Di Palma's adventures, Matera uses as a backdrop the transformation of sixties radicals into eighties Yuppies. Laura's husband, Hal, hospitalized after a stroke caused in part by a war wound sustained in Vietnam, walks out of his room and disappears. Frantic with worry, Laura searches for him while also trying to cope with defending a radical activist against charges that he murdered an FBI spy. Matters escalate when Laura gets cryptic messages from Hal on her answering machine, the activist commits suicide, and Laura's law partner is found dead. Matera manages to utilize the genre's conventions and to develop her theme without resorting to stereotypical characters or plotting (although the FBI gets cast as the villain in pure sixties' terms). Di Palma certainly belongs in the same league as Sue Grafton's Kinsey Milhone and Sara Paretsky's V. I. Warshawski when it comes to brains, determination, and guts. A sure winner. —*Stuart Miller*

Mathis, Edward.
Out of the Shadows.
Scribner, $17.95. 224p.

In this third Dan Roman mystery to be published posthumously—after *Another Path, Another Dragon* (Scribner, 1988) and *The Burned Woman*, —Mathis again meshes his remote Texas locale and loner hero to perfection. But when Dan hits the road in search of Loretta Arganian, missing for over 15 years and major-league trouble in large doses, the book loses a little of its focus. From Los Angeles to Vegas to rural Tennessee, Dan tracks the elusive Loretta, now calling herself Nancy Taylor. From there *Shadows* cuts away to Johnny, a proud Indian guy, boozing hard, still carrying a torch for Nancy, even after she left him for an L.A. bigshot. Is Loretta/Nancy still alive? And is she even worth finding? Mathis' prose sparkles in places but isn't as finely honed as in past works. He's more effective evoking harsh terrain than he is in detailing interrelationships; Dan's stormy relationship with Susan is once again on rocky ground, and the

Mystery & Espionage

author gets a mite close to weeping melodrama in charting its vicissitudes. But Roman remains a captivating shamus: uneasy in his own mind, driven by personal demons, hard, flawed, but always likable. —*Peter Robertson*

McBain, Ed.
Three Blind Mice.
Arcade, $17.95. 304p.

Matthew Hope, the suave Florida lawyer, is back in the latest of McBain's series of cynically titled nursery-rhyme and fairy-tale themed novels including *The House That Jack Built* and *Cinderella*. The title characters of this lean tale are three Vietnamese who have been charged with raping a wealthy white woman on the hood of her Maserati. They are acquitted, then gruesomely murdered. The revenge-seeking husband of the rape victim is jailed, and it looks like he's heading for the chair, but Hope and his handsome investigator, Warren, start nosing around, looking for leaks in the airtight case. While the mystery is solved at a leisurely, teasing pace, we're treated to loving descriptions of every visible article of clothing each sexy woman wears and critiques of men's physiques. Between murders, visits to his client, and tennis lessons, Hope ruminates over bittersweet memories of his divorced wife and mixed-race relationships. (He's falling in love with the beautiful and virginal Vietnamese interpreter.) With some 50 books in print, McBain is an undisputed master of the genre—slick, wry, and satisfying. —*Donna Seaman*

McCrumb, Sharyn.
The Windsor Knot.
Ballantine, $16.95. 288p.

With the multilayered incandescence of the earlier *If Ever I Return, Pretty Peggy O* and this, the first Elizabeth MacPherson mystery in hardcover, Sharyn McCrumb continues an impressive and rapid ascent into the forefront of mystery writers. A Southern girl, a confirmed anglophile, and an aspiring forensic anthropologist, Elizabeth is on a tight schedule to wed Scottish marine biologist Cameron Dawson. Once married, the happy couple will be able to attend a Royal Garden Party in Edinburgh. But before that, the wedding must occur, the bimbo TV weatherwoman must act as bridesmaid, cousin Charles must find a bride fast—to beat Elizabeth to the inheritance—and Cameron must track down the garden gnome, missing from his Edinburgh house, who is sending cute postcards from around the world. Oh, and a murder must be solved. Or is it a murder? (The man appears to have died twice.) Will his wife have to pay back the insurance money? Will the dress be finished on time? And will Elizabeth look as good as her beloved Fergie did on her special day? The frenzied crosscutting between wet, hidebound, genteel Edinburgh society, and blistering hot, secretive, genteel Georgia life is priceless, as are the gnome dispatches. McCrumb's prose has enough sparkle to sustain what seems like an eternity before a reluctant descent into the mystery proper. Most readers won't even notice the wait. —*Peter Robertson*

McCullough, David, ed.
City Sleuths and Tough Guys.
Houghton, $19.95. 587p.

Limiting a crime collection to the urban and the hard-boiled barely qualifies as a limitation—at least in the canon of American mystery fiction. It does, however, give editor McCullough the opportunity to throw together some choice cuts from the hard-boiled storehouse. As with most short fiction collections, random sampling proves the best method of perusal. For example, by reading Mickey Spillane ("The Gold Fever Tapes") before Jim Thompson ("This World, Then the Fireworks"), it is possible to jump from the hardheaded and hokey to the hard-boiled and hateful. Also included are works by such disparate authors as Paretsky and Poe (Auguste Dupin as the first "city sleuth"), McBain and MacDonald, and a special treat in the form of Raymond Chandler and Billy Wilder's drastic yet effective reworking of James M. Cain's *Double Indemnity* for the 1944 film. This brief but revealing sightseeing trip through the mean streets comes with an introduction by McCullough in which he ponders the definition of "sleuth" and provides a thumbnail history of the hard-boiled tale. Chandler's classic essay on crime fiction, "The Simple Art of Murder," is also included. —*Peter Robertson*

Moseley, Walter
Devil in a Blue Dress.
Norton, $18.95. 224p.

Los Angeles in the 1940s remains a popular setting for historically minded mystery writers. Stuart Kaminksy has been mining the territory for years, and, more recently, James Ellroy has staked his own claim, especially with *L.A. Confidential.* Walter Mosley and his creation, Easy Rawlins, now join the parade but with several significant differences. Rawlins is a black sleuth, so we get to see a very different side of L.A.—Watts instead of Beverly Hills, after-hours jazz clubs rather than art deco movie-star haunts. Rawlins is a reluctant detective, but after being fired from his machinist job for talking back to the foreman, he agrees to help find a mysterious white woman in a blue dress. In a plot reminiscent of the film *Chinatown,* Rawlins soon finds himself thrashing about in a quagmire of murder, cover-up, and corruption that extends from bootleg whiskey salesmen to high-level government officials. Race relations in the forties is a persistent theme, but Mosley never preaches. This is an impressive debut by a writer who puts a refreshing spin on the conventions of the genre. —*Bill Ott*

Murray, William.
The Getaway Blues.
Bantam, $17.95. 224p.

"I always seem to get caught up in the middle of some sort of intrigue or find myself standing hip-deep in somebody's mess," remarks Shifty Anderson, the horseplaying magician who makes his third appearance in as many racetrack mysteries penned by Murray. Shifty's words were never more apt. Short of a betting stake while between magic gigs, Anderson hires on as a temporary chauffeur for an elderly eccentric who just happens to own horses. He soon begins to suspect that the murders of a couple of stunning blondes, apparently the work of a serial killer, may be connected to a scheme to bilk his employer of his millions, and not being one to mind his own business, his suspicion just as quickly puts his own life on the line. Danger to Shifty, the most likable of protagonists, is enough in itself to keep us turning the pages, but a genuinely puzzling mystery adds to the compulsion. This is Murray's best effort yet, and as readers of *When the Fat Man Sings* and *The King of the Nightcap* are fully aware, that means it's a doozy. —*Dennis Dodge*

Nabb, Magdalen.
The Marshal's Own Case.
Scribner, $17.95. 224p.

The image of the Italian city of Florence is, of course, that of one vast museum: a concentration of art to a degree unknown in any other community in the world. But, as with all urban areas, even sublime Florence has its seamy side; and it is into the Florentine underground that police marshal Guarnaccia must descend to apprehend the perpetrator of a particularly gruesome and sensational crime—the dismemberment of a transsexual prostitute, Lulu, a prominent figure in the nocturnal segment of Florence's outré society. Everyone knows Lulu was widely despised, but the policeman's charge is to find the one person who hated her enough to kill her. Ultimately, the marshal not only identifies the murderer, but, from the sordidness he's gotten involved in, learns some universal truths about the need for people to connect. This latest in Nabb's Guarnaccia series will reinforce the devotion of her veteran readers as well as inspire new ones. —*Brad Hooper*

Nava, Michael.
How Town: A Novel of Suspense.
Harper, $16.95. 208p.

In the third Henry Rios adventure, Nava brings the gay lawyer-sleuth back home. Henry's defending an old friend's younger brother on a murder rap of which, of course, he's innocent. But who's framing the man? Henry smells a quite fetid rat when he learns of his client's earlier close call on a child-molestation charge. The California valley town of Los Robles is not the kind of community to let probable "preverts" go unpunished. What distinguishes this book no less than its predecessor, *Goldenboy*, is how good a novel it is. Henry is a complex, vital character. So are virtually all the other personae; it's easy to get as involved with their personalities and the tiny subplots they're part of as with the sleuthing and the convincing pretrial court scenes. A genuinely engrossing mystery that, as is Nava's wont, stretches the psychological and emotional boundaries of the genre. *And* it's literate: the title's taken from an e. e. cummings poem about the way small-minded communities stifle love. —*Ray Olson*

Palmer, William J.
The Detective and Mr. Dickens.
St. Martin's, $17.95. 320p.

This raucously bawdy novel is cast in the form of a secret memoir written by Wilkie Collins, a real-life compatriot and protégé of Charles Dickens. Drawn into a murder investigation, Collins and Dickens collaborate with Holmesian inspector William Field, staking out a circle of decadent, upper-class gentlemen with a penchant for kinky sex. In their trafficking in pornography and their scheme to buy and drug young girls for sexual pleasure, the amateur detectives come face-to-face with the hypocritical nature of Victorian society. Rounding out the colorful cast are a group of prostitutes, beggars, and thieves (whom Dickens' fans will recognize from his books) who provide the two novelists with plenty of grist for the mill as well as entrée into London's teeming underclass. Amazingly entertaining, suspenseful reading for both mystery aficionados and literature lovers. —*Joanne Wilkinson*

Paretsky, Sara.
Burn Marks.
Delacorte, $17.95. 352p.

The greening of V. I. Warshawski continues apace in Paretsky's latest detective drama. Fictional sleuths all go through a midlife crisis of sorts; after about the fourth book the pizzazz that garnered them an audience begins to run a bit thin. One of two things happens: either they continue to recycle the same plots and the same wisecracks, ultimately becoming parodies of themselves, or they acquire depth, vulnerability, and the kind of roundness you don't usually associate with characters in genre novels. Fortunately, V. I. has taken the second route. It began in Paretsky's last novel, *Blood Shot*, when the feisty heroine exhibited a crack or two in her hard-boiled veneer. Those humanizing fault lines are even more visible this time, as V. I. must deal with several skeletons in her familial closet while exposing a quintessentially Chicago scam—politicians, real estate developers, and construction companies all in bed together, fondling their way toward greater profits. V. I. puts the hanky-panky to a stop and manages to sort through a host of unresolved feelings about her alcoholic aunt, her police-lieutenant mentor, and her own devil-may-care attitude. Don't worry, though, she's not in danger of becoming so sensitive it hurts your teeth. V. I. may be vulnerable, but she's no wuss. —*Bill Ott*

Mystery & Espionage

Parker, Robert B.
Stardust.
Putnam, $18.95. 256p.

Enough already! The mystery genre is wallowing in incest. Once an unspoken evil, now the key plot ingredient in every third detective story, incest has become to the modern American mystery what brain fever was to the nineteenth-century British novel. Unfortunately, for mystery fans the shock value of incest is long gone; moving through the genre these days one just assumes that all family members are sleeping together until it's proven otherwise. Thus, it's hardly giving away much to reveal that the latest Spenser novel hinges on an alcoholic, nymphomaniac TV star's incestuous relationship with her father. (The incest bug seems to be biting Boston sleuths especially hard: first Brady Coyne, in William G. Tapply's *Client Privilege*; now Spenser. Will Linda Barnes' Carlotta Carlyle be next in line?) It's a shame Parker fell prey to the incest plot here, because all the other elements are in place for vintage Spenser fare: there's plenty of Hawk, Spenser's black compatriot, who steals every scene he's in; there's the right amount of Boston ambience; and, of course, the one-liners and witty banter just keep coming. Aside from its worn-out linchpin, even the plot (TV star threatened, Spenser hired to protect her, TV star kidnapped, Spenser pissed) is engaging enough. Don't give up on Parker, but *please*, start a petition, do something, to ban incest as a plot device. —*Bill Ott*

Paulsen, Gary.
Kill Fee.
Donald I. Fine, $18.95. 250p.

The scam is simple, profitable, and awful. Young children are abducted, drugged, abused, sold, used as "entertainment" for groups of wealthy businessmen, then thrown naked from a private plane, their bodies scattered at random all over the country. A Denver cop investigating the latest incident is suddenly pulled from the case. Major-league clout is at work, but it cuts no mustard with reporter-sleuth Tally Janrus. Tally has a body littered with scars, a book's worth of sad stories, and a taste for the truth, however nasty. With the help of a grizzly old-timer who spots the planes landing and loading, the plot is exposed along with the formidable catalog of sickos behind it. When award-winning children's author Gary Paulsen decides to write for adults, he usually pulls out all the stops. This gut-wrenching tale of perversity is no exception, but Paulsen wisely steers clear of graphic excess, and he brings the whole package together with a cunning and frenetic climax. —*Peter Robertson*

Pearson, Ridley.
Probable Cause.
St. Martin's, $18.95. 275p.

Forensic investigator James Dewitt takes a new job, as a police sergeant in Carmel, California, hoping to put his past behind him—a past that includes his shooting to death the man who murdered his wife and permanently disabled one of his daughters. But after little more than two months, he fears he has a serial killer on his hands, a *trapper* —someone who slyly sets out traps, baits them, and then draws his victims in. The rapid twists and turns in the plot soon establish Dewitt as a suspect, even while his daughters' lives, and his, are in jeopardy. Although the contrariness of almost everyone else involved in the investigation—from the overweight, pencil-chewing commander to the voluptuous and sexually aggressive public defender—seems somewhat contrived on occasion, this is fiction for true true-crime buffs, filled with clues, both planted and missed, fancy forensic footwork, and intriguing snares. Pearson, author of the best-selling novel *Undercurrents*, among others, combines a little romance, a little misdirected loyalty, and a whole lot of suspense. A satisfying, gripping police procedural. —*Eloise Kinney*

Peters, Ellis.
The Heretic's Apprentice.
Mysterious Press, $16.95. 192p.

The intricacies of medieval politics, religious and secular, are neatly exploited by Peters in her latest mystery starring Brother Cadfael. A young man, Elave, returns from a pilgrimage to the Holy Land determined to fulfill two missions of his late master, a once prominent merchant and generous donor to the Shrewsbury monastery. When Elave is deemed a heretic and a murderer, Brother Cadfael helps to seek the truth, aided by his friend Sheriff Hugh Beringar. Fascinating arguments over church beliefs and teachings unfold amid life-threatening adventures and calculated twists of plot. The ever-popular Brother Cadfael's literary origins were charted in the recent trilogy of stories, *A Rare Benedictine*. —*Denise Perry Donavin*

Peters, Ellis.
A Rare Benedictine.
Mysterious Press, $19.95. 118p.

Three classic stories featuring Brother Cadfael, Peters' medieval monk whose powers of deduction are practically miraculous. The first tale, which offers American readers their first glimpse of Cadfael's literary origins, finds him a scribe and soldier returning from war in 1120. He has an inclination to lead a more stable life, so after solving his first mystery and saving his master's neck (but not his property—which ends up in the hands of the church), Cadfael heads for Shrewsbury to join the Benedictines. Two equally tempting tales follow. All are aptly illustrated by Clifford Harper's color drawings. The mystery of Brother Cadfael's beginnings, now solved, will certainly delight his many fans. —*Denise Perry Donavin*

✓ **Pickard, Nancy.**
Bum Steer.
Pocket, $16.95. 240p.

The unusual bequest of a Kansas cattle ranch to the Port Frederick, Massachusetts, Civic Foundation sends director Jenny Cain, plucky heroine of *Dead Crazy* and *No Body* (Pocket, 1986), into decidedly foreign territory. The murder of ranch owner Cat Benet, his odd choice of inheritor, and rural Kansas in general soon have Jenny perplexed. Things only get worse: a private plane nearly crashes, shots are fired at night, and Jenny ruins a pair of red leather shoes delivering baby calves in the Kansas mud. Then there's the matter of ranch hand Quentin Harlan, who may be the killer but who also is deliciously appealing to the happily married Jenny. The earlier novels in the Cain series, while both delightful, were at times overly prim and mannered; here Pickard hits her stride with what may well be a breakthrough book. The switch in locale to the author's home state is a resounding success, and the plotting, always a treat in a Pickard novel, has taken several giant steps forward in terms of complexity. The ending, the old switched-identities gambit, is delivered with enough finesse to have the reader hastily skipping backwards to find missed clues. Naturally, they all check out perfectly. —*Peter Robertson*

Pronzini, Bill.
Jackpot.
Delacorte, $16.95. 224p.

It's ironic that the most dynamic, evolving, and human protagonist in detective fiction doesn't have a name. However entertaining Spenser, McGee, Scudder, Warshawski, etc., may be, they never change significantly. Pronzini's "Nameless" detective is always a little different, though, and here, in his eighteenth book, he's still recovering from the starvation ordeal he endured in *Shackles* when a young woman asks him to investigate the suicide of her brother. It seems the young man had just won $200,000 on a Reno gambling spree and had everything to live for. The trail leads Nameless to the Mob and personal treachery while he confronts his own personal limitations. More a leg in a psychic journey than a straight hard-boiled mystery, but it's deeply satisfying on both levels. —*Wes Lukowsky*

Putre, John Walter.
A Small and Incidental Murder.
Scribner, $16.95. 245p.

This excellent first novel gives readers a new hard-boiled protagonist and a fabulous setting for a murder and its solution. Doll is the man's name. Just Doll. Nothing else. He arrives on a little coastal island on the Maryland Eastern Shore at the request of his old buddy (sort of) Ellis LeCates. A clear and present stranger among the community of Chesapeake watermen, Doll sets out to investigate the death of LeRoy Carrow, a skipjack captain who made enemies among both his fellow fishermen and the outside real estate interests who threaten to buy up island property, build subdivisions, and consequently destroy the centuries-old traditions of the local drudgers, tongers, and eelers. Lots of atmosphere, solid writing, and a clear sense of mysterious mission drive this tale to a satisfactory conclusion. —*Martin Brady*

Randisi, Robert.
Separate Cases.
Walker, $18.95. 210p.

Miles Jacoby, a New York private eye, is flying solo after the death of his partner and mentor. Appearing as an expert witness, Miles is slashed to ribbons by opposing counsel. The resulting crisis in confidence has Miles floundering in an alcoholic haze until he reluctantly agrees to help the widow of a slain private eye. The police feel he was the victim of a serial killer; the widow believes that a sensitive case may have backfired, with the murderer using the serial killer's modus operandi to conceal the motive. Each Randisi book is better than its entertaining predecessor, and the thoroughly likable Jacoby may be on the cusp of a popularity enjoyed by series detectives Amos Walker, Nameless, and Spenser. —*Wes Lukowsky*

Reeves, Robert.
Peeping Thomas.
Crown, $18.95. 256p.

Boston's Combat Zone isn't what it was. It's smaller, for one thing, and seedier, if that's possible. But it stands in a desirable section of town. And Yuppie developers stand ready to swoop. In addition, the porn dealers face angry feminists battling hard for a restrictive city ordinance. Dissipated professor Thomas Theron proves the ideal guide to the seamy side for the strong-willed ladies as they picket a porn store. Then the place blows up, and Emma Pierce, their leader, is killed. Basking in his sabbatical, plenty of alcohol on hand, and only the faintest of emotions stirring in the presence of his delectable ex-wife, Theron finds himself both a tabloid sensation and a reluctant detective. This is the second work in a series that garnered impressive reviews with the first outing, *Doubting Thomas*. It's easy to see why—brisk, delirious dialogue; meticulously placed wit; and a lively spin on the by-now jaded academic mystery angle. Thomas is just the kind of professor you wish you'd had. —*Peter Robertson*

Rendell, Ruth.
Going Wrong.
Mysterious Press, $18.95. 260p.

If you want this one from *his* point of view, read the book. Instead, take a minute to see it from hers. To start with, she's young. On the street she meets a couple of working class boys, one of whom lets her have a puff of a joint. Her mother wouldn't approve, but she likes him. She even steals some things for him and turns a blind eye to his more shady dealings. Now cut to 10 or 12 years later. He's out of crime and *very* rich. But *trés nouveau*. No, worse than that. And she's changed. Her rebellion has become the standard artsy-liberal one. She even has a boyfriend. But Guy can't stand this. Sentimental, dull, cunning, he wants to know who turned her against him. Who he has to get rid of to assure her love. . . . Now look at it from his point of view and see the subtlety, control, and pity in Rendell's intelligent, dissecting craft. —*Stuart Whitwell*

Mystery & Espionage

Reynolds, William J.
The Naked Eye.
Putnam, $18.95. 288p.

The detective is named Nebraska. Yes, it's an odd name; confusing, too, since he lives and works in Nebraska. In this fifth entry in a critically acclaimed series, Nebraska goes to Minnesota, where he tracks down a young male runaway and splatters the nose of local blowhard Steven Dimand, the would-be abductor, all over his face. Dimand swears revenge. Operating under three separate aliases, Nebraska takes off for the Twin Cities. The trail soon leads to Joshua Fienman, a powerful businessman providing the muscle now chasing Nebraska. The detective gets friendly with Josh, they both end up chasing a suitcase full of cocaine, and the incognito dick finds himself getting friendly with Josh's sister, Sharon. The new locale makes a nice change for the Nebraska series, which tends to overdo the small-town quaintness. Despite an occasional misstep—Does combing one's hair back and donning a pair of funny glasses really make for an effective disguise?—Reynolds again offer a sizzling plot and a wealth of characters who seldom need much encouragement to fire off an affectionate parody of classic gumshoe-speak. A fine series. —*Peter Robertson*

Rivers, Caryl.
Indecent Behavior.
Dutton, $19.95. 416p.

The novel's title refers to its two lascivious heroes as well as the immorality they discover in pursuit of a news story. Sally Ellenberg and Boston Brahmin Jack Forbes Aiken are coworkers at the *World Herald* newspaper. They suddenly find themselves so passionately in love that sexual fantasy and erotic acts nearly consume their daily schedules. When not in bed, Sally and Jack are doing some heavy-duty investigative reporting about mind games (involving brain surgery and implants) that are authorized by higher-ups in the federal government and undertaken by a wacko neurosurgeon. Sally insistently evokes the names of journalism's demigods—Woodward and Bernstein—to justify her illegal acts and dogged pursuit of a story that her editors disbelieve. At least one form of indecent behavior is cleared up by the novel's end, but it would spoil the suspense to say which. Rivers never lets the social-issues message trip up the actions of her witty, lusty characters. —*Denise Perry Donavin*

Roberts, Les.
Full Cleveland.
St. Martin's, $15.95. 224p.

A simple scam turns complex. Fake ads are sold for a phony magazine, and a guy and his hooker wife take a powder with the money. Soon the small-change con has escalated, with thousand-dollar bills replacing hundreds, Mob connections surfacing, and blackmail and murder entering the picture. This is the second mystery, following *Pepper Pike*, to feature Cleveland detective

Milan Jacovich. Les Roberts is a talented new crime writer who already has the California-based actor-sleuth Saxon up and running in a concurrent series. The Slovenian Jacovich is an altogether more amiable, down-to-earth character than Saxon—uglier, unabashedly ethnic, considerably less ego-driven. In this outing, he is aided (if that's the right word) by one Rocky Bustamente, a Mob gofer forced on Jacovich as an assistant. Rocky favors polyester outfits accented by white-belt and shoe combos, unkindly referred to as the "Full Cleveland" ensemble. Like the Saxon novels, this is slick and tough and plotted to perfection. —*Peter Robertson*

Satterthwait, Walter.
At Ease with the Dead.
St. Martin's, $16.95. 256p.

Santa Fe, New Mexico, private eye Joshua Croft, fresh from *Wall of Glass* (St. Martin's, 1988), returns in this page-turner about the Navahos and a 60-year-old unsolved murder. Dignified and enigmatic Navaho Daniel Begay asks Joshua to find the remains of a fellow tribesman, removed from the Indian reservation in 1925 by an archaeological team and missing since the team leader was murdered shortly after returning to his home in El Paso. Joshua soon learns that looking into old crimes sometimes stirs up very bad trouble, as he and Daniel must race to a remote corner of a Navaho reservation in order to stop another murder. Using the potentially hackneyed plot device of an old, unsolved murder to excellent effect, the author produces a riveting, highly readable mystery. The vivid characters and evocative use of the Navaho setting are reminiscent of Tony Hillerman. Hope for further installments in this series; Satterthwait is an author to watch. —*Stuart Miller*

Schopen, Bernard.
The Desert Look.
Mysterious Press, $17.95. 256p.

This is a brave and unusual book, more textured than most mysteries, more concerned with visions and myths than straightforward seek-and-solve. The "desert look" is really more of a stare, seemingly blank but possessing an awareness of wide-open spaces, a respect for an alien environment. TV newswoman Miranda Santee finds Jack Ross in the Nevada desert, putting his P.I. career behind him and hiding out. Scared and desperate, she carries a picture of two Vegas showgirls and sports a gunshot wound in her shoulder. And she has a story. Pretty much every character in this multilayered novel has a story—some of them intersect, some diametrically oppose one another, a few are outright lies. Sometime in the past, a Reno hood was crossed by two women for money; one escaped, one died in a hotel brawl, one may be Jack's mother. The genealogical lines become hazy after a while, but that might just be the sun from Schopen's sparse, resonant desert background. Or perhaps it's the flashing neon from glittery Reno and Vegas, where Jack reluctantly goes in search of answers. What he finds is a dazzling array of venal, sexually driven criminal types—gamblers, killers, whores, or, worse, people pretend-

Mystery & Espionage

ing not to be gamblers, killers, whores, or some ugly, twisted combination. —*Peter Robertson*

Simonson, Sheila.
Larkspur.
St. Martin's, $16.95. 240p.

Regency romancer Simonson has turned her hand to mystery writing with very satisfying results. The heroine is Lark Dailey, part-time basketball coach at the local junior college and full-time owner of Larkspur Books in a small, remote town in Northern California. The Fourth of July weekend is spent at the elegant summer lodge of poet David Llewellyn, an old friend of Lark's mother. Also in attendance are Lark's lover and local policeman, Jay Dodge; a local newspaper and small press publisher and his wife and daughter; Llewellyn's niece (an English literature teacher) and her unpleasant husband (under indictment for drug growing); an always-on-stage ex-dancer; a surly Filipino cook; and a beautiful Mexican houseboy. Llewellyn's death by poisoning (a homemade decoction of larkspur in his Campari and soda) of course brings everything to a halt, and not surprisingly all the houseguests turn out to have had the means, motive, and opportunity for doing the deed. Simonson's use of standard plot devices and a romantic subplot are handled with surprising skill. Watch for the next one. —*Stuart Miller*

Skvorecky, Josef.
The End of Lieutenant Boruvka.
Norton, $18.95. 168p.

Bone-weary cops who carry the world's sorrows on their slumping shoulders are familiar figures in mystery fiction, but there is nothing hackneyed about Lieutenant Boruvka of the Prague police. The plight of this mournful detective, to whom "each murder victim seemed like a tragically unfinished novel," never feels like a literary device. Watching Boruvka struggle with the Communist bureaucracy in six stories set just before and after the "Prague Spring" of 1968, we share the burden of solving crimes in a society where the truth is usually something to be avoided. Whether the problem at hand involves a skeleton unearthed from a building site or the apparent suicide of an insignificant chanteuse, Boruvka battles his Party-member superiors with an ingratiating mix of cynicism and quiet cunning. Forced to take a personal stand in the last story, his action becomes not an abstract sacrifice for honor, but the piercing cry of an individual man who can't take it any longer. That the Iron Curtain has finally collapsed may have more to do with the unsung Lieutenant Boruvkas than it does with the policies of any politician. —*Bill Ott*

Sprinkle, Patricia Houck.
Murder in the Charleston Manner.
St. Martin's, $17.95. 288p.

Members of old-line Charleston, South Carolina, families have a reputation for exquisite manners. Sheila Travis gets an opportunity to observe whether this inbred tradition can triumph over the trials and tribulations that accompany murder when she visits her Aunt Mary's friends, Dolly Langdon and Marion Wimberly, two elderly sisters living near the Battery in Charleston. Fresh from her sleuthing in *Murder at Markham*, Sheila has reluctantly agreed to visit the sisters at her aunt's behest following a disturbing letter from Dolly detailing various accidents that have recently occurred to several family members. Sprinkle has turned out an entertaining story, replete with a wealth of likely suspects, all with motives, means, and opportunity—a distantly related judge drops dead, Dolly's nurse is murdered, a neighbor has her head bashed in, a granddaughter is poisoned, and the house is robbed of its silver and the family Bible. With its slower-paced, Charleston-like ambience, this mystery will perhaps best be enjoyed on a shady porch with a cooling drink of iced tea at one's side. —*Stuart Miller*

Stroud, Carsten.
Sniper's Moon.
Bantam, $18.95. 384p.

Frank Keough carries plenty of burdensome psychological baggage: his father's illustrious career as a cop; the death of his mother; and the gradual unraveling of his own life, which, if the mounting evidence against him is found true, will include conviction as a cop killer. Woven into the fabric of this first novel, in which sex and death are fodder for grim laughs, is the kind of cop-world detail found in the fiction of William Caunitz and in Stroud's previous nonfiction work, *Close Pursuit*. The tale may be a bit overloaded with angst and with the author's poetic, dirt-splattered gutter prose; Stroud can turn turgid without warning, but when not obsessed with Oedipal snakes and ladders, he expertly pilots his ambitious plot through seas of ambiguity, fueled by dialogue that strips away illusions the way a heat gun strips paint. A flawed but fearless, full-bloodied crime-thriller debut. —*Peter Robertson*

Sublett, Jesse.
Tough Baby.
Viking, $16.95. 195p.

As in Sublett's previous *Rock Critic Murders*, the plot here features every conceivable rock-music excess. Bass player and sleuth Martin Fender gets back to Austin, Texas, after a grueling tour. His steady girl wants space, so he ties one on, meets another girl, and heads off to a party. But a Mickey gets slipped, and Fender wakes up feeling groggy. The girl doesn't wake up. She's in a coma, after having been raped and beaten with an unusual choice of weapon—Martin's trusty Fender Precision bass. At this point, the plot takes off in all sorts of confusing directions, but most of the entertainment comes from following the antics of the boys in the band, rock 'n' roll rebels all, who are acting very strange (even for rock guys)—buying fancy new Gibson Flying V guitars, running naked through nightclubs after biker women, and simply vanishing. Like its predecessor, this novel has a rock 'n' roll heart and a

Mystery & Espionage

built-in gutsiness. Sublett's sleazy-side-of-Austin setting adds to the low-rent charm. —*Peter Robertson*

✓ **Symons, Julian.**
Death's Darkest Face.
Viking, $16.95. 272p.

A fictional "Julian Symons" receives a manuscript in which a dead actor friend describes his attempt to be "sort of a detective." Hoping to determine his father's role in the disappearance of a poet in England between the wars, Geoffrey Elder puts the pieces together in a puzzle that involves adultery, gambling, revenge, and possibly murder. The manuscript begins with Geoffrey's childhood—dreams of tennis, a beautiful girl, and a father struggling with strong emotions barely held in check. As the narrative jumps between Geoffrey's investigation in the sixties and his recollections of the thirties, we learn of affairs between servants and masters, of the relationship between Geoffrey's father and the poet's lover, of a whole tangled fabric of repression and secret lives. The novel is less a straightforward piece of detection than an emotionally turbulent journey into a father's love—a painstakingly detailed, multifaceted sojourn that brings with it both understanding and guilt. We are offered two "solutions": Geoffrey's, which is heartfelt, emotional, and lightly dipped in pathos, and Symons' own, which is cerebral and fiendishly clever. *Death's Darkest Face* stands as a quintessential example of how the mystery genre can function as a tool for the skilled prose craftsman to get at something considerably deeper and more resonant than whodunit. —*Peter Robertson*

Tapply, William G.
Client Privilege.
Delacorte, $16.95. 272p.

What Brady Coyne fans like about the exquisitely lazy lawyer-sleuth is the way he never lets ideas get in the way of a good time. He has principles, yes, but the most important ones involve tying flies and hitting five irons. A mystery series hero who knows the value of fun is something to be treasured, so you can't blame fans for starting to worry when they see that Brady's ninth case involves a lot of philosophical breast-beating over the principle of "client privilege." Brady's old law school pal, Chester ("Pops") Popowski is up for a federal judgeship, but a blackmailer has got wind of Pops' dallying in the secretarial pool. When the blackmailer turns up dead hours after a meeting with Brady, the fun-loving counselor becomes a murder suspect. Worse yet, it looks like good old Pops may be the killer, but Brady's lips are sealed due to client privilege. This isn't vintage Brady by any means—too principled for that—but there is enough endearing sloth, good-natured selfishness, and unrepentant Winston smoking and bourbon drinking to keep devotees happy. —*Bill Ott*

✓ **Thomas, Ross.**
Twilight at Mac's Place.
Mysterious Press, $19.95. 343p.

Thomas' characters are memorable rascals, his plots intricate yet elegant, his locales beautifully drawn, and his lean prose simply some of the best writing being done today. If that weren't enough, his genially cynical novels of political corruption celebrate people who hornswoggle corrupt governments. In this one, Thomas brings back McCorkle and Padillo and introduces the delightful, but dead, Steadfast ("Steady") Haynes and his quite alive son, Granville. Just before dying of natural causes, failed-Quaker-turned-government-destabilizer-extraordinaire Steady spreads the word that he's written his memoirs. The CIA is worried; they can't quash the book because Steady never officially worked for them. When they try to buy the manuscript from Granville, they discover another bidder. When the bodies start to pile up, Granville, a former homicide detective and truly his father's son, seeks help from Washington restaurateurs McCorkle and Padillo, no strangers to mayhem and chicanery and old friends of Steady's. Thomas fans will know Mac and Padillo from *The Back Up Men* and *The Cold War Swap*. They'll also know the dialogue will crackle, and the wit, action, and ambience will be as abundant as the portions served in Mac's Place. Sadly, Ross Thomas is under-appreciated. Fans of Elmore Leonard and Robert B. Parker are missing out on something special if they don't add Ross Thomas to their list of can't-miss authors. —*Thomas Gaughan*

Thornburg, Newton.
The Lion at the Door.
Morrow, $18.95. 288p.

It seemed to Tom Kohl like his life had finally bottomed out. After burying both his parents, having his wife leave him, and losing the family farm in rural Illinois, he moves to Seattle to live with boyhood pal Ken. He works long hours as a laborer, enduring contempt from upscale women in trendy bars and from Dianne, Ken's Yuppie girl friend. Things change when Ken gets drunk and kills a Mob-connected pedestrian in a hit-and-run accident. Ken falls to pieces, and Kohl finds himself with two lives to salvage—his own and Ken's. Women present further problems: there's Dianne, who rises in Kohl's estimations as Ken becomes more psychotic, and there's Bobbi, a waitress with an eye for the main chance, who may or may not have Kohl's best interests at heart. In the Elmore Leonard tradition, though lacking the master's light touch with dark humor, this novel by the author of *To Die in California* (Little, Brown, 1973) is fueled with enough enigmatically flawed characters and poignantly wasted dreams to engage our sympathy and hold our attention. —*Peter Robertson*

Mystery & Espionage

Turow, Scott.
The Burden of Proof.
Farrar, $22.95. 755p.

Turow's blockbuster *Presumed Innocent* is now being made into a feature film starring Harrison Ford, and this eagerly awaited follow-up novel should have 'em standing in line at the reserve shelf. It's a big, sometimes confusing, often riveting piece of fiction, and what failures it exhibits shouldn't deter the author's ardent fans. The hero is Alejandro Stern, the shrewd, silver-tongued, middle-aged defense attorney of Turow's debut novel. When he returns from out-of-town legal doings, Stern finds his wife, Clara, dead from her own hand, overwhelmed by car fumes in the garage. Stern's uneasiness at this event is compounded when he finds a medical report revealing that Clara had genital herpes. Furthermore, his brother-in-law is being investigated for insider-trading abuses, and his additional probes into matters of family and friends reveal tawdry sexual, business, legal, and medical episodes that complicate his personal and professional life unmercifully. (They also hasten Stern's rush into various romantic affairs, which add to torturous self-evaluation yet at the same time appear to fulfill the fantasies of his mid-life-crisis-beset mind.) Getting through the many overwritten passages of narrative reflection won't be much fun, but the rewards of Turow's thoroughly contemporary outlook on life and his generally potent prose are many indeed. —*Martin Brady*

Turtledove, Harry.
A World of Difference.
Ballantine, $4.95. 309p.

A joint U.S.–Soviet space probe encounters aliens on a distant planet, leading to a joint manned expedition. Unfortunately, the aliens are involved in their own hot war, and human intervention threatens to revive the cold war back on earth. There is nothing surpassingly brilliant about this novel and the pacing lags a bit in spots. But there is care, thought, and intelligence throughout. Another well-told tale from an author who has managed to combine quality and quantity. —*Roland Green*

Vachss, Andrew.
Blossom.
Knopf, $17.97. 236p.

You can usually find Burke cruising the neon hell of New York's grungiest streets, hunting down abused children with the help of his network of scum experts, hookers, and crazed society rejects. The fifth novel in Andrew Vachss' series of unrelenting comic-book-scenarios-gone-noirishly-berserk finds Burke flying solo in the alien heartland of Indiana, without his friends and without his invaluable grid map of contacts. At the summons of a former cellmate, whose nephew is the chief suspect in a serial-murder case, Burke must test the boy's innocence and then prove it. Further complicating matters is the beautiful Blossom, posing as a waitress at a local diner but actually looking for her sister's killer. Like his close friend and fellow crime writer

Eugene Izzi, Vachss is fervently committed to aiding the victims of child abuse and exposing the abusers; that commitment shows up here as the distinction between moral ambiguity (Burke) and profound emotional sickness (the killer). *Blossom* isn't perfect. Vachss' women seldom emerge much beyond the familiar hooker-with-a-heart-of-gold composite. Despite that flaw, though, the Burke series remains one of the brightest lights on the mystery horizon. Vachss continues to explore our secret darkness in strikingly stylized yet gut-wrenching fashion. —*Peter Robertson*

Vine, Barbara.
Gallowglass.
Crown/Harmony, $19.95. 288p.

The fourth novel British mystery writer Ruth Rendell has published under the Vine pseudonym displays to advantageous degree her expertise at dissecting dysfunctional psychology with clinical accuracy. Twisted people (and, accordingly, a twisted plot) are the hallmarks of Vine/Rendell. In this instance, the reader comes to know the perversities of lamebrain Joe and his malicious friend, Sandor, who concoct—Sandor actually drawing up the plans, Joe just following along out of dumb adoration—a scheme to kidnap a wealthy woman. Events transpiring in the woman's household—particularly, her relations with and the backgrounds of the people in her domestic employ—add double and triple layers to the conflict, all to the good of the reader of this totally engaging thriller. —*Brad Hooper*

Wallace, Pamela.
Small Town Girls.
St. Martin's, $19.95. 448p.

A potboiler with pretensions by the co-scriptwriter for the film *Witness*. Wallace has whipped up a frothy tale of four gals from a smothering California town bound by a deep, dark secret. Shelly, illegitimate daughter of the town tramp, is gang raped. Her girlfriends come to the rescue and end up killing the ringleader. They vow never to tell and go their separate ways. Shelly hightails it to L.A. where she quickly becomes a *Playboy* centerfold, fashion model, and after a husband's death, head of a cosmetic firm. Val becomes a hotshot TV talk show host and after years of experimenting finally finds true love with another woman. Barbara stays behind in an unhappy marriage, takes to the bottle, and winds up having an affair with one of the rapists. While under the influence, she spills the beans. When he blackmails her, she kills him and commits suicide. The fourth member of the group, Kate, an Oscar-winning screenwriter, is so moved she decides to write about the whole sorry mess. A genre lover's delight: scoops of sex, glamour, and intrigue sprinkled generously with clichés. —*Donna Seaman*

Washburn, L. J.
Dog Heavies.
Tor, $17.95. 288p.

Silver-haired Lucas Hallam may be a Tinseltown extra and low-budget Hollywood sleuth, but his past—as a Texas Ranger, a gunslinger, and a Pinkerton man—is downright mythical. Hallam's latest job—guarding the spoiled son of a famous director while the kid is sent to a Texas ranch to learn cowboy tricks for an upcoming part—is tolerable only because it offers the sleuth a free trip home. The youngster, predictably bumptious beyond all belief, learns fast, flirts with the daughter of the ranch owner, and, in common with the other movie stuntmen along for the trip, annoys the local ranch hands to distraction. When things heat up with some rustling, Lucas finds himself reluctantly repeating some of the heroics of his past. Part western, part history lesson, and part (a very small part) mystery, this warm, likable hybrid doesn't have much to do with crime, but there's plenty of movie and cowboy lore and even a few scalpings. Best of all, there's the slow-talkin' Lucas, as chivalrous and low-key a hero as ever strapped on a six-shooter.
—*Peter Robertson*

Wilhelm, Kate.
Sweet, Sweet Poison.
St. Martin's, $16.95. 240p.

Al and Sylvie don't belong here. They're Bronx-born and -bred, working stiffs. So when they hit the lottery jackpot and buy an abandoned mill in rural upstate New York, local feathers are ruffled, or, rather, fur because first the watchdog the couple buy is poisoned. Then the young man who helped them buy the property overdoses. Then their financial advisor is stung to death. All this, to say nothing of the very unfriendly letters they're receiving. This is the fourth case for retired cop Charlie Meiklejohn and his wife, Constance (three novels and one short story), and marks a welcome return to crime writing for Kate Wilhelm, a Nebula Award–winning sf author. She offers studied prose, an almost too heavy dose of local color, and tightly knit plotting in a novel that isn't like most mysteries. Here, hidden fantasies emerge from the subtext, and narrative detours that would lose most crime writers are handled adroitly. Her elderly detectives arrive on the pages fully formed, their marriage a picture of compatibility at once believable and uncheapened by sentiment. —*Peter Robertson*

Wilson, Barbara.
Gaudí Afternoon.
Seal Press, $8.95. 196p.

Fans of Wilson's antiauthoritarian detective, Pam Nilsen (featured in *Murder in the Collective, Sisters of the Road,* and *The Dog Collar Murders*) will be only temporarily disappointed by her absence in this book, in which heroine Cassandra Reilly unravels the mystery of a missing child in a gender-bending romp through Barcelona, Spain. There hasn't been this much cross-dressing, confusion, and hilarity since Rosalind entered the Forest of Arden. Add a subplot about the magic realist novel Cassandra is translating, throw in conventioneers from the European Society for Organ Transplantation and a foot therapist with the unlikely name of April Schauer, and you have a novel that (to paraphrase one of the characters) is a little unconventional, but works. As in her other books, Wilson manages to shoehorn in the feminist perspective on a larger social issue—this time, tolerance for diversity and ambiguity. —*Marie Kuda*

✓ **Wright, Eric.**
A Sensitive Case.
Scribner, $17.95. 224p.

Moments of tranquility seldom disturb the life of Toronto policeman Charlie Salter. Chronically understaffed on the job and more than a shade perturbed on the home front by his wife's apparent affair, Charlie is gamely trying to cope when the murder of psychotherapist Linda Thomas is thrown onto his already full plate. His unlikely savior is an unassuming career copper, Mel, only days from retirement. The Thomas death requires treading softly: her clients included a television personality and a prominent politician, her lover was a college president, and her profession carries the pervasive hint of possible prostitution being served up on the side. Seventh in the winning Salter series, *A Sensitive Case* is really a showcase for Mel; we watch the older man's hopes and dreams—a log cabin, peace from tiresome relatives, long walks with Willis the Dog—all fall into place in ways both expected and otherwise. Adept sleuthing, down-to-earth humor, offbeat charm, and surprising warmth—the Charlie Salter books have it all. —*Peter Robertson*

Science Fiction

Anthony, Piers.
Phaze Doubt.
Putnam, $17.95. 304p.

Phaze/Photon is taken over by the Hectare, a ruthless race of game players with a distinctive code of honor, in this high-spirited conclusion to the Apprentice Adept series. It's up to Nepe/Flach, one of the few "adepts" still at large, to fulfill the three-part quest to save the planet and to persuade Lysander, an agent for the Hectare, to play his part in the prophecy. It's not easy to step into this series. Although Anthony spends the first portion of the book recapping the merging of the two worlds Photon and Phaze and explaining how science and magic have melded, most of the inhabitants are shape-changers with dual personalities; consequently, it's hard to keep them straight. Always imaginative, Anthony has invented some intriguing games and tasks for his characters. By weaving in themes of love and honor, he imbues the story with an appealing, fairy-tale quality. Followers of the series won't be disappointed. —*Candace Smith*

Anthony, Piers.
And Eternity.
Morrow, $15.95. 356p.

Having dealt with Satan in *For Love of Evil*, Anthony takes on God in the seventh and final novel in his enormously popular Incarnations of Immortality series: "After God, all else is anticlimactic," he says in an afterword. Three women (two ghosts and one mortal teenager) join together in a quest that leads them, ultimately, to a replacement for the Incarnation of God, who actually is offstage for the duration of the story—"contemplating His own greatness, to the exclusion of all else." In part, Anthony is using the novel as a platform to speak out on the state of the world—pollution, overpopulation, war, etc.—and about the concepts of good and evil. Rather than being didactic, however, the tale is, by turns, rollicking, bawdy, sexy, and thought-provoking. Recommended for the series' many fans. —*Sally Estes*

Ash, Constance.
The Stalking Horse.
Berkley/Ace, $3.95. 304p.

In this sequel to *The Horsegirl* (Ace, 1988), Glennys, a trained horse handler, is working in the theaters of the capital city, St. Lucien, where she is caught up in both political and artistic intrigues, as well as war and romance. The book survives a somewhat predictable plot by superior characterization and outstanding world building, as Ash impressively brings St. Lucien to life. Highly recommended for most fantasy readers. —*Roland Green*

Asimov, Isaac and Silverberg, Robert.
Nightfall.
Doubleday, $19.95. 384p.

This novel is a first-rate expansion of Asimov's classic short story about a planet with six suns, where darkness comes only every few milennia and leads to mass panic and the collapse of civilization. The novel follows the original story closely but develops it further, putting on-stage much of the background to the original story. The actual time of nightfall is still as chilling as ever, and the aftermath is shown with a good many surprises. Using sf classics as springboards for new novels seems to be developing quite a vogue; this one should set the standard for the category for some time. —*Roland Green*

Asprin, Robert.
Phule's Company.
Berkley/Ace, $3.95. 240p.

The start of a new series by the prolific Mr. Asprin includes his first essay on military science fiction in some time. Captain Willard Phule, a wealthy playboy officer in the Space Legion, is sent as punishment to command a company of his fellow misfits. Before the story is done, Phule's men are a notably more effective and considerably wealthier organization. The tone is lighthearted without being stupid or silly, and Asprin's knowledge of the military (especially of fencing) is displayed to good advantage. —*Roland Green*

Asprin, Robert and Abbey, Lynn.
Stealers' Sky.
Berkley/Ace, $3.95. 256p.

The twelfth (and apparently concluding) book in the Thieves' World series—the longest-running and in many ways the best shared-world anthology. Here, the thieves roam the ruins of Sanctuary under cover of a dust storm. Many of the series regulars return with good stories, and about as many ongoing conflicts are resolved. An honorable coda to one of the ground-breaking projects in modern sf, and recommended for all Thieves' World fans. —*Roland Green*

Asten, Gail Van.
Charlemagne's Champion.
Berkley/Ace, $3.95. 304p.

This retelling of the story of the French paladin Roland is a definite improvement over the author's *Blind Knight*. Roland is depicted as a surly youth of unknown parentage, and his sword, Durendal, is the incarnation of a sorceress who wants him for her lover. This is a first-rate combination of historical and mythical fantasy, with events plausibly and originally motivated (including Ganelon's betrayal at the Pass of Roncesvalles). Fantasy readers will love it. —*Roland Green*

Auel, Jean M.
The Plains of Passage.
Crown, $24.95. 752p.

Finally! After a five-year wait, Auel's fans are rewarded by the latest in the Earth's Children series. Ayla and Jondalar begin the long journey back to Jondalar's people, the Zeladonii. Along the way, they meet different groups of people, including members of another clan, and discover the true depths of their love for each other. More than just another adventure storyteller, Auel continues to offer a wealth of information about the prehistoric world. Her detailed descriptions of animal and plant life, of tools and tool-making, and of the general life-styles of prehistoric societies provide a relaxed pacing that not only mirrors Ayla's and Jondalar's journey but makes important anthropological information accessible to the general public. The protagonists are a bit too perfect, a bit too talented, but Auel's readers will be willing to overlook those flaws in favor of a good story, travel with familiar companions, and a learning experience. —*Jill Sidoti*

Science Fiction

Bova, Ben.
Voyagers III: Star Brothers.
Tor, $18.95. 352p.

This novel concludes a trilogy that is emphatically Bova's most important work to date. The astronaut Stoner, who assimilated the powers of an alien he encountered in an asteroid, must now use those powers to preserve peace on Earth, while facing myriad crises. The pacing is brisk and the technological extrapolation well thought out and impressively detailed. Bova continues to subordinate characterization to other story elements, but readers of hard-science or space-advocacy sf will be enthralled. —*Roland Green*

✓ **Brin, David.**
Earth.
Bantam, $19.95. 640p.

In the middle of the twenty-first century, Earth may have only two years more to survive, thanks to a close encounter with wandering black holes. This ambitious novel by the acclaimed Hugo and Nebula award winner mines the classic "Earth in peril" plot. Happily for Brin's many fans, it is conceived and executed on a gigantic scale, in a style that affirms why he is considered one of the more gifted writers in the field. As with any panoramic novel of this size, the inherent faults are present: keeping track of too many events and too many characters can be daunting. But in all other respects, this saga must be ranked very highly, perhaps second only to *The Postman* among Brin's ever-impressive canon. —*Roland Green*

Bujold, Lois McMaster.
The Vor Game.
Baen, $4.50. 345p.

Miles Vorkosigan returns in Bujold's latest novel, recently graduated from the Imperial Academy on Barrayar. He must rapidly meet and beat a criminal commanding officer, find a missing emperor, outthink mercenaries and Cetagandans, and preserve life, limb (fragile as his may be), honor, and sanity at the same time. While not quite at the level of *Brothers in Arms*, this is still an extraordinary book, deserving of the highest recommendation and certain to be enjoyed by all sf readers. —*Roland Green*

✓ **Card, Orson Scott.**
Maps in a Mirror: The Short Fiction of Orson Scott Card.
Tor, $19.95. 675p.

Without question, this is *the* outstanding science fiction collection of the year, featuring 46 pieces by an exceptional writer. Card's talents are represented by fantasy, science fiction, horror, poetry, and the stories that launched his sagas of Alvin Maker and Ender Wiggins. A substantial amount of autobiographical discussion of each story's origin enhances the volume's high value. Highly recommended for any collection. —*Roland Green*

Clarke, Arthur C. and Lee, Gentry.
Rama II.
Bantam, $18.95. 320p.

It's been 16 years since the publication of Arthur C. Clarke's multiple-award-winning *Rendezvous With Rama*, and eager sf fans have been waiting anxiously for another opportunity to explore the huge, mysterious alien spacecraft that drifted into our solar system only hinting at its true purpose. In *Rendezvous*, Clarke truly excelled himself, with several bold extrapolations on existing scientific theory and with layers of metaphysics applied to the painstakingly crafted alternate world within the spaceship. In *Rama II*, Clarke again collaborates with NASA engineer Gentry Lee (they worked together on the flawed *Cradle*), and the results are decidedly mixed. This time another *Rama* appears in our galaxy, with the same shape, the same unearthly vistas, and even more creatures running wild over its spacescapes. A childlike genius, a beautiful medical officer, and a deeply religious military man form the nucleus of the good guys, anxious to explore, befriend the creatures, and discover the true purpose of the spacecraft. Surprisingly, measured against Clarke's usually streamlined plotting, the novel is a shockingly lethargic tale. Interestingly, the brusque, occasionally starchy Clarke dialogue has been replaced by lengthy speeches loaded with earthy undertones. Lee seems to favor florid characterizations, with many characters introduced purely for color and placed in scenes of effective, if somewhat misplaced melodrama. *Rama II*'s storyline is somewhat transitional in nature, obviously part of an ongoing series (the Clarke-Lee team is contracted to Bantam for a trilogy.) With two more books in the pipeline, it goes without saying that *Rama's* true purpose will stay mysterious for a few more years.
—*Peter Robertson*

Clayton, Jo.
Shadowplay.
NAL/DAW, $4.50. 400p.

Clayton's latest well-told tale of space adventure begins a new saga spun off from her popular Diadem series. Shadith, imprisoned in the Diadem itself for centuries, has now regained her human form. She promptly becomes involved in a struggle against a perverse villain who starts wars so that he can sell movies of the results. There is plenty of action in this book—with the promise of more to come—so that Clayton's fans and fans of space adventure in general will not be disappointed. —*Roland Green*

De Haven, Tom.
Walker of Worlds.
Doubleday, $19.95. 341p.

This volume of modern-day fantasy begins what may prove to be a major saga in the field, the Chronicles of the King's Tramp. An investigative reporter, a wealthy pharmacist, and the woman caught between them become involved with Jack, the King's Tramp, and assorted sorcerers. The book will not satisfy

Science Fiction

those who like to know who is doing what to whom, but it contains so many nuggets of superior characterization and use of language and so many good scenes that readers may well prove tolerant. —*Roland Green*

✓ **Dickson, Gordon R.**
Wolf and Iron.
Tor, $18.95. 512p.

In a postholocaust America, a young man who anticipates economic collapse is trying to reach safety. But that safety lies in Montana, across 2,000 miles of hostile countryside, which he must cross with only a wolf as his companion. If he can communicate with the animal, however, he will add substantially to his repertoire of survival skills—and to what he can contribute to rebuilding society. Dickson has done his homework on wolves, but more, his writing is up to the level that has made him one of the giants of the field. —*Roland Green*

DiSilvestro, Roger L.
Living with the Reptiles.
Donald I. Fine, $18.95. 284p.

An "eco-novel" from the author of the comic fantasy *Ursula's Gift*. Meet Jackson Black, a man with the gift of total recall who is bamboozled into helping the megalomaniacal mogul Mr. Ritz track down a UFO in the Brazilian rain forest. Ritz, paralyzed except for the use of a finger, is hoping aliens can cure him. Instead of finding aliens, they discover a human time traveler, Tyler Blake, and his *chronocraft* (time machine). Blake has returned, illegally (time travelers are only supposed to travel to prehistoric eras so that they don't alter history), to bring back a cure for Beach Disease, a pollution-based plague ravaging the population of Earth in the year 2075. The antidote is derived from a rain-forest plant, which is, of course, extinct in his time. Leaving Blake and Black to rot in the jungle, Ritz steals Blake's chronocraft so that he can go into his own past, before his accident. Once whole again, he travels back to medieval times and sets himself up as a king. The plot gets good and gnarly with time police, time waves, and old and new histories. The travelers witness both the Earth's prehuman past—pristine and peaceful—and the hideous, people-infested, filthy future. DiSilvestro lays it on pretty thick, but can we blame him? As editor for *Audubon* magazine and chief staff writer for the Audubon Society television specials, he has more on his mind than dishing up sf fun. Fortunately, the message doesn't overpower the fiction. With a cast of quirky characters and "Star Trek"–style suspense, this is an inventive and droll tale, begging for the silver screen. —*Donna Seaman*

Herbert, Brian.
Race for God.
Berkley/Ace, $4.50. 304p.

Frank Herbert's son returns to print with this successful, humorous sf novel. God, discovered living on a distant planet, summons an oddly assorted group of earthlings to hear his message. The perils of the journey are exceeded only by the perils of the personal rivalries to obtain a personal blessing. Herbert handles the whole thing with a cheerful irreverence that manages to avoid being tasteless and is frequently original. —*Roland Green*

Kerr, Katharine.
The Dragon Revenant.
Doubleday, $18.95. 384p.

Katharine Kerr's latest novel of the Celtic realms of Deverry is well up to the high standard of earlier entries in the series. When the heir to the throne of Aberwyn is kidnapped, it turns out to be at least partly a trap set by the wizard Nevyn's ancient enemies in order to lure the immortal mage to his doom. Kerr is a thoroughly accomplished writer and an authoritative Celtic scholar. The resulting combination is so felicitous as to recall Katharine Kurtz's best-selling Deryni novels. Guaranteed to be popular with fantasy readers. —*Roland Green*

Kerr, Katharine.
Polar City Blues.
Bantam, $4.50. 262p.

Kerr's first attempt at science fiction, after four successful volumes of Celtic fantasy, is up to the high standards of her other work. Here, an unknown alien is found murdered in Polar City, the only remaining habitation on an overheated Earth. Kerr manages plenty of action, solid prose and characterization, a superbly depicted world (one of her hallmarks), and a challenging mystery, all in one book. —*Roland Green*

✓ MacAvoy, R. A.
Lens of the World.
Morrow, $17.95. 288p.

MacAvoy begins the projected multivolume saga of Nazhuret, a dwarfish, illegitimate orphan brought up in a military school, taught by an eccentric nobleman to be a lens maker (and much else), and by the end of this tale, trained as a seasoned warrior who saves his king's life. MacAvoy has just about every skill of the accomplished fantasist at her command and in this volume displays them all. The book bodes exceedingly well for the rest of the series, which may eventually rank with Donaldson's Thomas Covenant, Wolfe's Latro, and Card's Alvin Maker sagas. —*Roland Green*

Mason, Lisa.
Arachne.
Morrow, $17.95. 263p.

Following the path into a sleazy, technology-based future blazed by William Gibson, Mason explores the field of jurisprudence from a cyberpunk perspective. Artificial-intelligence (AI) entities and humans cruise a symbolic logic network called telespace, a computer-driven creation similar to Gibson's cyberspace. Carly Nolan, a young, fast-track telespace lawyer, finds her career

Science Fiction

and finally her life in jeopardy as she becomes enmeshed in an AI scheme to steal human souls. An innovative, solidly written addition to the growing volume of cyberpunk sf. —*Elliott Swanson*

Morris, Janet and Morris, Chris.
Threshold.
Penguin/ROC, $16.95. 256p.

Inadvertently time-traveling astronaut Joe South arrives at a far-future orbital depot. He lands in the middle of a crisis caused by smuggled telepathic aliens, the runaway teenage daughter of a right-wing Moslem leader, an alien artifact, and the general cussedness of both human and nonhuman sapient beings. At the end of the story, most of these crises are solved, and South has a place in the new world, but there is clearly enough story left to justify the trilogy of which this is the first volume. Good space adventure. —*Roland Green*

Scott, Melissa.
Mighty Good Road.
Baen, $3.95. 320p.

Free-lance salvage operators Gwynne Heikki and Sten Djuro find themselves commissioned by a major corporation to recover a cargo lost on a savage, uninhabited planet. Unfortunately, both the local animals and their corporate bosses are even more savage than expected, and this sets off a sequence of fast-moving intrigues and adventures. Scott writes well and includes her hallmarks—a believably feisty female protagonist and meticulously detailed world building. Fans of adventure sf won't be able to put this one down. —*Roland Green*

Sheffield, Charles.
Summertide.
Ballantine/Del Rey, $16.95. 272p.

An excellent, tightly written hard-science piece, ostensibly the first in a series. The twin planets of Opal and Quake are about to be subjected to massive earthquakes because of a rare astronomical conjunction ("Summertide"); in fact, Quake will become uninhabitable. For some reason, a variety of both human and nonhuman travelers wants to visit Quake at the height of Summertide. This turns out to involve the Builders, a long-vanished race in whose interstellar empire Quake clearly played a major role—but what was it? That mystery is left for further volumes. In this one, Sheffield tells a complete, thoroughly absorbing story. —*Roland Green*

Silverberg, Robert.
The New Springtime.
Warner, $19.95. 368p.

Robert Silverberg seems to be a more effective novelist working on a large canvas, and this latest novel supports that notion. This sequel to *At Winter's End* continues the tale of a far-future Earth recovering from a massive ecological catastrophe. Two city-states have become bitter rivals, each has its own internal divisions, and an insectoid species threatens both. A sprawling story, but one full of ingenious pieces of characterization and world building. Certain to appeal to Silverberg's many faithful readers. —*Roland Green*

✓ **Simmons, Dan.**
The Fall of Hyperion.
Doubleday, $18.95. 480p.

In this eagerly awaited sequel to *Hyperion* (Doubleday, 1989), Simmons continues to play out the future of man and machine on a grand scale. Humanity's fate is in the hands of a small band of pilgrims trapped on the besieged planet Hyperion. Their attempts to discover the secrets contained in artifacts called Time Tombs are monitored through the dreams of a computer-designed human containing the persona of poet John Keats. Further complicating the plot are Machiavellian intrigues taking place between factions of humanity and powerful self-evolving artificial intelligence constructs. The richly evoked characters coupled with fully realized far-future settings make this ambitious series one of the most satisfying of its kind, rivaling even Asimov's Foundation novels for world-building skill. —*Elliott Swanson*

Stirling, S. M.
The Stone Dogs.
Baen, $4.50. 528p.

This volume concludes Stirling's generally superior alternate-history Draka saga. A panoramic novel covering the two generations following the end of *Under the Yoke* (Baen, 1989), it uses two families, one American and one Draka, as viewpoints for the steadily escalating confrontation between the expansionistic Draka and the increasingly desperate Alliance. In spite of occasional lapses, Stirling remains skilled at characterization and world building and outstanding in battle scenes. The trilogy as a whole should establish the author as a major figure with military science fiction readers. —*Roland Green*

Vance, Jack.
Madouc.
Berkley/Ace, $8.95. 432p.

In the concluding volume of Vance's Lyonesse trilogy, Princess Madouc flees her father's court and lands right in the middle of a fine stew of battles and intrigues, magical and otherwise, all conducted in a world wrought with the abundant and imaginative detail very nearly unique to Vance. Near the end of one of the longer careers in American sf and fantasy, Vance proves that he still possesses talent of a high order. —*Roland Green*

Wilhelm, Kate.
Cambio Bay.
St. Martin's, $17.95. 294p.

The lives of assorted, disparate people interconnect in Wilhelm's latest supernatural tale through Miss Luisa's Victorian house at Cambio Bay, California. The house—"said to occupy land that once [was] the dwelling place of Great Chief and Squaw and their child"—is huge and disorienting, with gables, cupolas, balconies, stairways that appear and disappear, and an ocean view for every room. Drawn here are a professor of English on sabbatical to study the mythos of the West; a real-estate agent and the man she rescues when a sudden deluge washes his car off the road; a frightened young mother with a five-year-old mute daughter fleeing a mobster; and, eventually, the mobster himself and his deadly hitman. Influencing everything is the legend of Great Chief, Squaw, and their child—whose stories the enigmatic Miss Luisa recounts, linking the tales with the lives of her guests as they play out their roles in the continuing legend. Despite the many main characters, Wilhelm vitalizes each with care. Suspense and a sense of terror, tempered by touches of humor and romance, mount slowly but inexorably to a fitting conclusion that adheres to the mythological underpinnings of the compelling tale. —*Sally Estes*

Williams, Tad.
Stone of Farewell.
NAL/DAW, $21.95. 592p.

Book 2 in the Memory, Sorrow and Thorn series is another massive, colorful volume filled with a multitude of characters and plenty of action. Simon, the scullery boy turned sometime wielder of the sword Thorn, continues to play a large role in the battle to save the land from the undead Sithi ruler, Ineluki the Storm King. In the face of the terrifying onslaught of the Storm King's vicious minions, the unnaturally cold weather, and the ominously gathering storm clouds, Simon and his companions struggle to reach the distant and mysterious Stone of Farewell, where—they have been told—they will be able to find sanctuary for a time. Other ragged groups are also making their way there slowly. Some episodes seem contrived to offer yet another deadly incident, and the convoluted plot, switching between the many groups desperately seeking a place of safety and a chance to marshall their meager forces to combat the Storm King, is often confusing; however, there are a number of compelling scenes, and Williams maintains the atmospheric distinctiveness of *The Dragonbone Chair*. Readers of the first book will no doubt relish this continuation of a saga that promises to endure. —*Sally Estes*

Williamson, Jack.
Mazeway.
Ballantine/Del Rey, $17.95. 336p.

In the future, Earth is devastated when an alien causes the fall of all orbiting habitations. Then the survivors of humanity are excluded from interstellar space by a consortium of advanced aliens. One way to end this exclusion is to play the game of Blade and Stone, wherein two abandoned planets form a complex maze. Two men and a woman compete in this contest, alternately cooperating with and combating aliens, eventually discovering a hostile plot against the whole consortium. While Williamson basically offers a reworking of a typical sf plot, his considerable writing skills turn it into an excellent novel. Highly recommended. —*Roland Green*

Wilson, F. Paul.
The Tery.
Baen/Simon & Schuster, $3.50. 256p.

The Tery—a beast who appears to be a cross between a bear and a monkey, but who thinks, talks, and reasons like a human—is beaten and left for dead by soldiers under orders to destroy any variant life on the planet. The beast is rescued and nursed back to health by 17-year-old Adriel, an outcast from her clan because she is not telepathic, and Steve Dalt, an undercover agent for the Cultural Survey Service. Themes concerning myth, religion, revenge, and justice are woven into this story of an outsider's quest for humanity. A brief but related story, "Pard," in which Dalt's mind is linked with an alien in a beneficial partnership, concludes the volume. Thought-provoking science fiction. —*Candace Smith*

Wolfe, Gene.
Castleview.
Tor, $19.95. 400p.

In downstate Illinois, the small town of Castleview is shaken when the murder of a factory manager sets off a furious investigation into the mystery of the castle after which the town was named, a medieval edifice that appears and disappears randomly. (The castle is actually that of Morgan Le Fay, the nemesis of King Arthur, and the pursuit of its secret is immediately and totally perilous to the pursuers.) Wolfe doesn't entirely resolve the stated conflict, but he has created his usual splendid cast of characters, and he builds suspense admirably. —*Roland Green*

Zahn, Timothy.
Warhorse.
Baen, $4.50. 352p.

Zahn's latest novel postulates an encounter between an expanding human race and an alien species of consummate biological engineers who have appointed themselves defenders of all life. The species' arsenal, much to humanity's dismay, includes "live" spaceships (the "warhorses" of the title). This is Zahn at his best, mixing hard science and social-science extrapolation and supporting the whole with good prose, pacing, and characterization. —*Roland Green*

AUTHOR INDEX

Author Index

TITLE INDEX

Title Index

Title Index

Title Index

Title Index

Title Index

Title Index

Title Index

Title Index